Frontiers of Sociology

Annals of the International Institute of Sociology (IIS)

Since its foundation in 1893 the International Institute of Sociology (IIS) has played an important and at times crucial role in the international world of social science. The IIS was created as a forum for discussions among scholars whom we now think of as classics of sociology and social science. Among its members and associates were prominent scholars such as Franz Boas, Roger Bastide, Lujo Brentano, Theodor Geirger, Gustave Le Bon, Karl Mannheim, William F. Ogburn, Pitirim Sorokin, Georg Simmel, Werner Sombart, Ludwig Stein, Gabriel Tarde, Richard Thurnwald, Ferdinand Toennies, Thorstein Veblen, Alfred Vierkandt, Lester F. Ward, Sidney Webb, Max Weber, Leopold von Wiese and Florian Znaniecki. They shared a sense of urgency about social conditions but also a conviction that systematic inquiry would make human beings more able to grasp and overcome them. They also shared a belief that scholars from different nations and different theoretical traditions can form an international community and engage in intellectual contestation and dialogue while remaining respectful of each other's diversity. This is reflected in the publications of the Institute, the most important one being the Annals. The first volume of the Annals was published already in 1895. In recent years the IIS has increasingly come to play a role analogous to that of its early years. The congresses preceding the one in Stockholm in 2005 were held in Beijing (2004), Krakow (2001), Tel Aviv (1999), Köln (1997), Trieste (1995), Paris (1993), Kobe (1991) and Rome (1989). They have highlighted dilemmas of human existence and societal institutions amidst processes of globalization, cooperation and violent conflict. They have done so in the spirit which guided the formation of the IIS, namely that of an engagement and encounter between a variety of theoretical positions among members of a truly international community of scholars.

Frontiers of Sociology

Edited by

Peter Hedström
Björn Wittrock

BRILL

LEIDEN • BOSTON
2009

This book is printed on acid-free paper.

Library of Congress Cataloging-in-Publication Data

Frontiers of sociology / edited by Peter Hedstrom, Bjorn Wittrock.
    p. cm. — (Annals of the International Institute of Sociology ; 11)
    Includes bibliographical references and index.
    ISBN 978-90-04-16569-4 (hardback : alk. paper) 1. Sociology—Congresses. I.
Hedström, Peter. II. Wittrock, Björn. III. Institut international de sociologie. World
Congress (37th)
    HM421.F76 2008
    301—dc22

                                                                    2008038910

ISSN 1568-1548
ISBN 978 90 04 16569 4

CONTENTS

INTRODUCTION: FRONTIERS OF SOCIOLOGY

Peter Hedström and Björn Wittrock

Since its foundation in 1893 the International Institute of Sociology (IIS) has played an important and at times crucial role in the international world of social science. The IIS was created as a forum for discussions among scholars whom we now think of as classics of sociology and social science. They shared a sense of urgency about social conditions but also a conviction that systematic inquiry would make human beings more able to grasp and overcome them. They also shared a belief that scholars from different nations and different theoretical traditions can form an international community and engage in intellectual contestation and dialogue while remaining respectful of each other's diversity.

In recent years the IIS has increasingly come to play a role analogous to that of its early years. World Congresses of the IIS have highlighted dilemmas of human existence and societal institutions amidst processes of globalization, cooperation and violent conflict. They have done so in the spirit which guided the formation of the IIS, namely that of an engagement and encounter between a variety of theoretical positions among members of a truly international community of scholars.

There may be a greater urgency today than for a very long time for sociology to examine its own intellectual and institutional frontiers relative to other disciplinary and scholarly programs but also relative to a rapidly changing institutional and academic landscape. In this sense, current sociology may be in a situation more analogous to that of the classics of sociology and of the IIS than has been the case for a large part of the twentieth century.

The 37th World Congress of the IIS focused on theory and research at the forefront of sociology and on the relationship between sociology and its neighboring disciplines. This volume constitutes a sustained effort by prominent sociologists and other social scientists to assess the current standing of sociology. It is a stocktaking of the unique nature of sociology in the light of advances within the discipline itself and within a range of neighboring disciplines. Some of the chapters outline institutional and professional strategies for sociology in the new millennium. Others trace scholarly advances and propose ambitious research programs drawing on recent developments not only within traditional neighboring disciplines such as history, political science, and economics, but also within the cognitive, cultural and mathematical sciences.

A little more than half of the chapters of this book draw on texts that were originally presented at the 37th World Congress. They have all been subject to revision and rewriting. The other half is constituted by texts that have been written specifically for the book. In one case—the chapter by the late Harvard sociologist Aage B. Sørensen—there is a previously unpublished text which has been graciously offered to the editors by his widow, Professor Annemette Sørensen.

The volume is divided into six parts. The first part, *The Legacy and Frontiers of Sociology*, is constituted by a series of efforts to explore the cognitive, cultural and institutional commitments of sociology. They do so by way of an analysis of intellectual traditions in historical context but also by arguments for sociological research programs that encompass and expand core components of these traditions. Thus Hans Joas brings out the relevance to contemporary sociology of the legacies of two originally non-sociological traditions, namely those of the predominantly German tradition of historicism and hermeneutics and of the American tradition of pragmatism. He traces ways in which these two traditions influenced classical sociology but also how they may be related to each other in ways of the highest relevance to contemporary sociology. In particular he outlines a sociological research program for the study of what he calls "major innovations in the fields of values" and in particular of "The Emergence of Universalism". Such an "affirmative genealogy of moral universalism" will re-establish links between sociology and moral philosophy that were taken for granted in the period at the turn of the eighteenth century when modern social science emerged but which became increasingly tenuous already in the course of the nineteenth century. For any sociological analysis of any issue related to human rights and violations of such rights, a research program, which probes the frontiers of sociology, philosophy and history, seems indispensable.

Raymond Boudon explores the growth of two types of relativism, which he calls cognitive and cultural, within the social sciences in the course of the last thirty years. He traces their intellectual origins and the particular constellations of conditions that contributed to their rapid diffusion in the last decades of the twentieth century. Interestingly enough Boudon then cautiously proceeds to subject these two types of relativism to a sociological inquiry in the tradition of Durkheim.

In consequence, he comes to probe, or perhaps rather expose, the socially and constructed nature also of prevalent relativist assumptions and concludes by arguing how these presuppositions may indeed be transcended.

Joas and Boudon share an interest in the emergence and constitution of values both in daily life and in research practices. Piotr Sztompka's chapter is explicitly devoted to an inquiry in the return of values in sociological theorizing. He starts out by distinguishing two different views on the role of values, namely as a source of bias and as a facilitator of ideology. He then relates the role of values to different strands in current sociology sharing an anti-naturalistic stance and emphasizing the cultural, transformative, agential, reflexive nature of practices both at a micro-processual and at a global level. They all help to underpin an increasing emphasis on dialogue, on the constitution of meaning, on the role of values in social practices and on contributions of sociology to public debates, public actions, and ultimately to the way sociologists may contribute to a higher degree of collective rationality. Although different both in rhetorical style and in terms of theoretical tradition, the argument of Sztompka is largely parallel and complementary to that pursued by Boudon.

Whereas the focus of Joas, Boudon and Sztompka alike is on the historical evolution and current viability and promise of different intellectual traditions and of some key modes of sociological theorizing, the focus of the contributions by Jack Goldstone, and Dietrich Rueschemeyer is a different one, namely on the formulation of institutional strategies for the future development of sociology. Goldstone and Rueschemeyer have a similar view of the great potential and actual contribution of sociology to a well-founded understanding of central features of the contemporary world. Their prescriptions for the future success of sociology are, however, radically different. Both of them contrast the more open intellectual landscape of academic sociology to the clearly demarcated and compartmentalized institutionalization of disciplines such as economics and political science. Goldstone espouses a strategy that would entail an ordering of the teaching and research activities of sociology into four clearly demarcated subfields—sociology of the nation, macro-sociology, micro-sociology, and organizational sociology—in a mode reminiscent of that practiced within economics (micro-economics, macro-economics, international economics, and economic history) and political science (home country politics, comparative politics, international relations, and political theory). Goldstone argues that this would constitute an important step towards further development of sociology as a discipline and a profession and would make the impressive range of achievements of sociology more visible also to the public at large.

Rueschemeyer on the other hand argues that it is now time to overcome the long-term development of social science into panoply of different and diverging disciplines and specializations that have evolved since the late nineteenth century when a comprehensive social science, what we now call classical sociology, was fragmented into specialized fields of sociology, political science and ethnology/anthropology. Sociology as a discipline may still be more open to methodological and theoretical explorations than, say, political science, but both disciplines and others would profit from closer collaboration and from a systematic effort to strengthen macro-comparative research in the social sciences at large and to make their impressive achievements more apparent also to a wider audience.

A new comprehensive social science is however, Rueschemeyer argues, not just a program but rather something that has already been partially realized. This is clearly the case in the comparative study of revolutions and democratization or the comparative study of welfare societies or the study of economic transitions or the research program of institutionalism. In all these areas of frontier research, sociologists, economists, political scientists and scholars from organizational and cultural studies are already cooperating in comparative empirical research on a vast scale while exploring theoretical avenues at the frontier of their own and neighboring disciplines. A new comprehensive social science faces far less obstacles in intellectual terms than the corresponding program at the turn of the nineteenth century when it was largely "pre-empted by politics and simple ideological thrusts as was the case between 1914 and 1945".

The renewal and growth of a comprehensive social science would not replace but significantly complement the different existing disciplines and help bring out commonalities in their legacies and current orientations but also enhances further research advances beyond those which have already been achieved. It would, perhaps most importantly, help bring out the true potential of systematic research to an understanding and overcoming of the current dilemmas of humankind which, in Rueschemeyer's words, are "fundamentally the old problems writ large: extreme forms of poverty and inequality; coexistence of rich and poor nations; weak and ineffective institutions related to growth and distribution; a growing disconnect between inherited cultural templates and current developments; and, arising out of these, the chance of brutal domestic and international conflicts".

The second section, *Sociology and the Historical Sciences*, explores the curious ambivalence that characterizes the relationship between sociology and history. In a sense sociology and the social sciences at large are intrinsically historical. They have tended to portray themselves as part of an effort of human beings to achieve an understanding of the contemporary historical epoch so as to be able to exert an influence on its shape and development. At the same time, there has been a process over the past two centuries that has resulted in a deep divide between the social and historical sciences. In recent decades, however, there have been a range of advances in the social sciences which have brought history back into the core of social science. Björn Wittrock provides a historical overview of some of the mechanisms behind the emergence of a chasm between the social and historical sciences. He also explores three key avenues in the contemporary renaissance of historical reasoning in the social sciences. He argues that the full potential of research on the emergence and development of macro-societal institutions can only be realized if sociologists transcend the limits of historical institutionalism and engage in a study of the interplay between cultural crystallizations and the emergence of macro-institutional trajectories.

The chapter by S. N. Eisenstadt is devoted precisely to one such crucial period of cultural crystallization in the history of humankind, namely the so-called Axial Age, i.e. the period in the middle of the first millennium BCE which saw the emergence in widely different forms in cultures across Eurasia of cosmologies premised on a chasm between a mundane and a transcendental sphere entailing new relationships between rulers and subjects, between practices of interpretation and domination, between inscription and interpretation, between orthodoxy and heterodoxy. This period and its consequences for the emergence of radically new forms of political order, of new universal religions, and of an era in which, to paraphrase the German Egyptologist Jan Assmann, Kings could no longer claim to be Gods, only to rule with a Mandate of Heaven or by the Grace of God, i.e. on terms that entailed the principled possibility for claims that the mandate had been forfeited, that an interpretation bolstering established order was erroneous and illegitimate, that orthodox interpretations and institutions could never exorcise the possibility of heterodoxy and dissent.

The discussion of the hypothesis of the Axial Age and about the properties of the Axial civilizations, which emerged in the wake of it, have been one of the most persistent and sustained intellectual debates during the second half of the twentieth century with the most important protagonist being first Karl Jaspers and later Eisenstadt but with many other contemporary participants and with a range of precursors including both Max and Alfred Weber. The hypothesis of the Axial Age has had profound implications for the historical and comparative study of religious, cultural, social and political practices, and Eisenstadt's chapter brings out some of the most important dimensions of this, including discussions of patrimonial and feudal arrangements, forms of Empires and other political orders, as well as the nature of public spaces.

In the last decade interest in the hypothesis of the Axial Age and Axial civilizations has become more intense and more wide-ranging and is likely to play a crucial role in sociological discourse in the years to come. It is a delight to be able to include a contribution by one of the most significant protagonists in this debate during the past half century and more.

The chapter by Philip Gorski is written by a historical sociologist whose work on the reformation and the comparative study of state formations in early modern Europe immediately became a central reference point. In his contribution to this volume, Philip Gorski presents a sophisticated and extensive argument for his vision, or rather his detailed model, of how comparative-historical analysis should proceed in the social sciences. It is an argument that takes its point of departure in an overview of contemporary schools in the philosophy of science and in a forceful argument in favour of so-called critical realism, i.e. the form of anti-positivistic philosophy of science which has been developed by Rom Harré and Roy Bhaskar but which includes a range of prominent scholars in several fields, among them the sociologist Margaret Archer to take but one example.

Central to this position is the argument that scientific work cannot remain content with providing descriptions of various occurrences on the level of what is empirically observable and then to hope that empirical results will more or less automatically yield theoretical insights. On the contrary science always makes assumptions about generating mechanisms, which may not be directly observable themselves, but which may be real none the less and have observable consequences. Thus this position rejects both empiricism and an instrumentalist view of scientific theories and emphasizes the need to understand and to theorize generating mechanisms. Philip Gorski does just that by way of a detailed argument that starts from an examination of various uses of the term mechanism. He then elaborates his proposal for a critical realist program for a theory of causal mechanisms, the so-called ECPRES model, where "e" stands for "emergent", "cp" for "causal powers", "re" for "related entities", and "s" for "system". In the following step Gorski confronts this model for comparative-historical sociology with a range of rival theories that currently occupy a prominent role. The focus is on two broad types of such rival theories, namely firstly rational choice approaches, including those of Edgar Kiser, Michael Hechter, Jon Elster and Peter Hedström's version of a form of rational choice based theory of social mechanisms, and secondly historical institutional approaches, with special reference to the works of James Mahoney and Charles Tilly.

The third section, *Sociology and the Economic Sciences*, explores the frontier between sociology and economics. The chapter by Neil Smelser considers the evolving relationship between economics and sociology, starting with his and Talcott Parsons' 1956 book *Economy and Society* to the most recent developments in economic sociology and behavioral and institutional economics. While the disciplinary boundaries in certain respects have diminished over time, fundamental methodological differences remain intact suggesting that a theoretical synthesis is not likely to happen in many years to come.

These methodological differences between economics and sociology also are discussed in Richard Breen's chapter. He considers rational-choice theory in the broader context of formal theory and distinguishes between "thin" and "thick" versions of rational choice theory. The use of a thin version of rational-choice theory has the advantage of producing clear and precise explanations of social outcomes but they raise difficult and important questions about the explanatory status of theories which are founded upon knowingly false assumptions. Breen argues for the importance of closer links between empirical research and formal theory and sees agent-based modeling as an important new addition to the sociologist's theoretical toolbox.

Richard Swedberg explores the importance of Pierre Bourdieu's work for economic sociology. He focuses on Bourdieu's early studies of Algeria, his attempt to bring a normative dimension into the discussion of economic sociology, and his attempt to develop a sociological notion of interests. Swedberg argues that Bourdieu's combined focus on interests *and* relations and his use of subjective data on individuals' states of mind in his analyses of economic phenomena are likely to contribute to re-vitalizing the intellectual dialogue between sociology and economics.

In the fourth section, *Sociology and the Cultural Sciences*, Peter Wagner starts out by pointing to the limitations of a purely institutional analysis of "modern societies". He then goes on to highlight how sociology has in fact already largely achieved, to paraphrase his subtitle, "something like a cultural turn in the sociology of 'modern society'". Going beyond a purely institutional analysis also means rejecting the way in which sociology for a long time, from Weber through Giddens, has tended to focus on the unique experience of Europe and more broadly "Western civilization". Instead Wagner articulates an understanding of modernity as an interpretive relation to the world that involves "a range of problematiques to which a variety of responses are possible". The starting point must be the unique nature of a variety of situations in time and space and the cultural resources available in these situations. It is only in such a perspective that it becomes meaningful to explore wider issues of comparative historical sociology and anthropology. In this sense there can be no meaningful sociology at all which does not take the achievements of the cultural and philosophical sciences in recent decades seriously.

Ulf Hannerz's contribution is an exploration of relationships between sociology and the cultural sciences at large but also of a variety of imaginations of geocultural and geopolitical borders and flows. In particular he dissects waves of world scenarios and how current imaginations of cultural flows and influences relate to each other but also to classical sociology and anthropology which he argues is characterized by an emphasis precisely on "the interflow of cultural material between civilizations" to quote Alfred Kroeber. Thus today's theorizing of deterritorialization, virtuality, hybridity and creolization may be more at odds with contemporary imaginations in the social and political studies about homogeneous movements whether of modernization or civilizations than with the classical heritage of sociology and anthropology.

In this vein Hannerz also explores the possibilities for a transnational consciousness in a world not only of print capitalism but of media sound-bites and a variety of hybrid genres. His analysis, as always in his works, carefully couched and elegantly argued, provides the potential for a geocultural imagination where divisions between centres and peripheries and between dominating powers and subalterns are not able to resist a global conversation and a talking back and dialogue that may, to use Ulf Hannerz's expression, "point to a way out an empire of fear".

In the fifth section, *Sociology and the Cognitive Sciences*, the cognitive turn in sociological theory is considered from the viewpoint of sociology as well as cognitive science. Peter Gärdenfors points to the importance of going beyond Dennett's notion of the *intentional stance* and adopting a *social stance* to certain phenomena. This stance applies to situations that involve the ascription of social intentions or joint beliefs as causal factors. Gärdenfors argues that acknowledging the causal explanatory efficacy of social intentions does not mean that methodological individualism has to be sacrificed, however, since social intentions are supervenient on individual intentions.

Jens Rydgren's chapter is concerned with the importance of belief-formation processes for explaining why individuals do what they do. A focus on belief formation processes is crucial because individuals' beliefs are neither random nor do individuals form, on average, correct beliefs about the world in which they are embedded. Individuals' beliefs are biased but they are biased in systematic and understandable ways. Rydgren's chapter is particularly concerned with the importance of shared beliefs about the past, and how such beliefs shape individuals' predictions about future events and their strategies for dealing with new situations.

A focus on cognitive processes also is at the heart of analytical sociology and in his chapter Peter Hedström discusses the basic foundations of the analytical approach and the role of desires, beliefs, and opportunities in explaining action. He argues that society is like a complex dynamic system where actions and interactions among individuals explain the emergent properties of the system. He uses computer simulations to illustrate that aggregate patterns and associations often say very little about why we observe what we observe. Instead of examining aggregate-level patterns and associations, we must seek to link macro and micro levels to one another. That is, we must seek to take into account the reasons for why individuals do what they do, as well as the causes of the reasons and the effects of the actions that these reasons cause.

The fifth and final section of the book focuses on the frontiers between sociology and the mathematical and statistical sciences. Mathematics can be used for formalizing sociological theories and applied mathematics in the form of statistics is at the core of quantitatively oriented sociology. In his chapter on mathematical sociology, Christofer Edling focuses on the history and future of formal theory in sociology.

The chapter is centered on a series of interviews with six of the leading mathematical sociologists of the last few decades, Peter Abell, Philip Bonacich, Kathleen Carley, Patrick Doreian, Thomas Fararo, and Harrison White. The chapter highlights the considerable potential of formal theory in sociology but it also identifies many important institutional and intellectual barriers to the development of a large body of formal theory in sociology.

A recurrent theme in Aage B. Sørensen's chapter concerns the importance of providing tighter links between sociological theory and mathematical and statistical modeling. Sørensen is highly critical of what he perceives to be the conventional wisdom among quantitatively-oriented sociologists which essentially amounts to basing empirical research on standard off-the-shelf statistical models. In this mainstream tradition there is little or no concern about the mechanisms that produce change and the role of theory often does not extend beyond the task of justifying which variables are to be included in statistical models. Sørensen advocates a much more sociologically-grounded approach which starts with clear and precise ideas about mechanisms of change, and on the basis of these ideas formal mathematical models of social processes are specified. Once these mathematical models are at hand, empirical data can be used to estimate the size of various parameters. He illustrates what he has in mind in a critical examination of series of studies of social mobility and school effects on student achievement.

In recent discussions about causality a distinction often has been made between causation as *robust dependence*, causation as *consequential manipulation*, and causation as *generative process*. In his chapter, Hans-Peter Blossfeld clarifies the distinctions between these different notions and he illustrates how event-history models can be used for analyzing complex generative processes that unfold in time and space. He demonstrates the viability of the approach in a cross-national study examining the effect of first pregnancy/first birth on entry into first marriage.

Without the generous financial support received from the Swedish Collegium for Advanced Study, *Stiftelsen Riksbankens Jubileumsfond* ("The Bank of Sweden Tercentenary Foundation"), the Swedish Council for Working Life and Social Research, and the Swedish Research Council, this congress would not have been possible. We would also like to express our gratitude to Michelle Ariga for her help with organizing the event and, not the least, to all those who participated in the congress and made it into such a successful intellectual event. Finally, we owe a debt of gratitude to Dr. Sara Grut who played a key role in the final process of editing the text for publication.

Peter Hedström
Secretary General of IIS

Björn Wittrock
President of IIS

THE LEGACY AND FRONTIERS OF SOCIOLOGY

THE EMERGENCE OF UNIVERSALISM:
AN AFFIRMATIVE GENEALOGY

Hans Joas

In planning the session about "The Legacy of Sociology" at the 37th World Congress of the International Institute of Sociology, the organizers certainly had more in mind than a mere combination of representatives from different *national* sociological traditions when they decided to invite Margaret Archer, Raymond Boudon, and myself. They had good reasons to assume that Margaret Archer's critical realism and Raymond Boudon's open-minded version of a rationalistic action theory deserve to be called creative continuations of important strands of the sociological tradition. But what exactly could my role be in the dramaturgical plot they probably had in mind? In my sociological work, I see myself as deeply influenced by at least two different national traditions, namely the German tradition of historicism and hermeneutics on the one hand and the American tradition of pragmatism on the other. Two questions therefore arise immediately: 1. Can one be a representative of both these traditions at the same time? And 2. What exactly is the relationship of these two originally non-sociological traditions to "the legacy of sociology"? Let me first attempt to give brief answers to these two questions; I will thereafter try to exemplify my specific approach based on these two traditions in the field of my current research on the history of human rights.

I will start with the second question. There is no doubt that the philosophies of pragmatism and of hermeneutics influenced classical sociology, at least to some extent. Much has been written about the importance of pragmatism for the Chicago school of sociology, for example in W. I. Thomas, Robert Park, and, of course, the social psychology of George Herbert Mead and Charles Horton Cooley and its continuation in symbolic interactionism.[1] But pragmatism never became fully integrated into Talcott Parsons' ambitious attempt at theoretical synthesis, and for what really constituted the dominant

---

[1] See, for example, my own attempt: Joas 1993, 14–51.

type of American sociology after 1945, the combination of Merton's middle-range functionalism with Lazarsfeld's quantitative methodology, this approach always remained marginal. This is even more the case in Europe, where a traditional feeling of cultural superiority regarding the U.S. for a long time prevented a serious reception of pragmatist ideas in philosophy and the social sciences.[2]

In a similar way one could say that nobody can ignore the crucial importance of historicism and hermeneutics for sociological classics from Germany like Max Weber and Georg Simmel. But as the neglect of Peirce, James, and Dewey in the understanding of what a pragmatist sociology is proved to be enormously harmful, a study of these two authors (Weber and Simmel) without their wider intellectual contexts can only be misleading. Donald Levine, in his *Visions of the Sociological Tradition*, wisely decided to devote almost as much space to Wilhelm Dilthey as to Max Weber when he described the specificities of the German sociological tradition.[3] By including Dilthey, we can detect where Weber still depended on a (Neo-Kantian) "pre-linguistic turn" philosophy; by further including great sociological scholars like Ernst Troeltsch or Georg Jellinek or Otto Hintze, who nominally belonged to other disciplines, we can also learn to see how deeply idiosyncratic some of Weber's views, for example on religion or on democracy, were. My answer to the second question therefore is that pragmatism and hermeneutics played a constitutive role for sociology, but also got lost in the later development of the discipline. Sociology has to reconnect not only with the legacy of its founders, but also with the broader intel-lectual contexts out of which the works of these founders emerged.

And what about the first question? At first sight, the two traditions (of pragmatism and hermeneutics) seem to be very different. The pragmatists clearly were mostly interested in the natural sciences from physics to biology whereas the hermeneuticists obviously lived in an intense dialogue with theology, the history of philosophy, literature, and law. The American tradition, including the pragmatists, has always stressed the unity of science, whereas the German tradition emphasized an almost dichotomous distinction between "Geistes-" and "Naturwissenschaften"—which made the location of the social sciences

---

[2] See my chapter: "American Pragmatism and German Thought: A History of Misunderstandings", Joas 1993, 94–121.
[3] Levine 1995, 181–211.

somewhat uneasy. But it would be a very superficial view that took this
first impression too seriously. Behind these differences we find striking
similarities that have been elaborated by Richard Bernstein and Jürgen
Habermas in great detail.[4] Both pragmatism and hermeneutics are
anti-foundationalist, fallibilist, emphasize the social character of the
self, reflect on the conditions of inquiry, and are inherently pluralistic.
I will not further dwell on any one of these important points here. In
my writings, I have tried to spell out what a contemporary sociological theory based on pragmatism and hermeneutics looks like: Its main
feature is an emphasis on the creative character of human action—with
all the consequences this has for the sub-problems of action theory from
motivation to perception and the questions of the emergence of social
order out of the creative accomplishments of human beings.[5] This
must sound abstract as long as we do not enter the world of concrete
historico-sociological analysis. A last statement of faith here: One of the
great dangers of sociology is that it takes the empirical knowledge of its
classics for granted. How many students have learned things about Protestant ethics or the religion of totemism that are obviously wrong—but
frozen in the sociological heritage because Weber or Durkheim once
made certain claims? For positivists this means that we should finally
"put an end to ancestor worship" (Rodney Stark);[6] but in my view we
should not fall behind the basic hermeneutic insight that there is no
direct, unmediated access to "the facts". We have to do the synthetic
work that the classics once attempted again and again; they have not
done it once and for all. And we have to reflect on the continuities and
discontinuities between their attempts and ours.

Let me now switch to my attempt to illustrate these programmatic
remarks in a specific area of research, namely a historico-sociological
study of what I have called "The Emergence of Universalism". What I
mean by that is the cultural, political and social processes out of which
the first declarations of human rights emerged in North America and
France in the late 18th century and the later waves of a dissemination
of what Thomas Haskell called a "humanitarian sensibility".[7] My point
of departure—that all this began in the 18th century—may already
be debatable; some will claim a much earlier beginning, for example

---

[4] See, for example, Bernstein 1983 and Habermas 1983, 9–28.
[5] Joas 1996.
[6] Stark 2004, 465–475.
[7] Haskell 1992, 107–160.

already in the emergence of the so-called world religions. But although I see their point and would never deny the universalist "potential" of the Christian religious tradition, I find it sociologically unacceptable to think that we should see the more than 1700 years between Jesus Christ and the human rights declarations as a mere maturation of something that had somehow already ever been there.

The type of sociology I am representing here tries to understand—as I said—creative processes. The creative process that interests me most at the moment is the creation of new values.[8] I prefer not to speak of the *creation*, but of the *genesis* of values, because it is one of the seemingly paradoxical features of our commitment to values that we do not experience them as being created by us but as captivating us, attracting and grasping us ("Ergriffensein"). There is a passive dimension in all creative processes that has always been described in terms like "inspiration"; but in the case of values it is clearly only from an observer's standpoint that we can see values as created. The participants in these processes do not feel committed to an entity of their own making, but consider values as being discovered or rediscovered.

A sociological study of major innovations in the field of values is neither a philosophical attempt to offer a rational justification for these values nor a mere historical reconstruction of the contingencies of their emergence. Philosophical justifications do not need history. In the case of human rights, they mostly develop their argument out of the (alleged) character of reason or moral obligation as such, out of the conditions of a thought experiment or the fundamentals of an idealized rational discourse. The history of ideas is then mostly seen as the pre-history of the definitive solution that can be found in the work of Kant or Rawls or Habermas.—Historiography, on the other hand, certainly has some implicit elements of an evaluative character and of their justification and it can be a historiography of philosophical, political, or religious arguments concerning human rights and universal human dignity. But as historiography it seems to be nothing but an empirically tenable reconstruction of historical processes and not a contribution to the justification of values. In their division of labor philosophy and history support a strict distinction between questions of genesis and questions of validity.

---

[8] Joas 2000.

The role of sociology, at least in my eyes, could be to overcome this separation of philosophy and history. Let me first say in negative terms why I think such an overcoming is necessary. I do not believe in the possibility of a purely rational justification of ultimate values. If something is to be called an ultimate value, what should its rational justification be based upon? What could be more basic and still have an evaluative character? Many of those who are like me skeptical with regard to such ultimate justifications fear that this pragmatist non-foundationalist attitude will lead into historical or cultural relativism and open the door for postmodern arbitrariness. In the case of human rights, they rightly claim, we cannot afford a merely playful attitude. But the alternative of ultimate rational justification versus relativism again merely reproduces the sharp distinction of genesis and validity. If this distinction does not really hold with regard to values—as distinct from cognitive or normative validity claims—I can say in positive terms now what a sociological approach could contribute with here. Such a sociology can connect narration and justification in a specific way when it analyses the history of the emergence and the dissemination of certain values. As a narrative reconstruction of such a process it makes us aware that our commitments to values and our conceptions of the valuable are based on experiences and their interpretation. They thus become recognizable as contingent, i.e. non-necessary. No longer do they appear in this analysis as simply pre-given. But such a narration of a contingent process, of values as historical individualities does not weaken our commitment to them or destroy it.

This is the point at which I have to explain why the subtitle of this presentation is "An Affirmative Genealogy". The notion of genealogy is, of course, taken from Nietzsche.[9] Nietzsche is the pioneer of all studies about the genesis of values. He emphasized the contingency of this genesis, the role of power in it, and he assumed that we are always losing faith in these idols as soon as we see how they have been fabricated. I agree with his emphasis on contingency and power, but not with the destructive character of his genealogical method. Bernard Williams, in his last book,[10] has spoken of a "vindicatory" genealogy; I take from Paul Ricoeur's "hermeneutics of affirmation" the term "affir-mative" in order to emphasize that the insight into the contingency of

---

[9] Nietzsche 1883/1969, 761–900.
[10] Williams 2002.

the genesis of values can even strengthen our commitment to them. A brief example will suffice: Why should the fact that post-war Germans feel committed to human rights because of the Holocaust and other Nazi crimes lead to a weakening of their (our) value commitment as soon as we become aware of this contingent context? Why should the fact that power, namely the military power of the Allied Forces, played a crucial role in the democratization of Germany, why should this insight into the role of power weaken a German's commitment to democracy? Nietzsche and his followers, including Foucault, are plainly wrong in this regard. Sociology can contribute to the affirmative genealogy of values in a double sense. It has to study the dynamics that lead to value innovations and the institutionalization of values; this can be called the genesis of values in a *"chronological"* sense. But it also has to study this genesis in an *existential* sense. We do not feel committed to values for the simple reason that they have once come into the world. Human rights, for example, could have disappeared again after their emergence. We would consider them a mere curiosity of the Age of Enlightenment then, like Mesmerism. We always have to ask whether the cultural forces that once made the institutionalization of a value possible are still vital today, whether new cultural forces have come up that are able to compensate for the loss of weakened traditions, and, what is more, whether there are new experiences that reinvigorate old values and revitalize old traditions. Without experiences values are, according to Paul Valéry, nothing but "stuffed animals on a shelf".

Such a study has to do justice both to the positive, let's say enthusiastic, origins of value commitments and to the negative experiences out of which value commitments can arise. In my book *The Genesis of Values*[11] I have only paid attention to the positive roots, the "fascinans" and not the "tremendum" in the experience of the sacred, so to speak. In the following book *War and Modernity*[12] I have tried to analyze the experience of violence as the "perverse brother" of value-constitutive experiences, but again not with regard to the possible transformation of such "negative" experiences into "positive" commitments. This is the basic problem of the current project. What is the role of the experience of violence in the history of human rights? How can experiences of

---

[11] See fn. 8.
[12] Joas 2003.

violence be transformed into value commitments, and, more specifically, into a commitment to the values of moral universalism?

It is clear that I can only summarize the results of this research in a very brief manner here. I first had to study whether there are traces of the history of violence in important documents from the history of human rights. One has, in a second step, to turn around and ask which parts of the history of violence have indeed entered the discourse on human rights so far. If the result of this second step is negative, i.e. if it can be shown that the current human rights discourse is highly selective, then we need conceptual means for the analysis of what has not become part of the discourse, for the insufficiently articulated experiences (third step). The research on "trauma" has recently become prominent in the humanities and the social sciences as a means for that purpose. I share the belief that we have an important approach here, although I am deeply skeptical with regard to the notion of a so-called "cultural trauma". And, in a fourth and last step, one has to systematize the conditions for the successful transformation of experiences of violence into universalist value commitments.

A few remarks on all four steps now. 1. It is easy to demonstrate in the German case how, for example, the concept of human dignity formed a point of orientation in the plans of the German anti-Hitler resistance (the "Kreisau Circle") before 1945 and how it then permeated the preparations for new constitutions in the German states. They mostly refer to "barbarism" and "annihilation" and derive from this experience the justification for their value orientation. But the same is true on the global level. The charter for the foundation of the United Nations in 1945 connects human rights and barbarism. Several authors have meticulously studied how a shared repudiation of Nazism and Fascism influenced the drafts preceding the UN Declaration of Human Rights in 1948. One has called the experience of Nazism and the Second World War the "epistemic foundation" of this declaration, the common ground of various religious and non-religious world-views.[13] And this is not only true for the preamble, but for individual articles and specific formulations against servitude, for example, against "cruel, inhuman, or degrading treatment or punishment", for the right to seek asylum. The right to political participation (Art. 21) is directed against the Fascist conception of a substantive will of the people incarnate in

---

[13] Morsink 1993, 357–405.

the person of the "Führer", and the "internationalist" interpretation of human rights (Art. 30) cannot be understood aside from the fact that the international community realized that prior to 1939 (or 1941) the struggle against Nazism had not been considered the task of all other states.

2. As unambiguous as the picture then seems at first, it changes completely when we change the perspective. Although positive values can be distilled from negative experiences, it would be absurd to assume that injustice always leads to higher justice, violence to progress. Suffering can also lead to hopelessness, despair, revenge, a spiraling of violence. The less we think that Nazism is representative for state-organized and collective violence as such, the less a human rights discourse based on the experience of Nazism can be taken as comprehensive. Stalinism is to some extent analogous to Fascism and Nazism, but only to some extent, and the Stalinist Soviet Union at the time prevented any serious debate about its human rights record in the drafting of the relevant documents. And the same has to be said about the colonial powers and their role in this process. Even today, we have not yet arrived at an appropriate inclusion of the history of colonialism into the contemporary discourse about human rights.

3. In this situation the social sciences have to ask whether there are empirically verifiable traces of the experience of violence, long-term consequences of an experience that has successfully been excluded from official discourse. Research on "trauma" has proven to be one of the most fruitful endeavors in this regard, and in my book on war I have myself tried to contribute to it. But in the work of Jeffrey Alexander and others[14] the research on trauma has became "culturalized"—not just in the sense of the cultural preconditions for human experience and its articulation, but in the sense of the assumption that whole cultures can be traumatized; this conceptual move has been accompanied by a "subjectivation" of the concept of trauma itself so that a trauma seems to exist only "when members of a collective *feel* (my emphasis, H. J.) they have been subjected to a horrendous event [...]".[15] But can the notion of trauma really be extended to whole cultures? Is there such a thing as a "cultural" trauma? Does a trauma depend on being defined as such by those most affected by it?

---

[14] Alexander, Eyerman, Giesen, Smelser and Sztompka 2004.
[15] Alexander et al. 2004, 1.

I cannot really develop my argument here, but it leads me to negative conclusions in all three respects.[16] No doubt, there are claims of cultural traumatization to be found in our culture, and the sociological examination of the emergence and dissemination of these claims is certainly useful. However, this aspect should not be conflated with the question what the consequences of actual personal traumatization are. "Cultural traumas" are neither the presupposition for individual traumatization nor their consequences. Individual traumatization as such does not depend on its cultural definition as trauma. Such a "culturalism" has to be checked by an "experientialism"—this, I would say, is an important legacy both of pragmatism and hermeneutics.

4. For the analysis of successful transformation processes in this field of study we need two things. First a study of articulation processes, and second an integration of this study into the fields of power and interests. Neither a cultural nor a material determinism is appropriate here. In my current work I am concentrating on the rise of abolitionism as a case study in the "emergence of universalism". The dynamics of articulation refer to an interplay of processes on four levels: the situations of action and experience themselves with their own qualitative immediacy, our pre-reflective responses to such situations, our own articulation of these pre-reflective responses, and publicly available and established interpretations. Such a model for the articulation of experience has nothing to do with a naïve belief in an unmediated access to "experience as such".[17] And, at least in my case study of abolitionism, this model can be integrated with the dynamics of a social movement, its international features and the cognitive repercussions of an increased role of markets at the same time when the revolution in humanitarian sensibility took place.

All this had to remain relatively abstract here, but maybe it is sufficient to make the claim plausible that such an "affirmative genealogy" of moral universalism is a viable sociological project and does indeed fill a gap in moral philosophy as well. Since the force of "rational motivation" is only weak, moral progress depends on strong motivations, and the study of their sources is an important interest of sociology and moral philosophy alike.

---

[16] See Joas 2005, 365–374.
[17] Joas 2002, 506–515.

References

Alexander, J., R. Eyerman, B. Giesen, N. Smelser and P. Sztompka. 2004. *Cultural Trauma and Collective Identity*, Berkeley: University of California Press.

Bernstein, R. 1983. *Beyond Objectivism and Relativism: Science, Hermeneutics and Praxis*, Oxford: Basil Blackwell.

Habermas, J. 1983. "Die Philosophie als Platzhalter und Interpret" in J. Habermas, *Moralbewußtsein und kommunikatives Handeln*, Frankfurt/Main: Suhrkamp Verlag, 9–28.

Haskell, T. 1992. "Capitalism and the origins of the humanitarian sensibility" (Parts 1 and 2), in T. Bender (ed.), *The Antislavery Debate*, Berkeley: University of California Press, 107–160.

Joas, H. 1993. "American pragmatism and German thought: A history of misunderstandings" in H. Joas, *Pragmatism and Social Theory*, Chicago: University of Chicago Press, 94–121.

——. "Pragmatism in American sociology" in *Pragmatism and Social Theory*, Chicago: University of Chicago Press, 14–51.

——. 1996. *The Creativity of Action*, Chicago: University of Chicago Press.

——. 2000. *The Genesis of Values*, Chicago: University of Chicago Press.

——. 2002. "On articulation" in *Constellations*, 9:506–515.

——. 2003. *War and Modernity*, Cambridge: Polity Press.

——. 2005. "Cultural trauma?" in *European Journal of Social Theory*, 8:365–374.

Levine, D. N. 1995. *Visions of the Sociological Tradition*, Chicago: University of Chicago Press.

Morsink, J. 1993. "World War Two and the universal declaration" in *Human Rights Quaterly*, 5:357–405.

Nietzsche, F. 1883/1969. *Über die Genealogie der Moral*. vol. 2, F. N. Werke (ed.), München, 761–900.

Stark, R. 2004. "Putting an end to ancestor worship" (SSSR presidential address) in *Journal for the Scientific Study of Religion*, 43:465–475.

Williams, B. 2002. *Truth and Truthfulness: An Essay in Genealogy*, Princeton: Princeton University Press.

THE SOCIAL SCIENCES AND THE TWO RELATIVISMS[1]

Raymond Boudon

Among his many predictions, Tocqueville has foreseen that relativism would be a dominant worldview in modern societies. He was certainly right as far at least as the social sciences are concerned. In the last thirty years, they have much contributed making relativism legitimate in its two main forms: cognitive and cultural. Why is that so? Where does the influence of these two forms of relativism come from? Are they promised to the same future? Here are the questions I would like to explore. I will deal with cognitive relativism firstly and secondly with cultural relativism. I will evidently not try to treat this complex subject in its full extension, but rather concentrate my attention on some basic cognitive and social mechanisms responsible for the popularity of the two forms of relativism.

1. *Cognitive Relativism*

Kuhn's Role

An important source of cognitive relativism is the "new sociology of science", an intellectual tradition which was started with Kuhn's work (1962) on *The Structure of scientific revolutions*. More than any other, this thin book has given an entirely new orientation to the sociology of science.

The "classical" sociology of science, the sociology of science that was developed from Durkheim to, say, Merton, dealt with questions concerning the extrascientific origin of scientific concepts, as when Durkheim (1912/1979) wondered where the notion of force came from; it dealt with the role of institutions on scientific productivity, as when Ben David and Zloczower (1962) wondered why Germany was eminent in many scientific fields in the 19th century; it dealt with the impact on the development of science of ideas developed in politics,

---

[1] This communication leans heavily on a chapter of my book on *The Poverty of Relativism*, Oxford, Bardwell, 2004.

philosophy or religion, as when Merton (1938/1970) analyzed the influence of Puritanism on the development of science. None of these writers held the view that the impact of institutional or social factors on science would imply that scientific theories would be unable to reach objective validity.

After the publication of Kuhn's *Structure of Scientific Revolutions*, the sociology of science took a new turn. Kuhn's main thesis was that the history of sciences is much less linear than philosophers of science had maintained until Popper. As Kuhn rightly claimed, the detailed analysis of scientific discussions shows that they are less "rational" than philosophers of science have asserted. Beside logical criteria, aesthetical, political, religious or ideological factors also play a role in the fact that a scientist prefers a theory to an alternative one. But nobody would have accepted that, since *some* individuals can, in *given* circumstances, prefer a scientific theory for non scientific reasons, *all* scientific theories would in *all* circumstances be accepted or rejected on the basis of non scientific reasons. Kuhn did not draw this conclusion himself. But it was quickly drawn by his followers.

Some years after Kuhn's work appeared, Feyerabend (1975) went as far as to maintain that scientific theories would be "fairy tales". In France, Latour and Woolgar (1979) went further: scientific explanations are "constructions" and, as we see the world through these constructions, we cannot compare the images of the world they deliver with a "reality out there" that we have no access to.

Gusfield (1981) maintained that, as the relationship between drinking and automobile accidents is demonstrated by using correlation coefficients, it is "constructed" and thus should not be considered as a "fact". Rorty (1979) stressed that knowledge is not a "mirror of nature". This point had been recognized at least since Kant. Rorty drew novel conclusions from it, though: since knowledge is not a mirror of nature, it is a construction, always to some extent arbitrary.

Why has this cognitive relativism become widely accepted and has it taken extreme forms? The starting point of this process derives from the fact that Kuhn had developed his views on science on the basis of careful historical monographs, as the controversy on the phlogiston theory in the 18th century. So, Kuhn has started a revolution in the first place because his book rested on a robust core.

The Philosophy of Science in a Dead-End

A second factor contributes to explain Kuhn's influence and the radicalisation of his ideas by his followers: that, at the time when he exposed his theses, the philosophy of science appears as blocked in a dead-end.

The modern philosophy of science had raised notably one question: on the basis of which criteria can a scientific theory be distinguished from a non scientific one? A theory is scientific, according to Popper's famous answer (1934/1968), if and only if it can be contradicted—"falsified" in Popper's vocabulary—by observational data.

In spite of the intellectual modesty of Popper's theory, it has been shown though that it does not capture the distinction between scientific and non-scientific theories.

- Firstly, because many falsifiable statements are not normally considered as scientific, as: "the train from Paris to London is leaving at 8 a.m."
- Secondly, because many theories normally considered as scientific cannot be falsified, as all the theories which introduce the clause "other things equal" without proposing any clear criteria on the basis of which one can be sure that "other things" are actually "equal".
- Thirdly, because some scientific theories do not bear on actual phenomena, but deal rather with the question as to how phenomena of a given class should be explained. Thus, the neo-Darwinian theory of evolution deals with the way evolutionary facts should be explained: as the effect of mutation and selection. Such theories cannot be falsified since an advice cannot be properly falsified.
- Fourthly, a crucial point of Popper's theory is that it introduces a radical asymmetry between truth and falsity. As the so-called Duhem-Quine thesis states, it is not easier to be convinced that a theory is false than to be convinced that it is true.
- Fifthly, scientific theories contain concepts which have the status of non empirical constructs. They are included in statements which for this reason cannot be falsified.

In summary, the intellectual conjuncture of the 1960s and of the following decades is characterized on the one hand by the wide attention granted to Kuhn's theory and, on the other hand, by a growing scepticism towards the idea that it would be possible to draw a clear demarcation line between science and non-science.

Misusing the No Middle Term Principle

At this point, a cognitive mechanism played a crucial role. When a number is odd, it cannot be even. The two terms are contradictory. By contrast, when a pen is not black, that does not mean that it is white. "Black" and "white" are *contrary*, not *contradictory* terms.

As already noted by Pareto (1916/1964–1988), the confusion between "contrary" and "contradictory" is a basic cognitive mechanism responsible for many false beliefs. It leads to a misuse of the no middle term principle. It inspires illegitimate questions taking an *either/or* form.

This is the case here: the basic question behind the works of the "new sociology of science" can be formulated: is the selection of scientific ideas rational *or not*? The answer of the "new sociology of science" to this question is "no", since Kuhn has shown that the selection of scientific ideas can be inspired by irrational motivations. The same is true of the other question underlying the "new sociology of science", the question as to whether a clear demarcation line can be drawn between science and non-science *or not*. If it cannot, then the binary form of the question leads to the conclusion that the distinction between science and non-science is an illusion. Hence some went as far as to conclude, as Feyerabend (1975) or in Germany, Hübner (1985), that mythical explanations of the world are as valid as scientific ones. On the whole, the misuse of the no middle term principle led from the acceptable views of Kuhn to much more radically relativistic views of science, as Feyerabend's.

Pareto's Distinction between "Truth" and "Usefulness"

Beside this cognitive mechanism, a social mechanism is responsible for the influence of cognitive relativism. It was also identified by Pareto (1916/1964–1988): some beliefs become influent, he states, not because they are "true", but because they are "useful", in other words, because they serve social interests.

This mechanism is relevant here. The relativistic view on science produced by the "new sociology of science" (Bunge 1999) was developed in an intellectual conjuncture when the collusion between science and politics became a central issue in intellectual circles. Consequently, theories which showed that the authority of science and scientists is treated as more legitimate than it should be were "useful" in Pareto's sense.

So, the growing radicalisation of cognitive relativism from Kuhn to his followers can be explained by a three phase process.

- Phase 1: it gets started with the mobilisation of objectively credible core ideas;
- Phase 2: these core ideas are then hyperbolised thanks to cognitive mechanisms as the confusion between contrary and contradictory terms;
- Phase 3: finally, the hyperboles become popular because, besides looking credible, they also appear as "useful" to some audiences.

I leave aside the point that this "usefulness" can be exogenous but also endogenous and give birth to cycles: when a hyperbolized idea starts arousing doubts, it tends to be replaced by the opposite hyperbolized idea, as suggested by Pareto or Sorokin (Boudon 1989).

The Decline of the New Sociology of Science

The new sociology of science is no more as influential as it was. Durkheim (1912/1979:624) has identified in his *Elementary Forms of Religious Life* the main socio-cognitive mechanism responsible for this type of decline: it often occurs, he claims, that an idea is endorsed by most people in a first stage because it is collectively accepted, while in a second stage it remains collectively accepted only under the condition that it can be held as objectively grounded.

The case of the "modern sociology of science" illustrates this mechanism. Cognitive relativism was in a first stage held as true because its main intuitions were collectively accepted, notably among the sociologists of science. Doubts on the solidity of the "new sociology of science" appeared from the moment when Sokal, a physicist, had the idea to submit to a professional journal devoted to the "new sociology of science" a paper defending its views, but containing a number of statements and equations which were mere nonsense for any educated physicist. The paper was published without hesitation, though. Sokal's successful hoax contributed a great deal to discredit the "new sociology of science" (Sokal and Bricmont 1997). Thanks notably to Sokal's hoax, its claims appeared as ungrounded. Two arguments are essentially responsible for this disqualification.

1. As rightly stated by Kuhn, the selection process of scientific ideas is *in the short term* much less rational than handbook writers assume. But handbooks are right *in the long term*. Lavoisier's theory of the composition of the air is objectively more solidly grounded than Priestley's phlogiston theory. But this certainty emerged *in the long term*, while in the *short term* Priestley's arguments appeared as credible. As soon as this distinction between the long and the short term is taken into account, the question as to whether the selection of scientific ideas is rational *or not* becomes meaningless: it is not rational in the short term; it is in the long term (Boudon 1994).

2. The same type of argument can be developed as far as the question of the demarcation criteria between science and non-science is concerned. They were not found. Nobody succeeded providing clear general criteria on the basis of which it would be possible to distinguish a scientific from a non scientific theory. But the fact that there are no *general* demarcation criteria does not lead to the conclusion that the distinction between science and non-science is illegitimate: we know that there are scientific and magical explanations of a number of phenomena and we are able to make the difference.

On the whole, the decline of the "new sociology of science" is an effect of the mechanism identified by Durkheim. We realise clearly now that the cognitive relativism it supports is ill-grounded. Sokal's hoax has accelerated the process. But it worked because the "new sociology of science" was unable to defend its claims against the arguments which had been opposed to it.

2. *Cultural Relativism*

I turn now to cultural relativism. It is much more influent and widely spread than cognitive relativism. In spite of this difference, the two forms of relativism have a common feature. In the two cases, relativism has become established under the effect of the general three phase process I have described in the cognitive case: 1) mobilization of hard core ideas; 2) derivation of hyperbolic conclusions from these core ideas with the help of cognitive mechanisms as the confusion between contrary and contradictory terms and the misuse of the principle of the no middle term; 3) diffusion of the hyperbolic conclusions thanks to their "usefulness", i.e. their congruence with collective material or symbolic interests.

I will start with the core ideas. Cultural relativism is grounded notably on three core ideas to which three great names can be associated: Montaigne, David Hume and Max Weber. They have all much inspired modern analysts: philosophers as well as anthropologists, political scientists or sociologists.

Core Idea 1: Montaigne

The prominent American anthropologist Clifford Geertz (1984) is the author of an influential article entitled "Anti-anti-relativism". It rests explicitly on the famous thesis of Montaigne's *Essays* according to which the diversity of norms through cultures proves that they are conventional: as some say, they are "culturally arbitrary". According to Geertz, Montaigne would have discovered an essential truth, consolidated by modern anthropology: the truth according to which there would be no normative truth, but only customs, variable from one culture to another. People see their normative beliefs as grounded on reasons. But these reasons would be mere justifications rather than the causes of these beliefs. They would be unconsciously endorsed by people because of their functional psychological value.

Beside Geertz (1984), many before and after him, as Granet (1990), Whorf (1969), Needham (1972), Shweder (1991) or Lévi-Strauss (1952) and political scientists as Goldhagen (1997) or Huntington (1996) clearly endorse the same idea.

In this vein, an article by Richard Shweder (2000)—the author of fascinating studies in cognitive psychology as well as anthropology—evokes the case of an African anthropologist. She was raised in the US, went back to her country, Sierra Leone, after graduation and submitted herself to genital mutilation. In a communication to the American anthropological society, she stated that most women in her tribe, the Kono tribe, draw from excision a feeling of enhanced power. From this fact, Shweder concludes that people consider a norm as positive or negative because they are exposed to cultural forces emanating from the cultural environment. These forces would be powerful enough as to make that a scholar educated in a modern culture and going back to her original culture would experience genital mutilation as a "positive" experience. Shweder goes even further. The negative medical effects of genital mutilation would have been greatly exaggerated, according to a study conducted by a Harvard anthropologist, he states. This study would indicate that the negative feeling toward genital mutilation Westerners normally experience is the mere product of their own socialisation.

Thus, Montaigne offers to cultural relativists a first *core idea*: the diversity of norms and values through cultures would imply that they are mere socio-cultural unconscious conventions that are transmitted to individuals through socialisation.

Core Idea 2: David Hume

A second core idea has had a more diffuse but still powerful influence: the famous theorem we owe to David Hume according to which no system of assertive statements can lead to a prescriptive conclusion. The theorem is true. From this theorem the view has been drawn that prescriptive statements cannot, by essence, be objectively grounded. There would be an unbridgeable gap between facts and values.

This idea has had a considerable influence. Hume's theorem gives, so to say, a powerful theoretical ground to Montaigne's empirical observation that norms and values appear as highly variable among societies.

Core Idea 3: Max Weber

The social sciences owe to Max Weber a third core idea. He is some-times presented as a relativist on the basis of two famous metaphors: "value polytheism" and the "war of Gods" (Weber 1919/1995). These metaphors suggest that social life would be essentially characterised by value conflicts with no solution.

3. Do We Need to Believe in the Hyperbolic Interpretations of the Three Core Ideas?

Montaigne

I turn now to the cognitive mechanisms responsible for the hyperboliza-tion of these core ideas.

Montaigne's core idea takes with Geertz a radical form thanks to the introduction of the *either/or* principle, i.e. of the principle of the "no middle term": norms are *either* conventional *or* rationally grounded. Obviously, Geertz ignores that *some* norms and values are conventional, while others are not; that a rule can be arbitrary and grounded in *tradition*, while it expresses a value or a norm which is rational in the sense that it derives from *reasons*. To take a trivial example: there are no reasons, except conventional, to shake hands as Frenchmen use to do, while there are reasons to be polite: the norm "be polite" is itself grounded on a value, i.e. the respect due to other people in reciprocity of the respect we expect from them.

The case of female genital mutilation illustrates the importance of these distinctions. Shweder (2000) seems to accept that the feeling of indignation normally aroused by the practice of excision in the mind of Westerners would be "cultural": their negative feeling would be an effect of their socialisation to values typical of Western societies.

It is perhaps simpler to assume that Westerners have some *reasons* to have a negative reaction against female genital mutilation. All societies tend to develop rituals, the function of which is to integrate the youngsters into the world of adults and to help them to develop their personal identity. One can accept the idea that female genital mutilation has a function of this type in the Kono society. But we know also that personal identity and integration can mobilize other devices and that these devices can legitimately be preferred if they appear as equally efficient and less cruel than the devices generating a corporal mutilation.

When Westerners learn that in some societies thieves can have their hands cut off, they have normally a reaction of indignation. No anthropologist has actually dared, to my knowledge at least, to extend to this other case the cultural explanation of this reaction some of them, among the most prominent, treat as evident in the case of excision. Probably because the *rational* explanation appears in this case as clearly much more acceptable than the *cultural* one.

The implicit theory which I propose to introduce here into the mind of Westerners is no other than the theory Durkheim (1893/1973) has explicitly developed in his *Division of social labour*. Social control tends to become softer over time because when a new device of social control is found which is as efficient as the existing devices and more respectful of human dignity, it tends to be socially selected (Boudon 2002).

So, if we follow Durkheim, we can suppose that Westerners perceive the practice of excision negatively, not because they would have been socialised to values incompatible with such practices, but because they have strong reasons of doing so.

The assumption introduced by culturalists that normative beliefs should be held either as cultural *or* as rational rests actually on the undesirable *a priori* that there would be no middle term.

David Hume

So, the relativistic conclusions drawn from Montaigne by culturalists need not to be accepted. The same is true of the relativistic conclusions drawn from Hume. The correct formulation of his theorem is that it is impossible to draw a prescriptive conclusion from a set of statements which are *all* descriptive. Reciprocally: a prescriptive conclusion *can* be derived from a set of statements, provided *one of them at least* is prescriptive, whence it results that a normative argument can very well be discussed at the light of factual considerations. The unbridgeable gap between facts and values is a myth.

Thus, the pseudo-corollary currently drawn from Hume's theorem according to which prescriptive conclusions cannot be drawn from descriptive statements is a mere sophism. But the influence of this sophism contributes to explain that the false idea according to which normative and axiological beliefs would be conventional has become widespread.

Max Weber

As I said earlier, Max Weber is sometimes represented as a hard relativist: he would have insisted on the point that societies are endemically threatened by endless and merciless value conflicts. But he has also repeatedly insisted through his notion of "diffuse rationalization" (*Durchrationalisierung*) on the fact that political, social or moral ideas tend to be rationally selected in the long term.

The apparent contradiction can be solved in the following way: Weber was aware that every theory, including the most solidly established physical theory, rests necessarily upon undemonstrated principles. Otherwise, the basic statements of a theory would not be principles. He sees in other words principles as provisional assumptions which are kept up or rejected according to the interest of the consequences they generate.

On the whole, I would submit that Weber sketches in his various writings a theory of the selection of social norms which I would qualify as "programmatic". Thus, when a political institution seems to lead to an increased respect for the dignity of individuals, it tends to be perceived as legitimate, to be collectively approved and, if the circumstances are favourable, to be socially selected. One can think of the recognition of unions or of the right to strike. These institutions have become established in a growing number of places because they generate in principle a protection of workers and employees. Now, the general principle according to which every member of a community should be equally protected cannot be demonstrated. It represents the first element in a chain of arguments. Being the first one, it cannot be grounded on other principles. But it inspires political life constantly. This is exactly what Durkheim (1893/1973) meant on his side when he asserted that "individualism"—the need of any human being to see his dignity respected—has always been a central value, in all times and all societies.

This does not say that political and social life is peaceful. It took a long time and many struggles before the right to strike was accepted. Before it was accepted, the "polytheism of values" ruled: some actors explained that strikes would ruin the economy, while others maintained that the economic system would run more smoothly if power was more evenly distributed among the various economic actors. Today, the "polytheism of values" and the "war among Gods" are over as far as this issue is concerned. Many issues have in the same way given birth to a situation of "polytheism of values" in a first stage and to a solution to the conflict of values in the long term: think of the separation of the State and the Church, of the notion of *Rechtsstaat*, of the subsidiarity principle, of the equality between genders, of the division of powers, etc. My guess is that Weber had such examples in mind when he evoked both the "war among Gods" *and* the process of "diffuse rationalisation".

4. *Toward the End of Cultural Relativism*

To conclude on cultural relativism: it results from a hyperbolic treatment of core ideas developed notably by Montaigne, Hume and Weber. It draws hyperbolic conclusions from these core ideas thanks to cognitive mechanisms, as the misuse of the no middle term principle, the overgeneralization of given ideas or the derivation of doubtful consequences from true theories, as in the case of Hume's theorem. These cognitive mechanisms are crucial for the sociology of ideas: they explain why many false or fragile beliefs are endorsed by people. Of course, other cognitive mechanisms would be at work in other examples.

But in order to understand why false or fragile beliefs can become collective, another mechanism, a non cognitive one, should be introduced beside the cognitive mechanisms, the mechanism identified by

Pareto according to which collective beliefs are reinforced when they are "useful": when they serve the interests of some social groups.

As cognitive relativism, cultural relativism is effectively "useful" in Pareto's sense. The culturalist analysis of the reaction to excision is certainly palatable to those in Sierra Leone who have the impression that this tradition is an essential feature of their culture. It is also palatable to the Westerners who have the of course fully justified impression that a moral obligation of our time is to respect all cultures. Colonialism was possible, they claim rightly, because cultures were considered as unequal. This view justified the imposition of the Western culture on other cultures. If cultural relativism is right, no culture is better than any other and no society better than any other. In Pareto's vocabulary cultural relativism is in that sense "useful": it legitimizes ideas which are morally fully justified.

One can, however, be a strong opponent of any institution or enterprise hurting the dignity of men without accepting cultural relativism since it is both wrong from a scientific point of view and incompatible with the obvious observation that the wellbeing and the dignity of people are better preserved in some societies than in others.

References

Ben David, J. and A. Zloczower. 1962. "Universities and academic systems in modern societies" in *Archives Européennes de Sociologie*, III, 45–84.
Boudon, R. 1989. *The Analysis of Ideology*, London: Polity Press.
——. 1994. *The Art of Self-persuasion*, London: Polity Press.
——. 2002. *Déclin de la Morale? Déclin des Valeurs?*, Paris: Presses Universitaires de France et Québec, Nota Bene.
Bunge, M. 1999. *The Sociology-Philosophy Connection*, New Brunswik/London: Transaction.
Durkheim, É. 1912/1979. *Les Formes Élémentaires de la Vie Religieuse*, Paris: Presses Universitaires de France.
——. 1893/1973. *De la Division du Travail Social*, Paris: Presses Universitaires de France.
Feyerabend, P. 1975. *Against Method*, London: N.L.B.
Geertz, C. 1984. "Distinguished lecture: Anti anti-relativism" in *American Anthropologist*, 86(2): 263–278.
Goldhagen, D. J. 1997. *Hitler's Willing Executioners: Ordinary Germans and the Holocaust*, New York: A. Knopf.
Granet, M. 1990. *Études Sociologiques sur la Chine*, Paris: Presses Universitaires de France.
Gusfield, J. 1981. *The Culture of Public Problems: Drinking-Driving and the Symbolic Order*, Chicago: University of Chicago Press.
Hübner, K. 1985. *Die Wahrheit des Mythos*, Munich: Beck.

Hume, D. 1741/1972. *Essais Politiques*, Paris: Vrin. Translation of. *Essays, Moral and Political*, London: printed for A. Millar, third edition, 1748.

Huntington, S. 1996. *The Clash of Civilizations and the Remaking of the World Order*, New York: Shuster and Shuster.

Kuhn, T. 1962. *The Structure of Scientific Revolutions*, Chicago: University of Chicago Press.

Latour, B. and S. Woolgar. 1979. *Laboratory Life: The Social Construction of Scientific Facts*, London: Sage.

Lévi-Strauss, C. 1952. *Race et Histoire*, Paris: UNESCO. Repr.: Paris, Gonthier.

Merton, R. 1938/1970. *Science, Technology and Society in Seventeenth Century England*, New York: Howard Fertig. First published 1938 under the title "Studies on the History and Philosophy of Science" in *Osiris* 4(2).

Needham, R. 1972. *Belief, Language and Experience*, Oxford: Blackwell.

Pareto, V. 1916/1964–1988. *Traité de sociologie générale: Oeuvres Completes*, vol. 12, Genève: Droz.

Popper, K. R. 1934/1968. *The Logic of Scientific Discovery*, London: Hutchinson. First published 1934 under the title *Logik der Forschung*, Vienna.

Rorty, R. 1979. *Philosophy and the Mirror of Nature*, Princeton: Princeton University Press.

Shweder, R. A. 1991. *Thinking through Cultures: Expeditions in Cultural Anthropology*, Cambridge: Harvard University Press.

——. 2000. "What about 'female genital mutilation' and why understanding culture matters in the first place" in *Daedalus*, 129(4): 209–232.

Sokal, A. and J. Bricmont. 1997. *Impostures intellectuelles*, Paris: O. Jacob.

Weber, M. 1919/1995. *Wissenschaft als Beruf*, Stuttgart: Reklam.

Whorf, B. L. 1969. *Linguistique et Anthropologie: Les Origines de la Sémiologie*, Paris: Denoël.

THE RETURN TO VALUES IN RECENT SOCIOLOGICAL THEORY*

Piotr Sztompka

Why "the Return"?

The problem of value judgments and their role in sociological thinking is one of the perennial riddles of sociology. Already for the founding fathers of the discipline in the 19th century the distinction of scholarly, fact-oriented and moral, normative discourse created grave difficulties. Their intellectual roots were in philosophy—political philosophy, philosophy of history, philosophical anthropology, ethics—and hence they were ready to speak about "good society", "social progress", "human nature", "justice" etc., all these notions infused with valuations. At the same time their ambition was to create a "science" of society, and in their days it was synonymous with "positive science", focusing on facts, data, and at most observable relations of coexistence or temporal sequence among facts. They were not able to solve this dilemma and in their writings we can find parallel, sometimes overlapping, sometimes separate forms of discourse: just reporting but also critical, descriptive and prescriptive, explanatory and visionary, fact-oriented or stipulating values.

Then, in the 20th century the aspiration to be truly "scientific" in order to safeguard for sociology the legitimate position in the academic institutions, became dominant. For a long time the positivist creed has been ruling, with the attempt to purge values from sociological, empirical inquiry, and either ignore them altogether or allow only as data of social consciousness disclosed by value surveys and opinion polls, and treated just like any other facts, at a distance, with "cold", detached, and purely descriptive attitude. This was typical for the whole epoch of narrow empiricism, trapped in the futile attempt to catch up with

* This article was previously published in the *Polish Sociological Review*, 3 (2007): 247–261 and is reprinted in this volume with permission of the Editorial Board of the *Polish Sociological Review*.

the standards of the natural sciences. Any trace of value judgments was considered unscientific.

And it is only recently that sociology opens again toward values and embraces values again as an integral, legitimate component of sociological work. But it does not indicate a simple return to the masters who were torn—as we have seen—by ambivalence, because the riddle of valuations is approached in an entirely new way. To render this novelty clear I will leave a historical overview and introduce an analytic typology of three ways in which values have been treated in sociology: (a) as a bias, (b) as an ideology, (c) as a part of meaning.

Values as a Bias

The first position treats values as personal and subjective biases, which sociologists, being human, cannot avoid and which interfere in research. They are the nuisance, the obstacle to valid, many-sided and "objective" knowledge. Therefore they must be bridled, tamed, controlled or if possible entirely eliminated from the domain of science.

Let us look at some influential examples of such an approach. Herbert Spencer in *The Study of Sociology* (1894) gives a list of pernicious biases to which researchers should be sensitized and which should be avoided. They create "difficulties in the way of sociological science which arise from the various emotions excited by the matters it deals with" (Spencer 1894/1903). He discusses the educational bias, the bias of patriotism, the class bias, the political bias, the theological bias etc. The remedy he proposes, in a typical positivist mood, is rigorous traininng of sociologists in some fields of natural science which would provide them with the requisite discipline of thought insulating against biases.

In a similar vein Emile Durkheim in *The Rules of Sociological Method* (1897) recommends suspending all presuppositions, coming to research with open, clear and unprejudiced mind and assuming a detached, objective attitude "treating social facts as things" (of course not in the ontological sense of material objects, but as a methodological posture akin to that of the natural scientists). "The sociologist must emancipate himself from the fallacious ideas that dominate the mind of the layman" (Durkheim 1897/1962: 32).

A more sophisticated solution is proposed by Max Weber in the famous doctrine of "Wertfreiheit". First, he distinguishes teaching from research, demanding complete neutrality and objectivism of educational, pedagogical work. It is illegitimate to assert values from the lectern, the students must only be given intellectual resources for their own valuational conclusions. The role of the academic teacher must be separate from the role of the active citizen. Entering the lecture hall professors should leave their ideological views, like a coat in the cloakroom. Second, within the research process proper, Weber distinguishes the heuristic phase (what Hans Reichenbach called later "the context of discovery" [1949]) and the research phase (in the language of Reichenbach "the context of justification"). Whereas values are admitted and even indispensible for the selection of problems and the shaping of tentative hypotheses, the solving of problems, testing of hypotheses and the validating of solutions must be entirely value-free. "There must be a rigorous distinction between empirical knowledge and value judgments" (Weber 1949: 49). "An empirical science cannot tell anyone what he should do—but rather what he can do—and under certain circumstances what he wishes to do" (Weber 1949: 54). Third, values that the people hold to (as different from the values of the researcher) are the crucial subject matter of sociological research, because human reality, in Weberian account, is pervaded with values, which are its indispensable, constitutive dimension. But values can be studied in a value-free, scientific mood. Sociology of religion is not the same as theology or sociology of morals, not the same as ethics or political science and not the same as ideological doctrine.

In the 20th century sociology we find a very characteristic pronouncement of similar approach in Gunnar Myrdal's little book *Objectivity in the Social Sciences* (1969). He focuses on stereotypes, prejudices and folk wisdom which influence the researcher and argues that "disinterested social science has never existed and for logical reasons can never exist" (1969: 55). The only road to objectivity in the social sciences is not to hide inevitable valuations, but "to raise the valuations actually determining our theoretical as well as practical research to full awareness" (1969: 5), and then to reveal them frankly and openly together with research results. In other words: "to expose the valuations in full light, make them conscious, specific and explicit" (1969: 56). The open disclosure of valuations, the debate and clash among competing biases will neutralize and eliminate their impact, leading to a more objective picture of the social world.

Values as Ideology

The second traditional approach to values treats them as synonymous with ideologies, i.e. not as pernicious individual, subjective biases but just the reverse—as cognitively beneficial and enlightening collective perspectives, not blocking but actually facilitating the access to true knowledge. The central claim is rooted in the so-called sociology of knowledge and goes as follows: the existential social situation of researchers and different cognitive horizons which attach to that, give them unequal opportunities for reaching full and adequate knowledge about society. Social knowledge is therefore always perspectivistic, ideological, and reflects interests and values. But—and this is a crucial proviso—not all ideologies are equal in cognitive chances. One should identify the conducive, fruitful perspectives from which society should be approached to obtain best cognitive results.

This implies a search in two directions. The first direction is taken by Karl Mannheim: he identifies groups whose existential condition makes them least polluted by particularistic interests and values. Their universalistic *Weltanshauung* guarantees impartiality. In *Ideology and Utopia* he points to the "free-floating unattached intellectuals" as those who are predisposed for objectivity (Mannheim 1960). The second direction is taken by Karl Marx and some later Marxists, as well as other brands of left-wing scholars. They search for groups whose particularistic perspective is most revealing, giving privileged access to the truth about society. In other words: instead of affirming universalism, they affirm some, supposedly eye-opening particularism. There are two suggestions. According to one it is the positions of those oppressed, excluded and discriminated against, the underdogs which open the eyes to true problems of society. They do not hide realities, just the reverse, it is in their best interests to reveal the mechanisms of exploitation, identify the exploiters, and debunk their ideologies. The classical formulation comes from Marx himself and is elaborated by Georgy Lukacs in *History and Class Consciousness* (Lukacs 1971); the sociologist should adopt the perspective of the proletariat. Members of this class, the most oppressed, exploited and de-humanized in the capitalist system "have nothing to lose but their chains" as Marx and Engels put it in the *Communist Manifesto* (Marx and Engels 1848/1998), so they do not have any interest in hiding oppressive social realities. Some more recent version of this approach can be found in the radical sociology which calls for the adoption of the perspective of the minorities, as well as in the feminist sociology which considers the perspective of women as cognitively privileged and demands purging sociology of the one-sided and distorting "masculine gaze". The alternative way to search for privileged epistemological position is suggested by the proponents of what Robert K. Merton ridicules and criticizes as the doctrine of "insiderism", namely the belief that knowledge can be attained only by direct experience, revealing the social situations from the inside (e.g. that Blacks may only be understood by Blacks, women by women, homosexuals by homosexuals) (Merton 1973).

Areas of Commonality between Two Approaches

At the first glance the negative view of values as detrimental bias, and the positive view of values as facilitating ideology, are fundamentally opposite. But in their extremism neither seem to be fully satisfactory. In order to overcome both extreme positions one must unravel some basic, deeper-lying assumptions that they both share. Only by identifying and then rejecting such assumptions shall we be able to formulate a third approach, more adequate than the other two (for the explication and various applications of this strategy see: Sztompka 1979).

There are several common assumptions of both traditional approaches. First, and most importantly, they take for granted the radical dichotomy of facts and values, categorical statements and value judgments, so strongly advocated by positivist, neo-positivist and all other "scientistic" models of science. As we remember one position claims that in the context of inquiry values are bad, another that values are good, but none questions the fundamental distinction of values from facts. They are particularly adamant in emphasizing that no facts can ever imply values. And equally strongly that no values can imply facts. Second, both approaches focus on researchers, the values they personally hold, rather than the values pervading their subject-matter, shared by the members of society, embedded in a culture and acquiring the quality of Durkheimian "social facts" (Durkheim 1897/1962). Third, both approaches locate values in the research process, as its distorting or enabling factor, rather than in the content of the research results, as the component of their meaning. Fourth, both approaches seem to believe in the strict separation of research process from the subject of research, an external relationship between students of society and the society being studied.

Taken for granted, one may say paradigmatic for a long time, these assumptions started to be undermined by two kinds of developments. The new approach to the riddle of valuations has been made possible by the intellectual, intrinsic changes in the discipline of sociology, linked to the ontological, real changes in sociology's subject matter, the human society.

Some Tendencies of Current Sociology

Already long ago the discipline witnessed the anti-naturalistic and anti-positivistic turn, symbolized by names such as Max Weber, George Herbert Mead, Florian Znaniecki, Talcott Parsons, then followed the subjectivist turn in the sixties with the work of Erving Goffman, Harold Garfinkel, or Alfred Shutz, then the culturalist turn announced by Jeffrey Alexander, Steven Seidman and the whole school of "cultural studies". As a result, by the end of the 20th century the humanistic sociology, or as some called it "the second sociology" (Dawe 1970), gained ascendance and now seems dominant. It focuses on human action and conceives of it as meaningful, with a particular stress on normative and axiological orientation drawn from a culture.

The relatively new tendency is the treatment of society as an incessant process, rather than stable system, as a fluid field of forces in permanent transformation, rather than a fixed structure, or metaphorically—as social life rather than social organism. Examples of such perspectives can be found in Anthony Giddens' idea of structuration rather than structure, Norbert Elias' concept of figurations rather than forms, Pierre Bourdieu's focus on practices, or my own on emphasis on social becoming rather than social being (Sztompka 1991).

Third trend is the break away from evolutionism, developmentalism and all other deterministic, fatalistic and finalistic views of change (which Karl Popper put under the label of "historicism") and instead focusing on constructing, making history by human agency (Sztompka 1993). Most sociologists would now treat the people, either individual or in collectivities, and their actions either single or collective, as the ultimate driving force of all social processes, with every stage seen as construction, achievement by social actors, and the direction of the process as contingent on what people choose and do. A highly elaborated statement of this perspective is provided by Margaret Archer in the theory of morphogenesis (Archer 1986, 1995, 2000). I join the same stream of theorizing with my theory of social becoming (Sztompka 1991).

As the fourth novelty we have witnessed the discovery of the phenomenon of reflexiveness (pre-figured by the Mertonian concepts of
self-fulfilling and self-destroying prophecies), indicating that in the
human society, as distinct from the world of nature, the very knowledge about society feeds-back on its subject matter, directly influencing
people's beliefs, their motivations and consequently their actions. This
idea became the foundation of the whole theory of reflexive modernity
by Anthony Giddens, Ulrich Beck, Scott Lash and others.

Fifth, we observe the refocusing of the attention of sociologists from
the macro-structural to the micro-processual level, or in other words
to the domain of everyday life or the "life-world", as the central area
of social functioning. The switch started with Goffman's dramaturgical
theory, Garfinkel's ethnomethodology, Schutz's and then Berger and
Luckman fenomenological sociology, and is currently represented by the
theory of "interaction ritual chains" by Randall Collins (Collins 2004),
the "radical microsociology" of Jonathan Turner (Turner 2002), and
the proclamation of the new "performative turn" by Jeffrey Alexander,
Bernd Giesen and others (Alexander et al. 2006).

The last and sixth tendency is the extension of the notion of society from the level of nation-state to the global level of humanity, and
demonstrating how the processes of globalization impinge upon the
life-world of common people and their consciousness and imagination. Extending their horizon, providing with spatially unlimited and
rich information and opinions via mass media and new techniques of
telecommunication, they radically transform awareness of the masses.
Running under the label of cosmopolitan vision this view of current
societies is particularly strongly elaborated by Martin Albrow and Ulrich
Beck (Albrow 1997, Beck 2006).

New Tendencies in Human Society

Such intellectual trends within sociology are never detached from the
actual course of social life. They were to a great extent responsive to
the changes in the nature of human societies in the current period
known as late modernity, reflexive modernity or simply second modernity. After all, sociology is nothing else but the intellectual reflex of
society. As Jeffrey Alexander puts it: "Understanding and changing
the world simply cannot be separated. [...] If the world is itself based
on collective understandings, then changing the world always involves,

in some large part, changing these understandings" (Alexander 2003: 193). The changing of society and the changing of social theory to some extent coincide. And at the turn of centuries sociologists have observed a number of new crucial phenomena.

First, the acceleration and growing pervasiveness of social change as such, including its peak revolutionary manifestations, resulting in phenomena of anomie, trauma, anxiety, uncertainty and disorientation. These makes common people more often ask the questions: where we are, where we are coming from, where we are moving, and is it good or bad? Among other sources they turn to sociology for enlightenment.

Second, we are witnessing expanding democratization and liberalization, crucially enlarging the field of opportunities and options for making history by human agents, individual or collective (voters and consumers, social movement and political parties), and making their choices decisive for future developments. Recognizing their growing power people want to use it rationally, and among other sources they also look to sociology for advice.

Third, there is the educational revolution, which has made masses of people generally more knowledgeable and particularly more sensitive and receptive to the knowledge about themselves, to the self-awareness provided among other fields—by sociology.

Fourth, there is the growing saturation of the life-world with mass media, as well as new communication and telecommunication technologies opening unprecedented opportunities for public debate, in which sociology becomes an important resource.

Last but not least, there is the ongoing process of globalization which sensitizes the people to the universal dimensions of human fate, global solidarity, human rights, and pushes them to search solutions for the new scale of problems in, among other sources, sociological knowledge.

Some Steps Toward a New Perspective on Values

As a result of all these sociological and societal changes the problem of values returns to the fore of sociological debate. There are several steps leading to the new solution of this old issue. Again, let us start from a historical overview, to turn later to analytical considerations.

At the end of the century we observe the revival of the influence of C. Wright Mills, and particularly his book on *Sociological Imagination* (1959). In the plebiscite for the books of the century among members of

ISA in 1998, this book came close to the top, right after Max Weber's *Economy and Society*. Mills collected works have just been re-edited, his biography has been rewritten. And Mills was quite straightforward about the problem of valuations: "By their work all students of man and society assume and imply moral and political decisions. [...] There is no way in which any social scientist can avoid assuming choices of values and implying them in his work as a whole" (1959: 76, 177).

In 2000 Ben Agger argues in his *Public Sociology* for a personalized and normative style of sociology which can go into dialogue with wider publics. "Scholarly rigor would be mixed with perspective and passion, turning sociology outward toward a world that calls it forth" (Agger 2000: 264). In his view if an author writes in the genre of public sociology "she acknowledges that her text both constructs the world and intervenes in it deliberately" (ibid.: 258). "Good sociology is unashamed of its advocacy, grounding objectivity in choices" (ibid.: 257).

A year later in 2001 Bent Flyvbjerg publishes *Making Social Science Matter*, where he formulates the principles of—what he calls after Aristotle's distinction of *episteme* (i.e. cognitive account), *techne* (i.e. application of knowledge) and *phronesis* (prudent advice on practice referring also to values)—the phronetic approach. "The point of departure for classical phronetic research can be summarized in the following three value-rational questions: 'Where are we going?', 'Is this desirable?', 'What should be done?'" (Flyvbjerg 2001: 60). The whole point of the study is to enter into a dialogue with individuals and society and to assist them—after they have assisted the researchers—in reflecting on their values. The aim is to make moral debate a part of public life" (ibid.: 63).

In 2003 Jeffrey Alexander declares in *The Meanings of Social Life* that "unless we recognize the interpenetration of science and ideology in social theory, neither element can be evaluated or clarified in a rational way" (Alexander 2003: 197), and argues for the new brand of theories which "must be pushed to maintain a decentered, self-conscious reflexivity about their ideological dimensions even while they continue in their efforts to create a new explanatory scientific theory. For only if they become aware of themselves as moral constructions—as codes and as narratives—will they be able to avoid the totalizing conceit" (ibid.: 228).

In 2004 The British Journal of Sociology organizes a debate about "making social science useful" where the leitmotif is the role of sociology as "part of a democratic conversation" (Lauder, Brown and Halsey 2004: 8). The participants are almost unanimous: "The concept of self-reflexivity suggests that agents can now be more knowledgeable about themselves and their place in the world and should be included in any debate about policies concerning fundamental social problems" (ibid.). Therefore the role of sociology in democratic public debate is growing.

The same year 2004 Michael Burawoy delivers a presidential address at the American Sociological Association centennial convention in San Francisco titled "For Public Sociology" (Burawoy 2005a). He claims that because sociology is now of course firmly established and has acquired a solid corpus of knowledge, the time has come to return its debt to society, and it can afford to return to the consideration of values.

> We have spent a century building professional knowledge, translating common sense into science, so that now we are more than ready to embark on a systematic back-translation, taking knowledge back to those from whom it came, making public issues out of private troubles, and thus regenerating sociology's moral fiber. (Burawoy 2005a: 2).
>
> Reflexive knowledge interrogates the value premises of society as well as our profession (ibid.: 8).
>
> Public sociology brings sociology into a conversation with publics, understood as people who are themselves involved in conversation. It entails, therefore, a double conversation (ibid.: 4).

In his perspective public sociology builds a bridge between sociologists and common people, and therefore constitutes a new development complementary to three traditional brands of sociology: professional sociology and critical sociology engaging exclusively the sociologists, and policy sociology linking sociologists in a service relationship with the clients dictating goals. Burawoy identifies the forerunners of public sociology: W. E. B. DuBois of *The Souls of Black Folk* (1903), Gunnar Myrdal of *American Dilemma* (1944), David Riesman of *Lonely Crowd* (1950)—the all time sociological bestseller—and Robert Bellah's *Habits of the Heart* (1985).

Very soon after publishing Burawoy's 'manifesto' the rich debate evolves on pages of *The British Journal of Sociology* (vol. 56, No. 3/2005). Craig Calhoun indicates the possible contributions of sociology to public debate:

> part of what sociology brings to public discourse is greater capacity for critical analysis of the possibilities open beyond existing circumstances, of the social conditions for realizing those possibilities, of the interests served by existing institutions, and of the reasons for the blindspots in many intellectual arguments (Calhoun 2005: 358).

Richard Ericson is explicit about the necessity of valuations in public sociology and he singles out the points where valuations inevitably enter:

> as analysts of principled courses of action, sociologists cannot escape making choices among preferred principles and thereby contribute to policy. They make such choices in the topics they select for research, the classifications they construct, the analyses they undertake, and the techniques through which they structure their research communications (Ericson 2005: 368).

Amitai Etzioni ridicules value-free experts:

> public sociologists who believe they can contribute to dialogues on public matters by merely relying on and referring to evidence (which by itself tends to reflect normative assumptions) are mistaken. Whatever position they take has normative implications (Etzioni 2005: 374).

Saskia Sassen emphasizes the heuristic role of the dialogue with sociology's subjects, common people, as a corrective for some blind spots of professional sociology:

> part of having a vigorous public sociology is that we can work at theorizing with our publics accepting that they also can theorize—can see, and may indeed see what we cannot see, because we are blinded by the enormous clarity of our theories (Sassen 2005: 403).

In summarizing the discussion Burawoy puts an emphasis on the normative (valuational) dimension of public sociology: "Public sociology [...] makes both dialogue and normative stances central to its preoccupation" (Burawoy 2005b).

The New Approach: Valuations as Construction of Meaning

I submit that in all these recent statements and comments, values are no longer treated as a bias, nor as an ideology, but as the immanent part of meaning that informs human individual and collective action. This is the third, new approach to the role of values. More specifically it involves four claims. First, an obvious point for the whole humanistic, anti-positivist sociology—that people endow their actions, situations, institutions with meaning. Second, that meaning is drawn from various sources (tradition, religion, mass media etc.). Third, that meanings are shaped in the dialogue, debate—what I like to call "meaning industry"—both direct through conversation and indirect through mass media, literature, art, movies and dramas. The scope for such dialogue is growing. Fourth, that one of the sources of meaning attaining growing importance in this dialogue, an important component of "meaning industry" in our time, is sociology: its data, concepts, models and theories. And fifth, that sociological research results of all kinds include or at least imply values.

If we accept such an approach to values, all assumptions of the traditional approaches, common for both the view of values as a bias, and the view of values as ideology are reversed. First, the focus is now on the values held by the members of society, and the way in which values help them to make sense of their life, rather than on the values held by sociologists.

Second, the role of sociology in promoting values as tools for the meaning-construction by common people is recognized. And accordingly the role of a sociologist is redefined. The question of Alfred McClung Lee: "Sociology for whom?", who are the addressees of sociological knowledge, (Lee 1976) is answered in a new way, by adding one more type of audiences. Most often two roles, and their respective audiences were mentioned before. The sociologist as an explorer, pure scholar—was seen as addressing other sociologists, subjecting the results to the scrutiny of the "peers". That was a typical role in the domain of pure social science, serving Aristotelian "Episteme". On the other hand the sociologist as an expert was seen as addressing the power holders with instrumental advice concerning sociologically justified means to ends as defined by them. This kind of service-role was treated as typical for applied social science, social engineering, socio-technique etc. It served Aristotelian "Techne". Now, in the third role, the sociologist as a mentor is seen as engaging with common people with both factual and unashamedly axiological messages. One purpose of this contact is promoting certain values. Another is debunking, unravelling the false assumptions and pernicious implications of prejudices, stereotypes, "derivations" (Pareto), "false consciousness" (Marx). Doing all this the sociologist is serving Aristotelian "Phronesis" i.e. providing prudent practical wisdom, or to put it in different terms is involved in Dahrendorf's "representative actions" (Dahrendorf 1980) indicating the pool of possible futures for the wider public. Whether knowingly or not a sociologist becomes a Burawoy's "public sociologist" involved in axiological dialogue with the common people. Taking up this kind of role is ever more common. "Public sociology is flourishing. It simply does not have a public profile but operates in the interstices of society in neighbourhoods, in schools, in classrooms, in factories, in short, wherever sociologists find themselves" (Burawoy 2005b: 426).

The next traditional assumption which falls down has to do with locating valuations in research practices. The new approach locates values in research results, which become the resource, pool of values to be used by common people in the construction of meaning (rather than by professional sociologists in the process of research). What types of results can sociology provide that may either directly include valuations, or indirectly imply values? Here another famous question posed by Robert Lynd (1939) is relevant: "Sociology for what?" There are five types of such results.

Sociology articulates special vocabulary, the language, concepts that are necessary for thinking about society and for identifying phenomena and events, pinning down the significant aspects of social life. Many sociological concepts entered the vernacular. Some are new, invented by sociologists, e.g. social role, role models, status, self-fulfilling prophecy, social capital, stigma, social class, exclusion, habitus. Others have acquired new sociologically clarified meaning e.g. ideology, culture, deviance, identity. Among them we find a special category of concepts with strong valuational content e.g. justice, equality, meritocracy, consensus, democracy, equilibrium, trust, development, modernization, trauma, progress and many others. They immediately "smuggle" values into public debate.

Sociology provides descriptions: the mirrors in which society can look at itself, recognize its traits, distribution of beliefs, degree of conflict etc. Statistical data, survey data, opinion polls, value studies etc. are intentionally objective, detached. Even when they report about values, they do not articulate valuations themselves. And yet, as I shall argue they often have indirect valuational implications.

Sociology constructs models and theories, the maps of social terrain which specify the mechanisms, regularities of social phenomena, the overall, generalized pictures of social life. Again, we shall argue that they have strong valuational implications.

Sociology may paint the visions of the future, the images of the good society, social utopias, scenarios of possible development discerning progressive from regressive alternatives. Here valuations are directly formulated.

Finally, sociology may formulate the agendas of problems to be solved. Here it answers directly the question "Sociology of what?". It identifies coming challenges, vital social issues, pressing concerns as

defined by the members of society, in a word real "social problems",
rather than intra-disciplinary "sociological problems" attended to
by sociologists. Here the strongest input of common people may be
discerned. And of course the choice of problems, their hierarchy of
importance assumes and implies values.

Sociological Syllogism

Thus we come to the strongest, primary assumption shared by traditional
approaches, namely that values do not follow from any facts (research
results), nor any facts follow from values. This is a strict dichotomy of
facts and values fundamental for positivist view of science.

Even assuming that it is true in the natural sciences, in the social
sciences the peculiar epistemological relation of the researcher (the
sociologist) and the object studied (society, consisting of self-aware
people), inescapably brings valuations into the cognitive process. Even
assuming that logically, in the deductive sense values do not follow
from facts, one should accept that they are implied by sociological
claims in the other way which I would call "sociological syllogism"
rather than "logical implication". It operates in five ways. First, the
sociological results may provide the language for speaking about society
which favors certain values. This is the valuational load of sociological
concepts. For example discussing community, consensus, cooperation,
democracy, trust promotes some values, contrary to the language of
hatred, struggle, suspicion or xenophobia.

Second, sociological results may mobilize emotions and moral
impulse strengthening attached values. This is the role of sociological
descriptions and diagnoses. For example learning about the scale of
human poverty and degradation may mobilize compassion or altruism,
unraveling the atrocities of war may galvanize the value of peace, finding out about the beliefs and opinions of others may break "pluralistic
ignorance" and mobilize solidarity and activism. Here we may also
recall the early intuitions of Emile Durkheim in his paradoxical claim
about the positive functions of crime. Namely the criminal act, and
the information about it, awakens moral impulse, allows the people to
draw a clear border between behavior which is good, and behavior
which is bad, to define the limits of virtue and of sin. Currently in the
widely reported phenomenon of "moral panics" as mass reactions to

particularly shocking or widespread deviances or social pathologies, we observe the same situation when facts "sociologically imply" values.

But the truly central role as the suggestive source of values, is played, third, by sociological models and theories. They persuade that certain values are functional and other dysfunctional for the operation of society, and even that some are necessary imperatives. For example the theory of social becoming which emphasizes the role of agency in permanent self-transformation of society, implies the values of activism, freedom, equal life-chances, democratic constitution of the field of opportunities—as pre-requisites for the creative making of history. On the other hand all brands of evolutionism or developmentalism assuming some inexorable Laws of History working above human heads, imply passivism, adaptation and wait-and-see attitude. Models and theories may also show the link between—what C. Wright Mills called—"private troubles and public issues" (Mills 1959), or in other words between the micro-experiences of everyday life and macro-structural and historical processes. In this way they help to shape "sociological imagination" sensitive to public issues and concerned with the huge social and historical tendencies as they impinge on our fate. To pay attention, to participate, to be active—become valuational implications of such a perspective. Finally, theories demonstrate that in our time most phenomena and processes attain global dimensions, and that human fate is decided no longer within the tribe, local community, ethnic group, or even nation-state, but at the level of humanity as a whole. Theories of globalization produce "global awareness", or "global imagination", which in turn imply such values as cosmopolitanism, transnational solidarity, tolerance, pluralism and diversity, inclusion, personal dignity, human rights etc. Their important quality is that they are universalistic, rather than particularistic values. They do not represent certain classes (like Marx's proletariat), or certain groups (like Mannheim's "unattached intellectuals", or Becker's outsiders) but the humanity as a whole. The quintessential codification of such values is provided by the catalogues of "human rights".

Fourth, sociological results may suggest which scenarios for the future action are beneficial for society and which are destructive, by unravelling the whole spectrum of unintended and unrecognized consequences, side effects, boomerang effects and the whole "balance of functions and dysfunctions" of various alternatives. This is the role of sociological visions. For example the projections of the consequences of unfettered growth and unrestrained exploitation of resources, allow to stipulate sustainable development, harmony with nature and other ecological values.

Finally, sociologists may sensitize the people to the neglected or ignored values by including them in their research. Through articulating and ordering values in a set of preferences in the research instruments (interviews, questionnaires, focus-group debates etc.). they may influence societal, common-sense definition of pressing problems and issues, and change priorities of individual or collective actions. This is the role of sociological agendas. For example the very study of poverty, or corruption, or injustice may mobilize the research-subjects to ponder about these pathologies of social life and take measures to eradicate them.

All these five situations demonstrate how scientific results may carry in themselves or imply values. In other words how "facts" widely understood, due to the "sociological syllogism" are consequential for values. But "sociological syllogism" has also the reverse vector. It shows contrary to positivistic claim that values may engender facts. How come? This seems more obvious. The early intuition was phrased already by Karl Marx: "Ideas become material forces if they mobilize the masses" (Marx 1844/1964). This claim may be unpacked in the following way. If we assume the standpoint of humanistic "second sociology" society is constituted of human actions—individual and collective. Society becomes what it is only due to certain actions taken up by its members. People act on their beliefs, incorporating them in the motivations, reasons, incentives, justifications for action. Among their beliefs we find values which push people to action in their defense or for their affirmation. Thus values which people hold to, which become widespread, embedded in a culture as Durkheimian "social facts", in important sense determine what people do, and thus what the society is like. Innumerable illustrations from history show how acting on such values as justice, equality, sovereignty, solidarity etc. people were basically and fundamentally changing their societies, eg. through revolutions. Thus values "sociologically imply" hard, factual realities of social life.

Sociological Ethics

The valuations accepted and applied by the common people in their choices and decisions make up the ethos of a group, community or society. The clearly articulated and organized sets of values proposed

by the intellectuals, philosophers, moralists, politicians—and sociologists—make up the various ethical systems. They are tantamount to
good, right, proper, in a word condoned ethos. This obviously involves
a sort of meta-evaluation: judgement about the merit of some values
as opposed to others.

There are many ways to justify, legitimize ethical systems and argue
for their preponderance, e.g. by reference to God, revelation, intuition,
to natural law, common emotions. And thus many ethical systems,
variously justified, compete for social attention and acceptance, for the
chance of being turned into dominant ethos.

I propose a sociological justification: values worth defending are
inferred by what I have called "sociological syllogism" from the mechanisms of social life as unraveled by sociology, its concepts, diagnoses,
explanations, visions and agendas. This is a variety of the argument
from Natural Law. Except that it focuses on something akin to the
Social Law, the ways society really operates which are slowly unraveled
by sociology. The "sociological ethics" should enter as an important
competitor into the contest of ethical systems. As its strength one may
indicate that it does not derive from faith, or intuition, or whims of
emotions, but from scientific study of society. As long as we believe in
the privileged status of science as the way to knowledge, this argument
has to be taken seriously.

Choice is the fundamental human predicament, values as criteria
of choice are indispensable components of human existence. People
draw values from various pools, articulate values, apply values and
make choices in incessant dialogue, debate, conversation with their
fellows—both direct and indirect, both with living and dead. In this
way they give meaning, make sense of their personal situations and
biographies, social environments and histories of their society. There is
no reason why sociologists should stand aside, excuse themselves from
this universal human game of meaning-construction, and remain passive, detached onlookers. According to the new conception of valuations
that I have tried to present in this article, they should rather engage
their wisdom—together, aside or against other voices—in the public
axiological debate, contributing with their sociologically grounded values
to higher collective rationality.

References

Agger, B. 2000. *Public Sociology*, Lanham: Rowman and Littlefield.

Albrow, M. 1997. *The Global Age: State and Society Beyond Modernity*, Stanford: Stanford University Press.

Alexander, J. 2003. *The Meanings of Social Life*, Oxford: Oxford University Press.

Alexander, J. et al. 2006. *Social Performance: Symbolic Action, Cultural Pragmatics and Ritual*, Cambridge: Cambridge University Press.

Archer, M. 1986. *Culture and Agency*, Cambridge: Cambridge University Press.

———. 1995. *Realist Social Theory: The Morphogenetic Approach*, Cambridge: Cambridge University Press.

———. 2000. *Being Human: The Problem of Agency*, Cambridge: Cambridge University Press.

Beck, U. 2006. *The Cosmopolitan Vision*, Cambridge: Polity Press.

Bellah, R. et al. 1985. *Habits of the Heart: Individualism and Commitment in American Life*, Berkeley: University of California Press.

Burawoy, M. 2005a. "For public sociology" in *The British Journal of Sociology*, vol. 56, no. 2:259–294.

———. 2005b. "Response; Public sociology: Populist fad or path to renewal?" in *The British Journal of Sociology*, 56(3): 417–432.

Calhoun, C. 2005. "The promise of public sociology" in *The British Journal of Sociology*, 56(3): 355–363.

Collins, R. 2004. *Interaction Ritual Chains*, Princeton: Princeton University Press.

Dahrendorf, R. 1980. "On representative activities" in T. Gieryn (ed.), *Science and Social Structure: A Festschrift for Robert K. Merton*, New York: New York Academy of Sciences.

Dawe, A. 1970. "The two sociologies" in *The British Journal of Sociology*, 21(2): 207–218.

Durkheim, E. 1897/1962. *The Rules of Sociological Method*, New York: Free Press.

Du Bois, W. E. B. 1903. *The Souls of Black Folk*, New York: A. C. McClurg.

Ericson, R. 2005. "Publicizing sociology" in *The British Journal of Sociology*, 56(3): 365–372.

Etzioni, A. 2005. "Bookmarks for public sociologists" in *The British Journal of Sociology*, vol. 56(3): 373–381.

Flyvbjerg, B. 2001. *Making Social Science Matter*, Cambridge: Cambridge University Press.

Lauder, H., P. Brown and A. H. Halsey. 2004. "Sociology and political arithmetic: Some principles of a new policy science" in *The British Journal of Sociology*, 55(1): 3–22.

Lee, A. McClung. 1976. "Sociology for whom?" in *American Sociological Review*, 41:926–936.

Lukacs, G. 1971. *History and Class Consciousness*, Cambridge: MIT Press.

Lynd, R. 1939. *Knowledge For Whom?*, Princeton: Princeton University Press.

Mannheim, K. 1960. *Ideology and Utopia*, London: Routledge.

Marx, K. 1844/1964. *Early Writings*, New York: McGraw Hill.

Marx, K. and F. Engels. 1848/1998. *The Communist Manifesto: New Interpretation*. (M. Cowling ed.), New York: New York University Press.

Merton, R. 1973. "Insiders and outsiders" in N. Storer (ed.), *The Sociology of Science*, Chicago: University of Chicago Press.

Mills, C. Wright. 1959. *The Sociological Imagination*, New York: Oxford University Press.

Myrdal, G. 1944. *An American Dilemma: The Negro Problem and Modern Democracy*, New York: Harper and Row.

———. 1969. *Objectivity in Social Research*, New York: Pantheon Books.

Riesman, D. 1950. *The Lonely Crowd*, New Haven: Yale University Press.
Sassen, S. 2005. "Digging in the penumbra of master categories" in *The British Journal of Sociology*, 56(3): 401–403.
Spencer, H. 1894/1903. *The Study of Sociology*, New York: Appleton.
Sztompka, P. 1979. *Sociological Dilemmas*, New York: Academic Press.
——. 1991. *Society in Action: The Theory of Social Becoming*, Cambridge: Polity Press.
——. 1993. *The Sociology of Social Change*, Oxford: Blackwell.
Turner, J. 2002. *Face-To-Face: Toward a Sociological Theory of Interpersonal Behavior*, Stanford: Stanford University Press.
Weber, M. 1949. *On The Methodology of the Social Sciences*, Glencoe: Free Press.

SOCIOLOGY AND POLITICAL SCIENCE: LEARNING AND CHALLENGES

Jack A. Goldstone

Let us start with a paradox. Political science is generally a larger, better-supported, and more prestigious field than sociology. No doubt, part of this attaches to the subject matter—people seek power, particularly through effective control of states and political office, and therefore turn to the science of power in search of answers. Similarly, economics has prestige and support not because economists are particularly good at predicting or explaining things like inflation, interest rates, and economic growth (they are not), but because people seek money, and therefore turn to the science of economics for insights on how money is made. Sociology has been seen as having a 'residual' subject matter—deviance, gender, religion, race/ethnicity—and such things are not high on the agenda of things that mainstream establishment groups or individuals wish to acquire.

Given this institutional relationship, one might expect that political scientists would receive more deference, respect, and recognition from sociologists than vice-versa. Yet this appears not to be true. At least two sociologists that I know of—my predecessor as Hazel Professor at Mason University, Seymour Martin Lipset, and my mentor at Harvard, Theda Skocpol—have been elected Presidents of the American Political Science Association. Sociologists such as Dietrich Reuschemeyer and James Mahoney have received major prizes for their work from the APSA. Although there have been many distinguished political scientists whose work is read and admired by sociologists, I am not aware of the same degree of sociologists' electing political scientists to be their leaders or win their prizes.

I think the reason for this is obvious. Sociologists study power *in general*, organizations *in general*, and social behavior *in general*. Thus for sociologists, political power, states, and political behavior are just special cases in their field—or more accurately, political sociology, the sociology of the state, and studies of political mobilization are subfields of specialization in sociology. But the converse is not true—it is hard to think of any subfield of Political Science that would correspond to a major field of inquiry in sociology!

I make these introductory comments not because I wish to offer another article on how sociology is the "queen of the social sciences." It is not—at least empirically, it clearly is not. And it is precisely on empirical matters of fact that I wish to focus. In this regard, I wish to point to the somewhat embarrassing failures of economics, political science, and sociology, and to ask what lessons one can draw from these as to how to build on sociology's strengths, make it more productive, and restore (or claim for it) a primary position among the social sciences, on par with economics and political science.

What Sociology Can Do

Both economics and political science have relatively simple structures to their academic fields. Economics divides itself, roughly, among micro-economics, macro-economics, trade or international economics, and economic history. Of course there are myriad specialties that cross these lines: labor economics, price theory, general equilibrium theory, development economics, finance, welfare economics, experimental economics, health economics, environmental economics, the economics of public goods, the economics of innovation/R&D, etc. etc. Nonetheless, economics gives itself great coherence as a field by having a simple four-fold division to guide its basic undergraduate and graduate foundation courses, and its staffing of departments.

Political science similarly has a four-fold division: American (or other home country) politics, comparative politics, international relations, and theory (actually the history of political thought). This can be even more simply conceptualized as the politics of my country, the politics of other countries, the relations among various countries, and the intellectual history of the field. Again, political science has myriad subfields that operate within and across these divisions: comparative democratization, legislative politics, the presidency, deterrence, political psychology, opinion research, public administration, etc. etc. But the basic four-fold division gives a certain coherence to structuring pedagogy and hiring.

Sociology, sadly, has no such internal structure. There is no reason for this, except for the history of the field as succumbing alternately to grand unifying visions (Marxism, Weberianism, Functionalism) and fractioning into a large number of different specialties. Sociology certainly could set itself up as having four basic fields: American (or the national society in which the department is located) society, comparative macro-sociology (the sociology of other societies and their relationships, including most of development and political sociology), micro-sociology (social psychology, small-groups, social identity, race/ethnicity/gender), and organizational or meso-sociology (professions, organizations, networks, business, religion, education, medicine, etc.).

Of course sociology, like economics and political science, could retain its hundreds of sub-specialties that cut across these divisions. But requiring all students to take a course in each of these four areas, and specialize in one of them, would give much greater coherence and institutional structure to the field. Right now, sociology presents itself through one vast intro survey course and an unstructured mass of specialized courses that have little intellectual organization.

What Sociology should NOT Do

The rejoinder to this is that the greater prestige and coherence of economics and political science is not simply a matter of self-presentation or the organization of the field into a few primary areas. Economics has prestige because of its advanced methods and models, and political science in turn follows precisely because it is borrowing methods from economics.

Yet in fact sociology has more sophisticated methods and models than economics or political science—these are just not perceived as being as central to the mission of sociology as they are in these other fields. For example, most economics models remain based on comparative statics, and econometrics and political science remain focused on regressions. Sociology has innovated with various log-linear analyses, markov analyses, network analysis and block-modeling, path analysis, and event-history analysis. Indeed, sociology faculties have many methodological specialists devoted to developing and improving formal models and statistical analyses that have been as innovative and broad ranging as any counterparts in political science or economics. Many of these techniques—such as event-history and markov analysis (Beck 2001; Przeworski et al. 2000)—have been borrowed by political scientists from sociology, not from economics.

Moreover, we must realize and appreciate that the models of economics and political science are not like the models of the natural sciences. The natural sciences focus on measurement and classification, and develop models and theory only to explain, very precisely and exactly, empirical data. Economics and political science typically develop models as heuristic devices, to elaborate relationships, and then use anecdotes or plausible 'stylized facts' to illustrate the models. This is because such models aim, unrealistically, to explain 'economic behavior' or 'political behavior' *in general* rather than the behavior of any particular, concrete, empirical economies or states. The result is models that cannot be falsified, and that therefore do not describe, much less explain or predict, any real phenomena.

Political scientists in particular often struggle to measure such basic features of political life as democracy, state power, political mobilization, or revolution. Economists, by contrast, are able to quite accurately measure such items as unemployment, inequality, economic growth, and interest rates. Yet despite this accuracy, they are unable to explain, much less predict, them to more than an order of magnitude, often missing even the direction of these crucial outcomes. Economists cannot explain or tell us, with any empirical verifiability, how to create economic growth; what interest rates will be; or when financial crises will occur. Political scientists, similarly, cannot tell us, with any empirical verifiability, how to create democracies, avoid state crises, or end corruption.

Sociologists clearly do not have much to gain by following in the path of economists and political scientists, who are developing more and more abstract models that tell us less and less about what is happening, or what is going to happen, in the actual societies in which we live.

Therein lies the challenge for sociology—how can we build on the methodological and substantive strengths of our discipline to do what economics and political science are not doing, namely to better analyze and explain behavior within and of actual empirical societies?

Towards Greater Recognition and Rigor for Sociology

To a surprising extent, I would argue, sociology already in fact does this. It is therefore no accident that political science departments raid comparative sociologists for their knowledge of welfare states, revolutions, or development; or that business schools hire sociologists for their knowledge of organizations, or that sociologists lead the way in empirical studies of religion, education, the professions, race, poverty, and many other aspects of social life. What is distressing is how little sociology *as a whole* is able to exploit this advantage, and make it evident to the world of scholarship in general.

I believe that this is because outsiders have a very difficult time perceiving what sociologists actually study, and where they have their expertise. We are widely perceived as experts on such fields as deviance and marriage, poverty and inequality, social mobility and gender and sexuality. Yet for all their popular appeal and scholarly importance, these fields seem fragmented. As a set of discrete specialties, each appeals to a certain limited audience. Unlike economics, which can be conceived of as the study of how societies and firms prosper; or political science, which can be understood as the study of how power is exercised, sociology does not have a clear focus that conveys all that sociologists do.

To overcome this deficiency and change this situation, I offer three suggestions as starting points for directions that sociology might take to improve its place in the academic and practical world:

1) *Adopt a simple internal organizational framework for all departments and programs*, with no more than four divisions. This will present a cleaner, stronger 'face' of sociology to the world, and emphasize that sociologists are experts in the broad fields of social relations and social change. My recommended four-part division would be: (1) Sociology of the nation in which the department is located (including power and gender relations, demography, culture, stratification and inequality); (2) Macro- and comparative sociology (the historical evolution of societies, differences among major regional/cultural/political/economic systems, political and economic sociology); (3) Micro-sociology (social psychology, gender and deviance, ethnography, the urban environment, networks); and (4) Organizational Sociology (Organizations, Corporations, Social Movements, Professions, Education).

Of course, these lines are somewhat fuzzy, as are the lines between comparative politics and international relations, and many specialties in sociology cut across them, just as 'growth theory' cuts across both micro- and macro-economics. But the point is not to find 'perfect boxes' for dividing the discipline. That can never be done. Rather, the point is to have a simplified organization of the discipline for public presentation that will highlight how much we do and how well we do it; sociology should be known as the pre-eminent field for the study of social relations and social change. If we accomplish that, we will gain students and the public will turn to us for answers on issues ranging from reducing poverty to promoting democratization to combating discrimination.

2) *Do not go overboard in generalized ambitions for universal truths or abstracted models remote from any reality.* Explanations of "society" as such are less important than explaining the forms, trajectories, similarities, and differences among *actual, historical* societies and sub-societal units.

The introductory textbooks we use aim too high, but too shallowly as well. They seek to present an overview of all that sociology does in a semester or even a quarter (much more rarely in a full year). They thus can rarely present students with all the insights that sociologists can offer about how their own society operates; about specific differences between their own and other societies; or about how organizations and professions function; or the varieties of small-group dynamics and the power of network theory. Precisely because political science and economics divide their fields into broad areas, they are able to offer introductory sequences of micro and macro-economics (a full semester each, a full year of each for more advanced work); or of American politics and comparative politics or international relations (again a full semester of each). If sociologists similarly focus on what they can teach about actual, concrete societies, rather than about 'society' as such, their courses will have more useful information, and be more rigorous and interesting. They will also naturally divide into a set of semester or quarter-long courses, each with a distinct focus, rather than a rushed and overly abstract tour of the entire field in a dozen or so weeks.

3) Measure and gather data as carefully as possible on as many aspects of social life as possible, in many different countries, and use the best statistical and modeling tools that can be devised to arrange and explain *that empirical data.*

Sociologists gather an incredible amount of valuable data, through surveys, the census, ethnographic field work, and other tools. Yet our courses rarely present this material, much less provide exercises with it, in introductory courses. Unfortunately, this leaves students unaware of the richness and rigor that sociological research offers. If sociology presents itself through a set of major areas, and each course introduces students to some of the data collection and analysis typically used to advance knowledge in that area, sociology will become known more as a true 'social science,' rather than as an abstract field of theoretical speculation and 'relabelling' of common sense.

I believe that if we build on these strengths, already widespread in our field, and present them more effectively to those outside our discipline, we will not only continue to be looked to by political science, business schools, and other fields for leaders, we will be widely recognized overall as a leading discipline among the social sciences.

References

Beck, N. 2001. "Time-series cross-section data: What have we learned in the past few years?" in *Annual Review of Political Science*, 4:271–293.

Przeworksi, A., M. E. Alvarez, J. A. Cheibub and F. Limongi. 2000. *Democracy and Development*, Cambridge: Cambridge University Press.

TOWARD A NEW COMPREHENSIVE SOCIAL SCIENCE

Dietrich Rueschemeyer

If I speak about the "frontier of sociology" that separates the field from and links it to political science, I should make clear from the start that it is precisely this borderland where my own work—as well as the work of colleagues and friends with whom I share many research interests—is located. As will become apparent, this location informs my view of the present state and the prospects of the two fields.

In order to establish a perspective within which I can say something meaningful about these two vast enterprises in a brief talk, I first look back a hundred years. At that time, an institutionally oriented, comprehensive social science responded to an increasingly self-limiting field of economics that proved unable to respond meaningfully to the social and economic transformations—and the disruptions—of the industrial revolution (Wagner 1990). This comprehensive social science was what we now call classic sociology, the origin of modern sociology.

From Comprehensive Social Science to Specialized Disciplines

Political science had evolved—in Germany as well as in other continental countries—earlier than sociology. Under different designations, it developed in conjunction with the rise of the modern state. The German *Staatswissenschaften* became one of the foundations on which at the end of the nineteenth century the new social science could build.

In the United States, political science responded to the emergence of a state with rapidly expanding operations. It focused on the tension between efficient governance and individual autonomy (Katznelson and Milner 2002). This American version of political science, inspired by the ethos of a non-partisan liberalism, was better able to retain a fundamental stability during the next generations than the historical social science represented by classic sociology. The social science of Max Weber, building on the dramatic accomplishments of modern history during the nineteenth century and embracing the analysis of government and law as well as of religion, community, and political economy—that social science was lost.

The comprehensive social science of the turn of the century turned into a number of specialized fields. Sociology, Political Science, and Ethnology/Anthropology were now separated from History as well as from the pioneer of disciplinary specialization in the study of social life, neo-classical Economics. Why did the multifaceted social science inquiry not prosper? There were, first, the imperatives of competitive institutionalization in the national university systems. These became powerful factors in the twentieth century. There were also complex intellectual reasons to which I will return. And a third causal condition, if I may hazard a historical guess, seems to have been that after the First World War politics preempted the interpretation of historical developments and crises. That made a "value-free" conception of social inquiry welcome to many.

Intellectually, the deepest divisions revolve around the role of model building with radical assumptions, theoretical generalization, and historical particularity. These concerns cemented—and continue to reinforce—the boundaries separating economics from the more institutionally oriented disciplines of Sociology, Political Science, and Anthropology and those boundaries that set History off from the fields more strongly defined by theoretical ambition.

I will argue that it is time to give another chance to an integrated social science. In fact this return is well under way. It can build on methodological and theoretical gains in actual research. The most promising developments are taking place in Political Science and Sociology, though they find partners in Economics and History. It is even possible to claim that such a return responds to a critical historical conjuncture of similar magnitude and urgency as the constellation that formed the background condition of the comprehensive social science conceptions represented by Pareto and Weber.

Learning from Political Science

Let me preface that argument with a few comparative observations about Political Science and Sociology and with some suggestions for change in Sociology. I will not be able to justify them in any detail. But the issues, if not my arguments, will be familiar to most social scientists.

Less bound to conventional ideas than Political Science, Sociology has explored methodological and theoretical issues more widely. Ranging from small group research through large surveys on many issues to societal system theory, it has been a proving ground for painstaking method development as well as attempts to grasp complex interdependencies through qualitative work, for big theoretical ambitions as well as the confrontations between alternative general theories. And both in methods and in theory Sociology has exerted significant influence on Political Science in the past.

I see two features that Sociology could and should adopt to its advantage from the way Political Science is currently institutionalized: the continued concern with normative theory, and the insistence on cross-national comparative research.

The first of these seems to run against the ideal of a value-free social science. Yet social thought radically "free" of values has been shown to be impossible. What is possible is to *differentiate* value judgments and their justifications from empirical judgments of what is the case and how things work. The insistence on a value-free social science has not rid us of blatantly ideological arguments parading as empirical judgments. Nor is political science significantly more plagued by such ideological orientations than sociology, in spite of the fact that "political theory" consists largely of a history of normative ideas from Aristotle to John Stuart Mill and current discussions about justice and community. To institutionalize in Sociology the consideration of alternative theories of "good societies"—the theories of, say, Habermas, Nozick, Rawls, and Sandel, with or without a complement from the history of social thought—would define large empirical problems of possibility, impossibility, and trade-off. At the same time, it would—as a clearly differentiated discourse—limit the commingling of empirical theory and ideology, if for no other reason than that it clearly identifies different value positions and the associated fusions of empirical postulates and value claims (otherwise known as ideologies).

Sociology also can and should learn from the fact that comparative politics is a pursuit that any respectable Political Science department is obliged to cultivate. Strangely enough, the standard program of Sociology gives macro-comparative work a much weaker priority. Sociologists tend to be preoccupied with issues pertaining to their own country, while macro-analysis rarely examines real countries other than one's own. Instead, Sociology proceeds too easily to arguments about "societies" in general. It is not that Sociology lacks macro-comparative studies; there are many and excellent ones. But the discipline as a whole does not demand realistic comparative macro-analysis as a steady pursuit and obligation in every self-respecting department.

The argument for institutionalizing macro-comparative research more strongly in Sociology is not unrelated to the first suggestion. Macro-comparative analysis can elucidate the range of variations across countries on issues relevant for the discussion of good societies. It can give clues about what is possible under specifiable conditions, what is impossible, and which trade-offs are likely between different desirable features.

Giving macro-comparative sociology greater emphasis is, of course, also closely related to my main theme, the return to a comprehensive social science as an emergent development and a major undertaking in the coming decades. Macro-comparative work that deals with such issues as state building, revolutions, the conditions of democracy, policies of social provision, or contrasts and transformations in gender relations cannot come to valid conclusions if it neglects power relations, law and other political and social institutions, cultural templates, economic conditions and developments, historical continuities and so on.

Toward a New Comprehensive Social Science

Advocating a return to a comprehensive social science, I will briefly indicate four arguments—that it has been partially realized, why it faces now less intellectual problems than a century ago, why it is important, and how it responds to a historical conjuncture that presents problems of similar complexity and urgency as the historical situation around the past turn of the century.

A new comprehensive social science has been partially realized. The problems of international development and the transformation of the command economies of Communist countries are similar in character to the issues faced by the early, undifferentiated political economy that dealt with the early and partial emergence of capitalism. The narrowing of economic analysis that came with the establishment of an institutional framework for capitalism in western Europe and its global offshoots is now giving way to a renewed appreciation of the institutional conditions of economic growth. This brings economic analysis closer to political economy work in political science and sociology.

The other major dividing line, defined by the tension between historical particularity and theoretical generalization, also has been crossed in ways few would have anticipated fifty years ago. Comparative historical work in the social sciences has made great strides with trans-disciplinary work on revolutions, democratization, and welfare state policies, to name just a few broad areas (Mahoney and Rueschemeyer 2003).

There is no question that the overall institutionalization of separate social science disciplines is here to stay, if not necessarily in unchanged fashion. The return to a comprehensive social science is and will most likely remain a partial return rather than a wholesale transformation of all the social science disciplines. But it seems a safe bet that it is here to stay and that it will make influential contributions.

A new comprehensive social science now faces less intellectual obstacles than a century ago. The development of overlapping research interests in the relations between Economics as well as History and the other social science disciplines has resulted in a sharing of analytic tools across the major dividing lines. One paradigmatic instance of this is the simultaneous emergence of institutionalism in economics, rational action theory, comparative history as well as in organizational and cultural studies in sociology (North 1990, Hall and Taylor 1996, Katznelson and Weingast 2005). Other examples are new analytic tools to deal with history in political analysis (Pierson 2004) and the florescence of economic sociology. The contrasts in the mode of analysis that separated economics and history from the other social sciences are weakening.

It is true that these developments are driven by theoretical ambitions that remain to a great extent unfulfilled. Yet if exemplars of what textbooks might recognize as full-fledged empirical theories are rare, there have been significant advances in focused theory *frames* that often come as interlinked and nested sets (Rueschemeyer, forthcoming). There also have been significant advances in research methods, for instance in comparative historical work where what a century ago could be attained only by genius now seems open to the cooperative work of yeomen.

The new developments do not constitute forms of intellectual imperialism (even though one volume advocating rational choice modeling adopted that label). What is happening in reality is just regular border crossing and much closer cooperation, so regular and close that the borders lose their significance.[1]

---

[1] Comte's sociology was conceived in imperialist terms; and the critique of economics around the turn of the last century also had an imperialist cast. Rational action theory sometimes presents itself as "economic imperialism", but it has been indigenized in Political Science and Sociology with major modifications. Neither Political Science nor

Why is the new comprehensive social science important? The simple answer
is that tackling social and political problems requires comprehensive
answers because their causal conditions are multi-faceted. The same
can be said about many important questions that are not directly
inspired by pragmatic issues for instance questions about the sources
of revolutions. The answers that social science has to offer often may
remain incomplete and fail to present ready-made solutions; one fre-
quent reason is that an answer is found in long-term developments
that are beyond the leverage and/or the time horizon of politics. Even
if this is the case, multi-faceted assessments by social scientists do not
leave the diagnoses to the purveyors of ideological shortcuts. In addition, putting Humpty Dumpty together again, beginning to integrate
insights of the specialized disciplines, is an intellectual challenge that
is unreasonably left to post-adolescent undergraduates unless it is also
made a scholarly task.

*Does the new comprehensive social science respond to a historical conjuncture
that presents problems of similar complexity and urgency as the historical situation
around the past turn of the century?* It is fundamentally the old problems
writ large: extreme forms of poverty and inequality; coexistence of rich
and poor nations; weak and ineffective institutions related to growth and
distribution; a growing disconnect between inherited cultural templates
and current developments; and, arising out of these, the chance of
brutal domestic and international conflicts.

There is a possibility that what a social science has to offer against
this background will again be preempted by politics and simple ideological thrusts as was the case between 1914 and 1945. What we have to
say has to compete with religious beliefs and their derivations—some
radicalized, some uncertainly searching for new orientations—but also
with a politically powered market fundamentalism and with simplistic
appeals to freedom as an all-purpose remedy.

Sociology ever had the standing to launch an imperialist enterprise. An anecdote from
the history of my department at Brown University illustrates this: When a senior professor of sociology in the late 1800s claimed in Comtean fashion that as the representative
of the "queen of all disciplines" he should have a say in all major appointments, the
university decided to discontinue Sociology.

References

Hall, P. and R. C. Taylor. 1996. "Political science and the new institutionalisms" in *Political Studies*, 44: 936–957.

Mahoney, J. and D. Rueschemeyer (eds.). 2003. *Comparative Historical Analysis in the Social Sciences*, New York and Cambridge: Cambridge University Press.

Katznelson, I. and H. V. Milner (eds.). 2002. *Political Science: The State of the Discipline*, New York: W. W. Norton and Company.

Katznelson, I. and B. Weingast (eds.). 2005. *Preferences and Situations: Points of Intersection between Historical and Rational Choice Institutionalism*, New York: Russell Sage.

North, D. C. 1990. *Institutions, Institutional Change and Economic Performance*, New York and Cambridge: Cambridge University Press.

Pierson, P. 2004. *Politics in Time: History, Institutions, and Social Analysis*, Princeton: Princeton University Press.

Rueschemeyer, D. Forthcoming. *Usable Theory: Analytic Tools for Social and Political Research*. Princeton: Princeton University Press.

Wagner, P. 1990. *Sozialwissenschaften und Staat: Frankreich, Italien, Deutschland 1870–1980*, Frankfurt: Campus Verlag.

SOCIOLOGY AND THE HISTORICAL SCIENCES

HISTORY AND SOCIOLOGY: TRANSMUTATIONS OF HISTORICAL REASONING IN THE SOCIAL SCIENCES

Björn Wittrock

History and Sociology: A Legacy of Ambivalence

Social science emerged as a form of reflection on the fundamental transformations that shaped the societal institutions later regarded as characteristic of the modern world. This image was part and parcel of the self-consciousness of the generation of scholars that—following Talcott Parsons' monumental rewriting of the history of social science in the mid-1930s[1]—we have come to think of as the "classical" social scientists': Weber's, Durkheim's and Pareto's. It has been equally typical of social scientists ever since. In this sense sociology and the social sciences at large are intrinsically historical. Yet their evolution as academic disciplines in the course of the nineteenth and twentieth centuries has, if unevenly and with many exceptions, been marked by a growing distance to history as an intellectual pursuit and by a lingering ambivalence among sociologists towards historical analysis.

This ambivalence is reflected already in the stance towards the constitutive transformations of modernity that can be found in scholars as different as Eric Hobsbawm and Reinhard Bendix.[2] They capture these transformations in terms of a "dual revolution" in, on the one hand, industrial and technological practices and, on the other, the political practices inherent in the French revolution and the ensuing waves of democratic demands which had repercussions throughout the nineteenth and twentieth centuries. However these technological, economic, and political transformations were paralleled and partly underpinned by transformations in intellectual and cultural practices and in the institutions which served as vehicles for such practices.

These intellectual transformations have been taken up in a range of studies of individual disciplines or proto-disciplines, of individual intellectual environments—be they the Edinburgh of the late Scottish

---

[1] Parsons 1937.
[2] Bendix 1967, 292–346.

Enlightenment (e.g. in studies by Nicholas Phillipson) or the Göttingen of German Enlightenment (e.g. in studies by Peter Hanns Reill). Thus the powerful imagery of Roy Porter and G. S. Rousseau, when they described the eighteenth century, is no longer entirely valid. Historians of science no longer see this period "as a tiresome trough to be negotiated between the peaks of the seventeenth and those of the nineteenth century; or as a mystery, a twilight zone in which all is on the verge of yielding".[3]

Already in the volume *Romanticism and the Sciences*, published in 1990, two prominent scholars, Andrew Cunnningham and Nicholas Jardine, argued that "[t]wo 'Scientific Revolutions' are now commonly recognized—a first revolution around the turn of the sixteenth century, in which new mathematically and experimentally oriented branches of natural philosophy were created, and a second revolution around the turn of the eighteenth century, in which was formed the federation of disciplines we call 'science'. Science, in our sense, once held to be more than two thousand years old, is now credited with less than two hundred years of history."[4]

However, even though there have been in the last decades a large number of studies of the emergence and transformation of the human sciences,[5] the social and human sciences have not in their self-understanding come to articulate a notion of a conceptual and epistemic revolution coterminous with the formation of the political and technological practices that we have come to associate with the world of modernity. This relative neglect is even more striking considering the fact that in social and political theory today, social knowledge is not only regarded as a form of reflection on the secular transformations that have shaped modern institutions. Social knowledge is seen as essential for the very constitution of these institutions. This is, to take but one prominent example, what Anthony Giddens is referring to when he argues that "the social sciences play a basic role in the reflexivity of modernity". 'Institutional reflexivity' in the sense of the regularized use of knowledge

---

[3] Rousseau and Porter 1980.
[4] Cunningham and Jardine 1990, 1. An important volume discussing the writing of the history of disciplines is Graham, Lepenies and Weingart 1983.
[5] One paradigmatic example from the mid-1990s is Fox, Porter and Wokler 1995.

about the circumstances of social life is indeed a constitutive element
of the institutional practices of modernity itself.[6]

In this perspective an understanding of the formation of the societies of modernity requires a sustained effort to analyze the emergence
and evolution of societal order relative to discourses and to various
social-scientific projects that have helped underpin (but also undermine)
prominent modes of institutional reflexivity. All such forms of reflexivity
have involved an interpretation of historical context, not only of the
immediate context of a particular institutional constellation or of a given
political community. Much more broadly, the entire political project of
modernity is permeated by visions of the place of humankind and of
interventions into the world in historical context.

Such reflexivity is relevant not only for the constitution of societal
order and its institutional practices but also for its span of policy options.
At key junctures the range of such options may be critically premised
on discourses on society, indeed on social science itself.[7]

Sociology and the social sciences at large are however characterized
by a curious ambivalence in their relationship to history. They tend to
portray themselves as part of an effort of human beings to achieve an
understanding of the contemporary historical epoch so as to be able
to exert an influence on its shape and development. At the same time,
there has, as pointed out, been a process over the past two centuries
that has resulted in a widening chasm between the social and historical sciences. Three key periods leading up to this divergence can be
pinpointed.

Diverging Paths: Three Periods of Increasing Separation between History and Sociology

The Rise of the Social Sciences

Ever since scholars have called themselves social scientists, with the
first recorded uses occurring in France in the 1790s, they have also
seen these new forms of knowledge as characterised by an effort to

---

[6] Giddens 1990, 14ff.

[7] A number of the contributions to Ashford 1992 as well as to Rueschemeyer and
Skocpol 1996 effectively illustrate this feature of modern polities. See also Wagner et al.
1991 and Wagner, Wittrock and Whitley 1991.

understand the world of modernity. They have tended to describe key features of this new world in terms of processes of industrialisation, urbanisation, and political upheaval, originating at the north-western edge of the Eurasian landmass but eventually having repercussions on a world-wide scale.

In this context there occurs, as just argued, a fundamental transition from earlier forms of moral and political philosophy into social science.[8] This transition is also linked to an institutional restructuring not only in forms of political order but also in the forms in which human knowledge is brought forth and in which claims to validity are ascertained. One feature of this institutional transition is the emergence of public sphere that gradually comes to replace arenas of a more closed nature such as aristocratic literary salons. Another one is the rise of new or reformed public higher education and research institutions that come to replace both the laboratories of wealthy amateurs and the academies under Royal patronage and partial control.

Social science is, from its very inception, characterised by an inherent duality.[9] On the one hand it is a form of knowledge that is premised on a previously unknown openness and contingency of the world. It is a world in which human agency and interventions may crucially contribute to a transcendence of the legitimacy of tradition and the familiarity of local experiences and inherited bonds and communal obligations. In this sense the new social science also serves to supply concepts that came to be constitutive of a set of new institutional projects of a specific nature.[10] Thus, there emerged institutions that were not just new but came to be vehicles for the enhancement of a continuous process of innovation. On the other hand, these institutional frameworks and the social sciences themselves were to be endowed with a certain degree of stability. One way to achieve this was to demonstrate that the new forms of knowledge, in contrast to the cameral concerns of an older absolutist state, were premised on universalistic rather than

---

[8] For perspectives on long-term developments of forms of regulative knowledge see Kelley 1990 and Raeff 1983. Brian 1994 is an important study of the transformation of the interplay between developments in geometry and statistics in relationship to processes of state transformation (autonomisation vis-à-vis the personal rule of the King and efforts at a more detailed statistical description so as to facilitate state interventions).

[9] Cf. Wagner 1994 and 2007.

[10] Wittrock 2000.

on particularistic assumptions about human beings, human agency and human societies.

The rise of the social science disciplines must then be cast in terms of this early history of their emergence in conjunction with the fundamental transformation of European societies that the formation of modernity entailed. One shift in intellectual and cultural transformation in this period pertains precisely to the concepts of society and history, and to the new awareness of the structural and constraining nature of societal life beyond the domain of communicative interactions, in the political sphere proper. Thus, there is a transition to a social science that transcends the boundaries of the political sphere proper but also traces the implications and conditions of that sphere much further than the old political philosophy. Pierre Manent has put forward the notion that society is a "postrevolutionary discovery".[11] True enough, and as is convincingly demonstrated by Keith Baker, the term 'society' undergoes a long conceptual development in the French context in the course of the seventeenth and eighteenth centuries—with a dramatic increase in the utilisation of the term in the mid-eighteenth century. It is also true that, in his critique of Louis Dumont's analysis of Western individualism and holism, Marcel Gauchet argued that (this is Baker's elegant summary):

> Individualism was not simply a symptom of the dissolution of the primacy of the social whole, as that had been understood in traditional religious terms. It was also a necessary condition for what he once again called (following Karl Polanyi) the "discovery of society"—its discovery in strictly sociological terms, disengaged from the religious representations in which it had hitherto expressed its existence. Not until the ideological primacy of individual interests was postulated, he argued, could constraints upon these interests be discovered in the operation of an autonomous social order subject to its own laws.[12]

Johan Heilbron has pursued an inquiry into the constitution of individual interests.[13] In the course of the seventeenth and eighteenth centuries, such interests were conceived as amenable to the constraints of various notions of sociability. In particular, given a human condition short of true religious virtue, was there a prospect for a human existence beyond the borders of a Leviathan-like imposition of absolute order

---

[11] Manent 1998, 51 but see also Manent 1994, 80–83.
[12] Baker 1994, 112.
[13] Heilbron 1995; 1998, 77–106.

that would involve socially acceptable outcomes of the pursuit of the self-interests of human beings? Such inquiries were pursued in various ways in the different parts of Europe throughout the late seventeenth and the eighteenth centuries. However, Heilbron and many others today agree that, even if there is a long process of gestation of the modern concept of society, the unique event of revolutionary upheaval requires that discursive controversy and political practice become joined in the formation of a distinctly modern era. Pierre Manent has elaborated a similar argument: "The Revolution offered the original spectacle of a political change of unheard-of scope, yet having no stable political effects, of a political upheaval impossible to settle, of an interminable and indeterminate event".[14]

This description of the Revolution as an irreversible and interminable process of fundamental change was formulated perhaps most clearly by one of the most well-known thinkers of the nineteenth century, Alexis de Tocqueville. In his memoirs, *Souvenirs*, written in the summer of 1850, he describes the Revolution as one long upheaval "that our fathers have seen the beginning of and which, in all likelihood, we shall not see the end of. Everything that remained of the old regime was destroyed forever".[15]

In fact, Reinhart Koselleck's conception in his early work *Critique and Crisis* is quite similar. He also links the temporal duration of the process of upheaval to its spatial, and indeed world-wide, extension, as well as to its increasing intensity in terms of modernity as a process that affects all human beings, not just, say, those in central political institutions or certain major cities:

> The eighteenth century witnessed the unfolding of bourgeois society, which saw itself as the new world, laying intellectual claim to the whole world and simultaneously denying the old. It grew out of the territories of the European states and, in dissolving this link, developed a progressive philosophy in line with the process. The subject of that philosophy was all mankind, to be unified from its European centre and led peacefully towards a better future.[16]

The late eighteenth century witnessed the creation of a political project encompassing the whole world and at that shattered the existing absolutist order. In this process horizons of expectations opened up that were

---

[14] Manent 1994, 82.
[15] Tocqueville 1964, 30.
[16] Koselleck 1988, 5f.

previously unknown. In the words of Koselleck: "The eighteenth century can be seen as the antechamber to our present epoch, one whose tensions have been increasingly exacerbated since the French revolution, as the revolutionary process spread extensively around the globe and intensively to all mankind".[17] However, it is also this sense of openness and contingency that serves as a forceful impetus to an examination of the structural conditions of the political body and entails a passage from political and moral philosophy to a social science.[18]

This transition entailed that the role of historical inquiry became crucial but also ambivalent. Historical reasoning was an integral part of the intellectual transition, and even abstract reason itself became historicised in early-nineteenth-century philosophy. However, as the moral and political sciences were being, if slowly and with lags and discontinuities, broken up into a variety of new discourses, which in the course of the nineteenth century came to coalesce and become reduced to a number of social science disciplines, the stage was also set for a divergence of the paths of disciplinary development of history and of the new social sciences.[19] Toward the end of the nineteenth century a permanent divide had emerged between history and the social sciences. This divide had largely been unknown to the late-eighteenth-century moral and political philosophers. Today it remains as a major chasm. It also came to influence the orientation of historical reasoning itself.

Paradoxically both the historical and social sciences came to share an analogous shift in terms of the perception of the place of Europe in global context. Already from the mid-eighteenth century onwards the type of critical historical reflection on the European political experience relative to that of other parts of the world, and in particular that of East Asia and China, as epitomized by Voltaire, disappeared. In its stead came first a distinctly Eurocentric conception of world history with Hegel's lectures on the philosophy of history as an emblematic expression. When history emerged as a clearly delimited academic discipline it had a focus on the European experience of the formation of a range of nation states. In the foundational works of Ranke, the

---

[17] Koselleck 1988, 6.

[18] Heilbron, Magnusson, and Wittrock 1998 is an effort to provide an overview of the rise of the social sciences in the period 1750–1859. In this volume Wokler 1998 is perhaps the one who argues for the closest relationship between the birth of social science and the political rupture of the French Revolution.

[19] For an analysis of the development of historical inquiry in the course of the nineteenth century see Kelley 2003.

main theme was the shaping of Europe through the confluence of the cultural traditions of Latin and Germanic peoples.[20] Later many, if not most, European historians would write narratives of the trajectories of individual nations. In majestic works by Meinecke and Hintze at the turn of the nineteenth century, there was a strong comparative orientation that went far beyond the achievements of any particular nation or indeed any constellation of European nations. Analogously, the emerging social sciences largely came to be preoccupied with the policy concerns of the new industrializing and nation-forming states. Parallel to the wide comparative grasp of Hintze's historical contributions were those of some of the most prominent social scientists, with Weber's essays on the sociology of religion as an exemplary case. However, such wide-ranging research tended to be exceptional both in the historical and in the social sciences.

Academic Institutionalization and the Crisis of European Modernity

In the late nineteenth century, at a period in time when European global pre-eminence was at its peak, history largely came to be a scholarly exercise that served as a discursive parallel to the formation or reform of European nation states. The new investigations of social conditions and the back side of processes of industrialisation, urbanisation and modernisation were to become institutionally embedded, if in a slow and uneven process, in the research-orientated universities and other new higher education institutions.[21] They largely developed in parallel to the efforts of those nation states to cope with "the social question".[22] Thus the relationship of the new social sciences to an historical conception, other than that, which took the life of a given nation state as its starting point, could not be but a tenuous one. The notion that the European experience should not be taken as the self-evident yardstick for the achievements of a civilisation was even more remote.

---

[20] A succinct analysis of this aspect of Ranke's work is to be found in Gilbert 1990.

[21] Wittrock and Wagner 1992 and 1996. For overviews of the changing role of higher education systems and the emergence of research universities see Jarausch 1983, Geiger 1986, Rothblatt and Wittrock 1993, and Rothblatt 1997.

[22] Rueschemeyer and Skocpol (1996) contains a number of interesting studies of the complex relationships between the development of the social sciences, the emergence of modern social policies and reforms of state structures.

The key institutions of modernity—archetypically exemplified by a liberal market economy rather than a regulated mercantilist economy, by a modern nation state and a constitutionally limited polity rather than an absolutistic police state and by modern scientific discourses and a research-oriented university—had all emerged in the wake of the deep-seated economic, political and discursive transformations of the late eighteenth and early nineteenth centuries. The evolution of these institutional projects in the course of the nineteenth and twentieth centuries was a highly uneven process and the turn of the nineteenth century in many ways marked a profound crisis of modernity. A liberal economy was no longer—in the wake of the long depression from the mid-1870s to the mid-1890s—seen to guarantee wealth and growth, a liberal nation state no longer peace and freedom. Weber's image of humankind being threatened by the iron cage of an inevitably advancing bureaucracy is but one amongst many examples. Evidently, modern science was no longer able to yield a cognitively meaningful map of the fragmented life of modern urban, mass society: what Nietzsche, Kafka and Bergson had expressed in literary and philosophical terms was echoed by countless writers analyzing the anomie and rootlessness of modernity, discarding the search for knowledge and eulogizing aesthetic experience and the display of the power of will. In fact the writings during this "first crisis of modernity"—*pace* Peter Wagner[23]—prominently carried some key themes that have recurred in present-day postmodernist theorizing.

It is in this context that some of the pioneers of early social science, including Max Weber, articulated a comparative and historical perspective that was deeply critical in its self-reflexivity and that in many ways remains unsurpassed. However even if Weber's most seminal works, such as his collected essays on the world religions, are masterpieces of global history, they stand in a complex and never quite resolved tension to other parts of his works. In the interpretation of his legacy for future generations of social scientists, as handed down most prominently perhaps by Talcott Parsons, it were these latter parts, emphasising the unique nature of Western modernity and its historical trajectory, that became the most visible and most frequently cited ones.[24]

---

[23] Wagner 1994.
[24] See Heilbron et al. 1998, Wagner et al. 1991, Wittrock and Wagner 1992 and 1996, Wagner 1999, Wittrock 1999. An analogous line of argumentation is pursued

It was not in Europe, however, that a full-blown professional separation occurred of what had previously been a broadly conceived
movement of social science into a range of individual social science
disciplines. This took place in the United States already at the turn of
the nineteenth century.[25] One of its consequences was a more secure
professional position for the practitioners of these forms of scholarship.
Another one, however, was the emergence of a widening chasm between
on the one hand history and on the other hand different social science
disciplines such as sociology and political science.[26] A corresponding
development did not take place in most European countries until well
after the Second World War. There can be little doubt that in the wake
of this development an interest in history, and particularly an interest in
global history, came to occupy a less prominent part within the newly
differentiated social science disciplines than had previously been the case.
In a number of European countries, political and sociological studies
had from the mid-nineteenth century onwards remained intimately
linked to historical research. However the focus had, as argued above,
been on the development of nations and national polities rather than
on global developments.

The Internationalisation and Americanization of the Social Sciences

Late nineteenth century American social scientists, many of them Ger-
man-trained, defined their intellectual projects in a society undergoing
a process of rapid transformation: industrialisation, urbanisation, and
concomitantly emerging massive social and political problems. As social
scientists with a professional legitimacy, they tried to mark out their
own scientific territory and establish their own systems of credential-
ing. These ambitions entailed the clear establishment of separate social
science disciplines.[27] In Europe, on the other hand, the professoriate
often already had an established position; one writer[28] even uses the

---

in Wallerstein et al. 1996. For a discussion of the role of universities in this process
see Rothblatt and Wittrock 1993.

[25] Some key studies on this development are Furner 1975, Haskell 1977, and Ross
1991.

[26] A classical work which demonstrates the continued role of historical reasoning in
the emerging science of politics in the case of Britain is Collini, Winch, and Burrow
1983. Reba N. Soffer has provided interesting inquiries both into the emergence of
the social sciences (Soffer 1978) and the crucial role of the reconstitution of history as
a key discipline in forming a new elite in Victorian England (Soffer 1994).

[27] Manicas 1987.

[28] Ringer 1969.

term "a Mandarin class" to describe the situation of the leading German academics at the turn of the nineteenth century. The situation in
some other countries, such as Sweden and Norway, was no different
than in others, especially in countries where reforms of the State had
not been implemented equally comprehensively, the situation was not
identical but yet different enough from that faced by early American
social scientists.

The full-blown institutionalisation of the social science disciplines
on a global scale is to a large extent a phenomenon of the era after
the Second World War. It is a development that occurs both at the
international and the national level.[29] One manifestation of this was
the establishment, originally under the auspices of *UNESCO*, of the
International Political Science Association (IPSA) and the *International Sociological
Association (ISA)* in 1949. There was also a gradual process whereby the
social sciences came to be introduced or fundamentally redefined in a
diversity of national settings, including the Netherlands, Norway and
West Germany but also in Latin America, Australia, India and Japan
and several other Asian countries. These developments often meant
that elements of the sociological-behavioural tradition came to affect
research in the social sciences but rarely to such an extent that other
earlier traditions were totally marginalised. A process of professionali-
sation was set in motion and came to exert a truly profound influence
world-wide in the wake of the expansion of higher education systems
in a range of countries in the 1960s and early 1970s.

In the 1960s there occurred a dramatic expansion of higher education systems, not only across Western Europe and North America but
in many other parts of the world as well. In these parts of the world
there also occurred sweeping processes of administrative reform, which
furthermore in many countries coincided with the coming to power
of new political majorities. Major new public policy programmes were
launched across the board in these countries. It is in this context that
the social sciences finally and firmly came to be entrenched as academic
disciplines in university settings. In this same age of great public policy
programmes, disciplines such as political science and sociology were
able to secure a firm basis in a series of European countries. In some
cases this occurred for the first time—as in Denmark—in others—as
in Britain, Germany and Sweden and Italy—in a renewed and greatly
expanded form. This expansion was paralleled by a growth of the

---

[29] Trent 1982.

social science disciplines on a global level that for the first time tended to make the international associations truly international.

On all continents, the full array of disciplines and subdisciplines appeared. This impressive expansion occurred parallel to a growth in the research methods being utilised. Thus a previously predominant—and more so in Latin America, Europe, Australia, Japan and India than in the United States—concern for institutions and processes on a national level was gradually being complemented by a stronger research orientation towards the study and management of clearly quantifiable processes. In terms of research methods, the 1960s was the period of the breakthrough of the behavioural revolution which had been pending and partly also prepared by European scholarly efforts in the interwar period (in the early work on electoral geography by André Siegfried in France, by the early sociological and socio-psychological studies by Paul Lazarsfeld and his collaborators in Austria, and by Tingsten's and Wold's minor classic on political behaviour). No longer could historical, juridical and philosophical reasoning alone or in combination be considered sufficient for the analysis of social and political phenomena. Methods and techniques previously elaborated in statistics, sociology, psychology, and economics were now being tapped by social scientists on a vast scale.

This shift in research methodology coincided with the numerical expansion of the social science disciplines and in Europe was often complemented by the introduction of more formalised graduate education programmes, normally with compulsory courses in research methodology. At the same time it became possible to see the emergence of an informal "invisible college" of younger scholars in Europe and in other continents as well, in marked contrast to the much more national orientation of scholars of an earlier generation. In those universities and countries where this shift was most decisively pushed through, there were certainly instances where the older juridical, historical and philosophical competences were either partially lost or could at least not be developed on par with developments in these neighbouring disciplines. Thus they became gradually antiquated and lost touch with what had been the rationale for the use of these traditional methods in the first place.

Apart from external political-societal reasons for this prominence of one mode of disciplinary identity, the fundamental fact of the early pre-war period was that only in the United States did the social science undertakings have sufficient size and scope to make wide-spread international emulation appear feasible. Thus, to take but one example, the American political science association had more than five thousand members in the early 1950s, when corresponding figures for European nations were generally only on a scale of one percent or less of that number. Even in the early 1990s the combined enrolment of West European political science associations was but roughly one third of that of the American association.

These professional and institutional developments had important repercussions also for the relationship between history and social science. First of all, social science became less historical than it had tended to be in most parts of Europe in the nineteenth and early twentieth century. Secondly, and more importantly, social science disciplines, and most notably so perhaps sociology and political science, tended to adopt one particular form of historical understanding that in its theoretical core seemed to reflect the pre-eminent position of the United States in the post-Second World War world.

This is obvious in the form of theorising about world history that came to be known as modernisation theory. This type of theorising was articulated in the form of a view of world history cast in terms of a set of dichotomies between the traditional and the modern, the Western and the non-western, the rural and the urban, the stagnant and the dynamic. Implicitly it tended to be premised on a view of the world in which the particular experiences of one country, notably the United States, was taken as the yardstick against which the achievements and failures of other countries were measured.

Thus even if social science, in its own long-standing self-conception, remained a discourse of modernity, disciplinary developments in the course of the twentieth century came to make it reticent to theorise either world history at large and even those upheavals that came to constitute the particular Western trajectory. Thus the particular Western trajectory to modernity tended to be assumed rather than examined. Furthermore, the relationship of a European trajectory to global historical developments tended to be ignored or simply dismissed. These types of questions, so prominent in earlier and overtaken forms of philosophy of history, were simply irrelevant to the behavioural sciences of modern industrial societies and their increasingly urbanised and differentiated forms of organised social life.

It is only when this particular mode of historical theorizing became increasingly criticized and seemingly unable to account for major shifts in historical and contemporary developments that a significant re-examination of relationships between history and sociology took place. This re-examination came to have a wide array of expressions ranging from an increasing interest in the history and ethnography of everyday events over efforts to critically rewrite national narratives to the rise of world systems theory and global history. These different articulations also came to range from explicitly culturalist and contructivist accounts of micro-interactions to radically structuralist and systemic accounts of long-term trends on a global level. The following section will highlight three components of the renaissance of historical thought in the social sciences.

The Renaissance of Historical Thought in the Social Sciences: Three Moments

In the present context attention will be focused on three broad strands of research that have exerted a deep-seated and lasting influence on the renaissance of historical thought in the social sciences. The first of these is perhaps the best example of a reconstitution of forms of historical reasoning which have introduced new standards of scholarly rigour for historical work in the form of a highly sophisticated form of historical inquiry inspired by speech act theory and the philosophy of Wittgenstein and Austin. It has transformed the study of the history of political thought and thereby the core of at least one social science discipline, namely political discipline, but with repercussions also for historical inquiry in sociology, economics, anthropology and statistics. In doing so, linguistic contextualists in general, and Quentin Skinner in particular, have been extremely careful to point out the limits and nature of the claims they make. This may have contributed to their success in transforming the study of political thought in a way that has for ever changed criteria of what constitutes acceptable scholarship in the field. Thus in this case, it is not a case of grafting historical analysis onto social science but rather of achieving a symbiotic merger of social science and history in one particular realm of research.

The second instance, so-called historical institutionalism, is a shorthand for a variety of scholarly undertakings which however share some basic features. They have all emerged from within social science disciplines rather than from history. Furthermore they all have the analysis of societal institutions as their point of departure and have the ambition to achieve an understanding of the emergence and development of these institutions by way of presenting their historically embedded nature. Analyses in this tradition are often theoretically and methodologically ambitious, and it is perhaps not surprising that this tradition has become the preferred mode of historical analysis in sociology but also in other disciplines, including political science and organization and business studies. Historical institutionalism rests, however and as will be reiterated below, on presuppositions which are more limited than many of its advocates seem to admit. Put bluntly, it is a form of analysis that for all its comparative orientation tends to take the particular shape of macro-institutions, as they have developed in Western Europe and North America, as a yardstick and that rarely has a clear interest in the cultural constitution and underpinnings of the origins of these institutions. As a result the analyses tend to become increasingly problematic the further away in time and space they move from the birth-places of the particular shape of a macro-institution, whether it happens to be "the modern state" or a modern public sphere or a modern class system.[30]

The third broad tradition taken up is one which holds out a promise to overcome some of these particular dilemmas. This tradition, conceptual history, emerged as an integral part of the discipline of history, but has been increasingly successful in attracting the interest and attention of social scientists and humanists at large. In addition it has an interesting, if often unexplored, relationship to a kind of universal philosophical anthropology, which points to ways out of the dilemma of engaging in deeply contextual analysis while allowing for the possibility of a strong comparatively historical stance.

Linguistic Contextualism

Firstly, the last three decades have witnessed what can only be described as a revolution in the writing of intellectual history. In particular the contributions by the strands of research, which are often identitifed with the term linguistic contextualism, have entailed that new and much

---

[30] Historical institutionalism has given rise to a more lively debate within the social sciences than between social scientists and historians. One important contribution to the debate within sociology was an article by the prominent Oxford sociologist John E. Goldthorpe (1991). An interesting stocktaking of the debate about historical analysis in sociology is the volume *Social Time and Social Change* (1999), edited by Engelstad and Kalleberg.

stricter standards have been set for the way in which an account may
be given of the emergence and transformation of intellectual contributions and traditions. For an understanding of the history of the social
and human sciences this has meant that it is simply no longer possible
to write such histories in the form of accounts of personal anecdotes
or a more or less arbitrarily enumerated line of alleged predecessors
leading up to the contemporary achievements with which the protagonist
identifies her- or himself. Instead there is an insistence on the need to
locate intellectual achievements against the background of a careful
reconstruction of what at the time constituted the dominant canons of
thought, of the ways in which such a canon was upheld and transmitted
in teaching and writing, of the ways in which such an orthodoxy might
be challenged and what did and what did not constitute a breach of its
main tenets and how such a brief was achieved by the performance of
acts of speech or of writing in specific institutional contexts.

This programme, sometimes described in terms of the so-called
Cambridge school, developed by scholars such as John Pocock, Quentin Skinner and John Dunn, has entailed a profound challenge to the
conventional history of ideas. According to Pocock "[...] if we are to
have a history of political thought constructed on authentically historical principles, we must have means of knowing what an author 'was
doing' when he wrote, or published a text".[31] Hence, to understand
what an author—or an entire "school"—really "meant" we must make
intelligible the langue he inhabits which gives meaning to the *parole* he
performs in it. According to Pocock, at least three consequences follow
from the involvement with "language" which have wide implications
for intellectual history. First, its history must be *événementielle* because the
scholar "is interested in acts performed and the contexts in and upon
which they were performed". Secondly, it will be textual and concentrate
upon printed utterances and responses. Thirdly it will deal mainly with
idioms and rhetoric rather than with grammar; with the affective and
effective content of speech rather than with its structure.[32]

There can be no doubt that the linguistic contextual approach to
the analysis of political texts, perhaps most closely associated with
the works of Quentin Skinner, has resulted in works that are among

---

[31] Pocock 1985, 5. For Skinner's position, which is derived from the Austinian notion
of speech acts, see Tully 1988.
[32] Pocock 1987, 19–38. For a critique of the contextualist approach see e.g. Bevir
1992, 276–298.

the most seminal scholarly ones of recent decades, works that have contributed to a profound renewal in the study of intellectual history and political philosophy.[33] Scholars in this tradition, and maybe most clearly so Skinner himself, have been careful to warn against a belief that their approach purports to solve all kinds of problems in the historical study of texts and societal practices. Thus it may be only fair to highlight three types of features that might be relevant in a study of the discourses of social science in their institutional contexts but that require an analysis that go beyond what has been the focus of interest of the Cambridge historians.

One such feature pertains to the role of macro-societal institutions in historical transformations, although again it is only fair to say that Pocock, rather than Skinner, and to some extent Istvan Hont have also dealt with such macro-societal institutions. By and large, however, intellectual historians in the contextual tradition have tried to focus the analysis on particular texts and their more immediate institutional and intellectual contexts.

Another feature that, maybe for pragmatic rather than methodological reasons, has not been the main focus of interest of the linguistic contextualists but that must be highly relevant for any social theory that takes reflexivity seriously, has to do with the political and institutional consequences of intellectual contributions. Even if contributions of social theory and science are seen in terms of speech acts, ensembles of such speech acts also may have per-locutionary force that must be analyzed in the study of the institutionally constitutive effects of political language. Thus ranges of policy options are often conceptually made possible or constrained in this way and so may the very existence of important institutional practices be, as already indicated in the previous section.

Thirdly, and maybe most important in theoretical terms, even if ideas are seen in context, we are not just dealing with a hyper text in cyber space but with ideas that are not expressed or inscribed by themselves but by someone with a body, with dreams, hopes and memories, someone who moves in space and time, someone who has to be theorized by a social theory that takes agency seriously. Again, it is certainly no "deficiency" in contextual intellectual history that it has tended to

---

[33] An excellent review of some key aspects of Skinner's work can be found in Palonen 2003.

assert the role of agency rather than to theorize it. However, there is
an unresolved tension in this tradition between *on the one hand* taking
the writing, speaking and acting human beings that produced the texts
seriously and *on the other* to reject a hermeneutical understanding of
the agent as both impossible and unfruitful. Instead of an individually
particular producer of speech acts, we then have an agent that is simply
structured by the properties of the cultural and institutional setting of
the context of the speech acts, an agent that may appear as almost as
standardized as that of modern rational choice theory.

However, the observations cannot detract from the fundamental
achievements of linguistic contextualism. Firstly, the history of the social
and human sciences must be contextually understood, and contextual
in a double sense of the word. It must be contextual in the sense that
it is not meaningful to write the history of what in our own age may
be termed sociology or anthropology or political science in the belief
that these particular denominations may simply be extended backwards
in a meaningful way. Instead it is necessary to consider shifts of various discourses and idioms across terminological boundaries. The lines,
to take but one example, between psychology, literature and medicine
were by no means, as so elegantly shown by Wolf Lepenies in his *Die
drei Kulturen* (1985), stable in the course of the nineteenth century. This
leads up to a second observation.

Secondly, then, the social and human sciences should be seen not
only in the context of their own shifting boundaries. They must also
be understood as forms of understanding and coming to terms with
societal transformations, and there are interesting and important links
to institutions in that larger context. In fact, many of the institutions
and modes of speech that we tend to take for granted have emerged in
intimate interplay with developments in the social and human sciences.
Obvious cases are provided by the very concepts of society and of
unemployment, to take but two examples. The same is true of a range of
techniques and methods for, e.g., sampling, national accounting, regional
and educational planning, but also for the relationship of a discipline
such as anthropology to colonial experiences and to migrations.

Thirdly, as argued above, it is becoming increasingly clear that the
particular period in which the basic conceptual apparatuses of the
social sciences went through maybe their most formative period, i.e.
the period of the late nineteenth and early twentieth centuries was in
some ways a unique period in history, characterised by a European
pre-eminence as never before, and never again to be achieved. For a

historical understanding of conceptual changes, of cultural mobility, of identity formation, of ideas of what constitutes a civil society and a public sphere, of what we understand when we speak of modernity and, in more general terms, how to understand our own societies in a global historical context, this particular characteristic of the history of the social and human sciences is an important one.

Historical Institutionalism

A large group of social scientists have during the past two to three decades brought back in not only history but the serious study of the state and other societal macro-institutions—to paraphrase the title of one of the most quoted volumes of this group.[34] The group explicitly and strongly rejects the previously dominant mode of functional-evolutionary theorizing as characterized by e.g. the modernization theory and convergence theory developing during the 1950s, 60s and 70s. Instead they advocate a historically informed social science that may draw on historical examples and analogies but that is premised on a rejection of all notions of linear evolution or theories of the existence of different historical "stages" or "phases". This body of historical, institutional social science has in recent decades come to exert an ever greater influence and has become a dominant, if not near-hegemonic mode, of historically orientated analysis in both sociology and political science.

However it raises some fundamental problems. Thus there seems to be no need to let the rejection of accounts in terms of a linear process of societal evolution mean abandoning all efforts to develop theories of the characteristics of a nexus of institutions at a particular point in a particular historical era. In fact such modes of analysis seem possible, fruitful and indeed necessary for understanding the interaction between political institutions, most importantly the modern nation state, and such societal institutions that primarily focus their activities on scientific, discursive practices; the modern research oriented university being a primary example.

Within the range of efforts to bring history back into the core of sociology and social science we find scholars who have taken the agential, the discursive and the linguistic constitution of social institution

---

[34] Evans, Rueschemeyer and Skocpol (eds.) 1985. For an overview of the state of the art in comparative historical research see Mahoney and Rueschemeyer (eds.) 2003.

seriously into account. However, a careful inquiry into these features of social life is more or less reserved for the study of the micro-settings where day-to-day practices are being reproduced or violated, whereas macro-societal institutions and change tend to be studied in ways that are just as systemic and overarching as those of the neo-functionalists—and often with a weaker theoretical, more ad hoc, justification.

For this chasm between microanalysis and macroanalysis to be closed, a much closer link seems to be required between intellectual and institutional history-writing.[35] For this reason, however, a purely neo-inductivist position, i.e. a position according to which the social sciences should limit themselves to a careful and preferably quantitative account of institutional practices and to seek to establish more general patterns on that basis, will ultimately lead to a dead end. Unless a link between agency and institutional transformation is established, institutional practices can be carefully recorded, but they cannot be accounted for except in terms of their own standard operating procedures, i.e. in terms of an account that is ultimately circular. This is in the last instance the dilemma of institutional analysis in the tradition of both the classical Carnegie and Stanford schools and that of so-called neo-institutionalism. There are only three ways out of this dilemma:

Firstly, the ambition level of institutional analysis may be limited to that of description. This is a sympathetic stance but not an intellectual solution.

Secondly, some theory of agency may be grafted on to the institutional analysis in a way that does not affect the basic properties of institutional understanding.

Thirdly, the formation of institutional practices may be cast in terms of an analysis of a theory of agency that allows for qualitative change.

To put it as bluntly as possible, it seems that many academic practices have opted for the first alternative. Institutional analysis then becomes a meso-level theory which is useful but ultimately not grounded.

On the other hand, many scholars in some of the key social sciences, in particular within political science and sociology, have chosen the

---

[35] Some of these issues are taken up from a broad functionalist perspective in Alexander 1989 and in Eisenstadt 1995.

second option. This often takes the form of an historical institutionalism where the description of institutional practices is linked to a heuristic use of some form of rational choice theory. Such forms of analysis tend to be illustrative and imaginative. However, they are in the last instance metaphorical and suggestive. In this sense they tend to avoid the basic dilemma rather than to face it head on, i.e. they do not take up the challenge of locating the *topos* where historical, linguistic and institutional analysis meet in a developed category of agency. In the last two sections, I shall outline an argument that tries to overcome this dilemma in a way that takes agency seriously while retaining a focus on the study of comparative-historical analysis of macro-institutions.

Conceptual History

Having done earlier work on the Enlightenment and German social history,[36] the historian Reinhart Koselleck, in 1967, published detailed instructions for a lexicon on changes in the political and social vocabulary. The *Geschichtliche Grundbegriffe* was to be a collective enterprise, co-directed by Otto Brunner and Werner Conze, mapping conceptual change in the German language between approximately 1750 and 1850. These conceptual changes would, according to Koselleck, be characterized by four tendencies:

1. *Democratization.* Concepts previously bound to specific social strata and professional corporations spread to other social groups. This process of social diffusion was generally accompanied by a loss of terminological precision.
2. *Temporalization.* Whereas traditional vocabularies were largely static, new conceptualizations were dynamic, indicating processes and often oriented towards the future, expressing expectations and aspirations.
3. *Ideologiesierbarkeit.* Because concepts were no longer bound to specific social groups and professions, they became more general and more abstract, especially in the form of -isms and singular nouns

---

[36] These two books, *Kritik und Krise* (1959) and *Preussen zwischen Reform und Revolution* (1967a), were both path-breaking studies, which were largely ignored outside of Germany for a long time. *Kritik und Krise* was translated into French in 1979 and into English in 1988. Together with Habermas' *Strukturwandel der Öffentlichkeit* (1962), translated into French and English in respectively 1979 and 1989, it gained an important role in the recent debate on the rise of a public sphere and the formation of public opinion. See, for example, La Vopa 1992, 79–116 and Goodman 1992, 1–20.

("liberty"). Concepts generally became less specific and particular,
therefore more diffuse and consequently more open to various
interpretations and usages. Meaning thus became more dependent
on the users and the context of usage.
4. *Politicization*. In connection with the *Ideologiesierbarkeit* there was a
   clear trend to politicizing language use, which was especially clear
   in the growing use of political slogans and political propaganda.[37]

Not all of these characteristics have received equal attention or have
proved to be equally fruitful. The best documented issue is probably
that of temporalization, *Verzeitlichung*. This aspect was close to the
professional interests of the historians, and in Germany in particular
had a long scholarly tradition (especially with respect to historicism).[38]
Koselleck, in any case, has devoted many subtle essays to it.[39] In his
view the *Sattelzeit* not only marks the transition to a new period, but
actually to the first era in human history characterized by a predominant
sense of historical time. This temporal structure of human experience
is visible in an unprecedented sense of change and renewal (emergence
of concepts like progress and development), in the notion of an open
future which calls for human intervention and "planning", and in the
separation of "experience" and "expectation."[40]
   These changes are apparent in various ways. Old and static concepts
may be redefined and thus become more dynamic, often simultaneously
expressing a movement or process and an expectation. Old topoi, more
generally, either loose their meaning, change in a more dynamic sense,
or are overshadowed by new terms and concepts.

---

[37] Cf. Koselleck 1967b, 81–99.

[38] Cf. Reill 1975.

[39] See especially the essays collected in *Vergangene Zukunft. Zur Semantik geschichtlicher Zeiten*, Koselleck 1979a. In 1985 it was translated it into English by Keith Tribe as *Futures Past*; see also Tribe's "The Geschichtliche Grundbegriffe project" in *Comparative Studies in Society and History*, 1989, 180–184. For the issue of temporalization in the sciences see especially Lepenies 1978.

[40] For a more extensive statement see Koselleck 1987a, 269–282. An interesting collection of essays by Koselleck is contained in his book *The Practice of Conceptual History: Timing History, Spacing Concepts* (2002). The significance of the Sattelzeit for the rise of historicism is far from being undisputed. Scholars such as Donald Kelley, Julian Franklin and John Pocock have argued that this view particularly obscures the work of French legal scholars of the Renaissance, see Schiffman 1985, 170–182. See also the collection of essays in Koselleck's honour edited by Palonen and Kurunmäki, *Zeit, Geschichte und Politik/Time, History and Politics. Zum achtzigsten Geburtstag von Reinhart Koselleck* (2003).

The programme as it was outlined by Koselleck has, in fact, only partially been fulfilled in the volumes of the lexicon. In a certain sense the method of the whole enterprise—a new form of conceptual history—has been more successful that its initial thesis. In the lexicon, the theme of the *Sattelzeit* is most apparent in the issues which touch upon the question of time and temporalization, and in the analysis of neologisms (revolution, conservatism, socialism, etc.). But a great deal of the effort has actually gone into very detailed analyses of ancient and medieval terminology, leaving relatively little time and space for the issues specifically related to the transformations between 1750 and 1850.[41] Another reason why the theme of the *Sattelzeit* may not have received the attention initially suggested, is the lack of a comparative material. In his detailed analysis of the concept of society, for example, Manfred Riedel demonstrates that it was only in Hegel's philosophy of law that the modern notion of society was first systematically articulated.[42] From a broader, European perspective, however, this was comparatively late and not in any way restricted to the German states. What is lacking from Riedel's analysis is such a treatment of conceptual developments in the English and French speaking world.[43]

In the reception of the lexicon abroad, considerations of conceptual history, as a specific type of intellectual history and historical scholarship, have often received more attention than the *Sattelzeit*. The methods and results of the *Begriffsgeschichte* were compared to somewhat similar approaches like historical semantics,[44] the tradition of the history of ideas,[45] and the study of political languages and vocabularies as advocated by the Cambridge school.[46]

In Germany, or so it seems, one actually finds the same tendency. Since the publication of the *Geschichtliche Grundbegriffe*, Rolf Reichardt, a former assistant of Koselleck, launched the *Handbuch politisch-sozialer Grundbegriffe in Frankreich 1680–1820* (1985–). Reichhardt and his collaborators have limited themselves in time, and have broadened the approach, among others, to include French contributors and their

---

[41] In due course Koselleck came to argue that the initial presuppositions of the project have grown into an "intellectual straightjacket", see Koselleck 1994, 7–16.

[42] Riedel 1972, 672–725.

[43] See Baker 1994, 95–120.

[44] Veit-Brause 1980, 61–67. For an early German debate on this issue see Koselleck 1979b.

[45] M. Richter 1987, 247–263.

[46] M. Richter 1990, 38–70.

historical traditions. An initiative which has preceded the *Geschichtliche Grundbegriffe* is the *Historisches Wörterbuch der Philosophie* (1971–). This lexicon, mainly produced by philosophers, represents a more traditional form of conceptual history as was conceived by Erich Rothacker, Hans-Georg Gadamer and Joachim Ritter. It contains many more and shorter entries, but lacks the attention for the social history of conceptual change that is present in the *Geschichtliche Grundbegriffe*. As Melvin Richter notes: "The GG originated in a style of historical inquiry that stressed hermeneutics and hence the importance of conceptual apparatus, horizons and self-understandings of historical actors. However, as a result of incorporating social history in its framework, both Brunner and Conze helped shift *Begriffsgeschichte* away from a philosophical and hermeneutic method towards another, incorporating social history of a sort more acceptable to historians."[47]

An internalist and predominantly philosophical style of intellectual history was thus opposed to a more historical mode of analysis which was more sensitive to contextual questions.[48] This opposition was also relevant in the English setting, where the Cambridge school of intellectual historians developed its programme, in part, as a critique of the way Oxford philosophers treated the history of political theory.

Curiously enough Koselleck's ideas about the *Sattelzeit* have received particular attention from system theorists in sociology. Niklas Luhmann and some of his colleagues have been anxious to recast their functionalist theory in a more historical manner, and for that purpose have extensively drawn on Koselleck's work. Luhmann's interest in the

---

[47] M. Richter 1990, 45. See M. Richter 1986, 604–637 and the critical exchange between him and Jeremy Rayner: see Rayner 1988, 496–501; Richter 1989, 296–301. Recently Michaela W. Richter has published a translation of Reinhart Koselleck's article on crisis in *Geschichtliche Grundbegriffe*. In an introduction to this article Melvin Richter and Michaela W. Richter (2006) present a comprehensive statement about the relevance of Koselleck's work from the vantage point of a tradition of history of ideas.

[48] For a critical exchange on the philosophical assumptions underlying Koselleck's project relative to those of philosophical hermeneutics see the lecture, in the Old Aula of the University of Heidelberg, by Koselleck and the response by Gadamer in connection with the celebration of Gadamer's eighty-fifth birthday on December 6, 1986, subsequently published in Koselleck and Gadamer 1987, with Koselleck's contribution called "Historik und Hermeneutik" and Gadamer's response "Historik und Sprache—eine Antwort". This exchange makes quite clear the degree to which Koselleck's historical inquiry is premised on the validity of a kind of transcendental Katergorienlehre, or a set of ontologically transcendent dichotomies—in some ways reminiscent of categories familiar from both Heidegger and Schmitt—that help structure the process of imputing meaning to conceptual and historical occurrences.

semantics of modern time was certainly shaped by the tradition of the *Begriffsgeschichte*, but he has also extensively drawn on Koselleck's ideas of the *Sattelzeit*. Luhmann reinterpreted the *Sattelzeit* as a period of societal transformation in which the hierarchial system of estates and orders was replaced by a system which is "functionally differentiated" in a plurality of subsystems.[49] This notion of modernization as a process of "functional differentiation" provided the starting point for Stichweh's work on discipline formation and similar studies on the cultural transformations during this period.[50]

For a long time conceptual history was seen as an integral part of the research programme for the kind of social history, *Gesellschaftsgeschichte*, which has sometimes been labelled the Bielefeld school (with Hans-Ulrich Wehler and Jürgen Kocka as two other prominent representatives). This may, as already indicated, to at least some extent have contributed to its diffusion and acceptance among wide circles of historians and social scientists. However, at the same time, Koselleck's conceptual historical programme, despite international acclaim remained, relatively speaking, marginal to the larger programme of *Gesellschaftsgeschichte* (social history, or perhaps better, the history of societal constellations). This school has had a strong influence among historians far outside of Germany as well. However, in the early twenty-first century it has also met with a mixture of critique and indifference among parts of younger generations of scholars in the human and social sciences to whom it has appeared too focused on empirical accounts of a social reality cast in terms of stable macro-structural categories and too little interested in the life-worlds of human beings and in the ambiguities and ambivalence of social and political categories and in the processes of their construction and reinterpretation. Somewhat paradoxically it was in this context that *Begriffsgeschichte*, conceptual history, with its focus on the construction of societally relevant categories in time and with its links to hermeneutics as a method in historical research, to phenomenology as a philosophical method, and to programmes of philosophical anthropology, received increasing

---

[49] See the different volumes of *Gesellschaftsstruktur und Semantik*, 1980, 1981, and 1989.

[50] See, for example, Schmidt 1989. Crucial for Luhmann's analysis of functionally differentiated subsystems are mechanisms of self-organization. On this notion see Krohn, Küppers and Nowotny (eds.) 1990.

interest and attention.[51] To many it seemed as if linguistic contextualism and conceptual history presented not two rival approaches but rather two complementary and mutually reinforcing programmes of inquiry—one derived from the philosophy of the late Wittgenstein, the other with some links to classical hermeneutics but also and perhaps more importantly, if in often unacknowledged ways, both to Hegelian historicism and to a philosophical tradition of phenomenology. In this sense, conceptual history could also be seen to provide the outlines of a conception of history that was an alternative both to older forms of empiricism and to various forms of poststructuralist subjectivism. In fact, Koselleck himself argues explicitly against such forms of subjectivism; to him they seem to entail that historical research will not only begin but also end with the given multiplicity of subjective impressions and their linguistic expressions:

> Eine subjektivistische Extremthese, die aus diesem Befund abgeleitet werden könnte, läge darin, jede Geschichte in der Vielfalt ihrer Wahrnehmungen aufgehen zu lassen (ähnlich den Romanen von Faulkner). Die tatsächliche Geschichte wäre dann nur soweit tatsächlich, als sie jeweils für wahr genommen worden ist.
>
> Eine weitere Konsequenz dieser subjektiven Wahrnehmungshypothese läge in Hayden Whites Theorie, dass sich die Realität in ihrer sprachlichen und kulturellen Aufbereitung erschöpft, so dass sie sich nur im Medium des sogenannten Diskurses literarisch fixieren und damit auch rhetorisch aufschlüsseln ließe. Dann erschöpfte sich die Wirklichkeit der Geschichte in der jeweils sprachlich vermittelten Sinnstiftung. Damit freilich würde verfehlt, was ehedem in der Pluralität der Ausgangslage enthalten war.[52]

If so, is there a way of avoiding both a teleological imposition of meaning and the reproductive fallacy of extreme subjectivism? One obvious alternative is that presented by historical research inspired by speech-act theory. This type of theory provides a method for reformulating questions of meaning in history as questions of language use in particular contexts. Koselleck and most conceptual historians share an interest with speech-act theorists in the way we do things with words. In this sense linguistic contextualism and conceptual history are complementary. Both speech-act theorists and conceptual historians will interpret texts and utterances against the background of conventions of language use and

---

[51] An excellent collection of essays is contained in Bödeker (ed.) 2002.
[52] Koselleck 1997, 324f.

canons of discourse that are obtained in a given context. The problem is, however, to what extent such an analysis permits statements that go beyond the analysis of a range of particular speech-acts.

Most speech-act theorists would probably say that this is a question that should be tackled pragmatically and as best as can be done given our knowledge of conventions in given contexts. What cannot be handled in this way falls outside of the realm of questions that it is interesting to pose from a scholarly point of view. This is reasonable enough, but it may not be sufficient for us to give a focus to such wider questions. In the field of social theory, Habermas solves the problem, as it were, by elaborating a form of universal pragmatics that takes the most general preconditions of dialogical speech as its starting point. That is an obvious advantage for normative analysis but less so for empirical research, particularly of a historical nature.

It is here that Reinhart Koselleck—and also Karl Jaspers—raise important questions beyond those that most speech-act theorists find interesting or indeed legitimate. Thus beyond the speech acts proper and beyond the given conventions, there are certain unavoidable dilemmas posed by our very existence as reflecting human beings. One inevitable fact is the finite nature of our physical existence but equally inevitable is the need to adopt some kind of position relative to a few basic phenomenological dimensions. These existential dimensions, that are inevitable to us as human beings, pertain to the finitude of our own existence, to universal anthropological necessities of drawing boundaries between the inside and outside of a community and of recognising the temporal and social location of our own existence relative to that of others.[53] This stance highlights basic properties inherent in our existence as biological creatures. However it is also an articulation of the phenomenology of reflexive human existence. This stance opens up the possibility of a comparative-historical analysis of macro-societal institutions in terms of the institutional implications of cultural crystallizations in world history. In the final section, I shall only be able to suggest the nature and promise of a research programme of this orientation that is currently being pursued.

---

[53] See Koselleck 1987b and 1989.

Cultural Crystallizations and the Formation of Macro-Societal Institutions

Our capacity to reflect upon our own situation entails the inevitability of a boundary between the world and ourselves; the world is no longer a seamless web from which we cannot even reflectively distance ourselves. This, of course, is what Jaspers saw as the origin of history in the sense not of biological reproduction but of the self-reflexivity of humankind. Reflexivity entails the unavoidability of some boundary between inside and outside, no matter where this boundary is drawn and how it is constructed. Our realisation of the finitude of our own existence entails a reflection on our temporal and historical location. These types of reflexivity and our realisation of the existence of orderings in relations between oneself and other human beings entail the potential of concepts of changing states of the world, of what social scientists today would call agentiality.

Here two statements of caution are necessary. Firstly, the recognition of these phenomenological dimensions does not entail any single specific theory of historical meaning. It is compatible both with an analysis—as that of the Cambridge contextualists—that emphasizes the role of conventions and rejects that of hermeneutic interpretation as well as a hermeneutic or historical intentionalist analysis. Secondly, the particular positions adopted along these phenomenological dimensions may of course vary dramatically across historical epochs and civilizations.[54] Maybe a critic might then say that these dimensions are so general as to be of little real interest or importance. Such a comment would, however, be mistaken. On the contrary, a historical phenomenology of this type has two invaluable characteristics. Firstly, it provides an analytical focus to the study of individual speech acts and contestations.[55] I have suggested the term cultural crystallization

---

[54] See e.g. Arnason, 2003; Eisenstadt 1986, 1987 and 1992 as well as Arnason, Eisenstadt and Wittrock 2005; Wittrock 2001 and 2006.

[55] Dietze (2008) seems to be advocating an analogous stance based on a line of argument drawn from Helmuth Plessner's philosophical anthropology. She uses this as a basis for a critique of Dipesh Chakrabarty whom she accuses of radical historicism. However, Chakrabarty does not reject the need for a kind of universal philosophical anthropology, nor the usefulness of a discourse in terms of universals *per se*: "To provincialize Europe was precisely to find out how and in what sense European ideas that were indeed universal were also, at one and the same time, drawn from particular intellectual and historical traditions that could not claim any universal validity" (Chakrabarty 2008: 96). This is a position analogous to the one I have been advocating in a series of essays from Wittrock 1998 and 2000 onwards.

to denote periods of fundamental reconceptualisations of positions on these phenomenological dimensions, leading to basic reconfigurations or reassertions of macro-institutional practices. Secondly then, in this sense an analysis in, what might be called, the Jaspers-Koselleck tradition of historical phenomenology opens up for the possibility of reintroducing civilizational analysis into empirical historical research.[56]

Fundamental redefinitions along the dimensions of reflexive consciousness, of historicity and agentiality—to use once again the language of social theory—are precisely what characterize periods of deep-seated cultural crystallization, be they the Axial Age as interpreted by Max and Alfred Weber, Eric Voegelin, Karl Jaspers and S. N. Eisenstadt, or be they the formative moment of a new era in late eighteenth century Europe in the analysis of Reinhart Koselleck, the conceptual historians and historical sociologists. These dimensions are no mere cumbersome ontological additions to conceptual history. It is existentially unavoidable for us as reflecting human beings to relate to them. However, precisely for that reason, they are also analytically necessary presuppositions for a historical phenomenology that is able to engage with conceptual change in global history.

Ultimately, the cultural crystallizations, which constitute formative moments in global history, involve an institutional articulation and interpretation of the human condition, of what it means to conceptualise the finitude of our own existence in a world premised on assumptions of the potentially infinite malleability of the world upon which and into which our actions impinge and what historical existence may mean in such a world.

Such a methodological stance does not presume an idealistic or subjectivist theory of history. On the contrary, the comparative materials at hand suggest that there are three key conditions that have to be fulfilled for the formation of radically new institutional practices and constellations, namely the following ones. *Firstly*, such transformations and reformulations tend to be cast against the background of a profound crisis of established political order. *Secondly*, potentials for deep-seated change of macro-societal institutions also seem to depend on processes that open up new possibilities in the realm of economic practices, including trends towards increasing productivity and growth

---

[56] For an ambitious stocktaking see Arnason 2003 (and my review essay Wittrock 2006).

in key sectors of the economy. *Thirdly*, there must exist or emerge arenas that grant a certain degree of autonomy to intellectual practices, a certain degree of protection from the powers-that-be to groups of literati who try to articulate conceptions of new societal arrangements or rather arrangements that are seen to safeguard key components of a cultural legacy or cultures of a threatened life-world.

This seems to be the case whether we focus on events during the so-called Axial Age[57] or on the period in the tenth to thirteenth centuries when new macro-institutional patterns emerged on the far Western and far Eastern edges of the Old World, i.e. in Western Europe and in China during the Song-Yuan-Ming transition, or in Japan in the crucial period of the emergence of Japanese "feudalism".[58] It is also true for the period of the transition from early modern more or less absolutistic polities to other forms of order during the emergence of multiple modernities in the course of the eighteenth and nineteenth centuries. However, the institutional practices, which emerged out of these formative periods, were proposed on the basis of reinterpretations of social practices in terms of key dimensions of the historicality, agentiality, and cosmology by means of which human beings interpret their conditions of existence. In this sense, articulations of new potentials and of new institutions cannot be severed from an analysis of the thoughts and actions of human beings.

Finally, however, the ways in which various institutional projects were being realized—or, to use another terminology, the ways in which promissory notes became institutional realities[59]—are protracted contestations and confrontations. The outcome of these contestations rest on the ability of different actors to draw on and to mobilize available resources. However resources themselves do not articulate institutional choices, only human beings do and they do so in terms of conceptions what it means to be a human being with a finite existence and endowed with capacities to act in the world and to change it.

---

[57] See e.g. Arnason, Eisenstadt and Wittrock (eds.) 2005.
[58] See Smith and von Glahn (eds.) 2003 and Arnason and Wittrock (eds.) 2004.
[59] Wittrock 2000.

References

Alexander, J. C. 1989. *Structure and Meaning: Rethinking Classical Sociology*, New York: Columbia University Press.

Arnason, J. P. 2003. *Civilizations in Dispute: Historical Questions and Theoretical Traditions*, Leiden: Brill Academic Publishers.

Arnason, J. P. and B. Wittrock (eds.). 2004. "Eurasian transformations, tenth to thirteenth centuries: Crystallizations, divergencies, renaissances", Special issue, *Medieval Encounters*, 10(1–3).

Arnason, J. P., S. N. Eisenstadt and B. Wittrock (eds.) 2005. *Axial Civilizations and World History*, Jerusalem Studies in Religion and Culture, vol. 4. Leiden: Brill Academic Publishers.

Ashford, D. E. (ed.). 1992. *History and Context in Comparative Public Policy*, Pittsburg, PA: University of Pittsburgh Press.

Baker, K. M. 1994. "Enlightenment and the institution of society: Notes for a conceptual history" in W. Melching and W. Velema (eds.), *Main Trends in Cultural History: Ten Essays*, Amsterdam: Rodopi, 95–120.

Bendix, R. 1967. "Tradition and modernity reconsidered" in *Comparative Studies in Society and History*, 9:292–346.

———. 1978. *Kings or People: Power and the Mandate to Rule*, Berkeley, CA: University of California Press.

Bevir, M. 1992. "The errors of linguistic contextualism" in *History and Theory*, 31(3): 276–298.

Bödeker, H. E. (ed.). 2002. *Begriffsgeschichte, Diskursgeschichte, Metapherngeschichte*, Göttingen: Göttinger Gespräche zur Geschichtswissenschaft, Band 14, Wallstein Verlag.

Brian, Eric. 1994. *La Mesure de l'Etat: Administrateurs et Géometres au XVIII Siècle*, Paris: Albin Michel.

Chakrabarty, D. 2008. "In Defense of *Provincializing Europe*: A Response to Carola Dietze" in *History and Theory*, 47(1):85–96.

Collini, S., D. Winch and J. Burrow. 1983. *That Noble Science of Politics: A Study in Nineteenth Century Intellectual History*, Cambridge: Cambridge University Press.

Cunningham, A. and N. Jardine (eds.). 1990. *Romanticism and the Sciences*, Cambridge: Cambridge University Press.

Dietze, C. 2008. "'Toward a history on equal terms: A discussion of *Provincializing Europe*" in *History and Theory*, 47(1):69–84.

Eisenstadt, S. N. (ed.). 1986. *The Origins and Diversity of Axial Age Civilizations*, Albany, NY: State University of New York Press.

———. (ed.). 1987. *Kulturen der Achsenzeit. Ihre Ursprünge und ihre Vielfalt. Teil 1, Griechenland, Israel, Mesopotamien; Teil 2, Spätantike, Indien, China, Islam*, Frankfurt am Main: Suhrkamp.

———. (ed.). 1992. *Kulturen der Achsenzeit II. Ihre institutionelle und kulturelle Dynamik. Teil 1, China, Japan; Teil 2, Indien; Teil 3, Buddhismus, Islam, Altägypten, westliche Kultur*, Frankfurt am Main: Suhrkamp.

———. 1995. *Power, Trust, and Meaning: Essays in Sociological Theory and Analysis*, Chicago, IL: University of Chicago Press.

Eisenstadt, S. N., W. Schluchter and B. Wittrock. 2001. *Public Spheres & Collective Identities*, New Brunswick, NJ: Transaction.

Engelstad, F. and R. Kalleberg (eds.). 1999. *Social Time and Social Change: Historical Aspects in the Social Sciences*, Oslo: Scandinavian University Press.

Evans, P., D. Rueschemeyer and T. Skocpol (eds.). 1985. *Bringing the State Back In*, Cambridge: Cambridge University Press.

Fox, C., R. Porter and R. Wokler (eds.). 1995. *Inventing Human Science: Eighteenth Century Domains*, Berkeley, CA: University of California Press.

Furner, M. O. 1975. *Advocacy and Objectivity: A Crisis in the Professionalization of American Social Science 1905–1965*, Lexington: The University Press of Kentucky.

Geiger, R. L. 1986. *To Advance Knowledge: The Growth of American Research Universities 1900–1940*, New York: Oxford University Press.

Gilbert, F. 1990. *History or Culture: Reflections on Ranke and Burckhardt*, Princeton, NJ: Princeton University Press.

Giddens, A. 1990. *The Consequences of Modernity*, Cambridge: Polity Press.

Goldthorpe, J. E. 1991. "The uses of history in sociology: Reflections on some recent tendencies" in *British Journal of Sociology*, 42(2):211–230.

Goodman, D. 1992. "Public sphere and private life" in *History and Theory*, 31:1–20.

Graham, L., W. Lepenies, and P. Weingart (eds.) 1983. *Functions and Uses of Disciplinary Histories, Sociology of the Sciences Yearbook*, vol. 7, Dordrecht: Reidel.

Habermas, J. 1962. *Strukturwandel der Öffentlichkeit: Untersuchungen zu einer Kategorie der bürgerlichen Gesellschaft*, Darmstadt: Neuwied.

Haskell, T. 1977. *The Emergence of Professional Social Science*, Urbana, IL: University of Illinois Press.

Heilbron, J. 1995. *The Rise of Social Theory*, Cambridge: Polity.

Heilbron, J., L. Magnusson, and B. Wittrock (eds.). 1998. *The Rise of the Social Sciences and the Formation of Modernity: Conceptual Change in Context, 1750–1850, Sociology of the Sciences Yearbook*, vol. 20, Dordrecht: Kluwer.

Jarausch, K. 1983. *Transformations of Higher Learning, 1860–1930*, Stuttgart: Klett.

Kelley, D. R. 1990. *The Human Measure: Social Thought in the Western Legal Tradition*, Cambridge: Cambridge University Press.

——. 2003. *Fortunes of History: Historical Inquiry from Herder to Huizinga*, New Haven, CN: Yale University Press.

Koselleck, R. 1959. *Kritik und Krise: Eine Studie zur Pathogenese der bürgerlichen Welt*, Freiburg: K. Alber.

——. 1967a. *Preussen zwischen Reform und Revolution: Allgemeines Landrecht, Verwaltung und soziale Bewegung von 1791 bis 1848*, Stuttgart: Klett-Cotta.

——. 1967b. "Richtlinien für das Lexicon politisch-sozialer Begriffe der Neuzeit" in *Archiv für Begriffsgeschichte*, 11:81–99.

——. 1972. "Einleitung", in O. Brunner, W. Conze and R. Koselleck (eds.), *Geschichtliche Grundbegriffe*, vol. 1, Stuttgart: Klett-Cotta, XVI–XVIII.

——. 1979a. *Vergangene Zukunft: Zur Semantik geschichtlicher Zeiten*, Frankfurt am Main, Suhrkamp. English translation by Keith Tribe, 1985. *Futures Past: On the Semantics of Historical Time*, Cambridge, MA: MIT Press.

——. (ed.). 1979b. *Historische Semantik und Begriffsgeschichte*, Stuttgart: Klett-Cotta.

——. 1987a. "Das achtzehnte jahrhundert als beginn der neuzeit" in R. Herzog and R. Koselleck (eds.), *Epochenschwelle und Epochenbewusstsein*, München: W. Fink Verlag, 269–282.

——. 1987b. "Historik und Hermeneutik" in R. Koselleck and H.-G. Gadamer (eds.), *Hermeneutik und Historik. Sitzungsberichte der Heidelberger Akademie der Wissenschaften*, Heidelberg: Carl Winter Universitätsverlag; also reprinted in Koselleck. 2000, 97–127.

——. 1988. *Critique and Crisis: Enlightenment and the Pathogenesis of Modern Society*, Oxford: Berg. First German edition in 1959.

——. 1989. "Sprachwandel und Ereignisgeschichte" in *Merkur*, 8:657–672.

——. 1994. "Some reflections on the temporal structure of conceptual change" in W. Melching and W. Velema (eds.), *Main Trends in Cultural History*, Amsterdam: Rodopi, 7–16.

——. 1997. "Vom sinn und unsinn der geschichte" in *Merkur*, 51:319–334.

——. 2000. *Zeitschichten: Studien zur Historik*, Frankfurt am Main: Suhrkamp.

——. 2002. *The Practice of Conceptual History: Timing History, Spacing Concepts*, Stanford, CA: Stanford University Press.

Koselleck, R. and H.-G. Gadamer. 1987. *Hermeneutik und Historik: Sitzungsberichte der Heidelberger Akademie der Wissenschaften*, Heidelberg: Carl Winter Universitätsverlag.

Krohn, W., G. Küppers, and H. Nowotny. 1990. *Selforganization: Portrait of a Scientific Revolution, Sociology of the Sciences Yearbook*, vol. 14, Dordrecht: Kluwer Academic Publishers.

La Vopa, A. J. 1992. "Conceiving a public: Ideas and society in eighteenth century Europe" in *Journal of Modern History*, 64:79–116.

Lepenies, W. 1978. *Das Ende der Naturgeschichte: Wandel kultureller Selbstverständlichkeiten in den Wissenschaften des 18. und 19. Jahrhunderts*, Frankfurt am Main: Suhrkamp.

———. 1985. *Die drei Kulturen: Soziologie zwischen Literatur und Wissenschaft*, München: Hanser; English translation 1988. *Between Literature and Science: The Rise of Sociology*, Cambridge: Cambridge University Press.

Luhmann, N. 1980, 1981, and 1989. *Gesellschaftsstruktur und Semantik. Studien zur Wissenssoziologie moderner Gesellschaften*, Bd. 1, 2, 3. Frankfurt am Main: Suhrkamp.

Parsons, T. 1937. *The Structure of Social Action*, New York: The Free Press.

Mahoney, J. and D. Rueschemeyer (eds.). 2003. *Comparative Historical Analysis in the Social Sciences*, Cambridge: Cambridge University Press.

Manent, P. 1994. *An Intellectual History of Liberalism*, Princeton, NJ: Princeton University Press.

———. 1998. *The City of Man*, Princeton, NJ: Princeton University Press.

Manicas, P. T. 1987. *A History and Philosophy of the Social Sciences*, Oxford: Blackwell.

Palonen, K. 2003. *Quentin Skinner: History, Politics, Rhetoric*, Cambridge: Polity.

Palonen, K. and J. Kurunmäki (eds.). 2003. *Zeit, Geschichte und Politik/Time, History and Politics: Zum achtzigsten Geburtstag von Reinhart Koselleck*, Jyväskylä: Jyväskylä University Printing House.

Phillipson, N. 1983. *Universities, Society, and the Future*, Edinburgh: Edinburgh University Press.

Pocock, J. G. A. 1985. *Virtue, Commerce and History*, Cambridge: Cambridge University Press.

———. 1987. "The concept of language and the métier d'historien: Some considerations on practice", in A. Pagden (ed.), *The Languages of Political Theory in early-Modern Europe*, Cambridge: Cambridge University Press, 19–38.

Raeff, M. 1983. *The Well-Ordered Police State: Social and Institutional Changes through Law in the Germanies and Russia 1600–1800*, New Haven, CT: Yale University Press.

Rayner, J. 1988. "On *Begriffsgeschichte*" in *Political Theory*, 16(3):496–501.

Reill, P. H. 1975. *The German Enlightenment and the Rise of Historicism*, Berkeley, CA: University of California Press.

Richter, M. 1986. "Conceptual history (*Begriffsgeschichte*) and political theory" in *Political Theory*, 14(4):604–637.

———. 1987. "*Begriffsgeschichte* and the History of Ideas" in *Journal of the History of Ideas*, 48: 247–263.

———. 1989. "Understanding *Begriffsgeschichte*: A rejoinder" in *Political Theory*, 17(2): 296–301.

———. 1990. "Reconstructing the history of political languages: Pocock, Skinner, and the *Geschichtliche Grundbegriffe*" in *History and Theory*, 24:38–70.

Richter, M. and M. W. Richter. 2006. "Introduction: Translation of Reinhart Koselleck's 'Krise' in *Geschichtliche Grundbegriffe*" in *Journal of the History of Ideas*, 67(2): 343–356.

Riedel, M. 1972. "Gesellschaft, bürgerliche" in O. Brunner, W. Conze and R. Koselleck (eds.), *Geschichtliche Grundbegriffe*, vol. 1, Stuttgart: Klett-Cotta, 672–725.

Ringer, F. K. 1969. *The Decline of the German Mandarins*, Cambridge, MA: Harvard University Press.

Ross, D. 1991. *The Origins of American Social Science*, Cambridge: Cambridge University Press.

Rothblatt, S. 1997. *The Modern University and Its Discontents: The Fate of Newman's Legacies in Britain and America*, Cambridge: Cambridge University Press.

Rothblatt, S. and B. Wittrock (eds.). 1993. *The European and American University Since 1800: Historical and Sociological Essays*, Cambridge: Cambridge University Press.

Rousseau, G. S. and R. Porter (eds.). 1980. *The Ferment of Knowledge: Studies in the Historiography of Eighteenth Century Science*, Cambridge: Cambridge University Press.

Rueschemeyer, D. and T. Skocpol (eds.). 1996. *States, Knowledge and the Origins of Social Policies*, Princeton: Princeton University Press.

Schiffman, Z. S. 1985. "Renaissance historicism reconsidered" in *History and Theory*, 24:170–182.

Schmidt, S. J. 1989. *Die Selbstorganisation des Sozialsystems Literatur im 18. Jahrhundert*, Frankfurt am Main: Suhrkamp.

Smith, P. J. and R. von Glahn (eds.). 2003. *The Song-Yuan-Ming Transition in Chinese History*, Cambridge, MA: Harvard University Asia Center.

Soffer, R. N. 1978. *Ethics and Society in England: The Revolution in the Social Sciences 1870–1914*, Berkeley, CA: University of California Press.

——. 1994. *Discipline and Power: The University, History, and the Making of an English Elite, 1870–1930*, Stanford, CA: Stanford University Press.

Tocqueville, A. de. 1964. *Oeuvres Complètes, Tome XII, Souvenirs*, Paris: Gallimard.

Trent, J. E. 1982. "Institutional development" in W. G. Andrews (ed.), *International Handbook of Political Science*, Westport, CT: Greenwood Press, 34–46.

Tribe, K. 1989. "The Geschichtliche Grundbegriffe project: From history of ideas to conceptual history. A Review Article" in *Comparative Studies in Society and History*, 31(1):180–184.

Tully, J. (ed.). 1988. *Meaning and context: Quentin Skinner and his Critics*, Cambridge: Polity Press, 1988.

Veit-Brause, I. 1980. "A Note on *Begriffsgeschichte*" in *History and Theory*, 20: 61–67.

Wagner, P. 1990. *Sozialwissenschaften und Staat: Frankreich, Italien, Deutschland 1870–1980*, Frankfurt am Main: Campus.

——. 1994. *A Sociology of Modernity: Liberty and Discipline*, London: Routledge.

——. 1999. "The twentieth century—The century of the social sciences?" in A. Kazancigil and D. Matkinson (eds.), *World Social Science Report 1999*, Paris and London: UNESCO and Elsevier.

——. 2007. *Modernity as Experience and Interpretation: A New Sociology of Modernity*, Cambridge: Polity.

Wagner, P., C. H. Weiss, B. Wittrock and H. Wollmann (eds.). 1991. *Social Science and the Modern State: National Experiences and Theoretical Crossroads*, Cambridge: Cambridge University Press.

Wagner, P., B. Wittrock and R. Whitley (eds.). 1991. *Discourses on Society: The Shaping of the Social Science Disciplines, Sociology of the Sciences Yearbook*, vol. 15, Dordrecht: Kluwer.

Wallerstein, I. et al. 1996. *Open the Social Sciences: Report of the Gulbenkian Commission on the Restructuring of the Social Sciences*, Stanford: Stanford University Press.

Wittrock, B. 1998. "Early modernities: Varieties and transitions" in *Daedalus*, 127(3): 19–40; reprinted in Eisenstadt, Schluchter and Wittrock (eds.), 2001.

——. 1999. "Social Theory and intellectual history: Rethinking the formation of modernity", in F. Engelstad and R. Kalleberg (eds.), *Social Time and Social Change: Historical Aspects in the Social Sciences*, Oslo: Scandinavian University Press, 187–232.

——. 2000. "Modernity: One, none, or many? European origins and modernity as a global condition" in *Daedalus*, 129(1): 31–60.

——. 2001. "Social theory and global history: The three cultural crystallisations" in *Thesis Eleven*, 65:27–50.

——. 2006. "Review essay, *Civilizations in Dispute*" in *European Journal of Sociology*, 47(3): 407–416.

Wittrock, B. and P. Wagner. 1992. "Policy constitution through discourse: Discourse transformations and the modern state in central Europe" in D. Ashford (ed.), *History and Context in Comparative Public Policy*, Pittsburgh, PA: University of Pittsburgh Press, 227–246.

———. 1996. "Social science and the building of the early welfare state: Toward a comparison of statist and non-statist western societies" in D. Rueschemeyer and T. Skocpol (eds.), *States, Social Knowledge, and the Origins of Modern Social Policies*, Princeton, NJ: Princeton University Press, 90–113.

Wokler, R. 1998. "The Enligthenment and the French revolutionary birth pangs of modernity" in Heilbron, Magnusson, and Wittrock (eds.), *The Rise of the Social Sciences and the Formation of Modernity: Conceptual Change in Context, 1750–1850*, 35–76.

AXIAL VISIONS AND AXIAL CIVILIZATIONS: THE TRANSFORMATIONS OF WORLD HISTORIES BETWEEN EVOLUTIONARY TENDENCIES AND INSTITUTIONAL FORMATIONS

S. N. Eisenstadt

Introduction

1.

The emergence of Axial Civilizations constitutes one of the most revolutionary transformations in the course of human history. At the same time it constitutes a great challenge to sociological theory.

Robert Bellah has recently presented a succinct analysis of the cultural specificity of the Axial breakthrough.[1] At the core of this breakthrough are major transformations of basic cultural conceptions, a breakthrough to what he calls the theoretical stage of human thinking or reflexivity. The distinctiveness of these revolutionary breakthroughs does not lie, however, only in the emergence of such conceptions per se—though they have of course been crucial—but in their becoming transformed into basic and predominant, indeed hegemonic, premises of cultural programs and institutional practices of their respective societies and civilizations. However not in all places, where such conceptions or visions emerged, did they become transformed into hegemonic premises, and even where this did happen, such processes were usually—with the rise of Islam as the only partial exception—very slow and intermittent. It is only when these conceptions were institutionalized and became central and hegemonic components of the basic premises of cultural and social order that it is possible to talk about Axial Civilizations.

Axial conceptions have become hegemonic in many parts of the world—in ancient Israel, later in Second-Commonwealth Judaism and Christianity; Ancient Greece; very partially in Zoroastrian Iran; in a different mode in Ancient Greece, early Imperial China; and in regions dominated by different strands of Hinduism and Buddhism; and later

---

[1] Bellah (2005).

on in Islam. With the exception of Islam they all crystallized in the first millennium BC and the first centuries of the Common Era. It was this relative synchronicity that gave rise to the conception, first formulated by Karl Jaspers, of an "Axial Age", a conception which was imbued with a strong, even if only implicit, evolutionary orientation or premise.[2] In this conception the Axial Age was conceived as a distinct, basically universal and irreversible, stage in the development or evolution of human history. In fact the emergence and institutionalization of such civilizations heralded revolutionary breakthroughs which developed in parallel or similar directions in different societies. Yet the concrete constellations thereof varied greatly between different civilizations.

2.

The new and specific combination of cultural orientations and institutional formations which developed in Axial civilizations gave rise to distinctive societal dynamics that came to change the course of human history.[3]

The core of the Axial "syndrome" lies in the combination of two tendencies. The first one "was the radical distinction between ultimate and derivative reality (or between transcendental and mundane dimensions, to use a more controversial formulation)", [...] "connected with an increasing orientation to some reality beyond the given one; with new temporal and spatial conceptions"; with a radical problematization of the conceptions and premises of cosmological and social orders, and with growing reflexivity and second-order thinking, with the resultant models of order generating new problems (the task of bridging the gap between the postulated levels of reality)."[4] The second tendency was the disembeddment of many aspects of social activities and organizations. Relatively closed territorial units with ascriptive frameworks, like for instance kinship, turned into more complex social systems with "free" resources that could be organized or mobilized in different directions. This created potential challenges to hitherto dominant institutional formations.[5] These two tendencies entailed that established patterns of

---

[2] On Axial Age see Jaspers (1949/1953); also Voegelin (1956–1987) and *Daedalus* (1975); Eisenstadt (1982); and see also notes 3 and 4.

[3] This analysis is based on Eisenstadt (1982, 1986, 1987/1992); Arnason, Eisenstadt and Wittrock (2005).

[4] Arnason (2005); and also Eisenstadt (2000).

[5] On the concept of free resources, see Eisenstadt (1963).

social organization and of cultural orientations became open to reinterpretation and change. It was the combination of processes of change
involving both these types of opening and transformation that constituted the background for the crystallization of new Axial Civilizations
and their revolutionary implications.

The revolutionary implications of these combinations were rooted in
the fact that, in the words of a preparatory statement for the most recent
conference on Axial Civilizations, "[t]he civilizations in question experience a comprehensive rupture and problematization of order. They
respond to this challenge by elaborating new models of order, based
on contrasts and connections between transcendental foundations and
mundane lifeworlds. The common constitutive features of Axial Age
world-views might be summed up in the following terms: They involve a
broadening of horizons, or an opening up of potentially universal perspectives, in contrast to the particularism of more archaic modes of thought;
an *ontological distinction* between higher and lower levels of reality; and a
normative subordination of the lower level to the higher, with more or less
overtly stated implications for human efforts to translate guiding principles into ongoing practices."[6]

Put in other words, the Axial visions entailed the development of conceptions of a world beyond the immediate boundaries of their respective settings. Potentially these visions would entail the constitution of
broader institutional frameworks and the opening up of a range of possible institutional formations while at the same time making these formations objects of critical reflexivity and potential contestation. The
common denominator of these formations was a certain transformation
of the major institutional arenas with most of them becoming, even
in varying degrees, relatively autonomous arenas, i.e. constituted and
operating according to criteria of relative autonomy *vis-à-vis* the powers-
that-be.

The most important among such new types of institutional formations, which developed within all Axial Civilizations, were new types of
societal centers constituted as the major embodiments or sites of interpretation of the transcendental visions of ultimate reality. They became
major loci for the articulation of the charismatic dimension of human
existence. In contrast to non- (or pre-)Axial arenas of articulation, Axial

---

[6] From the preparatory statement for the conference report on which Arnason,
Eisenstadt and Wittrock (2005) is based.

centers attempted to permeate the periphery and restructure it according to the Axial visions.[7] Typically, distinct collectivities and key agents in relatively autonomous institutional arenas came to be seen as the most appropriate carriers of transcendental Axial visions. Another characteristic feature was the transposition of forms of attachments from various existing "primordial", "ethnic", local, political or religious collectivities to "civilizational", often "religious", ones. It has however been one of the most prominent features of these broader civilizational frameworks that they have not been tied to *one* political or ethnic collectivity. Instead they tended to encompass many such different collectivities between which there could develop not only political or economic contestations but also contestations about their relative "cultural" or "ideological" primacy within a wider but broadly shared civilizational framework. These new collectivities and frameworks have continually impinged on the existing—political, "ethnic", territorial and kinship—collectivities and institutional formations, have challenged them, and have generated innumerable tensions within them, often leading to continual reconstruction or radical transformations of their premises.

Such transformations were perhaps most clearly visible in the political realm.[8] The king-god, the embodiment of the cosmic and earthly order, disappeared, and a secular—even with strong sacral attributes—ruler, in principle accountable to some higher order or authority, God and Divine Law, appeared. As a consequence there also emerged the possibility of calling a ruler to judgment. One such dramatic appearance materialized in the priestly and prophetic pronunciations of Ancient Israel, to be transmitted to all monotheistic civilizations. Other such conceptions emerged in Ancient Greece, in India, and in China—most clearly manifested in the conception of a mandate of heaven.

A new type of reflexivity developed in these civilizations. It entailed new modes and criteria of justification and of legitimation of social, political and cultural orders. A central component of such reflexivity was the development of second-order thinking with an ensuing possibility of principled critical examination of these orders and of their premises.[9] This reflexivity furthermore promoted awareness of alternative institutional arrangements that might involve challenge and

---

[7] On the institutional implications of the Axial Age see Eisenstadt (1982, 1986); Arnason, Eisenstadt and Wittrock (2005).

[8] Eisenstadt (1981).

[9] Bellah (2005); Elkana (1986); Eisenstadt (1986).

change, including revolutionary change, of the existing institutional formation.[10]

The patterns of reflexivity that developed in these civilizations were also closely connected with the emergence of new forms of cultural creativity. On a purely "intellectual" level it was above all theological or philosophical discourse that flourished and became constructed in much more elaborate and formalized ways and generating continual developments within such frameworks. Within these discourses relations between new cultural conceptions and mundane reality became central and new types of collective memories and narratives thereof developed. Take for instance the relation between cosmic time and mundane political reality as exemplified in different conceptions of *historia sacra* in relation to the flow of mundane time and of sacred space in relation to the mundane one.[11]

The specific reflexivity, especially second-order thinking, which developed in these civilizations, entailed the development of internal antinomies or tensions as an inherent component. The most important of such antinomies were those focused, first, on the awareness of the existence of a great range of possibilities of transcendental visions and their possible implementation; second, on the tension between reason and revelation or faith (or their equivalents in the non-monotheistic Axial Civilizations); and third, on the problem of the desirability of full institutionalization of these visions in their pristine form.

3.

Guided by these modes of reflexivity, institutional frameworks and distinct "civilizational" collectivities were no longer perceived as "naturally" given, either by divine prescription or by the power of custom. Thus they could become foci of concomitant contestations between multiple elites and groups. The development of such contestations was also rooted in the fact that one of the most distinctive characteristics of these civilizations, attendant on the disembeddment of social actors and activities from existing frameworks, was the development within them of multiple, relatively autonomous, very often contesting actors—individuals, groups, and above all potential elites—which promulgated different conceptions of the implementation of such conceptions.

---

[10] Bellah (2005); Elkana (1986).
[11] Eisenstadt and Silber (1988).

New institutional formations, new forms of reflexivity, second-order thinking and the antinomies inherent in these cosmological visions paved the way for the most important aspects of the dynamics of Axial Civilizations. Potential challenges to the existing regimes and their legitimation were created through the possibility of principled, ideological confrontations between hegemonic and challenging groups and elites, through continual confrontation between orthodoxy and heterodoxy or sectarian activities, and through the potential combination of such confrontations with contestations over power with political struggles, with movements of protest, with economic and class conflicts. The confrontation between heterodoxy and orthodoxy has in these civilizations not been limited to matters of ritual, religious observance or patterns of worship. The various "orthodox" and most of the "heterodox" conceptions shared strong orientations to the reconstruction of the mundane world which were indeed inherent in the basic Axial visions. Contestations between different elites also came to transform many if not all of them into, to follow Weber's designation of the ancient Israelite prophets, potential "political demagogues", who often attempted to mobilize wider popular support for the visions they promulgated. Hence the contestation between them about such conceptions had far-reaching implications for the structuration of different institutional formations, a central aspect of the dynamics of these civilizations. The continual confrontation between hegemonic and secondary elites and between orthodoxies and sects or heterodoxies, and their linkages to different types of social conflicts, have been of crucial importance in shaping the concrete institutional dynamics of different Axial societies. These elites and counterelites have been the carriers of far-reaching, potentially revolutionary, changes and transformations. Of special importance in this context is the fact that sectarian activities often articulated the broader, universalistic orientations inherent in many Axial cosmological visions.

The implications of these developments were succinctly summarized by one of the convenors of the symposium with an invitation to a symposium resulting in a recent major publication on the Axial civilizations, Johan Arnason:

> The cultural mutations of the Axial Age generated a surplus of meaning, open to conflicting interpretations and capable of creative adaptation to new situations. But the long-term consequences can only be understood in light of the interaction between cultural orientations and the dynamics of social power. The new horizons of meaning could serve to justify or transfigure, but also to question and contest existing institutions. They were, in

other words, invoked to articulate legitimacy as well as protest. More specific versions of both of these alternatives emerged in conjunction with the social distribution, accumulation and regulation of power. The dynamic of ideological formations led to the crystallization of orthodoxy and heterodoxy, more pronounced and polarizing in some traditions than others. In that sense, the history of ideological politics can be traced back to the Axial Age. But this development of new cultural orientations should not be seen as evidence of more thoroughgoing cultural determinism; rather, the complex interplay of patterns and processes is conducive to more autonomous action by a broader spectrum of social actors and forces.[12]

4.

The tendency to continual reconstitution of institutional formations, up to revolutionary changes, and of different combinations of cosmological visions and institutional formations, structures of power and collective identities, was reinforced in Axial Civilizations by the fact that with institutionalization a new type of inter-societal and inter-civilizational world history emerged. Within all these civilizations there developed, in close connection with tendencies to a form of cultural reimagination of the world, a propensity to expansion, in which ideological and religious impulses were combined with political and to some extent economic ones. To be sure, political, cultural and economic inter-connections between different societies, including the development of some types of international or "world" systems, existed throughout human history.[13] Some conceptions of a universal or world kingdom emerged in many non-Axial civilizations, like for instance in the Mongol Empire of Genghis Kahn and his descendants, and many cultural interconnections developed between them.[14] A more distinctive ideological mode of expansion in which considerations of power and of economic interests became closely related to ideological ones are however characteristic only of Axial Civilizations. It emerged in the wake of the development of broad civilizational collectivities which encompassed different political and ethnic collectivities as well as their continual contestations.

The zeal for reorganization and transformation of social formations according to Axial transcendental vision, when connected with such expansions, made the "whole world" at least potentially subject

---

[12] Arnason (2005).
[13] On world systems see, among many others, Frank and Gills (1993); Friedman and Rowlands (1977); Wallerstein (2004).
[14] Biran (2005, 2007).

to cultural-political reconstructions. In these new developments movements of heterodoxy played a central role. Although often radically divergent in terms of their concrete institutionalization, the political formations which developed in these civilizations—which can be seen as "ecumenical"—comprised representations and ideologies of quasi-global empire, and some, at specific moments in their history, even the reality of such empire. This mode of expansion also gave rise to many attempts at creating possible "world histories" encompassing many different societies. But no one homogeneous world history emerged, nor were the different types of civilizations similar or convergent. Rather, there emerged a multiplicity of different, divergent, yet continuously mutually impinging "world" civilizations, each attempting to reconstruct the world in its own mode, according to its basic premises, and either to absorb the others or consciously to segregate itself from them. A continual aspect of the dynamics of these civilizations was the interrelations, contacts and encounters as well as the confrontations between different Axial Civilizations and between these civilizations and non-Axial ones. Such contacts were not only important transmitters of different cultural themes that gave rise to different patterns of syncretization of cultural and religious tropes. They could also be connected with the crystallization of new—both Axial and non-Axial—civilizations. This was the case in both the Achaemenid and the Hellenistic civilizations, as well as in several South East and East Asian civilizations and later of course in Islam.[15]

The development of these potentialities of change was in part generated by conscious attempts of different coalitions of elites, political activists and various social actors. The internal and trans-societal, "international" institutional formations, and their close interlinkage with economic and class conflicts, constitute the institutional core of the revolutionary transformations that developed in Axial Civilizations. "Ethnic", political, economic and class conflicts became articulated in ideological and civilizational terms. Hence conflicts between tribes or between political regimes could take on features of missionary crusades for the transformation of civilizations. In so doing they also came to entail the potential of processes of change far beyond hitherto existing formations.

---

[15] See the respective chapters in Arnason, Eisenstadt and Wittrock (note 7).

5.

The general tendencies of such new types of institutional formations were potentially inherent in the Axial visions themselves but only or mainly as potentialities. Within the settings of different Axial Civilizations there crystallized a great variety of institutional formations, often competing with each other and subject to processes of change. Their exact modes of actualization depended on conditions independent of the visions. Indeed the crystallization of specific institutional formations was a result of articulations and contestations among different activists and groups. Within the settings of different Axial Civilizations there crystallized a great variety of institutional formations, often competing with each other and subject to processes of change.

In order to understand the formation and dynamics of Axial Civilizations and the nature of their revolutionary impact on world history, we have to focus on an analysis of the crystallization and interplay of institutional and cultural formations. Such an analysis is of intrinsic interest but also poses crucial challenges for sociological theory on several levels.

Given the fact that the basic characteristics of Axial visions entail the opening of social structures and cultural orientations, as made fully explicit in Bellah's analysis, the first such level in the reexamination is that of evolutionary theory, of the place of evolutionary perspectives, in social analysis. The second, closely related problem is that of the relation between evolutionary tendencies, presumably inherent in human societies, and concrete constellations of institutional and cultural formations. An ensuing third level of analysis concerns the nature of the processes through which the institutionalization of visions is effected. Belonging to this third level are also problems of the nature of the agency which is central in effecting such institutionalization. Finally there is the general problem of the precise relationship between symbolic formations and social forces, between "culture" and "social structures", and between the latter and geopolitical conditions and historical contexts.[16]

These problems are not, of course, limited to the analysis of Axial Civilizations. They are inherent in the analysis of the process of crystallization of any institutional formation. However in the case of the Axial Civilizations, cosmological visions and distinctive "modes of thinking",

---

[16] These problems in sociological theory are discussed in greater detail in Eisenstadt (1995).

as well as the different social forces promulgating and upholding such visions, are immediately relevant for an understanding of the crystallization of concrete institutional patterns.

The Institutionalization of Axial Civilizations and the Evolutionary Perspective

6.

Let us start with the relevance of an evolutionary perspective for an analysis of the institutionalization of Axial Civilizations. The conception of Axial Age as promulgated by Jaspers was, as indicated above, imbued with a strong, even if only implicit, evolutionary orientation. In this conception a co-occurrence of a qualitatively higher degree of "openness" in the symbolic formations and in the structural dimensions of social organization is a key characteristic of the Axial Age. Let us however relate the analysis of the crystallization of Axial Civilizations to the central assumption of evolutionary approaches.

A central component of evolutionary theory—or to be more precise one might speak of the "developmental" version of evolutionary theory—has been an emphasis on identifying the major forces of change in human history. In this regard, research has concentrated on the extension of the range of human activity, on the generation of higher levels of resources, among them free resources, that allow for a decoupling of organizational and symbolic dimensions of human activities and for the development of more complex social and symbolic formations.[17]

On the social organizational or structural level such potentialities are generated by new technologies, by new encounters between different societies, in particular between societies of higher levels of resources and especially of potentially free resources, and by growing structural differentiation. Such differentiation is manifested in the development of distinct organizations, collectivities and roles that are no longer firmly embedded in different family, kinship or local settings. As a result there is a concomitant crystallization of more complex institutional patterns and the emergence of new integrative mechanisms and complex mech-

---

[17] On social evolution, see from the immense literature (in chronological order): Hobhouse, Wheeler and Ginsberg (1915/1965); Lenski (1924/1970); Ginsberg (1932/1961); Steward (1955); Sahlins and Service (1960); Bock (1963); Schwartz and Miller (1964); Parsons (1964); Eisenstadt (1964a, 1968); Service (1968); Runciman (1986, 1997); Banner (2001); Lenski (2005); Siegenthaler (2004); Domhoff (2006).

anisms of control. On the symbolic level the processes of such decoupling have been manifest above all in the emergence of a distinct sphere of activity for the articulation and interpretation in relatively abstract terms of the basic components of symbolic formations and cosmological visions as well as of criteria of justification of human activities and of social order. In the theoretical mode of symbolic orientations such development is manifest in a process of growing "rationalization" up to the emergence of what might be termed second-order thinking, entailing the potential for a critical examination of the premises of the cosmic and social orders.

In classical, and to some extent also in some contemporary, evolutionary analyses the different degrees of the extension of human activities have often been designated as constituting different stages of social evolution. Thus the crystallization of different patterns of social division of labor—such as tribal, archaic, Imperial and the like—or of symbolic representations, say in terms of episodic mimetic, mystic and theoretical modes of human thought, have tended to be cast as reflecting not only change but different stages that can be ordered relative to each other. As for institutional formations to be found in Axial Civilizations, above all Empires, and the modes of "theoretical" thought prevalent in them, have often been described as distinctive and in many ways as constituting the most "developed" stage of political and social order before modernity.[18]

Many of the evolutionary-developmental approaches were imbued with an implicit assumption that broad evolutionary tendencies explain the crystallization of concrete institutional and cultural formations. These approaches tended to conflate general evolutionary tendencies and the crystallization of specific institutional formations. Different constellations of social division of labor, as shaped above all by different technological and ecological developments, were for instance seen to explain also concrete institutional formations that developed in each evolutionary stage. This in turn tended to have as a corollary an assumption that developments in the symbolic realm provided little but the legitimation of the respective social formations.

Many of these premises or emphases of the evolutionary perspective have been sharply criticized in the social sciences and in historical research. This is true especially for the ways in which different stages of

---

[18] See for instance Ginsberg (1932/1961); Eisenstadt (1968); Parsons (1966).

evolutionary processes were being cast, e.g., in terms of a convergence of the symbolic and structural stages of evolution. Indeed these types of assumptions have also been critically examined in the more recent analyses of Axial Civilizations—as against earlier analyses of the Axial Age which entailed, as we have seen, a strong—if implicit—assumption of a universal Axial age, as the apogee of social and cultural evolution.

Moreover, it was also in the context of the analysis of the crystallization of concrete institutional formations that central problems of general evolutionary theory, which, with some exceptions,[19] have been neglected in sociological theory, have emerged as an important issue. I am referring both to the problem of the nature of the process of selection of different components of institutional formations, and their adaptability to different environments, and to the potentially destructive possibilities that are inherent in the evolutionary process.

These more recent discussions, on which the preceding analysis of the basic characteristics of the Axial Civilizations has been to a large extent based,[20] enable a much more diversified and contextualized approach to problems of the relationship between general evolutionary tendencies and the crystallization of concrete institutional formations. This more recent approach does not, I argue, throw out the baby (i.e., the recognition of the existence in human societies of broad evolutionary tendencies) with the bathwater—i.e., with the assumption of a convergence of the symbolic and structural stages of evolution, as well as the conflation of evolutionary tendencies with the crystallization of concrete institutional formations.

Axial Visions and Crystallization of Institutional Formations

7.

Thus, we are here back at the crucial theoretical problem referred to above—namely the relationship between general evolutionary tendencies and the crystallization of concrete institutional formations—in our case in the Axial Civilizations. In this context it might be worthwhile to have a somewhat more detailed look at the different institutional formations that have crystallized in the framework of Axial Civilizations. The

---

[19] Runciman (1986, 1997).
[20] See Eisenstadt (1963).

starting point of such an analysis is the emergence of distinctive Axial visions, the characteristics of their carriers and the nature of the processes through which these visions were institutionalized.

The most important characteristic of the carriers of the Axial vision is that they were promulgated by distinct relatively autonomous cultural carriers of models of cultural and social order—the different Kulturträger. Examples of such are the ancient Israelite prophets and priests and later on the Jewish sages, the Greek philosophers and sophists, the various precursors of the Chinese literati, the Hindu Brahmins, the Buddhist "monks" to become the later different Sanghas, and the nuclei of the Ulema among the Islamic tribes and societies.

The nuclei of such groups promulgating Axial cultural visions emerged in all the historical settings in which the Axial Civilizations became institutionalized. They constituted a new social element, a socio-cultural mutation, a new type of religious or cultural activists which differed distinctively from the ritual, magical and sacral specialists in the pre-Axial civilizations, and which entailed the possibility of far-reaching institutional transformations. The very emergence of such would-be activists and institutional entrepreneurs constitutes a distinct mutation. The conditions under which it arises have not been adequately addressed or systematically analyzed in the social sciences, although some indications can indeed be found in the literature—as for instance the fact, pointed out by Bellah, that Axial visionaries tend to emerge especially in various secondary centers in relatively volatile international settings, and the more general observation that charismatic tendencies tend to arise in periods of social turmoil and disintegration.[21]

Only some of them were successful in the sense that their visions became institutionalized and became influential or hegemonic in their respective societies. In many societies, as for instance in some Greek city states, in which such visions emerged, appropriate resources or appropriate organizational frameworks through which they could be institutionalized, were not always available and the nuclei of new cultural and political activists were not able to mobilize such resources for the crystallization of new institutional patterns.[22] Beyond this, even when some such visions were institutionalized there developed great variations in the Axial institutional formations, not only between different

[21] Bellah (2005).
[22] Raaflaub (2005); Eisenstadt (1963).

Axial Civilizations but also within the framework of the same civilization—be it Jewish, Islamic, Hindu, Buddhist or Christian.

Thus within different Axial Civilizations there developed a great variety of institutional patterns, of institutional choices. These included full-fledged empires—in various forms (such as the Chinese, Byzantine or Ottoman ones) but also rather fragile kingdoms and tribal federations (e.g., ancient Israel) as well as combinations of tribal federations and city-states (e.g., ancient Greece). There are also the complex decentralized pattern of the Hindu civilization and the specific imperial-feudal configurations of Europe. Moreover, all these institutional formations were continuously changing—albeit in different tempi and directions—within Axial Civilizations.

8.

The institutionalization of the Axial visions was contingent, first, on the development of appropriate levels of free resources, which could be mobilized in the directions implied in these visions, i.e., in the direction of the development of autonomous centers, distinct institutional arenas and collectivities; and second, on the availability of organizational frameworks which could facilitate such mobilization.

Third, the institutionalization of these Axial visions was contingent on the development of coalitions between the original bearers of the Axial visions and other actors—especially political, economic or communal activists, i.e., potential elites which were active in the various arenas of their respective societies. These various political, economic, communal elites tended to become disembedded, though in different degrees in different Axial settings, from the major ascriptive frameworks and at the same time claiming autonomous access to the new order promulgated by Axial visions, thereby giving rise to continual contestation between them about their relative standing in relation to the new order.

Many of these elites were recruited and legitimized according to distinct, autonomous criteria, usually promulgated by themselves but in the shadow of the impact of the new visions. They saw themselves not only as performing specific technical, functional activities—be they those of scribes, or performers of rituals of initiation, and the like—but also as potentially autonomous carriers of a distinct cultural and social order related to the transcendental vision prevalent in their respective societies. They often acquired a potentially trans-regional consciousness of their own, but developed claims for an autonomous place in the constitution of the institutional formations and important components of the hegemonic coalitions thereof.

At the same time the carriers of the transcendental Axial visions became transformed into members of ruling coalitions, participating in the activities of mechanisms of control, in the regulation of power and of the flow of resources in their respective settings.

Thus, perhaps paradoxically, the institutionalization of Axial visions often entailed far-reaching transformations in the characteristics of the major social and political elites, but at the same time challenging the monopoly of the carriers of these visions over the processes of their institutionalization—i.e., over the formation of concrete institutional formations.

Simultaneously different institutional frameworks in many societies also acquired autonomous dynamic characteristics, perhaps most clearly seen in the case of Empires,[23] but also in other political formations, such as for instance in patrimonial ones.

Many of these formations were, in their basic structural characteristics, seemingly similar to parallel ones which developed in pre-Axial or non-Axial civilizations—such as for instance the patrimonial societies of South East Asia. However in patrimonial regimes, which crystallized within Axial civilizations, some distinct characteristics were of great importance, something we shall analyze in somewhat greater detail later on.

Cultural Orientations, Levels of Resources, and Modes of Control in the Crystallization of Patrimonial, Imperial and City-States Formations in Axial Civilizations

9.

The crystallization of the multiple institutional formations, which developed in the frameworks of the Axial Civilizations, was shaped by several factors. One such set consists of variations or differences in the basic cultural orientations promulgated by their respective hegemonic elites.[24]

---

[23] Eisenstadt, S. N., *Political Systems of Empires*, op. cit.
[24] On the different cultural orientations predominant in Axial Civilizations see in greater detail Eisenstadt (1986, 1987/1992, 2006); Arnason, Eisenstadt and Wittrock (2005).

A second set of conditions pertains to levels of resources, especially free resources, and the concrete structure of social arenas in which institutional tendencies can be played out. A third set is constituted by the processes through which different elites could regulate and mobilize available resources.

The most important differences from the point of view of institutional implications were those which had to do with different basic articulations of a tension between transcendental and mundane orders and modes of resolving it. There is first the distinction between cases where this tension is brought out in relatively secular terms (as in Confucianism and classical Chinese belief systems and, in a somewhat different way, in the Greek and Roman worlds) and cases in which the tension was conceived in terms of a religious and cosmological hiatus (as in the great monotheistic religions and Hinduism and Buddhism). In this respect a key distinctiveness of the Ancient Greek and Roman civilizations is the prominence of new conceptions of political order relative to that of transcendental "religious" articulations.

A second distinction within the latter context is that between the monotheistic religions, in which God tended to be portrayed as standing outside the Universe and potentially guiding it, and religions like Hinduism and Buddhism, in which the transcendental, cosmic system was conceived in impersonal, almost metaphysical, terms, and as being in a state of continuous tension with the mundane system. The "secular" conception of this tension was connected, as in China and to some degree in the ancient Mediterranean world, to an almost wholly this-worldly conception of salvation.

A third major distinction refers to the focus of the resolution of transcendental tensions, or in Weberian—basically Christian—terms, of salvation. Here the most important distinction was that between purely this-worldly, purely other-worldly and mixed this- and other-worldly conceptions of salvation. The metaphysical non-deistic conception of this tension, as in Hinduism and Buddhism, tended towards an other-worldly conception of "salvation", while the great monotheistic religions tended to emphasize different combinations of this- and other-worldly conceptions of the transcendental vision. Of special importance from the point of the impact of these orientations on the shaping of concrete institutional formations was the extent to which different institutional arenas—above all the political one, or some distinct collectivities—were designated as the arenas for the implementation of the respective cosmological vision.

These cultural orientations were promulgated by different elites and different coalitions within them. Such elites constituted bearers of different cultural orientations and played a crucial role in hegemonic as well as challenging coalitions. Different cultural orientations became hegemonic or predominant in different Axial Civilizations. Thus in the Greek and Hellenistic and in the Confucian (above all Chinese, but also Korean and Vietnamese) civilizations different types of this-worldly orientations were the dominant ones. In most of the South Asian and South Eastern Buddhist civilizations on the other hand it was above all other-worldly orientations that became predominant. The major monotheistic civilizations were characterized by the relative predominance of different and continually changing mixtures of this- and other-worldly orientations.

The concrete working out of potential institutional implications of different cultural orientations was dependent, as already argued, first, on resources and arenas available and, second, on processes of interaction between hegemonic elites and major groups and the carriers of the different Axial visions, and, third, on the processes through which different carriers or elites regulated available resources and were able to mobilize them in specific institutional directions.

It is, of course, beyond the scope of this essay to present a comprehensive comparative analysis of the different institutional formations that developed in Axial Civilizations. We shall however provide some illustrations of ways in which cultural orientations and their carriers, levels of resources as well as major coalitions and modes of control developed in some basic types of Axial institutional formations—patrimonial, Imperial and city-republican—and make comparisons with other such formations which developed in non-Axial ones. In all these cases we shall focus on the extent to which potentialities for relatively radical political change developed. Such potentialities were inherent in all Axial civilizations, but they developed in different degrees and directions. Our first illustration will focus on the comparative analysis of patrimonial regimes in non-Axial and Axial settings.[25]

Patrimonial regimes developed in many pre-Axial civilizations, be it Mesoamerica, South Asia or in Middle Eastern societies, in many Axial Civilizations, in which other-worldly orientations were predominant, such as in India and Hindu-dominated regimes of South Asia, and, as

---

[25] This is based on Eisenstadt (2006); idem., (1973, 1971); idem.

already indicated above, also in some this-worldly Axial Civilizations attendant on their expansion.

In contrast to Imperial and Imperial-feudal regimes, the differentiation between center and periphery in patrimonial regimes was, as we shall see, based mainly on the ecological distinctiveness of the center and on greater concentrations of populations within it, with a very limited degree of specialization between different groups, as well as of the autonomy of the urban communities.

The policies promulgated by the rulers of patrimonial regimes were mostly of an expansive character, i.e., aiming at expansion of control of large territories, rather than intrinsic ones (characterized by intensive exploitation of a fixed resource basis). They were also, to use Karl Polanyi's terms,[26] mostly redistributive ones, thus minimizing the development of a high level of free resources. The rulers of patrimonial regimes attempted to regulate the production and possible distribution of available free resources among the various groups of society in ways which would minimize the possibility of their being used by competing autonomous elites.

There developed great differences between patrimonial regimes with respect to levels of economic development as well as to the cosmological vision promulgated by their respective elites and the modes of control exercised by them. With respect to the first distinction, many of the concrete institutional power structures in patrimonial societies which developed in different Axial Civilizations were often similar to those that developed in "non-Axial" ones (as in Ancient Near East, Mesoamerica or pre-Hindu South Asia). They were often also attesting to the "persistence" of non-Axial components within Axial Civilizations. But the patrimonial regimes, which developed in other-worldly Axial Civilizations, differed greatly from the "classical" patrimonial ones in the sense that among the former there developed autonomous religious elites. The crucially distinct Axial component opened up possibilities of dissent and potential heterodoxy, which are endemic in Axial Civilizations. Thereby the stage was set for new types of contestations over power and material and ideological resources. Of special importance in this context is that such sectarian activities have often been among the most prominent articulations of the broader, often universalistic, Axial cosmological and institutional visions. Even if elites tended not to channel free resources

---

[26] Polanyi (1944).

into political arenas or into economic ones, they still had far-reaching impact on the reconstruction of their respective collectivities.

In parallel, important differences are also to be found between on the one hand Axial Civilizations, in which more patrimonial political systems and systems of political economy were predominant and in which other-worldly cosmological conceptions were promulgated by the dominant elites, and those on the other in which this-worldly or mixed this- and other-worldly orientations were predominant, above all in Muslim and Christian civilizations. In regimes where other-worldly orientations were predominant, as for example in the Hindu civilizations and to a large extent also in Buddhist and post-Reformation Catholicism, the political arena was not defined as crucial for the implementation of transcendental visions. The elites, who were the carriers of other-worldly orientations, tended to be highly autonomous in the "cultural" or religious arenas, but much less so in the political one. The elites also exhibited strong tendencies towards becoming embedded in existing power structures, thus generating tendencies to "non-revolutionary" potentialities of change. In these cases the basic structure and orientations of elites minimized the chances of growth of social movements oriented to the reconstruction of the political arena. At the same time, there tended to be a relatively accommodative form of participation of religious elites in the patrimonial political arenas of these regimes. Thus, in India and also in Buddhist and to some extent in post-Reformation Catholic societies, elites were not on the whole autonomous in the political arena. They were oriented more to the communal and religious cultural arena and much less in the direction of reconstruction of the overall political and economic one. Significantly enough, in these societies, as for instance in the case of the Maurya rulers in India, the tendencies of rulers towards expansion with potential Imperial implications was often hemmed in by coalitions of embedded cultural elites with wider ascriptive—kinship or territorial—settings.

The story was different in societies, like the Islamic ones or in Christian Eastern Europe (or in a different vein in Ethiopia), where the development of patrimonial regimes was more due to historical contingencies and political-ecological conditions, especially to different modes of expansion of these civilizations. In these societies there existed strong, even if for a long period only latent, orientations to the reconstruction of the political arena which could give rise to proto-revolutionary tendencies among the cultural and political elites, as in the case of Islamic societies. Given the basic premises of Islamic tradition, there developed in many if not most Islamic regimes after the establishment of the first Caliphates, in the Abbasid Empire and later after its demise, autonomous elites, often rooted in tribal traditions. These autonomous elites often developed a strong predisposition to transformative, proto-revolutionary ideologies and tendencies. However, it was but rarely that such elites came to mount a full revolutionary process or institution-alize a revolutionary regime. It was only at the core of the Ottoman Empire—and even there only to a very limited extent—that the ker-nels of an autonomous civil society and the concomitant revolutionary potential did develop.

10.

A different pattern of relations between cultural orientations, structural conditions and levels of resources and modes of control developed in Imperial and Imperial feudal regimes. In most of these regimes a development of different mixtures of this- and other-worldly orienta-tions as well as of an emphasis on the political arena, as at least one of the arenas for the implementation of transcendental visions, took place. This has been the case in most Christian (especially European and Byzantine) and Islamic civilizations, and in a different way in the Confucian-legal framework, in which other-worldly visions were of only secondary importance. Such orientations were usually connected with the development of multiple, potentially autonomous competing elites. It was the prevalence of such orientations, borne by multiple compet-ing groups, that generated conditions favorable for the development of potentially radical revolutionary orientations and patterns of change.[27]

The full institutionalization of Imperial and Imperial-feudal regimes such as the European, Byzantine, Russian, Abbasid and the Fatimid and late Ottoman cases, and the Chinese and Vietnamese ones, was to a high degree dependent on the development of a relatively high level of economic development. Another characteristic of these regimes was the relatively differentiated mode of political economy, in which rulers tended to promote economic policies, creating conditions for the devel-opment of relatively high levels of free resources and of relatively open social sectors. These conditions included a free peasantry and relatively autonomous urban groups, all of which generated wide spaces of free

---

[27] Eisenstadt (1963/1993); idem (1971).

economic resources and activities, not embedded in ascriptive, tribal or patrimonial settings.

Free resources generated within the various sectors of society could be channeled by competing elites into "this-worldly" political and/or economic arenas and in relatively radical directions. It was particularly in the Imperial or Imperial-feudal regimes described here, i.e., regimes in which the predominant transcendental vision was a this-worldly one or a combined this-worldly and other-worldly one, that this kind of development took place. In such appropriate historical contexts, resources of early modernity could be channeled in the direction of revolutionary developments.

The Imperial and the Imperial-feudal regimes, which developed in many of the Axial Civilizations, were characterized by the crystallization of distinct centers perceived as autonomous symbolic and organizational entities. They were also characterized by a continual interaction between center and periphery; by the concomitant development of multiple relatively autonomous primary and secondary—cultural-intellectual, religious and political—elites which tended to be in a process of continual contestation with one another. This in turn created a challenge to the attempts of the respective hegemonic elites to monopolize the production and above all the distribution and flow of free resources available in society.

There developed important differences between the institutional and political dynamics of different Imperial regimes, influenced by different modes of control exercised by these regimes. There tended first to be a difference in the dynamics of Imperial as against Imperial-feudal regimes. The rulers of the pure Imperial regimes, e.g., Byzantine and Chinese (and later also Russian), tended to develop concentrated modes of control. They also minimized the access of other elites and wider social strata to the center of the regimes. In Imperial-feudal regimes— the best illustrations of which have been Western and Central Europe and early Kievan Rus—there developed a continual struggle over such access and over the process of exchange between different resources.[28]

---

[28] See Eisenstadt (2006).

11.

Yet another illustration of the great variability and changeability of the institutional formations that crystallized in different Axial civilizations is the case of Athens and the formations in city-states. Mohammad Nafissi's[29] analysis thereof provides an important illustration of such variability and of its implications for sociological analysis and above all of the evolutionary perspective. Several aspects of the Athenian case as analyzed by Nafissi are important for the analysis of relations between evolutionary tendencies and crystallization of institutional formations.

The starting point for the analysis is his designation of the Athenian society as modern. This designation is based on several characteristics. The Athenian economy was a market based on private property where strong individualistic orientations developed. There was also the possibility of "private" citizens, above all peasants, mobilizing themselves and using their power to promulgate distinctive political social programs as well as acting as "autonomous agents with the capacity—discursive as much as coercive—for the collective construction and pursuit of ideal and material interests (especially with respect to arrangement of debts)". (p. 271).

Among the most important of such aspects are, first, the fact that the development of autonomous political actors in Athens was not connected with the development of the concept and institutional framework of the state as a distinct entity. Second is the fact that the critical reflexive attitude to the political arena which constituted the core of political mobilization was not connected, as was the case in other Axial civilizations,[30] with a distinct cosmology—although it was closely related to a critical evaluation of cosmological assumptions in general. Accordingly there did not develop in Ancient Athens heterodoxies as bearers of competing, cosmological orientations and political conceptions. Concomitantly the predominance of a market economy in Athens was connected with the *oikos* constituting the site of economic activity. "From this point of view, the Athenian economy was by definition embedded and, from the medieval and modern perspectives, primitive". Moreover the Athenian modernity did not lead to further evolutionary

[29] Nafissi (2005); idem (2004).
[30] Eisenstadt (1986); Arnason, Eisenstadt and Wittrock (2005); Bellah (2005). See also Eisenstadt, Abitbol and Chazan (1988); and idem, 168–200.

developments—but to regression, to breakdown and to incorporation in other institutional formations.

12.

Nafissi's detailed analysis and radical revaluation of the Athenian experience, as well as the brief analyses of patrimonial and Imperial societies presented above, have far-reaching implications for comparative evolutionary theory. They all indicate that Athenian modernity or the various Imperial or political regimes, while entailing evolutionary tendencies and potentials, cannot be designated as a distinct stage of social evolution. Rather they can be seen as a distinct historical constellation—in which institutional and symbolic evolutionary potentials crystallized in different ways. Moreover, these illustrations indicate that because the crystallization of any concrete institutional formation is dependent on the constellation of the different factors specified above, there exists a wide range of possible institutional formations, formations that were also open to continuous challenge.

Institutional formations are never preordained by cosmological visions or by general evolutionary tendencies, even if such tendencies do indeed provide the general framework for such crystallizations and create, as it were, the challenges for the formation of institutions.

Accordingly different institutional formations develop as selections from potentially multiple possibilities. Such selections are greatly influenced by modes of control, regulation and mobilization of resources developed by different activists and elites in their inter-relations with broader social sectors. There developed potential affinities[31] between cultural orientations and the characteristics of the elites—especially the scope of their autonomy and embeddedness in relatively closed social formations. In the most general terms, elites which were relatively embedded in closed frameworks tended to be more attuned to other-worldly orientations, while those which were embedded in relatively autonomous political frameworks—as was the case in China, and in a different way in the Greek case—were more attuned to this-worldly orientations. Elites which promulgated other-worldly orientations tended to be more autonomous and disembedded from closed frameworks. However the concrete outcome in any individual case depended on the combination

---

[31] Runciman (2005); idem (1986).

of structural characteristics of elites and of their cultural orientations with levels of resources and modes of control and regulation.

All the illustrations of different patterns, the multiplicity and change-ability of institutional formations are seemingly greater in Axial Civilizations than what can be found in other civilizations. Such multi-plicity and changeability is rooted in the combination of major cultural orientations with ecological and social settings. The potential multiplicity of institutional constellations was, as we have seen, exacerbated in Axial Civilizations by the fact that within all these civilizations there devel-oped, in close connection with the tendencies to reconstruct the world, a propensity to expansion, in which ideological, religious impulses were combined with political and to some extent economic ones. In all these settings contacts and confrontations between different Axial civiliza-tions—each with their own claims to some universality—and between them and non-Axial ones constituted a continual aspect of the dynam-ics of these civilizations.

13.

The crystallization of distinctive Axial institutional formations, rooted in the general tendency to the reconstruction of the world, with its sym-bolic-ideological and institutional repercussions, and their continual expansion, was common to all Axial Age civilizations. Yet, the concrete ways in which these tendencies developed, i.e., became transformed into specific institutional patterns, differed greatly between these civilizations and within them.

In more general terms the very potentialities of crystallization of Axial symbolic and institutional formations were contingent on the development of broad evolutionary tendencies. This in turn attests to a general tendency, not limited to Axial Civilizations, to continual expansion of the range of human activities, to a growing complexity of social structures and to a growing "rationalization" as well as prob-lematization of the symbolic realms[32] and of criteria of justification of human activities and of social order. At the same time, however, a close examination of the historical evidence indicates that such potentialities are not realized in all societies which seemingly "reach" a given evolu-tionary stage. Furthermore, and most importantly, the crystallization of

---

[32] Eisenstadt (2006).

any concrete institutional pattern or formation, including those which developed in different Axial Civilizations, is not assured or shaped by the "mere" emergence in any historical context of the appropriate symbolic and structural evolutionary tendencies. In other words, the different institutional patterns and cultural formations that crystallized in the Axial civilizations did not develop "naturally" or automatically as manifestations of a distinct stage in evolutionary history.

The institutionalization of any Axial visions was never a simple and peaceful process. It has usually been connected with protracted struggles between activists and groups with competing visions. Such struggles and contestations around the formation and the continuity of different institutional formations constituted a key aspect of the dynamics of Axial Civilizations.

The Distinctive Dynamics of Different Institutional Formations

14.

As in other historical cases, any institutional choice entails specific modes of relations between social structure and cosmological visions as manifest in the constitution of institutional boundaries and of different selective affinities between symbolic orientations and geopolitical conditions and structural formations.

Of special importance from the point of view of the openness of the relation between "cosmological" visions, ecological settings and institutional formations is the case of what Parsons called seedbed societies with early Ancient Greece and Ancient Israel as prime illustrations.[33] The central characteristic of these societies has been the discrepancy between the potential institutional range of their basic visions and the concrete possibilities of their institutionalization—giving rise to a situation in which many of the institutional potentialities of their visions were in a sense "stored", to be transmitted as components of institutional settings and dynamics of other civilizations.

Each of these institutional formations and choices also entailed different modes of incorporation of non- or pre-Axial symbolic and institutional components. Even in the new Axial settings, such non-Axial orientations and their carriers constituted important components of the

---

[33] Parsons (1977).

cultural and institutional dynamics thereof; creating autonomous spaces which could indeed be very influential within the frameworks of the Axial Civilizations, often persisting, as was the case in Egypt, through changes in the dominant Axial Civilizations. Many of the pre-Axial symbolic and institutional patterns crystallized as important secondary components in the Axial—in the way that Bellah has emphasized. They could also, as the case of Japan attests to, create their own very important niches in international frameworks dominated by Axial Civilizations.[34]

Accordingly, within each of these formations there emerged distinctive dynamics. These were generated by internal tensions in the wake of the institutionalization of Axial frameworks but also by tensions and contradictions between these processes and basic Axial premises and by ways in which different societies and civilizations were incorporated into international frameworks. The crystallization in these volatile settings of any concrete institutional pattern intensified the consciousness of tensions, antinomies and contradictions inherent in the Axial cultural programs and gave rise to reinterpretations by different social actors of the major premises of the Axial visions and programs. Within each of these formations there developed distinct relations between orthodoxy and heterodoxies, creating, or blocking, new developmental possibilities and paths. In one case—that of "Western" Christianity—these developments gave rise to the post-revolutionary transformation of the crystallization of the first modernity which then expanded throughout the world, and on its expansion encountered the other Axial civilizations in their respective historical institutional and symbolic settings with these encounters giving rise to multiple modernities.

Theoretical Implications: Evolutionary Tendencies,
Institutional Formations—Agency and Control

15.

The preceding analysis of the institutionalization of different Axial Civilizations has implications for the basic problems of sociological theory mentioned above—and for the analysis of world history.

First, these analyses indicate that the crystallization of any concrete institutional pattern entails, is contingent on, the development of

---

[34] Eisenstadt (1995).

distinct dimensions of social interaction which differ from the general
evolutionary tendencies—i.e., from the development of new resources
and new symbolic orientations. Second, the crystallization of institutional and symbolic formations is effected by distinct types of actors, the
emergence of which constitutes a socio-cultural mutation, which is not
predetermined by broad evolutionary tendencies. Third, the crystallization of concrete institutional patterns is contingent on the development
of patterns of interaction and of mechanisms of control and regulations between major social actors, above all between different would-be
elites and between them and broader social sectors. Fourth, historical
contingencies play indeed a very important role in the process of such
crystallization. Let us explicate, even if only briefly, these points.

The core of the crystallization of any concrete institutional formation
is the specification of the distinctive boundaries of social interactions.
As the human biological program is, to use Ernest Mayer's felicitous
expression, an "open" one,[35] such boundaries are not predetermined
genetically, but have to be constituted through specific modes of social
interactions. The openness of the human program entails the potentialities of the continual expansion of human activities. At the same time it
generates problematics which are managed through the constitution of
social boundaries—the core of which is the regulation of the continual
flow of resources and of relations between resources, different actors,
and their goals. Such social boundaries do not exist, contrary to some
more implicit assumptions in sociological, anthropological, and historical analyses, as natural ones delimiting closed systems. On the contrary,
such boundaries are open, continuously constructed and reconstructed,
and accordingly fragile.

Moreover, human consciousness of such indeterminacies generates
distinct problems, the most important of these problems being, as identified by the Founding Fathers of Sociology,[36] the constitution of trust,
regulation of power and provision of meaning and legitimation of social
activities and frameworks. Therefore the crystallization of institutional
formations—political, economic, "cultural"—and of different collectivities, involves contestations of power but also processes of economic
coordination and of the constitution of solidarity. The extent of their
autonomy or predominance varies in different societies according to the

---

[35] Mayer (1976).
[36] See on this in greater detail Eisenstadt (1995).

extent of their embeddedness in broader frameworks and the major orientations prevalent in them.

The inherent fragility of boundaries involves the creation of various mechanisms of social integration, regulation and control. Such regulation is effected by distinct social activists, "leaders", influentials or elites, and institutional empreneurs. The most important among these groups mentioned are first, those who structure the division of labor in a society; second, those who articulate collective political goals and a division of political power; third, those who specify the borders of different ascriptive social collectivities; and fourth, those who articulate the basic cultural visions and models predominant in a society or in sectors thereof.

Such processes of control and regulations entail the transformation of basic symbolic orientations, of the cosmological visions into "codes" or schemata. Such codes are somewhat akin to, but to take one example, what Max Weber called *Wirtschaftsethik*. A *Wirtschaftsethik* does not connote specific religious injunctions about proper behavior in any given spheres, nor is it merely a logical derivative of the intellectual contents of the theology or philosophy predominant in a given religion. Rather, a *Wirtschaftsethik* connotes a general mode of "religious" or "ethical" orientation which shapes the major criteria of evaluation and of justification of human activities and of institutional formations which serve as starting points for the regulation of the flow and distribution of resources in such an arena. Such regulation is effected by a combination of organizational means, especially of patterns of incentives and sanctions, with regulation of power, and with public and semi-public rituals—articulated in a variety of situations ranging from the latent rituals of daily situations to more official ones.

Such mechanisms of control are hierarchically composed of many stable lower-level and intermediate units that are strongly interconnected horizontally but less strongly coupled vertically. Furthermore, those vertical linkages diminish in strength according to their height in the hierarchical scale. Lower-level controls manage short-term and local affairs, while higher-level controls provide system-wide decision-making capability.[37]

---

[37] Simon (1965); idem (1977).

In all societies these kinds of mechanisms develop, but they differ with respect to the degree of their complexity. The more complex social and political systems and civilizational frameworks become, the more autonomous, but potentially also the more fragile, they become. Axial Civilizations provide one of the most important illustrations of the problems attendant on the development of relatively complex social systems rooted in evolutionary tendencies that led to potentially fragile modes of control and to enhanced possibilities for challenges of existing order and of their transformation. Axial Civilizations therefore by their very nature give rise to multiple and changing institutional formations.

16.

The preceding analysis has important implications for the analysis of the relation between broad evolutionary tendencies and the crystallization of concrete institutional formations.

It indicates first that any such formations, while rooted in evolutionary tendencies and potentials, cannot be designated as natural manifestations of distinct stages of social evolution. Rather they constitute historical constellations in which the institutional and symbolic potentials of human activity, inherent in broad evolutionary processes, crystallized in a distinctive way. In any historical context there exist multiple institutional possibilities. First is the fact that—contrary to some of the presuppositions of classical evolutionary analyses which have also influenced, even if only implicitly, some of the earlier analyses of Axial Civilizations—processes of social differentiation, technological development and a concomitant development of free resources and processes of a growing complexity of symbolic orientations and of the premises of cosmological order do not always go together in tandem. These two basic dimensions of social life in terms of practices of appropriation and of domination relative to practices related to symbolic and cosmological order, these two basic evolutionary universals, do not develop in any specific situation in a predetermined way; each of these dimensions of social action develops at least to some extent independently of one another; generated by its internal momentum, albeit, of course, continually influencing one another in a variety of ways. At most there develop certain affinities between these two processes, i.e., between the extent of openness of symbolic orientations and cosmological visions on the one hand and on the other hand processes of structural differentiation and a concomitant growth of free resources. (As already mentioned, it was the recognition of these facts that made Talcott Parsons designate Ancient Greece and Israel as seedbed societies, characterized by a strong discrepancy between their basic visions and the concrete possibilities of their institutionalization.)

Second, the development in any historical situation, at any stage of social evolution, of "open" spaces, of concomitant multiple institutional possibilities is strengthened in Axial Civilizations by the development of new resources, of specific patterns of social division of labor, as well as of symbolic orientations and of new forms of encounters with other societies across regions of greater spatial extension. All these processes opened up the possibility of a range of new institutional formations.

Third, and most important, is the fact that any crystallization of institutional formations is effected by distinct types of agency, by activities which mobilize available, especially free, resources in directions implied by the visions of different groups of agents, who try to regulate the flow of available resources. But the very emergence of such activities, carried by elite groups with their different visions, tends to give rise to a kind of mutations, which develop in different historical contexts in seemingly unpredictable ways, even if they all occur within the framework of the same process of symbolic and structural evolution.

This principled openness, in any historical situation and at any evolutionary stage, of a wide range of possible institutional formations, means that the attempts by different groups of entrepreneurs to crystallize any concrete institutional patterns entails a continual contestation for power and that there exist relatively autonomous practices of power, economic interest and constitution of solidarity, which jointly come to shape the institutional formations that emerge.

It is also because of the tendency to extension of the range of human activities, a tendency greatly enhanced in Axial Civilizations, that whatever equilibrium between the constitution of trust, regulation of power and legitimation of social order, which may have been achieved, tends to be undermined. The Axial Civilizations had as one of their most important legacies an inevitable enhancement of a consciousness of the arbitrariness of any social order. As a consequence they both created the potentials for new institutional formations with greater spatial extension and greater degrees of differentiation but also opened up the possibility for question and contestation around these formations of a qualitatively new type. Thereby they also entailed a complex interplay between constructive and destructive potentialities inherent in the charismatic dimension of human action—a fact which has not been given enough attention in sociological analysis.[38]

17.

Thus an analysis of the crystallization of different institutional formations of Axial Civilizations provides us with a truly differentiated and contextualized vision of world history; of the interlinkages between social and cultural evolutionary tendencies and concrete social processes in the crystallization of institutional formations in which human agency and historical contingencies play a central role; and of the continual confrontation between constructive and destructive tendencies inherent in these processes.

The preceding analysis puts into question the conflation of the crystallization of Axial Civilizations with the emergence of the "Axial Age" or "Ages." The extent to which developments in different parts of the world converge into a "global" or "semi-global" Axial Age has to be put as a question, as a problem to be investigated—and not as a given. There is no doubt that the emergence of Axial visions, with their universalistic transcendental orientations, with strong tendencies to the reconstruction of societies constituted a crucial social-cultural mutation and innovation in human history and that the Axial syndrome does constitute one of the most crucial and revolutionary components in the development of human societies. However, this component may develop in different ways in different contexts, in connection with other Axial and non-Axial societies or civilizations, characterized by different historical collective visions. No such vision does necessarily become hegemonic, nor does the crystallization of such hegemony necessarily exclude all other visions. There developed continual contestations between different visions and the civilizations in which they were implemented. Nor were all societies incorporated into the frameworks of Axial Civilizations but were in many cases able to develop their own spaces with distinctive dynamics, albeit in relation to and under influence from adjacent, as was for instance the case with Japan, or distant Axial Civilizations.

---

[38] For important indications about this problem, see Tiryakian (1999); Joas (2003); Eisenstadt (1968, 2003).

References

Arnason, J. P. 2005. "The Axial Age and its interpreters: Reopening a debate" in J. P. Arnason, S. N. Eisenstadt and B. Wittrock (eds.), *Axial Civilizations and World History*, 19–51.

Arnason, J. P., S. N. Eisenstadt and B. Wittrock (eds.). 2005. *Axial Civilizations and World History*, Leiden: Brill.

Banner, R. C. 2001. "Evolutionism, including social darwinism" in N. J. Smelser and P. B. Baltes (eds.), *International Encyclopedia of the Social and Behavioral Sciences*, Amsterdam: Elsevier, 7:5033–5038.

Bellah, R. N. 2005. "What is axial about Axial Age," op. cit. See also appropriate references in note 17.

——. 2005. "What is axial about the Axial Age" in *European Journal of Sociology*, 46: 69–89.

Biran, M. 2005. "The Mongol transformation: From the steppe to Eurasian Empire" in J. P. Arnason and B. Wittrock (eds.), *Eurasian Transformations, Tenth to Thirteenth Centuries: Crystallizations, Divergences, Renaissances*, Leiden, Boston: Brill, 339–363.

——. 2007. *Chinggis Khan*, Oxford: One World.

Bock, Kenneth E. 1963. "Evolution, function and change" in *American Sociological Review*, 28:229–237.

Daedalus. 1975. "The age of transcendence", 104:2 (Spring).

Domhoff, W. G. 2006. Review Essays on Gerhard Lenski's ecological-evolutionary theory. Principles and the essays included in *Contemporary Sociology Journal of Reviews*, 35 (November 6, 2006).

Eisenstadt, S. N. 1963/1993. *The Political Systems of Empires*, New York: Free Press of Glencoe. New edition with new introduction. New Brunswick: Transaction Publishers.

——. 1964a. "Social change, differentiation and evolution" in *American Sociological Review*, 29:375–386.

——. (ed.) 1968. *Max Weber on Charisma and Institution Building*. Chicago: University of Chicago Press.

——. 1968. "Social evolution" in *International Encyclopedia of the Social Sciences*, D. Shills (ed.), The Macmillan Company and the Free Press, 5:228–234.

——. 1971 (ed.), *Political Sociology: A Reader*, New York/London: Basic Books, Chapter 5, 138–178.

——. 1971 (ed.), *Political Sociology: A Reader*, New York/London: Basic Books, Chapter 7, 250–312.

——. 1973. *Traditional Patrimonialism and Modern Neopatrimonialism*, Beverly Hills/London: Sage Publications.

——. 1981. "Cultural traditions and political dynamics: The origins and modes of ideological politics", The Hobhouse Lecture in *British Journal of Sociology*, 32:155–188.

——. 1982. "The Axial Age: The emergence of transcendental visions and the rise of clerics" in *European Journal of Sociology*, 23(2):293–314.

——. 1986. *The Origins and Diversity of Axial Age Civilization*, Albany: State University of New York Press.

——. 1987/1992. *Kulturen der Achsenzeit*, 3 vols., Frankfurt: Suhrkamp Verlag.

——. 1995. *Japanese Civilization: A Comparative View*, Chicago: Chicago University Press.

——. 1995. *Power, Trust and Meaning: Essays in Sociological Theory and Analysis*, Chicago: University of Chicago Press, especially "Introduction: Social structure, culture, agency and change", 1–40, and Chapter 13, "Action, resources, structure and meaning", 328–389.

——. 2000. "The civilizational dimension in sociological analysis" in *Thesis Eleven*, 62 (August):1–21.

——. 2003. "Barbarism and modernity: The destructive components of modernity" in S. N. Eisenstadt, *Comparative Civilizations and Multiple Modernities*, Leiden: Brill, vol. 2, 561–577.

——. 2006. *The Great Revolutions and Modernity*, Leiden: Brill, especially chapter 13, 119–125.

——. 2006. *The Great Revolutions and Modernity*, op. cit., Chapter 12, 109–119.

Eisenstadt, S. N., M. Abitbol and N. Chazan (eds.) 1988. "The origins of the state reconsidered" in their *The Early State in African Perspective: Culture, Power and Division of Labor*, Leiden: Brill, 1–27.

——. idem, "State formation in Africa: Conclusions" in *The Early State in African Perspective*, op. cit., 168–200.

Eisenstadt, S. N. and I. F. Silber (eds.) 1988. *Cultural Traditions and Worlds of Knowledge: Explorations in the Sociology of Knowledge*, Philadelphia: JAI, Studies in Knowledge and Society.

Elkana, Y. 1986. "The emergence of second-order thinking in classical Greece" in S. N. Eisenstadt (ed.) 1986. *The Origins and Diversity of Axial Age Civilization*, Albany: State University of New York Press, 40–64.

Frank, A. G. and Gills, B. K. 1993. *The World System: Five Hundred Years or Five Thousand?*, London: Routledge.

Friedman, J. and M. J. Rowlands. 1977. "Notes towards an epigenetic model of the evolution of civilizations" in J. Friedman and M. J. Rowlands (eds.), *The Evolution of Social Systems*, London: Duckworth.

Ginsberg, M. 1932/1961. "The concept of evolution in sociology" in M. Ginsberg, *Essays in Sociology and Social Philosophy*, London: Heinemann, vol. 1, 180–199.

Hobhouse, L. T., G. C. Wheeler and M. Ginsberg. 1915/1965. "The material culture and social institutions of the simpler peoples: An essay in correlation" in *London School of Economics and Political Science Monographs on Sociology*, 3, London: Routledge.

Jaspers, K. 1949/1953. *The Origin and Goal of History*, London: Routledge and Kegan Paul.

Joas, H. 2003. *War and Modernity*, Polity Press: Cambridge.

Lenski, G. E. 1924/1970. *Human Societies: A Macrolevel Introduction of Sociology*, New York: McGraw-Hill.

——. 2005. *Ecological-Evolutionary Theory: Principles and Applications*, Paradigm Pub., S.I.

Mayer, E. 1976. *Evolution and the Diversity of Life*, Cambridge: Harvard University Press.

Nafissi, M. 2005. *Ancient Athens and Modern Ideology*, Institute of Classical Studies, School of Advanced Study, University of London.

——. 2004. "Class, embeddedness and the modernity of ancient Athens" in *Comparative Studies in Society and History*, 46(2):378–410.

Parsons, T. 1964. "Evolutionary universals in society" in *American Sociological Review*, 29:339–357.

——. 1966. *Societies: Evolutionary and Comparative Perspectives*, Englewood Cliffs, NJ: Prentice-Hall.

——. 1977. "Cultural legacies for later societies: The Hebrew and Greek concepts of a moral order" in *The Evolution of Societies*, Englewood Cliffs, NJ: Prentice-Hall, 99–114.

Polanyi, K. 1944. *The Great Transformation*. Beacon: Beacon Press.

Raaflaub, K. A. 2005. "Polis, 'the Political', and political thought: New departures in ancient Greece, c. 800–500 BCE," in J. P. Arnason, S. N. Eisenstadt and B. Wittrock (eds.), *Axial Civilizations and World History*, op. cit.

Runciman, W. G. 1986. "On the tendency of human societies to form varieties" in *Proceedings of the British Academy*, LXXII, 149–165.

——. 1997. *A Treatise on Social Theory*, Cambridge: Cambridge University Press.

——. 2005. "Not elective but selective affinities" in *Journal of Classical Sociology*, 5(2): 175–187.

Sahlins, Marshall D. and E. R. Service (eds.) 1960. *Evolution and Culture*, Ann Arbor: University of Michigan Press.

Schwartz, R. D. and J. C. Miller. 1964: "Legal evolution and social complexity" in *American Journal of Sociology*, 70:159–169.

Service, E. R. 1968. "Cultural evolution" in *International Encyclopedia of the Social Sciences*, D. Shills (ed.), The Macmillan Company and the Free Press, 5:221–227.

Siegenthaler, H. (ed.) 2004. *Rationalitat im Prozess kultureller Evolution*, Mohr Siebeck.

Simon, H. 1965. "The architecture of complexity" in *Yearbook of the Society for General Systems Research*, 10: 63–76.

——. 1977. "The complexity", Section 4 of *Models of Discovery and Other Topics in the Methods of Science*, Boston: D. Reidel, 175–265.

Steward, J. H. 1955. *Theory of Culture Change: The Methodology of Multilinear Evolution*, Urbana: University of Illinois Press.

Tiryakian, E. A. 1999. "War: The covered side of modernity" in *International Sociology*, 14:473–489.

Voegelin, E. 1956–1987. *Order and History*, Baton Rouge, LA: Louisiana State University Press, 5 vols.

Wallerstein, I. M. 2004. *World System Analysis: An Introduction*, Durham: Duke University Press.

SOCIAL "MECHANISMS" AND COMPARATIVE-HISTORICAL SOCIOLOGY: A CRITICAL REALIST PROPOSAL

Philip Gorski

The substance and goals of this article are contained in its title and sub-title: it uses the philosophy of science known as "critical realism" to develop a theory of causal mechanisms, both natural and social, in the hopes of clarifying certain ongoing debates within comparative historical sociology and comparative politics, but also in the social and historical sciences more generally. It is in four parts. By way of preface, I begin by outlining some of the key tenets of critical realism. Then, in the second part, I discuss a number of fallacies that arise when we think about causal mechanisms too mechanistically, using two paradigmatic mechanisms—the clock and the pin factory—as illustrative examples. In the third part, I introduce my own definition of mechanisms as *emergent causal powers of related entities within a system*, which I refer to as the ECPRES model. In the fourth section, I compare the ECPRES model with other models, specifically those developed by rational-choice theorists and structuralists (a.k.a. "historical institutionalists"), arguing that these models are ontologically inadequate and/or logically incoherent, even in their most developed and nuanced forms. Finally, in the conclusion, I enumerate and reflect on some of the issues facing a mechanismic approach to social science.

1. *Critical Realism: A Brief Overview*

The philosophy of social science known as "critical realism" is anchored by the work of Roy Bhaskar, particularly his path-breaking book, *The Possibility of Naturalism*, but must be seen as part of the broader resurgence of realist approaches that began during the early 1970s (Harré 1970; Mackie 1974; Harré and Madden 1975; Bhaskar 1979; Salmon 1984; Miller 1987; Salmon et al. 2005). The implications of critical realism for the social sciences have been most fully worked out by a group of English sociologists centered around Margaret Archer, whose seminal treatise, *Critical Realism: The Morphogenetic Approach* is probably the most nuanced and comprehensive treatment of this position to date (Collier 1989; Archer 1995; Archer 1998; Collier et al. 2004; Sawyer 2005).

Like modern, Western philosophy as a whole, the philosophy of science has been dominated by debates about epistemology—about what we *can* know, and how we come to know it. Realist philosophy of science, by contrast, involves a return to the question of ontology—about *what* we know, the actual objects of our knowledge. One of the things that sets critical realism apart from other realisms, particularly in the social sciences, is its emphasis on *emergent powers and properties* (Harré and Madden 1975; Sawyer 2005). The principle of emergence is well captured by the old adage that the whole is greater than the sum of its parts. It is not difficult to think of examples from the natural realm. Water, for example, can be used to extinguish a fire; applying hydrogen and oxygen to a fire, on the other hand, will cause an explosion. Thus, the causal properties and powers of water—e.g., its power to extinguish a fire—cannot be derived from those of its constituent elements. Critical realists contend that this same principle applies to the social world as well. Consider Adam Smith's pin factory. When one divides a complicated task up amongst a group of individual workers—the manufacture of a pin, say—their collective output as a group will be higher than their aggregate output as individuals.

A second important principle of critical realism, which follows directly from the above, is *ontological stratification*. This principle is a familiar one for social scientists, who often speak of the various "levels" or "dimensions" of a particular "system" or "phenomenon." But critical realism provides a basic principle for identifying these levels: namely, the principle of emergence. Consider the pin factory example once again. A modern manager or engineer could undoubtedly increase the output of the factory's workforce simply by making various kinds of organizational or technical adjustments—to the sequencing of tasks, the spatial layout, the introduction of new tools or machines, and so on. From the perspective of critical realism, then, the factory qua organization or institution is an autonomous reality.

This is not to deny that the output of the pin factory could also be increased by changing the composition of the workforce—e.g., by hiring more skilled or dextrous or energetic workers. The principle of stratification should not be confused with the principle of holism. To say that the whole is greater than the sum of its parts is not to say that the composition of the parts is of no consequence. This brings us to a third important principle of critical realism: *explanatory a-reducibility*.[1] A-reducibility is not the same as irreducibility. Irreducibility implies that one level or strata of reality cannot be explained in terms of another *at all*, that decomposing that strata into its constituent parts is useless; a-reducibility, on the other hand, merely implies that one level or strata cannot be *fully* explained in terms of another. So, to say that the output of the pin factory is a-reducible to the composition of its work force is not to say that the latter has no effect on the former, only that no individual-level property or power can fully explain the collective output of a factory, which is to say, that the factory has emergent powers and properties—that it is *real*.

Now, in what sense is "the factory" qua institution "real"? Well, certainly not by the commonsense criterion that it is a concrete object that can be perceived with the unaided senses. Of course, there are concrete factories—figuratively and literally speaking. But "the factory" is also an organizational *form* which exists independently of any of its concrete realization—in textbooks and blueprints, for example. Moreover, what makes a factory a "factory"—a certain organization of space, a certain division of labor—cannot be directly perceived without the aid of certain *symbolic* forms, such as the concepts of "spatial organization" and "division of labor" (Cassirer 1973). The claim that a factory has an emergent reality that cannot be perceived with the unaided senses and that is fully autonomous from its concrete realizations grates against the basic assumptions of the commonsense realist.

The above examples illustrate three more important principles of critical realism. The first is the *existence of non-observables*.[2] The term is precise: a non-observable is neither completely unobservable nor readily observable; rather, it is indirectly observable by means of its effects. This is the claim that the realm of the real extends beyond the realm of the senses. The argument for non-observables rests on two further suppositions. The first is the *causal criterion of reality*. This is the claim that some realms of the real can only be known by their effects; they cannot be directly observed. But if they cannot be directly observed,

---

[1] This concept is my own, though I believe it is broadly consistent with the viewpoint of Bhaskar, Archer and other critical realists.

[2] I prefer the term "non-observables" to the more conventional "unobservables" because the latter term tends to generate critical reactions, albeit misguided ones as in Sica 2004. Insofar as it suggests that such entities cannot be observed at all, when what is in fact being postulated is that they cannot be directly observed by means of the unaided senses.

then how do we know their effects? This brings us to the second part
of the answer and the third principle: viz., the *use of instrumental aids*
to observe and measure the causal effects of non-observables. Now,
the word "instruments" evokes examples from the physical sciences.
But the social sciences also possess an array of instruments: survey
instruments are used to observe and measure "public opinion" and
"social attitudes", censuses are used to measure "population growth",
"mobility tables" are used to measure social fluidity, and so on. Nor
are such instruments the sole preserve of quantitative researchers.
Scientific concepts—"bureaucracy", "field", "ritual", "binaries"—can
also function as instruments.

Now, concepts are important, not only for the scientific observer,
but also for social agents. Indeed, social reality is not simply captured
through concepts, but *constituted* through concepts—e.g., "the factory",
"bureaucracy." But concepts can come and go and exist in some societies but not in others; they are not fully trans-historical or universal.[3]
And that brings us to another cardinal principle of critical realism:
concept-dependence. Unlike their counterparts in nature, the existence
of many social entities is dependent upon the existence of a certain
concept. The consequences of this principle for our understanding of
social science are significant, for it implies that the ontology of the
social world—the entities that make up any particular socio-historical
world—changes over time and varies across space (this is true in physical
world, too, except the time scale is so vast that it can be ignored). This
means that history and culture set certain bounds to social-scientific
ambition and that one of the central aims of social-scientific research
must be to map these bounds—to record the life-cycles and trace the
perambulations of social structures.

---

[3] Building on the work of certain comparative linguists (see especially: Whorf,
B. L. 1984. *Language, Thought, and Reality: Selected Writings,* Cambridge, MA: MIT Press),
some social scientists have argued that there may be certain conceptual or ontological
universals that may be found in all languages (see e.g., Ruef, M. 2005. "The problem
of ontology in sociological analysis" in *Annual Meeting of the American Sociological Association.* Philadelphia, PA). Even if such universals exist, however, they are of an order of
generality that does not impinge on this argument.

2. *The Seductions of the Metaphor*

Mechanisms are "in the air" these days. Indeed, the term has become something of a buzzword of late at conferences and in journals. Long a part of the discourse in neighboring disciplines, such as biology ("cellular mechanisms"), economics ("the market mechanism") and psychology ("defense mechanisms"), the term "mechanism" is now routinely invoked in political science and sociology as well. On the whole, I regard this as a welcome development, insofar as it suggests a "return to reality" within the social sciences (Shapiro 2005). But it is not without dangers. One source of danger is the semantic baggage carried by the term, some of which, I will argue, is potentially pernicious. So, I begin this section by unpacking the mechanisms metaphor and discarding some unwanted semantic contents. This lays the groundwork for the next section, where I will present an analytical definition of the mechanisms concept which makes it clear what is inside my model and what should remain outside.

The reason that the term "mechanism" has accumulated so much baggage is that it has traveled so long and so far. Its origins extend back through Classical Latin to Ancient Greek, where it was used with reference to human contrivances—i.e., "machines" in the strict sense. It was then extended to the natural, behavioral and social realms beginning in the late 17th century by scientists, philosophers and theologians who espied divine designs in the material world. Thus, Robert Boyle referred to "the great System of the Universe" as a "Cosmical Mechanism." (*Free Enq. Notion Nature* 73, 1686; cited in *OED*, 2000), while his contemporary, the Anglican Bishop Edward Stillingfleet, emphasized that cosmic order had to have a divine designer, for it would be folly to "impure that rare mechanism of the works of nature to the blind and fortuitous motion of some particles of matter." (*Origines Sacrae* III. §15.401, 1662, cited in *OED*, 2000) Hobbes, of course, was one of the first to discuss human action in mechanistic terms ("the springs of action") (Hobbes and Macpherson 1968). So the mechanism metaphor enters into the natural and social sciences through the portal, not of atheism, but of deism. Since then, its meaning has continued to evolve, but it retains latent remnants of that earlier time that we should be careful about reactivating.

The paradigmatic example of a mechanism within deistic thought was, of course, the clock. It served as a metaphor for the universe ("celestial mechanics"), for divine creation (God qua "watchmaker") and for reformist ambitions (social and political institutions qua "well-oiled clocks"). And I suspect that it still serves as the root analogy in much contemporary thinking about social mechanisms. Thus, a closer analysis of the clock qua mechanism may help us to uncover some of the unstated assumptions that underlie contemporary thinking about social mechanisms and to discard those which are unwarranted. Indeed, we will see that the clock is a particularly instructive example, because it is at once a physical and a social mechanism.

A commonsensical definition of a clock—a traditional, mechanical one—might be as follows: "a clock is a mechanism made up of small, physically interconnected parts that translates stored energy into continuous and regulated motion in order to tell the correct time." Now, while this definition would probably be quite adequate for everyday communication, it turns out to be rife with perils for the would-be theorist of social mechanisms. In fact, the first four words are slippery enough to make us lose our balance. For while a clock is indeed a mechanism, the clock's "mechanism" is not its only mechanism, nor is a clock qua mechanism composed solely of "mechanisms." (Here, and in what follows, I employ scare quotes to set off folk understandings of "mechanism" from properly philosophical ones.) To put matters less coyly and more plainly, there are three points that bear emphasis here: a) a clock qua mechanism (in the philosophical sense) consists of the "mechanism" proper (in the physical sense) along with other components, such as a face, hands, and a casing, without which the clock's mechanism could not fulfill its function of "telling the correct time" any more than the face and hands could (continually) tell the correct time without an inner mechanism; the clock's power to tell time, then, derives from a certain set of elements in a certain type of relationship; b) the clock's "mechanism" can be broken down into various sub-mechanisms, which are, of course "mechanisms" in their own right; this is true, not only of the clock's inner workings, but of the hands and face, as well; it follows that c) the face and hands of the clock can also be thought of as a mechanism (in the philosophical sense), even if they are not a "mechanism" (in the commonsensical meaning of the term). In short, not all mechanisms are analogous to "mechanisms"; mechanisms are often composed of sub-mechanisms—they are internally stratified; and the proper operation of a mechanism typically involves the presence of several essential sub-mechanisms.

The next part of the definition is equally problematic. For a clock qua mechanism is not "made up of small, physically interconnected parts," not exclusively nor even necessarily. The face, for example, is not necessarily small, nor does it need to be physically connected to the mechanism; it only needs to be aligned with it. Further, the clock-face need not be physical. In order to achieve a certain, minimalist aesthetic, some clocks do not have a face; they rely on the "virtual" clock-face in the mind's eye of the human user. So while a clock is certainly a mechanism, it is not just a "mechanism." It does not necessarily consist of small, physically, interconnected parts. From which we learn that mechanism need not be (exclusively) mechanical, nor even (entirely) physical.

The third part of the definition—"that tells the correct time"—also turns out to be potentially misleading, and for at least two reasons. First, because the word "tell" implies that someone is "listening." This need not be the case. For example, if we were to give a clock to a tribe of hunter-gatherers who were unfamiliar with our system of hourly time, the clock would continue to tell the time (at least for a while), but the tribes-people might not listen (at least not in our sense). Several important conclusions follow from this example. First, a clock can operate "silently", without having its "normal" effects. This is because clocks are often sub-mechanisms within other, higher-order, social and physical mechanisms or systems, such as a system of wage labor or a radio alarm-clock. Thus, the presence or absence of a mechanism cannot necessarily be inferred from the presence of absence of its normal effects. Second, certain effects that we ascribe to clocks (such as regulating people's routines and/or waking them up) are in fact dependent on the presence of other mechanisms, which together constitute a system of some kind, a system of "time discipline" that we might find in a pin factory. Which brings us to the second danger lurking in the third part of the definition: the claim that clocks tell the correct time. This is not necessarily so. Factory workers sometimes complain that the factory's time-clocks do not work properly and that this is not accidental. One can imagine many different reasons why a clock might not tell the correct time. Someone might have intentionally manipulated the mechanism, the hands or the face in some way. Or, there might be a systematic problem in the manufacturing process. Or the clock might be worn out or broken. The general point here is that appearances can sometimes be deceiving, and that this may itself be part of a mechanism, as when a factory owner manipulates a time clock to lower his wage bill.

Based on the foregoing discussion, we can now list some of the errors which "mechanistic" thinking about mechanisms can lead to, the misunderstandings that arise when we construct our understanding of mechanisms out of sloppy analogies based on physical machines. I will distinguish between two different families of errors: atomism and mechanicism. Atomism is the claim that reality is ultimately composed of some kind of elementary particles, and it results in a particular understanding of ontology, theory and method. I will define an atomist as someone who makes one or more of the following kinds of claims: a) domain R of reality contains an entity E which is irreducible to any set of other elements sub-E; b) any legitimate scientific theory of domain R must contain references to E and need not and, indeed, should not, contain any references to sub-E's or supra-E's; c) any valid scientific explanation of processes or events in R must always contain references to E's and need not and should not contain any references to sub-Es or supra-E's in its statements about causes.

It is my view, that none of these claims can be sustained. Let us begin with claim "a." Consider the clocks example again. A usable mechanical clock is composed of at least three heterogeneous but necessary elements: i) mechanism ii) hands and iii) either a case or a face. However, each of these components is itself a mechanism (if not a "mechanism") that can be broken down into various sub-mechanisms, which can, in turn, be broken down further, perhaps *ad infinitum*. Thus, there are two or three hands, and these are composed of some kind of metal or alloy, etc.; the face is made up of some flat surface, markings and so on. Further, changes in the structure or function of any one of these sub-mechanisms or their components has the potential to affect the structure and functioning of the clock qua mechanism. A clock might break down because it was made of inappropriate materials (e.g., works made of a soft metal, like aluminum). A clock, then, is a mechanism composed of mechanisms composed of mechanisms. *It is a stratified entity with emergent properties.* I submit that this is a general feature of mechanisms, both natural and social.

Let us now turn to claim "b." Let us suppose, for the purpose of argument, that there is in fact some elementary particle or fundamental entity E_f out of which all matter is composed (even though it is not clear that there is such an entity or that this entity can be adequately conceived as a "particle"), and that this is a quantum entity. Claim "b" implies that a description of any entity E must contain references to E_f, so that a physical description of, say, a clock would have to be given in quantum terms. This is obviously absurd. Now, a weaker version of claim "b" might acknowledge the stratified and emergent character of clocks, but insist on pragmatic grounds that there is some level of reality which is always the most important when one is dealing with clocks. For example, it might be argued that all discussions of clocks must describe their constituent mechanisms. I do not think this position can be seriously defended either. Do we need a physical description of a clock's mechanisms in order to understand the role of clocks in a system of time discipline? Sometimes perhaps, but not usually.

Finally, let us examine claim "c", the claim that all valid explanations must contain references to some E_f. This argument also collapses for precisely the same reasons. Obviously, we do not need a quantum-level description of a clock to understand its normal functioning. Of course, it is possible in principle that the behavior of a clock might be influenced by quantum-level events. But this is a very, very unlikely occurrence, so it would be ridiculous to require that all explanations involving clocks be reformulated in quantum terms. Indeed, such a reformulation would require a very considerable degree of cleverness and effort—all of it mostly likely wasted. This is not to deny that (further) reduction can be a useful strategy; genetics and molecular biology provide ample proof of that. Rather, it is to insist that the grounds for reduction are pragmatic, rather than normative, and that the success of reduction is to be judged in terms of scientific productivity rather than methodological strictures.

Let us now turn to type b or mechanicist errors. While atomistic errors imperil our thinking about all mechanisms, both natural and social, mechanicist misunderstandings are more common in the social sciences (though they are not absent from the natural sciences, either.) Mechanicism is the view that reality consists of physically interconnected material entities that transmit energy to one another, or that it can at least be adequately conceptualized in these terms. Mechanicism, in other words, is the view that mechanisms are exactly analogous to machines. It can be further analyzed into two inter-related but distinct claims: physicalism and substantialism. Let us look at each in turn.

Physicalism insists on the physical interconnectedness of all of the "parts" of a mechanism. Now, this may apply to some mechanical mechanisms, but it not does hold for causal mechanisms *tout court*. For example, social interactions do not always, or even usually, involve actual bodily contact. Thus, in the social sciences, physicalism usually involves a somewhat weaker (and generally implicit) assumption that *spatio-temporal proximity* between human actors is a necessary condition for the transmission of causal effects. Now clearly, the relative importance of spatial proximity between human actors has been radically diminished within modern times by the development of electronic communications media. Still, it might be argued that: a) temporal proximity is still necessary, even in modern societies; and that b) spatial and temporal proximity are a sine qua non for the transmission of causal effects in pre-modern societies. However, this argument does not bear up under closer scrutiny. The requirement of temporal proximity, for example, is violated by the powers of memory and tradition, which allow distant or dead agents to influence present events. Nor are human agents necessary for the transmission of such influences. "Memory" and "tradition" can be embodied in symbolic forms such as mythological or historical narratives and religious or political rituals. The topic of symbolic forms brings us to the substantialist fallacy.

Substantialism insists that mechanisms are exclusively composed of concrete entities or, to be more precise, that the entities of which mechanisms are composed are primarily physical. The substantialist assumes that an entity only really exists if and to the extent that it exists materially; symbolic forms and representations are granted a solely epiphenomenal status. The earlier discussion of the pin factory qua organizational form has already given us reason to doubt this proposition. The argument, to recall, was that "the factory" exists apart from its material manifestation. I would now like to show that the substantialist position cannot be easily sustained even for a lower-level "material" mechanism such as a clock. I will do this by means of a thought experiment. Let us imagine that a radical sect decides that clocks are the source of all evil in the world and engages in a campaign of violent orlogo-clasm which succeeds in destroying all of the extant clocks in the world. Would "the clock" have ceased to exist? Not necessarily. For there would still be considerable knowledge of clocks stored in printed and virtual documents as well as in human brains, which could be used to make more clocks in a future, post-orlogo-clasmic age. Now, let us imagine another scenario, in which the orlogo-clasts successfully burn, wipe and kill all the knowledge of clocks embodied in books, bytes and brains, but fail to discover a trove of clocks that has been secreted in a vault. What would happen in a post-orlogoclastic age if these clocks were re-discovered? Would the future society still be able to make new clocks? Perhaps not. What if the vault contained books and computer files on clocks? These might prove more helpful, but only if their language could be deciphered. In both cases, then, information and knowledge—non-substantial entities—would be required. The point here is simple: *symbolic forms and other non-substantial entities can be necessary components of a social mechanism.*

3. *The ECPRES Model*

Having provided a philosophical backdrop, and explored some possible objections, I now turn to the ECPRES model proper. The central claim I will advance in this section is that each component of the model—each letter in the acronym—is necessary to a full and adequate definition of mechanisms immune from the kinds of fallacies just outlined. In order to defend the claim, I will unpack the model, looking closely at each term, identifying the potential misunderstandings that would result from its omission. At the same time, I will link the model back to the earlier discussion of critical realism, underling the senses in which it is "realist" and "critical."

Because there is no logical starting point for this discussion—the structure of the model is *onto*-logical rather than logical—and because each term takes on its full meaning only in relation to the others, I will simply unpack the model from left to right, beginning with the first "e", which stands for "emergent." The term emergence, as used here, points to the fact that the whole is sometimes greater than the sum of its parts or, somewhat more precisely, that a set of related entities sometimes has causal powers and properties that are greater than or different from those possessed by those self-same entities in isolation. Now, it should be clear that some or even most mechanisms possess emergent powers and properties. Still, one can imagine at least two objections to the inclusion of this term in a definition of mechanisms, one ontological, the other pragmatic. Thus, it might be objected that while some and perhaps even most mechanisms possess emergent causal powers or properties, nonetheless, there must be *some* that do not. The problem with this objection, is that it leads straight to the atomistic fallacy. For the only kind of mechanism that would lack any emergent powers and properties would be an elementary particle of some kind or another. And while it is possible that such particles exist, none have yet been discovered, not even in particle physics, and surely not for lack of trying. And even if such particles were to be discovered within the physical world, we know already that events in the social world are generated primarily by emergent mechanisms. Which brings us to the second objection, viz, that since the mechanisms that social science deals with are *all* emergent, to label them as such does not add anything to our understanding. Why not simply refer to a clocks' "mechanism" as "the mechanism", that is, as an entity with certain causal powers and properties? While usage of this sort is certainly convenient in substantive discussions and probably unavoidable, it can lead us into atomistic habits of thought, if we are not careful. The inclusion of the term "emergent" in our definition of mechanisms serves as a reminder that mechanisms can always be broken down further and, more broadly, that reality is stratified.

To say that a mechanism has "causal powers" simply means that it has the capacity to bring about change in the world—that its presence or absence, its activity or passivity, has effects that are real and (somehow) measurable. In thinking about what kinds of causal powers we should and should not ascribe to which mechanisms, it may be useful to draw two sets of distinctions, one between external and internal effects, and another between systematic and contingent effects. External effects are changes in entities and/or relations that are not constituents of the mechanism in question, as when an alarm clock goes off and wakes someone up. Internal effects involve changes in constituent entities and/relations. Thus, an analogue clock has the causal power to move its hands. In the ECPRES model, only external effects of a mechanism count as manifestations of its causal powers. Why? Because internal effects can usually be traced to the causal powers of one of the entities that constitutes the mechanism, to one of its sub-mechanisms. Thus, the power of a clock to move its hands is due to causal powers of the clock's "mechanism", not to the causal powers of the clock qua mechanism. We know this, because if we remove or disable the mechanism, the hands will not move. This may seem like a trivial point, but it is no mere quibble. Ontological elisions of this sort, in which the effects of one strata of reality are attributed to another, are a common mistake in scientific explanations—and a common strategy of theoretical inflation.

The distinction between systematic and contingent effects allows further clarification of the causal powers concept. By systematic effects I mean routine effects that occur under normal conditions. The power of an analogue alarm clock to "wake someone up" and of its "mechanism" to "move the hands" would both be examples of systematic powers in this sense. Contingent effects involve: a) mechanical breakdown, as when an alarm clock malfunctions, causing a person to be late for work, lose their job, etc.; and b) systemic interactions, as when the ringing of an alarm clock startles a burglar, causing him to draw his weapon, discharge it into the ceiling, thereby disrupting his "system" of night-time cat burglary. In the ECPRES model, only the systematic effects of a mechanism will be counted as manifestations of "causal powers." This is not to deny the existence or importance of contingent causal effects. The unexpected ringing or non-ringing of an alarm clock can certainly have consequences, sometimes important ones. Still, I do not think that we would want to include "losing jobs" and "discharging weapons" in the list of an alarm clock's causal powers, since the first is due to the failure of a lower-order mechanism and the latter to the intrusion of an external system. The key point here is that unusual or unexpected interactions between mechanisms can lead to "contingent" and "conjunctural" outcomes.

The concept of "causal powers" contains an ontological claim that poses a methodological problem. The ontological claim is that the real is not (solely) the (directly) observable but (also) the effective—that an entity is real if it can have (observable) effects. The methodological problem concerns observation of non-observables. How is such a thing possible? The answer is that scientific observation, unlike commonsense observation, often involves: a) physical or conceptual instruments, such as a telescope or a survey and b) physical or logical manipulations, such as an experiment, whether artificial or natural, or statistical controls. Instruments and manipulations allow social and natural scientists to "observe" non-observables. This has led some philosophers of science, and some critics of social science, to argue that all observations are mere constructions, created by the observer, by means of physical or conceptual instruments, and hence subjective rather than objective. Though overblown, these criticisms do have some bite: how *do* we know that an "observation" is actually a representation of reality rather than just an artifact of our instruments? Even the most sophisticated tests and instruments can generate false positives. The realist concept of causal powers allows us to transcend and refigure this debate. It allows us to acknowledge the existence of non-observables without giving up on the possibility of observation or inflating "observation" to the bursting point. For if we acknowledge that there *are* real entities that cannot be directly observed with the unaided senses, but whose existence *can* be assessed by aided or unaided observation of their *causal effects*, then we have taken a giant step beyond naïve empiricism and radical constructivism. That is the via media that critical realism seeks to follow: by allowing "causal effects" to serve as an ontological criterion, we can acknowledge the existence of non-observables, thereby bringing our philosophical assumptions into conformity with the practice of scientific researchers, which assumes the existence of non-observables all the time, without opening ourselves up to the critiques of the radical constructionists.

The third component of the ECPRES model is the concept of "related entities." Here, too, we find a crucial difference between realist and non-realist approaches. Non-realists typically speak about mechanisms in *phenomenal* terms, e.g., as "sequences of events" or "connections between variables." (Below, I argue the incoherence of this position.) Realists, by contrast, think of mechanisms in *ontological* terms, as relations between entities. In the ECPRES model, we are interested in systematic rather than contingent relationships. Here, it may be useful to distinguish between recurring and accidental relationships, on the one hand, and between necessary and incidental relationships on the other. The difference between recurring and accidental relationships is amply illustrated by the alarm clock examples given above, and involves "typical" or "normal" external effects as opposed to atypical or abnormal ones. The difference between necessary and incidental relationships concerns internal relationships within a mechanism. A necessary relationship is one that affects the causal powers of a given mechanism, as with the relationship between the "mechanism" and the hands of a clock. An incidental relationship concerns other relationships that do not influence causal powers of the mechanism in question—say, the color of a clock's housing. (Of course, if we are interested in a clock as a "decorative object" rather than as a "time-keeping device", then the color may indeed have an influence on its "effect" (in this case, an aesthetic effect.) As this example shows, the "same" entity can be part of different mechanisms and systems, often in virtue of different properties. (I will have more to say about this below.) For the moment, the key point is that the ECPRES model defines "related entities" as *entities and relationships that are necessary to the recurring effects of the mechanism in question*.

But what is an "entity"? In thinking about entities, we need to be wary of our ontological reflexes, which can be too much influenced by commonsense realism and Newtonian mechanics. These influences are manifested in the tendency to imagine entities as observable, physical objects—like billiard balls—and to equate observable, physical objects with entities. This approach is deeply mistaken and triply so: First, because so many of the objects that scientific researchers "observe" are actually non-observables, so that what is actually "observed" is some sort of observable *representation* of a non-observable, be it in visual, graphic, statistical or mathematical form. Second, because a good many of these objects, especially those studied by social scientists, are not "physical" in the same sense or to the same degree as a billiard ball. (Ironically, it is not even clear whether the electron—one of the inspirations for the billiard ball image—is physical in this sense, since it often behaves like a wave.) And third, because the entities that figure in mechanisms are often only parts or properties of more complex or higher-order objects that may also be entangled in other mechanisms as well.

Consider "preferences", an entity that figures prominently in economic models of social life. When economists speak of "observed preferences", they are of course actually referring to *inferred* preferences (i.e., preferences inferred from behavior on the basis of certain assumptions about human rationality). Preferences, in other words, are non-observables. This much would, I think, have to be conceded even by the most vulgar utilitarian, be it a neo-Hobbesian who viewed the human organism as a biological mechanism or a neo-Benthamian who saw all human action as a response to pain and pleasure. More controversial perhaps would be my second claim: that preferences are not straightforwardly physical. Let me be clear on this point: I do not mean to deny that preferences have a biological *substrate*, that they are somehow generated within brains and executed by bodies. I am simply arguing that one cannot feel or see a "preference" in the same way that one feels or sees a billiard ball or, for that matter, a strand of DNA. Now, an unrepentant physicalist might counter that preferences are really just neuronal connections in the brain and/or electrochemical impulses in the nervous system. But unless and until the epistemological gains of such a reduction have been demonstrated, there is no reason for the working social scientist to accept this claim; reduction, recall, is an explanatory strategy, not a methodological imperative. On this point, it seems to me, the burden of proof lies with the defenders of physicalism. In my view, "preferences" are best understood as a property of human agency which is itself an emergent causal power that derives, inter alia, from the combination of a brain, a body, and a language. To sum up: entities may be observable or non-observable; they must have a physical substrate, but they need not be described in physical terms; and they are often only parts or properties of complex objects with multiple properties.

The fourth and final component of the ECPRES model is the "system" concept. Like its counterparts, this concept signals a fundamental divergence between realist and non-realist approaches. Empiricists, particularly those of a positivist stripe, draw no ontological boundaries in space or time; they assume a universal and unchanging ontology, governed by universal and unchanging laws. The concept of "system", by contrast, allows for the existence of spatio-temporal boundaries. Constructionists, by contrast, would likely acknowledge the existence of such boundaries, but they would see them as the product of human agency. Realists, by contrast, are open to the possibility of systems that operate "behind the backs" of human actors, and not only in the natural world. The foregoing contrasts already provide some indication of what is intended here by the term "system." It has a structural or demographic dimension, as well as a dynamic or agentic one. The demographic aspect concerns the "population" of entities in a given spatio-temporal frame, insofar as the existence of certain entities forms a condition of possibility for certain mechanisms. Thus, carbon-based life-forms could not emerge until nuclear fission within stars had produced carbon atoms. Similarly, modern Western capitalism could not emerge, and cannot exist, at least not in the form that we know, without the existence of "free labor", which was the product, inter alia, of peasant expropriation ("enclosure"), or so Marx and Weber would have argued. The agentic aspect concerns the powers of properties, insofar as it is influenced by context. The conductivity of a metal is a causal power in some contexts (e.g., an electric motor) but not in others (a wind-driven turbine), where the powers of some other property become salient (e.g., weight or tensile strength). The same principle obtains in the social world. A patent of nobility may have very considerable causal powers in one socio-historical context (a feudal society) but relatively little in another (a capitalist society), and a very opposite one in yet another (a communist society). This is not because patents of nobility cease to exist; it is because other elements of the feudal system have disappeared (corporate estates, noble privileges, feudal forms of property, etc.). In a capitalist society a patent of nobility is like a Panda's thumb: a relic of a previous system which has now lost its function. Most systems have temporal limits; they usually have spatial limits as well. The power of a star qua "energy-generating mechanism" is an inverse function of distance, for example. The same relationship between power and space often obtains in social life as well. For example, the capacity of a state to project military power is inversely related to the distance from its intended target.

There is still one more thing we must do before we can compare the ECPRES model to rival models within sociology and political science, and that is to highlight certain important differences between natural and social mechanisms. Up until now, I have spoken about mechanisms in general, without making any such distinctions. But social mechanisms do have at least four features that set them apart from natural mechanisms: *activity dependence, concept dependence, mutability and time-space specificity.*

Activity-dependence. Unlike natural mechanisms, social mechanisms always involve human activity, be it physical, cognitive or discursive. The crucial question, of course, is in what sense they do so, and on this point, there is considerable disagreement amongst both philosophers and practitioners of social science. Here, the critical realist position can be usefully contrasted with two other points of view that are quite widespread within the social sciences which I will call *agentism* and *presentism.* By "agentism", I mean the claim that social mechanisms are composed exclusively of human agents or, more precisely, that the entities of which social mechanisms are composed can all be described and, indeed, should be described, as properties of biological individuals. In mainstream versions of rational-choice theory, for example, all mechanisms can be described in terms of "actors", "preferences" and "constraints", where constraints are understood as limitations on an actor generated by the preferences of other actors. Agentism is by no means confined to rational-choice theory, however. Less systematic and explicit versions of agentism can also be found within other traditions of theory and research. Activity dependence should not be confused with agentism. In the ECPRES model, as in critical realism more generally, social mechanisms may include non-agentic entities. Such entities might be non-human (e.g., a material artifact such as a clock or a church building, or a symbolic form such as "the clock" or "the church"), supra-individual (e.g., a group such as a class or confession or an institution such as a factory or a hierocracy) or sub-individual (e.g., a subjective disposition or psychic drive). In the ECPRES model, activity dependence is the claim that social mechanisms are composed exclusively of entities that are the *result* of human activity.

Here, we must guard against another error: presentism, the claim that social mechanisms are composed exclusively of entities produced by *living* actors. The problem with presentism, as Comte noted almost two centuries ago, is that some of the most powerful actors in any given society are already dead. To Comte's axiom we might add the further corollary that many of the non-human entities of which social mechanisms are composed were produced in the past. This is because actors can continue to act or, more precisely, to exercise causal powers, through the non-agentic entities which they helped produce. Even a resolute materialist such as Marx was insightful enough to recognize this. Recall the oft-quoted line from *The Eighteenth Brumaire*: "the weight of the dead generations hangs like a nightmare in the brains of the living."

Concept-dependence. Marx's "nightmare" provides a nice illustration of the second difference between natural and social mechanisms: concept dependence. Concept dependence is a direct corollary of activity-dependence. If human agency always involves concepts at some stage or level, then it follows that the operation of social mechanisms will involve concepts at some stage or level. But in what sense? The critical realist answer to this question can perhaps be best understood through a contrast with strong versions of hermeneutics and social physics (e.g., phenomenological and systems-theoretic approaches). The notion of concept dependence marks an obvious difference between the ECPRES model and a social physics in which agents' actions and reasons are simply the effects of other higher-order social processes of which they are either blithely or sadly unaware (e.g., Luhmann's "autopoiesis" (Luhmann 1995, 2002) or Black's social geometry (1973). But it also marks a subtle contrast with a cultural hermeneutics in which actions and reasons are the causes of everything and the task of the analyst is simply to recover the organic unity of actions and reasons. The notion of concept dependence can be seen as an effort to chart a middle way between these two positions and thereby avoid the errors to which they are prone. Social physics errs, not in claiming that there are higher-order social processes, but when it denies the activity dependence of such processes. Such higher-order processes exist only if, and only to the extent, that they succeed in steering human activity. And such steering processes inevitably involve concepts that are appropriated or internalized by human agents (e.g., "role", "rule", "order", "price", "contract", etc.). Cultural hermeneutics errs, not in claiming that human agents act in accord with concepts of which they are, or can become, conscious; rather it errs in imagining that all agents always have an *adequate* concept of why they do what they do. Marx's theory of capitalist exploitation provides an excellent example of this. The appropriation of surplus value by the capitalist is facilitated when the worker conceptualizes his relationship to the capitalist as a free contract between equals. As this example shows, there are instances in which an *inadequate* concept of the social world forms one entity within a social mechanism. Concept-dependent human activity can also have unintended consequences, as when particular norms about marriage and fertility have demographic consequences. One cannot understand the resulting demographic regime without attention to the marriage and fertility norms. But the norms themselves do not contain a concept of the demographic regime. Thus, we encounter the situation in which a lower-order concept forms one part of a higher-order mechanism, whose results cannot be seen as "intentional." In the ECPRES model, then, concept dependence is simply the claim that the operation of any social mechanism always involves the operation of at least one concept, though not necessarily one that is adequate or intentional.

Mutability. The principle of concept dependence leads directly to the principle of mutability—the claim that social mechanisms can and do vary, mutate and evolve. For if there is anything that the human sciences—social, cultural and historical—have incontrovertibly established it is that human worldviews vary across physical and social time and space, and if cultural concepts are a necessary ingredient of social mechanisms, this means that they too will be subject to variation, mutation, evolution—and extinction. Sometimes these changes are the result of intentional action, as when the re-conceptualization of workplace relations as class relations leads to the establishment of a system of collective bargaining that pegs wages to productivity, thereby attenuating the mechanism of capitalist extraction. Other times, they are not, as when the addition of new phases in the "normal" life-course (first "childhood", then "adolescence" and, most recently "young adulthood") change marriage patterns, and thereby influence fertility regimes and demographic equilibria. As this latter example suggests, conceptual changes lead to mechanism changes, not only by changing the relationships between existing entities (e.g., "labor" and "capital") but also by bringing entirely new entities into being. Thus, concepts like "class" or "state" do not simply name entities that already exist; they actually help to bring these entities *into* existence. This is not to endorse some sort of radical constructionism, in which social class has no reality or existence apart from the class concept. As Marx himself demonstrated in his historical analysis of "primitive accumulation", the genesis of

the modern working class was not just the result of cultural constructions; it was also the product of objective developments such as the
alienability of landed property, the emergence of monetary exchange
and the enclosure of common lands.

Time-space dependence. From this, the fourth and final difference between
natural and social mechanisms naturally follows: time and space specificity. This is the claim that most social mechanisms, maybe even all
of them, have a finite historical lifespan and can emerge and survive
only within certain "ecological niches" or "ecosystem parameters."
For example, the mechanism of capitalist extraction can emerge and
survive only so long as labor is a commodity that can be bought and
sold, whether in the form of "labor power", as in the modern variant
of capitalism analyzed by Marx, or in the form of slave labor, as in
the ancient variant of capitalism identified by Weber (1891), and it can
and will persist only so long as labor remains a commodity, as noted
by Polanyi (Polanyi and Dalton 1968; Polanyi 2001).

4. *The ECPRES Model and its Social Scientific Rivals*

Why all the talk about "mechanisms"? Why have sociologists and
political scientists suddenly become so enamored of this metaphor?
One part of the explanation is to be found outside these disciplines, in
changing power relations within the scientific field as a whole and, more
specifically, in the declining prestige and influence of physics and the
emergence of the biology as the new *Leitwissenschaft.* While the biological
sciences have made remarkable progress over the last several decades,
they have not discovered any new "laws", at least not the parsimonious
and mathematicized sort produced by Twentieth Century physics. What
they have discovered are "mechanisms." Thus, just as physics provided
the model which many social scientists once aspired to (and which
some economists imagine they have achieved), so biology provides the
paradigmatic science for many social scientists today.

Another part of the explanation for the mechanisms mania is to be
found within the disciplines of sociology and political science themselves
and, more specifically, in a growing disillusionment with empiricist and
positivist philosophies of science. This is not the place to tell the story
of how Hempel and Popper conquered Anglo-American social science.
That has been done ably enough elsewhere (Steinmetz 2005). And the
results of this conquest are inscribed in the positivist language of social

science, laden as it still is with talk of "prediction" and "deduction", and "theory-testing" and "falsification." The key point in this context is that there is a growing conviction in some quarters that positivism is a *canard*, that the covering-law model does not accurately represent "good social science" and that falsificationist methods do not necessarily lead to "scientific progress" (Gorski 2004).

But what comes after positivism? The mechanisms metaphor represents one alternative, and many of the disillusioned have latched onto it.

While mechanisms talk cuts across theoretical orientations and substantive specializations, the major programmatic statements have come from two quarters: rational-choice theory and qualitative comparative social science. Each group has its own reasons for championing a mechanisms approach. For rational-choice theorists within sociology and political science, mechanisms talk serves a dual purpose: first, it allows them to distance and distinguish themselves from two rival versions of rational-choice theory that have been quite influential within economics, and that were themselves strongly influenced by positivism: a) the more heterodox "instrumentalist" version associated with Milton Friedman, which claims that the psychological realism of rational-choice assumptions is of no import, so long as the empirical predictions it produces are accurate (Friedman 1953); and b) the more orthodox nomothetic version exemplified by Gary Becker, which seeks to subsume all facets of human behavior under a few basic laws (Becker 1976). A mechanisms-based version of rational-choice theory, by contrast, insists on the need for realistic assumptions (e.g., about human cognition and rationality) and/or replaces the search for laws with a search for mechanisms. By emphasizing mechanisms, advocates of rational-choice are also issuing a methodological and theoretical challenge to two of their intra-disciplinary rivals as well: first, to conventional statistical modelers, in the Columbia-Michigan-Wisconsin lineage, who analyze correlations between variables; and second, to conventional qualitative researchers, who focus on supra-individual level structures and processes. The rational-choice mechanizers argue that their approach is superior because it specifies causal "linkages" and identifies the individual-level mechanisms ("microfoundations") that underlie all macro-level phenomena.

A mechanismic approach also holds considerable appeal for qualitative comparative researchers in political science and sociology, albeit for rather different reasons. The collapse of structural functionalism and modernization theory during the early 1970s catalyzed a revival of qualitative comparative work in both sociology and political science (e.g., "comparative-historical sociology" and "comparative political economy"). Two of the most influential methodological apologias of the 1970s (Lijphart 1975; Skocpol 1979; Skocpol 1984) presented qualitative comparative analysis as fundamentally akin to quantitative statistical analysis. Initially ignored, these methodological self-representations were later subjected to blistering attacks from well-known quantitative methodologists in both disciplines (e.g., Goldthorpe 1991; Lieberson 1991; King et al. 1994; Goldthorpe 1997), who argued that qualitative comparative analyses did not meet certain basic standards for reliable causal inference: for example, there were too many variables, too few cases, too little independence between the cases, and an assumption of causal determinism. Comparativists often defended themselves in quite historicist terms, deploying terms like "conjuncture", "contingency", "narrativity", "events" and so on (Somers 1992; Savolainen 1994; Gotham and Staples 1996; Stryker 1996; Steinmetz 2004). While this defense protected the comparativist enterprise on one flank, it left it unprotected on another. In ceding the positivist ramparts to the statistical modelers, the comparativists blurred the boundary that had marked off their territory from the historians', and the division of scientific labor it underwrote: here, theory and explanation, there, data and interpretation. The mechanisms concept therefore serves a double function for the comparativists: it provides a methodological defense against the positivist critique launched by the statistical modelers, and it provides a *raîson d'être vis-à-vis* the historians.

To say that mechanisms talk in political science and sociology is a reaction against the long-standing hegemony of positivism and empiricism in economics and sociology is not a critique. On the contrary, in my view, the problem with most mechanisms talk in these disciplines is that it has not broken radically *enough* with positivism and empiricism. The ECPRES model can therefore be seen as one attempt to build on the existing momentum towards a mechanisms-based approach in order to complete the break with empiricist and positivist approaches. My view, in other words, is that the ECPRES model, and critical realism more generally, can be seen as the logical culmination, or at least as a logical continuation, of existing work. In this, the final, section of my paper, I will show how empiricist and positivist assumptions contaminate much of the current literature on mechanisms, rendering it both philosophically and methodologically incoherent; and I will argue that critical realism, as articulated in the ECPRES model, points the way towards a more consistent model of mechanisms and a more fully post-positivist vision of social science.

Rational-choice approaches. Let us begin by looking at how mechanisms have been conceived by several prominent scholars working within the rational-choice tradition. In a widely-cited and much-discussed article published in the *American Journal of Sociology*, Edgar Kiser and Michael Hechter (1991) use the mechanisms concept to critique the (then) current practice within comparative-historical sociology and develop an alternative vision of that sub-field. While the critique is somewhat overblown, it is not entirely inaccurate either; the alternative vision, however, is an unhappy and untenable symbiosis of positivism and realism.

Kiser and Hechter open their discussion by dividing comparative-historical sociologists into two main camps: "historicists" and "inductivists." The principal difference between the two camps, as they see it, lies in the empirical and theoretical generality of the explanations advanced by each camp. Historicists refuse both types of generality, while inductivists advance explanations that have considerable (if not universal) empirical scope, but do not embrace a single, general theory or provide explicit causal mechanisms. (Of course, this taxonomy leaves out at least one, very important school: the contentious politics tradition associated with the work of Charles Tilly and his collaborators. I discuss this tradition in the next section.)

Let us examine these charges more closely. Kiser and Hechter identify two exemplars of the historicist approach: Reinhard Bendix and Michael Mann. Both scholars, they say, "favor interpretations that stress the complexity, uniqueness, and contingency of historical events, and holistic approaches to the study of history" (Kiser and Hechte 1991: 10) and can be best seen as modern disciples of the interpretivist approach that stretches from Gadamer through Weber to Dilthey. As holists and interpretivists, then, they are in the same lineage as the original German Historical School of the late 19th century.

Is this genealogy accurate? I think not. First, it mischaracterizes Weber. As anyone familiar with the *Methodenstreit* well knows, Weber was not an orthodox historicist (Camic et al. 2005). On the contrary, he sought a via media between the German or Historical School of economics, on the one-hand, and the Austrian or Neoclassical school, on the other. Weber certainly thought that *Verstehen* or interpretation—understanding the meaning which actions have for actors—was an important tool in social science, that was necessary to constructing and assessing "valid" explanations. But he did not regard it as an end in itself. This (mis)characterization is all the more curious, given that Kiser (1999) has also tried to claim Weber for the rational-choice tradition.

So, the mere fact that Bendix was a Weberian does not make him, *ipso facto*, a historicist. Could we nonetheless argue that Bendix advocated a sort of historicist Weberianism? This characterization comes somewhat closer to the truth. For Bendix was interested in the motivations of social actors and the specificity of national historical trajectories (see e.g., (Bendix 1978). He was fond of particularizing comparisons and path-dependent explanations. But this does not necessarily make him an interpretivist or a holist. Like Weber, he used interpretation as a tool for developing and assessing causal explanations. So, he was no interpretivist, at least not in the usual sense of that term, which implies a strong rejection of causal explanation in the social sciences. Nor was he a holist. Like Weber, he emphasized the importance of social action—even of specific historical actors—in the production of social outcomes. It might be more accurate to describe him as a methodological individualist, albeit not of the rational-choice variety.

Now, Kiser and Hechter define "historicism" in a somewhat idiosyncratic and frankly, a-historical, way, as involving an emphasis on "the complexity, uniqueness and contingency of historical events." Was Bendix a historicist in *this* sense? I think not. His use of ideal-type methodology to map cross-national variations and identify recurring causal patterns makes clear that this characterization is at best one-sided.

Where Mann's work is concerned, the characterization is not simply one-sided; it is wildly off-the-mark. Certainly, Mann is no holist. On the contrary, he denies the very existence of "society" as a coherent whole, arguing that we should look at human history in terms of the development and interaction of multiple, overlapping "power networks" (Mann 1986). Nor is he an interpretivist. If anything, he could be charged with paying too *little* attention to what history "meant" to individual actors (Gorski 2006). And he explicitly rejects the characterization of his four "power sources" (ideological, political, economic and military) as Weberian ideal types. So he cannot be placed in the historicist lineage even to this extent. Nor is he a historicist in the idiosyncratic sense advanced by Kiser and Hechter. If Mann thinks that no historical sequence is precisely like any other, he evidently thinks that they are *enough* like each other, that they can all be analyzed within the same conceptual framework, namely, the IEMP model of social power. In sum, trying to hang the historicist label on a scholar who has tried to re-narrate the entirety of human history in terms of a single theoretical scheme is really just plain silly. And Kiser and Hechter themselves seem to realize that it is silly: later in their essay, they treat Mann as an inductivist.

Let us see whether the inductivist label has more sticking power than the historicist one. In fact, Kiser and Hechter jump back and forth between two labels: "inductivist" and "inductive generalist." An inductivist is someone who induces explanations from data, rather than deducing them from theory. An "inductive generalist" is someone who uses induction to develop generalizations. In other words, an inductivist is someone who induces empirical generalizations from historical data, rather than deducing them from general theory. Is Skocpol an "inductivist" in this sense? Yes and no. In her methodological writings, Skocpol does indeed describe her approach in inductivist terms (Skocpol 1979; Skocpol and Somers 1980; Skocpol 1984; Evans et al. 1985). Specifically, she argues that the comparative method employs the same methods of causal inference used by quantitative sociologists, only with a smaller "n." In her empirical work, however, she follows a somewhat different modus operandi. In the preface to *States and Social Revolutions* (1979), for example, she describes an interplay between "predictions" or expectations derived from various theories of revolution and the observed dynamics and outcomes seen in histories of major revolutions. So her actual method involves a complex interplay between deduction from theory and induction from cases. But are any of these theories "general" theories? What is more, at least one of the theories that explicitly informs Skocpol's own theory of revolution—Marxism—is described as a "general theory" by Kiser and Hechter themselves. Thus, while the claim that inductive generalists abjure general theory may appear plausible at first glance, it does not survive closer inspection.

While Kiser and Hechter's discussion of "historicism" and "inductive generalism" doesn't shed much light on Bendix, Mann or Skocpol, it does help illuminate what Kiser and Hechter mean by "general theory", namely, an *ontologically unified theory that generates universally applicable predictions/explanations*. They mention the following examples: structural-functionalism (Durkheim), historical materialism (Marx) and, of course, rational-choice theory (their preferred general theory). These theories are ontologically unified to the extent that they postulate a relatively small number of basic social entities and relationships (e.g., structures and functions, classes and production, individuals and interests). And they claim universal applicability insofar as they argue that all social phenomena in all times and places can be explained in terms of these basic entities and relationships. What irks Kiser and Hechter about the "historicists" and the "inductivists", then, is not that they refuse empirical generalizations and general theory—as we have just seen, they do not—but rather that they refuse *universal* empirical generalizations and *ontologically unified* general theory in favor of less-than-universal generalizations and ontologically pluralistic theoretical models. Thus, Skocpol's theory applies only to social revolutions that occur within agrarian regimes, and it draws on a variety of theorists (e.g., Marx, Weber, Tocqueville, Hintze and Huntington), none of whom, it should be added are rational-choice theorists. And while it could be argued that Mann's IEMP-model *is* ontologically unified, it certainly does not yield any universal empirical generalizations.

Why does this bother them so much? Why do we need a universal and unified theory? Isn't a general and pluralistic one good enough? Not if your understanding of what a "real" theory looks like is based on a positivist interpretation of the laws of physics, and an orthodox understanding of economic theory as the social science analogue of physics.

But Kiser and Hechter's orthodoxy only goes so far—namely, far enough to distance themselves from other comparativists. The problem is that their embrace of positivism not only sets them off from the "historicists" and "inductivists"; it also opens them up to the critique of "small-n" analysis launched by the quantitative positivists, a critique which they are not only aware of, but which they themselves approvingly cite in their critique of Skocpol. This is why they introduce the mechanisms concept: as a bulwark against their fellow-positivists. Rational-choice comparativists may not have big n's, but they do have little mechanisms.

Unfortunately, Kiser and Hechter thereby maneuver themselves into an unstable and ultimately untenable no-man's land between realism and positivism. The incoherence of their position is already evident in their wildly erroneous summary of Hume's epistemology: "following Hume", they claim, "it is generally acknowledged that causality can never be directly observed. Rather, it must be interpreted on the basis of observables" (Kiser & Hechter: 4). In point of fact, Hume categorically denied the very possibility of causal inference, arguing that we can *never* have reliable knowledge of causality. Causality, for Hume, was something that we imagine, not something we "interpret." Of course, as Andrew Abbot has wisely noted, this misinterpretation of Hume is a widespread one, originally propagated by quantitative methodologists anxious to reconcile an empiricist methodology with a positivist self-presentation (Abbott 1998).

The untenability and instability of their position is even more evident in their model of sociological explanation. "[A]dequate explanations", they essay, "must specify both causal *relations* between variables […] and the *mechanisms* responsible for producing these relations." This definition is both incoherent and redundant. It is incoherent, because a "variable" can never be a cause, because variables are, strictly speaking, observational categories, not ontological ones. Since variables are not real entities (except in scientific discourse), they cannot *do* anything (except in, say, a statistical model). Of course, social scientists do sometimes refer to real entities (e.g., interests, classes, institutions) as "variables." But this way of talking is nothing more than a clumsy gesture of obeisance towards positivism. Kiser and Hechter's definition is also redundant. It is redundant because a description in terms of mechanisms is always superior to, and therefore must always supersede, a description in terms of variables. What Kiser and Hechter seem to want to say, but say rather poorly, is that a recurrent conjunction or sequence of events suggests the operation of an unobserved causal mechanism, and that knowledge of causal mechanisms is more powerful than, and therefore preferable to, identification of recurrent phenomena. It is useful to know that catching pneumonia is often preceded by catching a serious chill, but it is far more useful to know that the underlying mechanism is typically a bacterial infection.

Kiser and Hechter are not the only ones who have tried to reconcile a mechanismic model of social-science explanation with a positivist understanding of the scientific enterprise. Jon Elster has also done so—three times: once in *Explaining Technical Change*, once in *Nuts and Bolts* and a third time in *Alchemies of the Mind* (Elster 1983, 1989, 1999). The evolution of Elster's views—frankly, "gyrations" might be a better term—nicely illustrate the inherent instability of such realist/positivist syntheses.

In *Explaining Technical Change*, Elster (1983) used the term "mechanism" in two different senses. First, to denote *underlying* mechanisms, which, for him, mean action-based and, specifically, rational-choice mechanisms. Here, "mechanisms" means "microfoundations." Second, to denote "causal connections", as opposed to mere correlations. Here, "mechanisms" means the "causal chain" that links two events or variables. In this version, let us call it Elster[1], Elster follows more or less the same strategy as Kiser and Hechter. On the one hand, he seeks to preserve the positivist understanding of laws as constant conjunctions between observable events, so as to distance himself from "soft" social scientists (e.g., interpretivists). At the same time, he introduces the "mechanisms" concept to distance himself from "hard" social scientists who might poke fun at his "small n" (e.g., statistical modelers) and assert his superiority *vis-à-vis* qualitative comparativists who don't have any micro-foundations. Both of these senses of mechanism are captured in the master metaphor in Elster[1]: the "black box." The black box contains the cogs and wheels, as it were, that are in between the statisticians variables and underneath the macro-sociologists descriptions. In Elster[1], then, a mechanisms-based explanation is simply a finer-grained version of a covering-law explanation.

In *Nuts and Bolts*, Elster (1989) has a second go at mechanisms. Let us call this approach Elster[2]. Elster[2] seems to drop the covering-law model altogether in favor of a mechanismic model of explanation, and on two grounds: "One objection is that the general laws might reflect general correlation, not causation. Another is that the laws, even if genuinely causal, might be preempted by other mechanisms." (1989: 6–7). In other words, a constant conjunction between observable events does not imply causation—unless we can specify the mechanisms. Conversely, an in-constant conjunction does not imply the in-operation of a law, because unobserved and countervailing mechanisms might be in operation. If these points are accepted, then the covering-law model of explanation and the falsificationist approach to theory-testing immediately collapse. Elster[2] seems to realize as much, when he states that "the emphasis in this book is on *explanation by mechanisms* (1989: 3, emphasis in original).

In *Alchemies of the Mind* (Elster 1999), however, he has a change of heart, giving birth to Elster[3]. For Elster[3], mechanisms are not a supplement to covering-laws, as in Elster[1], nor a replacement for them, as in Elster[2], but simply a second-best alternative to them. Elster[3] proposes that we see mechanisms "as intermediate between laws and descriptions" (1999: 1). "Intermediate" in what sense though? Apparently, in terms of regularity. Whereas a law implies constant conjunction ("if A, then always B"), a mechanism merely implies recurrent conjunction ("if A, then sometimes B"). Whence Elster[3]'s definition of a mechanism as "a recurring and intelligible causal pattern" (1999: ix) and, more specifically as a "frequently occurring and easily recognizable causal pattern that [is] triggered under generally unknown conditions or with indeterminate consequences" (1999: 1, emphasis removed). Mechanisms allow us to explain (retrospectively), but not to predict (prospectively) because we can tell if they have been triggered and what effects they have had, but we do not know why they are triggered and what other countervailing mechanisms might be operating. So, why the "plea for mechanisms?" Because they are the best that we can do, at least for now. We may aspire to nomothetic knowledge, says Elster[3], and we probably always will, but for now we must content ourselves with mechanismic knowledge, *faute de mieux*.

To sum up: Elster[1] argues that mechanismic knowledge deepens nomothetic knowledge by showing us how and why constant conjunctions come about. Elster[2] waxes skeptical about the very possibility of nomothetic knowledge and presents mechanismic knowledge as an alternative. Elster[3] then reinstates nomothetic knowledge as the Holy Grail of social science, but preaches the humbler pursuit of mechanismic knowledge until that millennial moment finally arrives. Why, one might ask, are there so many Elsters? The answer, I think, is that no one, not even Jon Elster, can stably bridge, much less logically reconcile, a covering-law model of explanation founded on positivism, with a mechanismic model anchored by realism.

The next question is: why try? After all, taken together, Elsters 1, 2 and 3 deliver a devastating three-point critique of positivist social science: 1) no universal laws of social life have yet been discovered, at least none that allow us to predict events in the way that physics does, not even by economists, their claims to the contrary notwithstanding; 2) while social scientists have certainly discovered many statistical correlations, they have not generated statistical "laws" that predict the exact frequency of particular outcomes, as the "laws" of quantum mechanics do; 3) absent laws, the falsificationist procedures outlined by Hempel and Popper are not a reliable method of theory-testing.

So, again, why try to reconcile realism with positivism? Indeed, why try to save positivism at all? Perhaps because rational-choice theorists have found it so useful in their quest for theoretical hegemony within the social sciences. Insofar as rational-choice theory seems to deduce "testable hypotheses" from a few basic axioms, it seemed to fulfill the positivist criteria for falsificationist and nomothetic science. And insofar as this positivist vision of "good science" enjoyed wide acceptance among social scientists, rational-choice theorists could argue that their approach was theoretically and methodologically superior. Critics rightly noted the fact that the laws of economic theory do not have anything like the explanatory power of physics (which is not to deny that they have a good deal of explanatory power in certain social and historical contexts). But for others, the argument was evidently persuasive, perhaps even for Elster himself. In any event, it is not hard to see why Elster and other rational choice theorists would be so hesitant to loosen their grasps on such a weighty rhetorical cudgel.

Peter Hedström is one of the few rational-choice theorists who has had the courage to do so. In *Dissecting the Social*, Hedström (2005) turns his back on positivism and presents a fully realist version of rational-choice theory that has many points of similarity with the ECPRES-model developed here. As we will see, however, there are also some important points of contrast as well, insofar as Hedström remains committed, at least programmatically, to a reductionistic and perhaps universalistic vision of explanation, and to an atomistic and possibly physicalist ontology of mechanisms. These stances—reductionism, universalism, atomism, and physicalism—are at odds with four core principles of the ECPRES model, namely: stratification, time-space dependence, emergence, and agent-dependence.

It should be stressed at the outset that Hedström's break with positivism and embrace of realism is complete and consistent. This can be seen, first of all, in the fact that he defines explanations in causal as opposed to logical or nomothetic terms. "A basic characteristic of all explanations", he argues, "is that they provide plausible causal accounts for why events happen, why something changes over time, or why states or events co-vary in time or space" (2005: 13). It can also be seen in his critique of statistical explanations in social science. All too often, he complains, when "a factor appears to be systematically related to the expected value on the conditional probability of the outcome, then the factor is often referred to as a (probabilistic) 'cause' of the outcome" (2005: 23). As the scare quotes show, he does not think that the "factors" or "variables" contained in statistical models have the ontological status of "causes." In this, he is very much at odds with his rational-choice colleagues, who flip-flop back-and-forth between positivist and realist language when discussing the subject of explanation. Indeed, he is so much at odds with the positivists that he approvingly cites Parsons' famous definition of "analytical realism", despite his own distaste for the sort of grand theory that Parsons later championed: "the general concepts of science are not fictional but adequately 'grasp' aspects of the objective external world [...]. Hence, the position here taken is, in an epistemological sense, realistic. At the same time it avoids the objectionable implications of an empiricist realism. The concepts correspond, not to concrete phenomena, but to elements in them which are analytically separable from other elements" (Parsons 1937).

Hedström's model of mechanisms is also broadly consistent with the one advocated here. In Hedström's definition, "mechanisms [...] consist of *entities* (with their properties) and the *activities* that these entities engage in, either by themselves or in concert with other entities" (2005: 25). Thus, there is considerable overlap with the ECPRES model, even with regard to basic terminology: "causality", "entities", and "properties", for example. There is even a tacit nod to the possibility of emergent entities and powers, insofar as Hedström acknowledges the possibility that "the properties of social aggregates" can influence individual behavior (2005: 70).

While Hedström's approach is broadly consistent with the ECPRES model, it is certainly not completely consistent with it. As noted above, Hedström sometimes advocates an atomistic and somewhat physicalist ontology as well as a reductionist and implicitly universalistic view of explanation. I say "sometimes", because Hedström vacillates a great deal on these issues. As a result, his position is either internally consistent or logically incoherent. As I will show, these contradictions can easily be resolved within a critical realist framework.

Let us begin with a brief outline of his position. At first glance, Hedström would appear to be a consistent atomist, insofar as he seems to insist that all social mechanisms are made up of a single elementary particle, namely "actors", along with their "desires, beliefs, and opportunities" (2005: 26). Similarly, although he is less explicit on this point, Hedström also strikes a physicalist pose, insofar as he conceptualizes the internal relations of mechanisms as "interactions", typically between individuals. This atomistic and physicalist approach to mechanisms goes hand-in-hand with a reductionistic and universalizing model of explanation. "From an explanatory point of view", Hedström insists, "it is not sufficient simply to postulate that one social phenomenon causes another [...]. One must also open up the 'black box' to reveal the social mechanisms that are believed to be at work" (2005: 68). Thus, Hedström adheres to a reductionist vision of rational-choice which insists that a valid, sociological explanation must always supply explicit, actor-based "micro-foundations." Finally, while Hedström does not make any of the usual claims about the universal scope of rational-choice explanations, neither does he give any indications that he is skeptical about such claims, and thereby at least tacitly affirms them. In sum, Hedström seems to embrace atomism and reductionism, and perhaps physicalism and universalism as well.

Upon further scrutiny, however, it soon becomes clear that Hedström's position is not nearly as consistent as it might initially appear. It is certainly not consistently atomistic. What, for example, is the real elementary particle of social mechanisms? Individual actors? Or desires, beliefs, and opportunities? If the former, then what is the ontological status of the latter? And, if the latter, then why even bother with the former? Which one is the really real? Evidently, Hedström thinks that both are real, insofar as he thinks that both have causal effects. On the one hand, his "DBO model" identifies and analyzes the various permutations and concatenations of desires, beliefs and opportunities—DBO, ODB, OBD, etc.—and the types of individual actions and strategies that result. So, he acknowledges the existence of a sub-individual strata of causal mechanisms or powers. And, of course, he also invokes intra-individual mechanisms of bargaining and exchange à la game theory. Thus, he implicitly acknowledges the stratified character of social reality, even if he wishes to limit his social ontology to two strata: what he calls "molecular" (i.e., sub-individual) and "cellular" (intra-individual). In the "Coda" at the end of *Dissecting the Social*, Hedström therefore urges that we make an "analytical distinction" between "elementary intra-actor mechanisms" and "molecular, inter-actor mechanisms" (2005: 145–6). And yet, he explicitly rejects the critical realist notion of stratification. To make matters still more confusing, Hedström sometimes seems to imply the existence of supra-individual mechanisms as well. For example, his computer simulations on social networks and group interactions show the causal powers of supra-individual structures. And he chides mainstream rational-choice theorists for focusing exclusively on the "micro" and "ignoring" the macro, recommending instead a "micro-macro-micro" form of explanation à la James Coleman, insisting that "individuals not only interact with other individuals; they also 'interact' with and are influenced by the properties of social aggregates" (2005: 70). Still, he is hesitant to accept the logic of his own argument, as his use of the term "aggregate" suggests: he does not want to acknowledge that groups or networks or any other supra-individual structures are real—that the whole is, in some sense, greater than the sum of its parts. Having acknowledged that these supra-individual structures have emergent causal powers, he seeks to deny their reality on other grounds. On the one hand, he resists any further reduction on purely conventionalist grounds, namely, that: "There exist discipline-specific relevance criteria and 'stopping rules'" (2005: 27). On the other hand, he eschews the reality of supra-individual strata on strictly empiricist grounds: "Most of us agree that individuals exist and that they have causal powers", he says. But, he counters, "[s]ince *society* cannot be observed as such, a perceptual criterion of ontological existence cannot be used" (2005: 72).

Alas, neither of these defenses is really defensible. The conventionalist defense fails for lack of conventions. Clearly, there is no consensus amongst social scientists about what the stopping rules are. There is certainly no consensus that the individual actor is the ontological stopping point for social science explanation, not even amongst economists, the ontological individualists par excellence: they have a long-standing and apparently growing fondness for psychological and biological reduction. One of the central goals of "behavioral economics"—the hottest subfield in that discipline—is to uncover such cognitive mechanisms by means of psychological experiments. And if such a consensus is weak at best in economics, it is completely non-existent in the other social sciences. As for the empiricist defense, it collapses for lack of observables. While "actors" qua persons are directly observable, "desires", "beliefs" and "opportunities" are not. Of course, it might be countered that we *can* observe desires and beliefs in ourselves by means of introspection and that it is therefore legitimate to impute them to others on that basis. Further, we can ask others about their desires and beliefs and we can compare what they say with what they do to assess the veracity of their self-representations. But this is clearly not "observation" in the strict, empiricist sense. Among other things, it involves the use of interpretation and instrumentation. And if our definition of "observation" allows for interpretation and instrumentation, then the reality of supra-individual entities can no longer be denied on empiricist grounds. For it is quite clear that we can "observe" groups, institutions and ideologies by various means, including survey research, network analysis or cultural hermeneutics. Nor is it even self-evident that such observations are less reliable or more inaccurate than our observations of individual actors. Clearly, people often err in their assessments of other people's persons "desires" or "beliefs" just as they often deceive others about their own desires and beliefs.

Thus far, my remarks have focused mainly on Hedström's inconsistent atomism and the resultant incoherencies in his ontology. But it should be clear by now that his physicalism, reductionism and universalism are equally subject to attack. Earlier, I suggested that Hedström is a closet physicalist to the degree that he describes all causal relations in interactional terms. Thus, Hedström insists that "individuals not only interact with other individuals; they also 'interact' with and are influenced by the properties of social aggregates" (2005: 70). Once again, the language is revealing. For in what sense does an individual "interact" with a "social aggregate"? Surely not in any straightforwardly physical sense. And as Hedström's own scare quotes indicate, he is not entirely comfortable about conceptualizing such top-down causal processes as "interactions", since individual's "interactions" with groups are clearly mediated by other entities (e.g., collective representations, social norms and institutional roles). As for Hedström's reductionist model of explanation, it is clearly inconsistent with his own stratified ontology, even the simple, two-layered ontology that he himself proposes. For what prevents a further reduction of desires, beliefs and opportunities to cognitive and even neurological mechanisms? Conversely, if a person's desires, beliefs and opportunities are influenced by their position within a network or membership within a group, then we must admit the possibility and validity of top-down or abductive forms of explanation, emphasizing "structure" and "culture." And once this is admitted, the dream of a universal social ontology collapses. For structure and culture are surely time-space dependent. Indeed, this may be precisely the danger that Hedström is guarding against by insisting on the unreality of supra-individual entities.

In sum, while Hedström clearly wishes to reconstruct rational-choice theory on a fully realist foundation, he does not entirely succeed in doing so. Numerous traces of the old empiricism and positivism have somehow found their way into the epistemological and ontological corner stones of his new "analytical sociology", creating weak-spots and fissures in the philosophical foundations that render the resulting sociological edifice unstable. The tensions and contradictions are numerous: economists are chided for being too reductionistic, sociologists for not being reductionistic enough. Non-observables are postulated ("desires" and "beliefs") but the existence of non-observables is disputed. The emergent properties of actors are acknowledged and highlighted, but the emergent properties of networks and groups are denied or downplayed. A two-layered social ontology is advanced in practice, but a stratified vision of social reality is rejected on principle.

Why does Hedström want to have it both ways? The answer, I suspect, is that the imperialistic pretensions of rational-choice theory, its aspiration to become the unified field theory of the social sciences, were harnessed early on to an empiricist epistemology—and to a libertarian politics—that denied the existence of "society" or of any supra-individual entities, and to a positivist methodology that insisted on the nomothetic and deductive character of explanation. One of the most common arguments in favor of rational-choice theory has long been philosophical, namely, that the rational choice approach accorded with the positivist vision of science more than any of its rivals. Fully embracing realism consequently involves abandoning a powerful argument in favor of rational-choice theory, and this Hedström is evidently and understandably reluctant to do. For once the emergent and stratified character of social reality is conceded, the rational-choice argument for atomism ("methodological individualism") and reductionism ("microfoundations") is rendered unpersuasive. Rational-choice theory then becomes a partial ontology and a partial methodology—in short, just one theory among others. That, however, is the price that must be paid if one wishes to rebuild rational-choice theory on a realist foundation.

While the rational-choice edifice has proven too narrow and too small to accommodate the whole of social life, the attention which its architects have paid to its ontological foundations is worthy of emulation. One of the great strengths of rational-choice theory is a parsimonious and explicit ontology susceptible of formal representation (if also vulnerable to superfluous over-formalization). As we will see, insufficient attention to social ontology has been one of the signal weaknesses of the vaguely structuralist model of mechanisms current among many comparativists in political science and sociology.

Historical institutionalist approaches. Proponents of a mechanismic approach hailing from the rational-choice tradition have gradually embraced a realist vision of social science, albeit somewhat reluctantly and incompletely, because they have not had an easy time letting go of positivism. This has not been so difficult for comparativists. The comparativist-positivist synthesis was always tenuous, as quantitative positivists were quick to point out. Having realized that the forms of causal analysis they practiced did not meet quantitative-positivist criteria of causal inference, many comparativists began to question the positivist criteria, themselves. "Mechanisms" seemed an attractive alternative. If comparative analysis couldn't produce general laws, so the thinking went, perhaps it could uncover mechanisms. And perhaps that was a more realistic goal, maybe even a more important one.

But what is a mechanism? To some degree, comparativists' thinking about this question paralleled that of rational-choice theorists. Some comparativists adopted the "intervening variable" version of mechanisms. One widely-read essay, by Margaret Somers, followed James Coleman in defining a mechanism as "a meaningful connection between events" (Somers 1998). This curious blend of empiricist ("events") and interpretivist ("meaningful connection") language is all the more curious, given that Somers' essay purported to defend a realist view of historical sociology. Other comparativists followed Elster[3] (who thought he was following Merton) in defining mechanisms as "middle-range theories", meaning theories that have more explanatory scope than narrative descriptions, but less scope than general laws. As we have already seen, neither view is coherent. "Events" and "variables" are categories of observation, not causation. Nor is the difference between a general law and a causal mechanism a matter of generality. Mechanisms are also governed by general laws. However, the ontological complexity and time-space dependency of the social world means that the causal laws governing mechanisms rarely yield empirical laws governing events (except in simple and/or closed systems). What they *do* generate are observable phenomenal regularities. The real task of social science, from a realist point of view, is to discover, describe and inventory the relevant mechanisms.

A few comparativists have been articulating, and arguing for, a consequently realist approach over the past decade. In this section, I will focus on two of them: James Mahoney, a political scientist, and Charles Tilly, a sociologist. Their writings on mechanisms reveal one of the main dangers as well as one of the biggest challenges facing a mechanismic social science. The danger derives from the mechanisms metaphor itself which can easily seduce us into atomistic, physicalistic, reductionistic and universalistic ways of thinking. The challenge lies in the ontological complexity of the social world itself and how best to tame it.

Tilly never subscribed to the comparativist-positivist synthesis advanced by Skocpol. Skocpol's attempt to hive off social revolution from kindred phenomena (e.g., riots, movements, and coups) was always at loggerheads with Tilly's vision of a historical social science that would situate the various types of "contentious politics" within a multi-dimensional "field of continuous variation" that stretched from the charivari to the *coup d'état*. As were her students attempts to develop a general theory of revolution through the addition of more and more new "variables." Indeed, in a seminal 1995 article, Tilly described such efforts as "a waste of time" which hindered "the accumulation of knowledge" (Tilly 1995: 1605). This was perhaps too strong a formulation. After all, one could argue that Skocpol and her students discovered some important causal mechanisms (e.g., state breakdown) that help produce a good many revolutions, even if they represented these discoveries in (misleadingly) nomothetic terms. But Tilly was correct in arguing that the quest for empirical laws was diverting the Skocpolians' attention from the search for causal mechanisms—that an inadequate methodological self-understanding was hampering theoretical advance. The metaphor he invoked in this early article was not the mechanism, however, but the "flood." The passage is worth quoting at length:

> I am arguing that regularities in political life are very broad, indeed transhistorical, but do not operate in the form of recurrent structures and processes at a large scale. They consist of recurrent causes which in different circumstances and sequences compound into highly variable but nonetheless explicable effects. Students of revolution have imagined they were dealing with phenomena like ocean tides, whose regularities they could deduce from sufficient knowledge of celestial motion, when they were actually confronting phenomena like great floods, equally coherent occurrences from a causal perspective, but enormously variable in structure, sequence, and consequences as a function of terrain, previous precipitation, built environment, and human response (Tilly 1995: 1601).

Thus, Tilly's critique of the comparativist-positivist synthesis did not issue in a rejection of historical explanation nor even of a certain sort of theoretical universalism. In order to combine theoretical rigor with historical nuance, Tilly argued, one should look for the smaller-scale causal regularities that underlie higher-order empirical variations. In that same article, Tilly juxtaposed this proto-mechanismic form of explanation to what might be called a monadological one, which he deftly described as follows:

> 1) assume a coherent, durable, self-propelling social unit; 2) attribute a general condition or process to that unit; 3) invoke or invent an invariant model of that condition or process; 4) explain the behavior of the unit on the basis of its conformity to that invariant model (1995: 1595).

Tilly's critique of the monadological approach, which he identified (rightly or wrongly) with the work of Shmuel Eisenstadt, was that it transformed processes into substances ("self-propelling social units") and explained higher-order events in terms of higher-order substances. In other words, the monadological approach, as he saw it, was substantialist and anti-reductionist. Let us call this position, Tilly[1].

But incisive as his criticisms are in some respects, Tilly[1] does not provide us with a general model of causal mechanisms that can be exported beyond comparative social science. On the contrary, the model of mechanisms that is implicit within this critique of monism is too much colored by the peculiar concerns of comparative-historical sociology. Consider Tilly's insistence on reduction. This is often a fruitful strategy when one is dealing with very high order phenomena, such as revolutions. But it should be obvious that abductive explanations which move from macro to micro can be quite fruitful as well, even in comparative-historical sociology. While Tilly may be right that revolutions are a lot like floods, there are other processes in social life that are, in fact, more like ocean tides. And just as ocean tides *are* well explained by celestial motion, so individual actions can often be well explained by social context. Tilly's attack on monism also leads him too far in the direction of atomism. While the activity of a higher-order entity (e.g., a state or a class) may often be better explained by lower-order mechanisms, this should not lead us to deny the emergent reality of such higher-order entities, as Tilly seems to do in this article. Often, it is quite reasonable to "assume a coherent, durable, self-propelling social unit" such as a state.

In his more recent writings (e.g., McAdam et al. 2001; Tilly 2001), Tilly develops a more fully and explicitly mechanismic approach to comparative social science. Let us call this Tilly[2]. His current position is well-described in the following definition and explication:

> Mechanisms are causes on the small scale: similar events that produce essentially the same immediate effects across a wide range of circumstances. Analysts often refer to large-scale social causes (poverty, widespread frustration, extremism, resource competitions, and so on), proposing them as necessary or sufficient conditions for whole episodes of collective violence. Here, in contrast, we search for recurrent small-scale mechanisms that produce identical immediate effects in many different circumstances yet combine variously to generate very different outcomes on the large scale (Tilly 2001: 20).

In truth, Tilly[2] is not that different from Tilly[1], save for the addition of the mechanisms metaphor, an addition which seems to have reinforced the tendencies towards reductionism and atomism already apparent in Tilly[1].

The reinforcement derives partly from the seductions of the mechanisms metaphor, which tends to (mis)lead us towards thinking of mechanisms as "small" and "hidden." But why reserve the term "mechanism"
for "causes on the small scale" and deny it to "large scale causes"? By
this logic, it would be legitimate to speak of, say, genetic mechanisms,
but not selection mechanisms—which would lead to the collapse of
the regnant synthesis in evolutionary biology, combining Mendel and
Darwin, certainly a degenerative paradigm shift.

There is perhaps also another reason for Tilly's lapse into reductionism: the quest for a universal social ontology. If one could find some
fundamental molecular mechanisms that were not time-space dependent, then the focus on small-scale mechanisms could be the salvation of
a universal social theory. Atomism, in other words, could be the rescue
of universalism. I regard this hope as somewhat over-inflated and very
probably misplaced. Even if such universal molecular mechanisms did
exist—and I am not at all sure that they do—the comparative analyst
would still be confronted with higher-order emergent entities (states,
regimes, religions, movements and so on) that were time-space dependent and whose dynamics could not be fully explained in reductionistic
terms. And are we to imagine that the emergence of new higher-order
entities has no influence on the lower-order ones? For example, does
the emergence of new institutions and networks not lead to new roles
and relations, which alter the nature of actors and action? Historical
sociologists and social historians have developed some very compelling
accounts to this effect (McAdam 1988; White 1992; Padgett and Ansell
1993; McLean and Padgett 1997; Goldstein 2005). Unless such analyses
can be definitively refuted, then the quest for a universal social theory
based on small-scale mechanisms is ultimately doomed.

There is also an increased incoherency in Tilly[2] which derives from
the insertion of a positivist language of "events" into the definition
of mechanisms and the characterization of large-scale social causes
as "necessary and sufficient conditions." As regards mechanisms qua
events: while it is true that non-observable mechanisms can only be
known through their observable manifestations, it is wrong to characterize mechanisms as "events"; mechanisms must be understood as real
entities and processes. Nor must an explanation that invokes "large-
scale causes" be stated in terms of necessary and sufficient conditions.
"State breakdown", for example, can just as easily be understood as a
mechanism (involving a relation between political rulers, social elites and

the means of physical coercion and fiscal extraction). Tilly's attempt to discredit a certain form of macro-historical explanation by equating it with a positivist philosophy of science therefore fails.

Another source of incoherence, evident in this essay and elsewhere (e.g., McAdam 2001), is Tilly[2]'s insistence that the real is the relational. I do not mean to suggest that Tilly is the only one to invoke this principle. And insofar as it "twists the stick in the other direction", away from a naïve physicalism, it is even to be applauded. However, it may also be a case of twisting the stick so far that it breaks. For how can a relationship be real if it is not between real entities? And if the relation involves real entities—human agents or social institutions, say—then don't the variable properties of these entities matter, as well? I have no doubt that Tilly would readily agree that they do. The problem is that the relationality concept stands in for, and misnames something else, namely, *emergence*, and not only in Tilly[2], but in a great deal of recent social theorizing (e.g., in Emirbayer 1997). In the ECPRES model, by contrast, entities, relations and emergence are all given their due.

Of course, it would be wrong to assume that Tilly's methodological self-representations are fully congruent with his actual theoretical analyses. In fact, the errors and inconsistencies found in the one are almost wholly absent from the other. One finds few if any traces of atomism, reductionism, atomism, physicalism or relationalism in Tilly's programmatic and empirical writings on contentious politics. On the contrary, they are full of emergent entities (social institutions and collective actors) whose causal powers and properties are often decisive. Further, these entities include non-physical ones (e.g., collective identities and symbolic boundaries) and the entities themselves are clearly specified and carefully characterized. But just because the errors and inconsistencies in Tilly's methodological pronouncements do not mar his own empirical analyses does not mean that they are not worth correcting. Such errors and inconsistencies can cause considerable mischief insofar as other, lesser scholars—and that includes most of us—unreflectively adopt them as recipes or strategies for their own work.

Within political science, the comparativist who has made the strongest case for a mechanismic approach is probably James Mahoney. Of the various approaches reviewed in this essay, Mahoney's is the one that most resembles the ECPRES model. But there are some important, and instructive, points of contrast as well. So it will be fruitful for us to engage in a brief compare-and-contrast exercise.

Like most proponents of the mechanismic approach, Mahoney's point of departure is a critique of statistical positivism in the social sciences, what he refers to as "correlational analysis." The problem with such analyses, he argues, is "that even non-spurious correlations in which the time order of variables is well-established may be inherently limited representation of causal processes" (Mahoney 2001: 575). Unlike certain advocates of a mechanismic approach, however, Mahoney is well aware of the deep tensions between realist and positivist philosophies of science, and is critical of efforts to overcome them, e.g., by defining causal mechanisms as "intervening variables" or "mid-level theories" (Mahoney 2001: 578). Instead, in this essay, he recommends that we conceive of a causal mechanism in realist terms as "an unobserved entity that—when activated—generates an outcome of interest" (Mahoney 2001: 580). Following Rom Harré (1970: 35), he rejects the atomistic claims of rational-choice theorists who argue that mechanismic explanations must necessarily be based on "an individual level of analysis" (Mahoney 2001: 581). In these four respects, Mahoney's position is identical to my own.

In other regards though, our positions are slightly different. These divergences emerge quite clearly in a later essay (Mahoney 2004), where Mahoney presents a positive formulation of his approach. The governing concept in this essay is not "causal mechanisms" but "general theories." Mahoney defines general theories as "postulates about causal agents and causal mechanisms that are linked to empirical analysis through bridging assumptions" (2004: 459).[4] Causal agents are "ontological primitives", the basic entities postulated by the theory, such as rational actors in rational choice or social systems in structural functionalism. As these examples show, agents need not be understood as irreducible atoms; they can be of large or small scale and may be composed of still other entities. A causal mechanism is "the particular feature of the causal agent that actually brings about outcomes and associations" (2004: 461). General theories, then, are not, and probably cannot be, general in the sense of being empirically deterministic or universal; they "may be probabilistic and apply to only a limited range of cases defined by scope conditions" (2004: 461). Rather, what

---

[4] The essay identifies five general theories: functionalist, rational-choice, power, neo-Darwinian and cultural (Mahoney 2004: 462).

makes a theory general, he contends, "is its use of an abstract causal mechanism that exists outside space and time" (ibid.). Accordingly, Mahoney contrasts general theories with less abstract and explicit forms of theorizing, such as "testable hypotheses, research orientations and general concepts" (2004: 462).

While I agree with much of the foregoing, I do have at least two quibbles with it, one large, one small. The largest concerns Mahoney's distinction between "causal agents" and "causal mechanisms" and the definition of the latter which follows from it. An adequate model of causal mechanisms cannot be built up out of entities ("agents") and their properties ("mechanisms"); it must also include the concept of relations. Indeed, the kind of relationship that exists between the entities often determines the kind of mechanism that results: the strength or pattern of ties in a social network, the payoff matrix or the number of iterations in a strategic game, the permeability and the directionality of the boundary between two fields, etc. In this respect, the ECPRES model is, I think, superior to Mahoney's. The smaller quibble concerns Mahoney's claim that a causal mechanism "exists outside space and time" or, as he puts it a little later, "outside specific spatial and temporal boundaries" (Mahoney 2004: 461). The first formulation—that mechanisms exist outside space and time—is patently at odds with realism. What is scientific realism, if not the claim that causal mechanisms really exist in space and time? Here, Mahoney appears to be conflating really, existing mechanisms with our theoretical representations of mechanisms, and thereby obscuring one of the most important methodological issues confronting the mechanismic approach, namely, how to negotiate the inevitable tradeoffs between theoretical parsimony and ontological complexity. The second formulation appears to blunt this anti-realist turn somewhat. Here, Mahoney seems to suggest that there must be more than one instance of a mechanism for it to *be* a mechanism. Now, some scholars may be more interested in studying frequently recurring mechanisms, and for some purposes this may be the wisest course. But there is no reason, ontologically speaking, why we should insist that real mechanisms be defined as recurring mechanisms, and there may be situations in which we may want to study one-time mechanisms, e.g., when they produce singular outcomes that are of particular interest to us. Conversely, some of the most common mechanisms may not be of great scientific interest, precisely because they are so obvious and well-understood. Finally, there are some mechanisms that are the result of conscious design (e.g., incentives within organizations), where the interesting question is not their construction, so much as their efficacy. In sum, the question is not whether one-time mechanisms exist, but whether it is useful to study them.

Conclusion

The aims of this article have been both constructive and critical. On the one hand, I have tried to construct an adequate and coherent model of causal mechanisms. On the other hand, I have criticized nomothetic and correlationalist approaches to social science as inadequate, and semi-positivist models of causal mechanisms as incoherent. Drawing on the critical realist philosophy of science, I have proposed that we define causal mechanisms as the emergent causal powers of related entities within a system. In addition, I have identified certain errors which the mechanisms metaphor seems to evoke, namely, atomism and physicalism. I then use the ECPRES model to critique positivist and empiricist visions of social science, which advance a nomothetic vision of explanation and a falsificationist method of theory-building, as well as semi-positivist and/or semi-empiricist understandings of causal mechanisms, that seek to bridge nomothetic and mechanismic approaches to explanation with deductivist and/or events-based ones.

What implications does the ECPRES model have for the working researcher? Before answering, let me emphasize that a critical realist or mechanismic approach is not a precondition of good social science. The annals of sociology and political science contain plenty of evidence to the contrary. The ECPRES is not a "method" in the sense of a recipe for doing good social science; rather, it is "method" in the sense of a model of what makes good social science good, and what does not. What makes good social science good, it claims, is a clear and explicit ontology that helps one to identify and describe important social mechanisms. Cultural interpretations and statistical correlations can be important means to achieving this end. The search for "general laws" in the sense of "constant conjunctions", however, while not necessarily a complete waste of time, is certainly not the best investment of our scholarly energies.

Although a mechanismic approach does solve certain intractable problems that have plagued nomothetic approaches, it also generates its own distinctive set of problems. In closing, I would like to highlight problems that are apparent to me, and sketch some very tentative answers to them. These problems concern: agency, abstraction, causality and contingency.

Agency and rationality. Two common objections to the mechanismic approach—and, indeed, to social *science* as such—are that it: i) denies the existence of human agency or ii) reduces actors to cogs in a machine. As numerous critics have pointed out, rational choice theory has very thin conceptions of "rationality" and "action." Action involves the conscious pursuit of goals, the maximization of utility; rationality is the conscious calculation of how to achieve these goals, given certain preferences and beliefs—the choice of an optimal strategy and nothing more. If an actor's preferences are fixed and ordered and strategies are rational and indeed optimal, then actors' choices will, in effect, be the product of constraints and, in more sophisticated models, of beliefs or information. Now, if this is what is meant by "action", "rationality" and "choice", then individual actors are indeed "cogs in a machine" who lack agency. They may have a subjective feeling of "agency" or "choice" but that is the only thing that separates them from, say, a pocket calculator. Once the information and constraints are put in, the outcome is certain.

Of course, it could in fact be that the only thing that separates a human actor from a pocket calculator is a subjective and illusory experience or feeling of agency and choice. Certainly, there are many neuroscientists who embrace such a view (e.g., Damasio 1994). I do not find their arguments persuasive, but this is not the place to take up that debate.[5] The only point I wish to make in this context, is that critical realism does provide room for a more robust understanding of agency, which allows for reasons over reasons (reflexive rationality) and dialogue about reasons (communicative rationality). Indeed, one of the central thrusts of critical realism in recent years has been to elaborate such an understanding. Here, Margaret Archer's work on the self is particularly relevant (Archer 2000, 2003). This does not mean that critical realism aligns itself with hermeneuticist or existentialist critiques of social science, which deny the possibility of causal explanation and turn agents into artists of their own lives. So, how can we reconcile the existence of agency with the operation of mechanisms? First, by acknowledging that the capacity for reflexive rationality, though inherent to human

---

[5] For two powerful critiques of neuroscience reductionism, see Searle 2001 and 2007.

subjectivity, is one that is susceptible to learning and training, and which therefore tends to be unequally distributed across social space and historical time (Bourdieu 2000). Second, by noting that the possibility of communicative rationality, though inherent to human language, is also heavily influenced by social context, by things such as freedom of speech and access to information. Third, by seeing that rational choices, in these more robust senses, are subject to external constraints imposed, not just by beliefs or information, but by resources and regulations. From this perspective, the question of whether individual actors are "cogs in a machine" or "transmission belts for social forces" is not one that can be settled *a priori*; it is a subject of investigation. From this perspective, actors are simply parts of causal mechanisms if, and to the degree that they a) act without engaging in rational reflection or communication (e.g., out of habit or out of self-interest); b) are highly constrained in or unable to act on their choices.

Parsimony vs. scope. If we accept the propositions that reality is stratified and that social reality is time-space dependent, then social science necessarily faces an unavoidable trade-off between theoretical parsimony and explanatory scope. That is, the fewer entities and levels contained in a given theory, the narrower the range of changes and events it will be able to explain. The history of economics provides a wonderful illustration of this dilemma—of how far a parsimonious ontology can be pushed. And formal modeling in political science shows just how thinly stretched the ontology eventually becomes. What to do? I do not think that there is a single, clear answer to this question. My own preference would be for a *via media* between economics and sociology: on the one hand, clear and explicit ontologies such as we find in economics; on the other hand, greater theoretical pluralism, such as we find in sociology.

Testing and adjudication. What comes after falsificationism? This is of course, a key question, maybe *the* key question, that confronts a mechanismic approach. Kuhn's (1962) well-worn distinction between "paradigm shifts" and "normal science" might provide a possible starting point for thinking about it. From a critical realist perspective, paradigm shifts could be understood as ontological shifts involving the theorization of new entities and/or the abandonment of prior representations of social reality. Marx's theory of "class" is a particularly influential example; Bourdieu's notion of "habitus" a more contemporary one. Normal science, by contrast, is about inventorying the mechanisms that can contribute to a given set of changes or events, and identifying which particular mechanisms produced a particular change or event. The history of Marxism is replete with work of this sort. The result is a less heroic, less individualistic vision in which scientific progress is mostly about retouching an existing representation of reality, and less about creating entirely new ones.

References

Abbott, A. 1998. "The causal devolution" in *Sociological Methods & Research*, 27(2): 148–181.

Ahlstrom, S. E. 1955. "The Scottish philosophy and American theology" in *Church History*, 24(3): 257–272.

Archer, M. S. 1988. *Culture and Agency: The Place of Culture in Social Theory*, Cambridge/New York: Cambridge University Press.

———. 1995. *Realist Social Theory: The Morphogenetic Approach*, Cambridge/New York: Cambridge University Press.

———. 1998. *Critical Realism. Essential Readings*, London/New York: Routledge.

———. 2000. *Being Human: The Problem of Agency*, Cambridge, UK/New York: Cambridge University Press.

———. 2003. *Structure, Agency and the Internal Conversation*, Cambridge, UK/New York: Cambridge University Press.

Becker, G. S. 1976. *The Economic Approach to Human Behavior*, Chicago: University of Chicago Press.

Bendix, R. 1978. *Kings or People: Power and the Mandate to Rule*, Berkeley: University of California Press.

Bhaskar, R. 1979. *The Possibility of Naturalism. A Philosophical Critique of the Contemporary Human Sciences*, Atlantic Highlands, NJ: Humanities Press.

Black, D. J. and M. Mileski. 1973. *The Social Organization of Law*, New York: Seminar Press.

Bourdieu, P. 2000. *Pascalian Meditations*, Cambridge, UK: Polity.

Camic, C., P. S. Gorski. 2005. *Max Weber's Economy and Society: A Critical Companion*, Stanford, CA: Stanford University Press.

Cassirer, E. 1973. *The Philosophy of Symbolic Forms*, New Haven: Yale University Press.

Collier, A. 1989. *Scientific Realism and Socialist Thought*, Boulder, CO: Lynne Rienner Publishers.

Collier, A., M. S. Archer et al. 2004. *Defending Objectivity: Essays in Honour of Andrew Collier*, London; New York: Routledge.

Damasio, A. R. 1994. *Descartes' Error: Emotion, Reason, and the Human Brain*, New York, G. P. Putnam.

Elster, J. 1983. *Explaining Technical Change: A Case Study in the Philosophy of Science*, Cambridge/New York/Oslo: Cambridge University Press: Universitetsforlaget.

———. 1989. *Nuts and Bolts for the Social Sciences*, Cambridge/New York: Cambridge University Press.

———. 1999. *Alchemies of the Mind. Rationality and the Emotions*, Cambridge, UK/New York: Cambridge University Press.

Emirbayer, M. 1997. "Manifesto for a relational sociology" in *American Journal of Sociology*, 103(2): 281–317.

Evans, P. B., D. Rueschemeyer et al. 1985. *Bringing the State Back in*, Cambridge/New York: Cambridge University Press.

Friedman, M. 1953. *Essays in Positive Economics*, Chicago, IL: University of Chicago Press.

Goldstein, J. 2005. *The Post-revolutionary Self: Politics and Psyche in France, 1750–1850*, Cambridge, MA: Harvard University Press.

Goldthorpe, J. H. 1991. "The uses of history in sociology: Reflections on some recent tendencies" in *The British Journal of Sociology*, 42(2): 211–230.

———. 1997. "Current issues in comparative macrosociology: A debate on methodological issues" in *Comparative Social Research*, 16: 1–26.

Gorski, P. 2004. "The poverty of deductivism: A constructive realist model of sociological explanation" in *Sociological Methodology*, 34(1): 1–33.

———. 2006. "Ideological power and the rise of the west: Reappraisal and reconstruction" in J. R. Hall and R. Schroeder, *An Anatomy of Power: The Social Theory of Michael Mann*, New York/Cambridge: Cambridge University Press: 101–133.

Gotham, K. F. and W. G. Staples. 1996. "Narrative analysis and the new historical sociology" in *Sociological Quarterly*, 37(3): 481–501.

Harré, R. 1970. *The Principles of Scientific Thinking*, Chicago: University of Chicago Press.

Harré, R. and E. H. Madden. 1975. *Causal Powers: A Theory of Natural Necessity*, Totowa, NJ: Rowman and Littlefield.

Hedström, P. 2005. *Dissecting the Social: On the Principles of Analytical Sociology*, Cambridge: Cambridge University Press.

Hobbes, T. and C. B. Macpherson. 1968. *Leviathan*, Harmondsworth: Penguin.

King, G., R. O. Keohane et al. 1994. *Designing Social Inquiry: Scientific Inference in Qualitative Research*, Princeton, NJ: Princeton University Press.

Kiser, E. 1999. "Comparing varieties of agency theory in economics, political science, and sociology: An illustration from state policy implementation" in *Sociological Theory*, 17(2): 146–170.

Kiser, E. and M. Hechter. 1991. "The role of general-theory in comparative-historical sociology" in *American Journal of Sociology*, 97(1): 1–30.

Kuhn, T. S. 1962. *The Structure of Scientific Revolutions*, Chicago: University of Chicago Press.

Lieberson, S. 1991. "Small N's and big conclusions: An examination of the reasoning in comparative studies based on a small number of cases" in *Social Forces*, 70(2): 307–320.

Lijphart, A. 1975. "Comparable-cases strategy in comparative research" in *Comparative Political Studies*, 8(2): 158–177.

Luhmann, N. 1995. *Social Systems*, Stanford, CA: Stanford University Press.

Luhmann, N. and D. Baecker. 2002. *Einführung in die Systemtheorie*, Heidelberg: Carl-Auer-Systeme-Verlag.

Mackie, J. L. 1974. *The Cement of the Universe: A Study of Causation*, Oxford: Clarendon Press.

Mahoney, J. 2001. "Beyond correlational analysis recent innovations in theory and method" in *Sociological Forum*, 16(3): 575.

———. 2004. "Revisiting general theory in historical sociology" in *Social Forces*, 83(2): 459–489.

Mann, M. 1986. *The Sources of Social Power*, Cambridge/New York: Cambridge University Press.

McAdam, D. 1988. *Freedom Summer*, New York: Oxford University Press.

McAdam, D., S. G. Tarrow et al. 2001. *Dynamics of Contention*, New York: Cambridge University Press.

McLean, P. D. and J. F. Padgett. 1997. "Was Florence a perfectly competitive market? Transactional evidence from the Renaissance" in *Theory & Society*, 26(2/3): 209–244.

Miller, R. W. 1987. *Fact and Method: Explanation, Confirmation and Reality in the Natural and the Social Sciences*, Princeton, NJ: Princeton University Press.

Padgett, J. F. and C. K. Ansell. 1993. "Robust actions and the rise of the Medici, 1400–1434" in *American Journal of Sociology*, 98(6): 1259.

Parsons, T. 1937. *The Structure of Social Action: A Study in Social Theory with Special Reference to a Group of Recent European Writers*, New York: McGraw-Hill Book Company, inc.

Polanyi, K. 2001. *The Great Transformation: The Political and Economic Origins of Our Time*, Boston, MA: Beacon Press.

Polanyi, K. and G. Dalton 1968. *Primitive, Archaic, and Modern Economies: Essays of Karl Polanyi*, Garden City, NY: Anchor Books.

Ruef, M. 2005. "The problem of ontology in sociological analysis" in *Annual Meeting of the American Sociological Association*, Philadelphia, PA.

Salmon, W. C. 1984. *Scientific Explanation and the Causal Structure of the World*, Princeton, NJ: Princeton University Press.

Salmon, W. C., P. Dowe et al. 2005. *Reality and Rationality*, Oxford; New York: Oxford University Press.

Savolainen, J. 1994. "The rationality of drawing big conclusions based on small samples—in defense of mill methods" in *Social Forces*, 72(4): 1217–1224.

Sawyer, R. K. 2005. *Social Emergence: Societies as Complex Systems*, New York: Cambridge University Press.

Searle, J. R. 2001. *Rationality in Action*, Cambridge: MIT Press.

———. 2007. *Freedom and Neurobiology: Reflections on Free Will, Language, and Political Power*, New York: Columbia University Press.

Shapiro, I. 2005. *The Flight From Reality in the Human Sciences*, Princeton, NJ: Princeton University Press.

Sica, A. 2004. "Why 'unobservables' cannot save general theory: A reply to Mahoney" in *Social Forces*, 83(2): 491–501.

Skocpol, T. 1979. *States and Social Revolutions: A Comparative Analysis of France, Russia, and China*, Cambridge/New York: Cambridge University Press.

———. 1984. *Vision and Method in Historical Sociology*, Cambridge/New York: Cambridge University Press.

Skocpol, T. and M. Somers 1980. "The uses of comparative history in macrosocial inquiry" in *Comparative Studies in Society and History*, 22(2): 174–197.

Somers, M. R. 1992. "Narrativity, narrative identity and social action: Rethinking English working-class Formation" in *Social Science History*, 16(4): 591–630.

———. 1998. "'We're no angel': Realism, rational choice and rationality in social science" in *American Journal of Sociology*, 104(3): 722–784.

Steinmetz, G. 2004. "Odious comparisons: Incommensurability, the case study, and 'small N's' in sociology" in *Sociological Theory*, 22(3): 371–400.

———. 2005. *The Politics of Method in the Human Sciences: Positivism and Its Epistemological Others*, Durham, Duke University Press.

Stryker, R. 1996. "Beyond history versus theory—Strategic narrative and sociological explanation" in *Sociological Methods & Research*, 24(3): 304–352.

The Oxford English Dictionary Online. 2000. Oxford, Oxford University Press.

Tilly, C. 1995. "To explain political processes" in *American Journal of Sociology*, 100(6): 1594–1610.

———. 2001. "Mechanisms in political processes" in *Annual Review of Political Science*, 4(1): 21.

Weber, M. 1891. *Die Römische Agrargeschichte in ihrer Bedeutung für das Staats-und Privatrecht*, Stuttgart: F. Enke.

White, H. C. 1992. *Identity and Control: A Structural Theory of Social Action*, Princeton, NJ: Princeton University Press.

Whorf, B. L. 1984. *Language, Thought, and Reality: Selected writings*, Cambridge, MA: MIT Press.

SOCIOLOGY AND THE ECONOMIC SCIENCES

SOCIOLOGY AND THE ECONOMIC SCIENCES

Neil J. Smelser

In asking me to reflect on the relations between sociology and the economic sciences, the organizers of the IIS-congress created a nice coincidence with the publication of the second edition of *The Handbook of Economic Sociology* (Smelser and Swedberg 2005). The first appearance of that book, one decade ago (Smelser and Swedberg 1994), was meant to capture and capitalize on the recent revitalization of that subfield; the second edition was to record and systematize the ongoing momentum of the area, which has continued to be one of the most vibrant in sociology. Its appearance provides a good occasion for me to offer some recent reflections. By no means do I intend to summarize the Handbook—that might cut into its sales—but I will take the moment to offer thoughts on what I consider to be some of the most salient themes emerging from its pages.

The Fate of Economic Man and Economic Rationality

In this portion of my remarks I will develop a series of paradoxes concerning the evolution of fundamental underpinnings of micro-economic (and by extension much of macro-economic) theory—namely the postulate of economic rationality, its behavioral manifestations, and the dynamics of how it works out in market situations. The first paradox is that, at one time regarded as a psychological universal and the basis for economics as a system of scientific laws, that original principle has now been distorted and compromised almost beyond recognition, even though *claims* concerning its generality still exist among some economists.

The second paradox will be that while the evidence responsible for dismantling that theoretical base of economics has accumulated in the work of economists, psychologists, sociologists, and anthropologists, most of the responsibility for its demise has to be laid at the door of *economists themselves*, talking among themselves, while at the same time resisting a mountain of confirming evidence from other disciplines. I will attempt to develop some reasons for this paradox.

Without attempting to spin a history of economic thought, one can identify the main impulses within economics that have led to this result. From an early time economists acknowledged that the postulate of economic man was better regarded as a heuristic device that gained analytic simplicity, theoretical elegance, and explanatory parsimony rather than as an economic universal. Even as orthodox a thinker as Milton Friedman defended it because it is valuable for prediction. For a long time, moreover, the variability of economic motivation has been part of the story of economic analysis. The great theoretical innovations of John Maynard Keynes, for example, in creating a model of an unemployment equilibrium, rested on his modification of the psychological assumptions of consumers (marginal propensity to consume), workers (withdrawal of labor from the market), and investors (marginal efficiency of capital and liquidity preference function). The economists of imperfect competition added the motive of long-term market position to short-term gain to the repertoire of economic actors' motivations.

The major innovations of several giants within economics also tended to be at the psychological boundaries of economists. The work of Frank Knight and George Stigler undermined the assumption of actors' complete market information; Herbert Simon challenged the assumption of maximization with his more pragmatic formulations, inventing "satisficing" and "bounded rationality" as alternatives. Finally, two major lines of innovations in the past twenty years have pressed this line of refinement and compromise further. The first is the development of behavioral economics, spearheaded by Amos Tversky and Daniel Kahneman and carried forward by what is now a small army of card-carrying and legitimate economists. Behavioral economics is based on two principles: that the assumptions of neo-classical economics were inadequate, and variations in risk and uncertainty as well as cognitive framing are decisive; and that the relative power of different psychological assumptions must be determined not *a priori* but rather by empirical demonstration. Most of the innovations by behavioral economists have been based on modification of psychological assumptions (Weber and Dawes 2005). Second, the development of new institutional economics took more seriously the role of economic institutions (including rules, norms, and ideologies) as significant elements of the environment of economic activity. Much of the focus of the new institutionalism, however, has been the application of traditional rational-economic analysis (in contrast to the older institutional analysis) to the creation of institutions relating to transaction costs. Douglas North, however, has taken this line of analysis a step further by referring consistently to the constraining effect of norms, institutions, and values on economic activity (Nee 2005).

The net effect of this accumulation of theoretical variations on the fundamentals of economic analysis has been to create a higher level of theoretical richness for the field, but, at the same time a theoretical diversity when compared with the neatness of neoclassical theory. It also provides the basis for challenging the assertion of scientific unity of economics, and moves economics more in the direction of the other behavioral and social sciences, all of which have long since given up the representation of themselves as possessing internal consensus, much less all of the accoutrements that the term "discipline" entails.

In the meantime, developments in economic sociology have demonstrated, in somewhat different fashion but with similar results, the assumption that tastes and institutions are "given" for purposes of economic analysis, and therefore not the subject of independent inquiry. Karl Marx (1859/1970) early demonstrated the fusion of economic activity and systems of class and political domination. While critical of Marx, Durkheim (1891/1984) also stressed the meshing of economic development (division of labor) with changing systems of economic integration and state regulative activity. Later Veblen (1919) launched a wholesale attack on "economic man" as a misguided conception of human nature. Weber (1922/1978) demonstrated the independent role of religious motives in facilitating or inhibiting economic activity, as well as the necessity of a facilitative administrative and legal apparatus for the development of rational bourgeois capitalism. A half-century later Parsons (1937) consolidated these contributions and argued consistently that what is reckoned to be economic motivation is not a matter of individual psychology but in fact the product of a complex moral and normative order. Finally, the entire impulse of the development of economic sociology in the past half-century, including the new sociological institutionalism, is that economic activity is embedded in and in large part determined by the network, institutional, political, ideological, and cultural environment of economic actors and the economy.

Economic anthropologists have pursued a similar line for more than a century. Bronislaw Malinowski (1922) and Marcel Mauss (1925/1990) early insisted on the intrusion of culture, kinship, and clan in primitive economic activity, little of which appeared to be based on economic calculation. Raymond Firth's monographic studies (e.g. 1946), as well as those of Melville Herskovits (1952) played on the same theme, Karl Polanyi (as much anthropologist as political scientist and philosopher), insisted on the embeddedness of economic activity in solidary and political arrangements (Polanyi, Arensberg and Pearson 1957/1971). Finally, much of the history of economic anthropology in the last half of the twentieth century has been based on a negative polemic against formal economics and an insistence on the intrusion of tradition and culture into the structuring of economic activities.

Despite the overwhelming accumulation of knowledge in sociology and anthropology, the paradox remains that economists, with very few exceptions (see Gibbons 2005), have remained remarkably deaf to their messages but, rather, have dismantled their orthodoxy by listening to themselves. One should ask why this has been so. It would be easy and plausible to write it off to disciplinary pride, jealousy, and status protecting—these factors no doubt play a role in all disciplines—but I would argue that the reasons run deeper. Three lines of argument have occurred to me:

- Almost all the innovations coming from within economics have been small steps that have pecked away at one or another parameter of classical economic rationality without challenging the fundamental notions of choice and calculation. Mainly they have carried the message that while some special assumptions regarding informa- tion, risk, or the rules of the game might be variable, the task of the economist is to take that line of variation and then calculate what rationality or reasonableness of behavior *within* the new posited context might be. Such changes do not undermine the fundamental methodological individualism of the economics tradition, and they do preserve the idea of choice, both individual and aggregated, as providing the analytic bases for explaining behavior. Such small steps are easier to absorb than the suggestions for more wholesale changes emanating from the traditions of economic sociology and economic anthropology, which often suggest that economists' psychology of economic behavior is some kind of fiction, and that the roots of all behavior—economic behavior included—reside in the over-arching structural and cultural constructions of social life. The latter entail paradigm changes rather than paradigm fiddling. Of course, the multitude of small steps taken by economists have in the aggregated amounted to a substantial—but often unnoticed or denied—revolution in the theoretical fundamentals of economics.

- Even if economists had been prepared to make wholesale modifications in their theoretical apparatus, the *forms* taken by the insights and findings emanating from sociology and anthropology have not been easily translatable into typical analytic economic models. Sometimes they have taken the form of general polemic attacks (for example, Polyanyi, Arensberg and Pearson 1957/1971); sometimes they have arisen from case studies or comparative studies with limited generalizability; and sometimes they have been so fundamental as to suggest that economic behavior, as such, really should not be defined as economic but as some *mélange* of socio-cultural manifestations.

- Perhaps most important, the accumulated critiques and reformulations by sociologists and economists are fundamentally at odds with the *philosophical* bases of the economics tradition. That tradition includes methodological individualism, as indicated, but in addition a philosophical preference for the principles of freedom and choice. These may be constrained, of course, but they remain the core items of disciplinary faith. The import of the sociologists' and anthropologists' stress of social structure and culture as determinants undermines all these principles in their stress on the primacy of macro-social determinism and the *impingements* on free choice via interpersonal influence, normative constraints, and cultural preferences.

This difference appeared no more clearly in the polemics of Coleman in his monumental effort to import economic theory into sociology (1990). He defended his choice of individualist theoretical assumptions by arguing that "[they] are grounded in a humanistically congenial image of man," by which he meant the classical liberal image—"the freedom of individuals to act as they will and an apprehension about "constraints that social interdependence places on that freedom" (p. 4). His polemic against alternative theories—technological, biological, and social determinism—and his critique of cultural psychology, sociological functionalism, normative explanations, and Weberian structuralism all boil down to his concern that they offend the principle of choice and individual contracts as the bases and explanations of human behavior.

At bottom, then, the disciplinary struggles are contests over basic images of human nature and organized society, and, as such, they are clearly philosophical, bordering on theological, oppositions of optimism versus pessimism and free will versus determinism. This, in my estimation, constitutes the most important and ultimate difference, and explains the relative impermeability of economics and sociology (and anthropology) to penetrations from the other.

The Story About Economic Institutions

We may be briefer in the discussion of institutions, because their story bears many similarities to the story of economic motivation.

The starting-point for analysis is the assumption that institutions, like tastes, are "given"—an assumption that served much of classical and neo-classical economics. The essence of this assumption is that institutions—such as a legal order which ruled out force and fraud and legitimized rules of property and contract, and legitimized and observed monetary system—are key conditions for the stability of markets and market behavior, as recognized by Adam Smith. By implication, their variations, including their collapse in episodes of political instability, would overwhelm routine economic activity. However, *for purposes of technical economic analysis*, they may be assumed not to vary, and, in consequence, analysis of economic behavior and its resulting of market equilibria can be carried out without the independent analysis of institutions. This key assumption of "givenness" renders institutions non-problematical.

A fundamental attack on this premise came first from within economics in the form of the institutional economists, Thorstein Veblen, John R. Commons, and Wesley Mitchell in the 1920s and 1930s ("within" is not exactly the right term, because they were read out of the field of formal economics so early and so decisively). In diverse ways these authors attacked the principle of methodological individualism (the individual as unit of analysis), developed an alternative stress on institutions as the basic unit of economic analysis, and treated these institutions mainly within the framework of evolutionary theory. While Hodgson (1994), a sympathizer, argued that these theorists were not atheoretical, he stressed the limitations of their theoretical structures, and critics as diverse as Gunnar Myrdal (1958) and Talcott Parsons (Parsons and Smelser 1956) laid the subsequent demise of the old institutionalism to its atheoretial and descriptive features.

Parsons and I carried on the sociological emphasis on institutions in the longest chapter in *Economy and Society* (1956) attempting to embed this analysis in a general theory of social systems, but insisting, above all, on the variability of institutions, and their directly regulatory impact on economic activity through the mechanisms of property and contract, and their full-blown characteristics as institutions—that is, involving normative (including legal) regulation, sanctions, the intervention of third parties (usually political authorities) in enforcement, and legitimizing values.

In the last two decades we have witnessed two "new" institutionalisms, one in economics and one in economic sociology. The principle characteristic of the former is that it makes use of the traditional tools of economic theory to ask why institutions arise. As indicated, this starting point does not break very radically with neo-classical economics. Its view of institutions, moreover, is that they tend to be purposively designed to facilitate economic activity and make it more efficient. Moreover, the derivative quality of institutions ("repeated games," mutually advantageous trust arrangements) stresses their facilitative rather than their regulative character. The new economic institutional sociology, however, returns to the emphasis of the independent significance of normative regulation, cognitive frames, cultural scripts (Nee 2005). While these brief descriptions violate the richness of these two new traditions, they do reveal—as in the case of economic motivation—that the differences between economic and sociological analysis are fundamental and paradigmatic, and do not lend themselves to synthetic bridge-building. Basically, this comes down to a difference in choice of the basic unit of analysis and its implications. The economic predilection is to stress the individualistic, atomistic, voluntaristic side of action, the sociological the constraining and determining features of an independent, social level of analysis. Equipped with this diagnosis, I can report, finally, that I am not optimistic about any major syntheses between the economic and sociological approaches to economic science in the near future.

Economic and Social Systems and the Global Economy

Because space is limited, I must give even more general treatment to the next-to-last set of my remarks—on the idea of system in economics and sociology.

The idea of system has always been at the core of macro-economics, expressed not only as interrelation among different parts but also in the notion that some kind of equilibrium (general, partial, stable, unstable) results from action among economic agents (sometimes including government, as in Keynesian analysis). The idea of system was also the key analytic linkage in the theoretical synthesis that Parsons and I (1956) attempted. It raised the ante of that idea in one respect—namely, treating the economy as one of four subsystems of the large system of society, a subsystem, moreover, which maintained systematic exchanges among itself and the other systems.

Parsons and I carried this system approach to great lengths. I would be less than faithful to the historical record, however, if I stressed anything other than its almost non-existent impact on formal economics, and its limited impact in sociology. There are many reasons for this, I am certain, but one of them is that, in sociology, social-system analysis was dragged down in part because of the general assault on and decline of Parsonian functionalism in the 1970s, even though the idea of systemic interconnectedness was not the main villain. Indeed, the neo-Marxist stress that came forward (and succeeded temporarily in challenging functionalism) retained the ingredient of systemic interconnections and the idea of capitalism as a system.

In contemporary economic sociology many of the ingredients of system survive. Both dependency theory (Cardoso and Faletto 1979) and world-systems theory (Wallerstein 1974) made use of it on the international level, the former implicitly and the latter explicitly. It is also found in the analysis of the transition from socialist to more-nearly capitalist alternatives, in which several "types" of systemic outcome have been identified (King and Szelényi 2005), and in the "varieties of capitalism" literature, though it is more the logic of system rather than the language and theory of system that characterizes these lines of analysis.

My own view is that the weakening and limited nature of the explicit applications of the system-perspective in sociology is unfortunate. In making this statement, I have in mind its clear and unequivocal relevance for the explanation of globalization. The idea of the international economy and the systematic interrelations between trade, flows of finance, and monetary developments is still strong, as is the idea of the growing economic interdependence among nations (Gereffi 2005). A certain "system-ness" is implied in most discussions of the governance of the global economy, which dominates the literature (e.g. Fligstein 2005), but these analyses tend to focus on the problematics of governance rather than on the general systematics of the relations between polity and economy. The areas where "system" is under-utilized are, in my estimation, (a) in the analysis of the relations among different *aspects* of globalization—economic, political, normative, and cultural and (b) in the theoretical treatment of national economies cultures as increasingly open systems (i.e., subject to outside influences) and political systems as in principle autonomous (as nation-states) but also constrained by the intrusion of forces beyond the control of the national polity from global sources, of economic, political, and cultural. These areas constitute what we like to call "under-theorized", and I would like to record my conviction that a resuscitation and new development of the logic of system is a major theoretical resource for understanding and explanation.

Relations Between Sociologists and Economists

I close with a few words about the prospects for good diplomatic relations between economists and sociologists and interdisciplinary synthesis between the two fields. The large sweep of history does not yield much cause for optimism, characterized as it has been by several intellectual seasons of economic imperialism and wholesale sociological denunciations of economics (see Swedberg 1990). The most recent of these have been, on the one side, the economic explanations of traditionally non-economic phenomena (marriage, crime, racial discrimination) of Gary Becker (1976) and the sociological variant of economic imperialism developed by James Coleman (1990), and, on the other side, the savage moral attack on the foundations of economics by Amitai Etzioni (1988). These are not without their intellectual merits, but from the standpoint of the creative synthesis of two fields, they yield more poison than fruit—rigidifying boundaries and diminishing mutually respectful discourse.

In contrast with this generally bleak history, the past half-century has yielded a number of incremental steps in both fields that are encouraging. I have reviewed these developments earlier in my remarks. On the side of economics, the relaxation of traditional parametric assumptions and the pursuit of analytically-based explanations on the basis of that relaxation has significantly opened the field to assumptions and empirical research from other disciplines, and, especially in the past 25 years economic sociologists, while never failing to attend to polemics, have turned to more craftsmanlike, empirically-based research on identifiable problems, a mode that generates more patient listening on the part of economics than does do broadside assaults.

Testifying from a biographical point of view, in the fifty years since the publication of *Economy and Society*, I can also record gratifying progress. When Parsons delivered his Marshall Lectures at Cambridge (on which the book was based) and when the book appeared, it was greeted mainly by non-noticing, with occasional fits of hostility from economists who generally regarded it as irrelevant to their technical concerns and perhaps threatening because it regarded economic theory as a special case of something grander. Slowly over time, however, I have witnessed the diminution of indifference and hostility, as well as a marginal accretion of respect on both sides of the disciplinary boundary. The reviews of the first edition of Richard Swedberg's and my *Handbook of Economic of Sociology* by economists contained an expected level of ambivalence, but economists as different as Kenneth Arrow and Samuel Bowles testified to its relevance for economic analysis.

I do not wish to make too much of this progress, however, and must end on a note of limited optimism about the future of theoretical synthesis. The basis for this caution, furthermore, lies in a point I stressed earlier—the fact that the differences between first-assumptions in the two fields are philosophical if not theological. That difference, to remind, is between (a) the persistent methodological individualism of the economic perspective and economists' insistence on *some* kind of rationality and choice however modified, and (b) sociologists' stress on relational factors and their focus on non-rational constraints on economic choice and behavior. Those differences remain so profound as to constitute a continuing paradigmatic chasm between the two disciplines. For economists and sociologists, respectively, to ingest either of these into their ways of thinking constitutes an act of acceptance and friendship that exerts too great a philosophical cost for each, and threatens their respective historically based disciplinary and professional identities. For this fundamental reason a counsel of patience seems the best posture.

References

Becker, G. S. 1976. *The Economic Approach to Human Behavior*, Chicago: Chicago University Press.

Cardoso, F. H. and E. Faletto. 1979. *Dependency and Development in Latin America*, Berkeley: University of California Press.

Coleman, J. S. 1990. *Foundations of Social Theory*, Cambridge, MA: Belknap Press of Harvard University Press.

Durkheim, É. 1891/1984. *The Division of Labor in Society*, New York: Free Press.

Etzioni, A. 1988. *The Moral Dimension*, New York: Basic Books.

Firth, R. 1946. *Malay Fishermen: Their Peasant Economy*, London: Kegan Paul, Trench, Trubner.

Fligstein, N. 2005. "The political and economic sociology of international economic arrangements" in N. J. Smelser and R. Swedberg (eds.), *Handbook of Economic Sociology*, Second edition, Princeton: Princeton University Press and Russell Sage Foundation, 183–204.

Gereffi, G. 2005. "The global economy: Organization, governance and development" in N. J. Smelser and R. Swedberg (eds.), *The Handbook of Economic Sociology*, Second edition, Princeton, NJ: Princeton University Press and Russell Sage Foundation, 160–182.

Gibbons, R. 2005. "What is economic sociology and should any economists care?" in *Journal of Economic Perspectives*, 19: 3–7.

Herskovits, M. 1952. *Economic Anthropology: A Study in Comparative Economics*, New York: Knopf.

Hodgson, G. M. 1994. "The return of institutional economics" in N. J. Smelser and R. Swedberg (eds.), *The Handbook of Economic Sociology*, Princeton, NJ: Princeton University Press and Russell Sage Foundation.

King, L. P. and I. Szelényi. 2005. "Post-communist economic systems" in N. J. Smelser and R. Swedberg (eds.), *Handbook of Economic Sociology*, Second edition, Princeton, NJ: Princeton University Press and Russell Sage Foundation, 205–229.

Malinowski, B. 1922. *Argonauts of the Western Pacific*, London: Routledge.

Marx, K. 1859/1970. *A Contribution to the Critique of Political Economy*, New York: International Publishers.

Mauss, M. 1925/1990. *The Gift: The Form and Reason for Exchange in Archaic Societies*, New York: W. W. Norton.

Myrdal, G. 1958. *Value in Social Theory*, New York: Harper.

Nee, V. 2005. "The new institutionalisms in economics and sociology" in N. J. Smelser and R. Swedberg (eds.), *The Handbook of Economic Sociology*, Second edition, Princeton, NJ: Princeton University Press and Russell Sage Foundation, 49–74.

Parsons, T. 1937. *The Structure of Social Action*, New York: McGraw-Hill.

Parsons, T. and N. J. Smelser. 1956. *Economy and Society*, Glencoe, IL: The Free Press.

Polanyi, K., C. Arensberg, and H. Pearson (eds.). 1957/1971. *Trade and Market in the Early Empires*, Chicago: Henry Regnery.

Smelser, N. J. and R. Swedberg. 1994. *The Handbook of Economic Sociology*, Princeton, NJ: Princeton University Press and Russell Sage Foundation.

———. 2005. *The Handbook of Economic Sociology*, Second edition, Princeton, NJ: Princeton University Press and Russell Sage Foundation.

Swedberg, R. 1990. "The New 'Battle of Methods'" in *Challenge*, January-February, 33–38.

Veblen, T. 1919. *The Place of Science in Modern Civilization and Other Essays*, New York: Huebsch.

Wallerstein, I. 1974. *The Modern World System*, vol. 1, *Capitalist Agriculture and the Origins of the European World Economy*, New York: Academic Press.

Weber, M. 1922/1978. *Economy and Society: An Outline of Interpretive Sociology*, Berkeley: University of California Press.

Weber, R. and R. Dawes. 2005. "Behavioral economics" in *The Handbook of Economic Sociology*, Second edition, Princeton, NJ: Princeton University Press and Russell Sage Foundation, 90–108.

FORMAL THEORY IN THE SOCIAL SCIENCES[1]

Richard Breen

Introduction

Rational choice is the single most widely used type of theory construction in several of the social sciences, though its status ranges from hegemonic in economics, through contested in political science and sociology, to almost absent in areas like anthropology. It is an approach based on methodological individualism, where the outcomes of interest, which usually refer to characteristics of aggregates, are held to depend on the action and interaction of individual agents or actors. Accordingly, much discussion of rational choice focuses on the assumptions that are made about these agents. I shall begin by comparing the way in which agents are conceptualized in two broadly sketched versions of rational choice: these are sometimes called 'thin' and 'thick', or 'narrow' and 'wide' versions. Then I draw further comparisons between these two and the depiction of agents in what are called agent based models or ABMs. Taken together these three—narrow and wide rational choice and agent based models—present quite different approaches to modelling agents in explanations based on methodological individualism. I argue that, despite their differences, there are two common criteria that should be used to assess the explanations that they provide: I call these criteria 'adequacy' and 'plausibility'. In the final section of the article I shall make some remarks about the role of empirical research in the development of theories that are both adequate and plausible. But I shall begin by highlighting some of the central features that characterise rational choice explanations. This will be useful when I discuss the way in which agents are depicted in rational choice theory and in agent based models.

[1] A version of this paper was delivered in January 2005 as the first in a series to inaugurate Oxford University's Centre for Advanced Study in the Social Sciences. I am grateful to audience members for their comments and Edmund Chattoe, John Goldthorpe, Peter Hedström, Kenneth MacDonald and Margaret Meyer for comments on an earlier draft.

Rational choice should really be called a theoretical perspective, rather than a theory, though for convenience I continue to use the shorter formulation: but although there are rational choice theories of specific phenomena there is no rational choice theory *per se*, at least not when theory is understood to mean explanatory theory. Rational choice is usually considered to be a type of formal theory; indeed, in American political science the term 'formal theory' is used to refer to rational choice and game theory. I prefer to use the term 'formal theory' in a rather broader sense to apply to theories that have two important characteristics: first, they are aimed at explaining something; and, secondly, that they are empirically testable. The first criterion might seem remarkably unexceptional if it were not that some contemporary social science denies the possibility of explanation. Much of what is labelled 'theory'—particularly contemporary social theory—does not in fact progress beyond the introduction and elucidation of concepts. The second criterion requires that a hypothetical explanation should be expressed in such a way that its consequences—or, at least some of them—can be deduced and tested. As an example, think of the finding that social class inequalities in educational attainment remained roughly constant over a long period in 20th century Britain. To provide an explanation for an empirical finding like this may call for considerable ingenuity, but if the explanation is developed to account expressly for that specific finding, then the fact that it does so is only a weak indication that it is correct. To gauge its adequacy we would either have to show that it was the only plausible explanation of the finding—which is a practical impossibility—or that it carried some implications that were testable elsewhere or which provided an explanation for another finding which had not been the original *explanandum*. So, in this case, we would have a greater deal of confidence in the hypothesised explanation of persistent class differentials if, for instance, it also yielded an adequate account of the observed trend in sex differences in educational attainment. To give another example, a theory developed to explain differences between countries in a particular phenomenon would gain much in persuasiveness if it also turned out to provide an explanation of temporal variation in that phenomenon.

The Structure of Rational Choice Explanations

I now want to turn to an outline of the structure of rational choice models. As I said in my introductory remarks, rational choice models are used to account for aggregate characteristics of the social world, rather than individual behaviour; or, as Hechter and Kanazawa (1997: 192) put it, social rather than individual behaviours. In economics one such social outcome is an equilibrium described by a set of prices; and while economists can legitimately claim to give a rational choice explanation of such an equilibrium, they do not—or, I believe, they should not—claim to be able to use rational choice to yield an explanation of the actions of any one of the particular firms or consumers whose actions, when aggregated with those of all the other firms and consumers, give rise to the equilibrium. Nevertheless, in line with methodological individualism, rational choice accounts of social outcomes are built up from the actions of individual agents and in rational choice models agents are depicted in the following way. First, they have certain preferences, or desires, which they seek to satisfy; secondly, they have a limited set of alternative courses of action open to them, among which they must make a choice; and, thirdly, they possess beliefs about the consequences of choosing each of the actions. This is sometimes called the 'Preferences, expectations and constraints' model.[2] Preferences and expectations are characteristics of agents, while constraints are characteristics of the endowments they possess and of the environment in which they are located. In accordance with the principle of methodological individualism, this environment is itself considered to be the product of the action and interaction of other agents, though for particular purposes we often treat the environment as given. For instance, we sometimes take as given the institutional settings within which choices are made, though we know that institutions themselves are the product of the actions and interaction of other agents.[3] Action follows from agents seeking to attain their most highly desired outcome, subject to the available opportunities and the beliefs they hold about the best way of doing this. But this process calls for some calculations

---

[2] Opp (1999: 173) notes that constraints and opportunities are, in effect, two sides of the same coin, and thus for convenience one might as well use one term or the other, rather than both.

[3] But in other cases we specifically seek to analyze the reciprocal relationship between individual actions and institutional structure.

to be made—the alternatives must be evaluated—and so another characteristic of the agents is what I will call their 'abilities', by which I mean their ability to identify the course of action which will yield the greatest satisfaction of their desires, or, in economic terms, to find the action that will maximize their expected utility. So the term ability is here used to capture both the agents' knowledge of the world and their ability to compute the utility maximizing course of action.[4]

This, then, is the basic rational choice model, but, as is well known, there are many variations on this theme. The strongest common element is the role played by opportunities or constraints. In almost all rational choice accounts variations in action—whether cross-sectional or temporal—are held to be entirely, or partly, the result of differences in opportunities: behaviour changes because of changes in the relative costs of alternative courses of action. While it is very plausible to see variation in action as driven by variation in opportunities in this way, such an emphasis is greatly helped by the fact that opportunities are much more easily measured than are desires, beliefs or abilities, which are all internal to the agents themselves. This emphasis on opportunities, for want of any information on the other elements of the model, is well captured in the following quotation from R. H. Coase (1988: 4). 'It may be' he writes,

> ...that ultimately the work of sociobiologists...will enable us to construct a picture of human nature in such detail that we can derive the set of preferences with which economists start...In the meantime, whatever makes men choose as they do,...in almost all circumstances a higher (relative) price for anything will lead to a reduction in the amount demanded (parentheses in original).

Varieties of Rational Choice

Rational choice approaches differ mainly in their treatment of preferences, beliefs and abilities. Quite commonly a distinction is drawn between 'thin' and 'thick' models (Ferejohn 1991; Hechter and Kanazawa 1997) or between 'narrow' and 'wide' versions (Opp 1999) of

---

[4] There are various ways that these distinctions might be drawn: for instance, knowledge, which I include under abilities, might be considered under the heading of beliefs, though I prefer to keep them separate and restrict beliefs to refer to those things that the agent possesses some information about.

rational choice. As a practical matter, one can identify a thin or narrow version of rational choice in which agents' preferences are stable,
materialistic and self-interested; beliefs are perfect; information is complete; and agents possess computational skills sufficient to allow them
to locate the utility maximizing choice, no matter how complicated it
may be to do so.[5] To see more concretely what this means, consider
the following example of a model of educational choice, which I have
taken from a paper by Cameron and Heckman (1998: 285) published
in the *Journal of Political Economy* in 1998.[6] The issue here is to explain
variation between people in their educational attainment, and Cameron
and Heckman argue that this comes about through individual students
(and their families) making different choices of the optimal amount of
schooling in which they should invest. Students make their choice by
solving the following equation:

$$\max_{j}\{R(j) - c(j|X)\}, j = 0,\ldots, S,$$

Here j indexes years of schooling, running from zero to a maximum
value, S; R(j) is the discounted lifetime return to j years of schooling;
and c(j|X) is the direct costs of j years of schooling, given characteristics
of the student, X. The optimum schooling choice is then the value of
j which solves the equation.

If this is taken as a model of what students do, rather than as a
way of representing the outcomes of choices they make on a different
basis, then it must be assumed that students know R(j)—the returns
to a specific amount of education—that they know how to discount
these returns to their present value at the time the decision is being
made, and that they know c(j), the costs of education. These are all
large assumptions, but the one about educational returns is particularly
big: economists' estimates of the returns to schooling show considerable disagreement, so one might wonder how students can know the
returns to schooling (Manski 1993). Finally, it is assumed that students
are able to solve the equation: that is to say, they compute the difference between the discounted lifetime returns to a certain number of

---

[5] Sometimes this is referred to as the economic model, though, even if it was the
dominant model in economics in the past, nowadays, and indeed for the past 20
years or so, one can probably find as wide a range of types of rational choice within
economics as within any other social science.

[6] This example is chosen to be quite general and thus typical of many other applications.

years of schooling and the costs of that number of years of schooling, conditional on their own characteristics, such as their ability. They do this for all possible years of schooling and pick, as their chosen level of schooling, that number of years of schooling for which this difference is greatest (assuming it is always positive). In fact, as a piece of mathematics this particular problem is not so difficult, at least not when compared with decisions that agents are supposed to make in other models which require them to have a knowledge of calculus or some facility with Bayes' rule, and so forth.

In thin models of rational choice like this one, preferences, beliefs and abilities enter into the explanation as assumptions, rather than as empirically warranted characteristics. One of the advantages of this version of rational choice, and of those that lie close to it, is that it allows its proponents to make clear, and often testable, predictions about what should be observed. On the other hand, as Green and Shapiro (1994) point out in their well known book *Pathologies of Rational Choice*, in many cases these predictions prove to be wrong, nowhere more evidently than in the so-called 'paradox of voting'. Nevertheless, thin models are sometimes defended on the grounds that strong assumptions of rationality provide a yardstick in the form of the actions that an idealised agent would be predicted to undertake, against which real behaviour can be compared. We might be tempted to go further than this and say that thin models provide some general theoretical predictions in much the same way that the laws of physics make predictions about the behaviour of idealised systems which seldom, if ever, occur in the real physical world. But, in my view, the analogy does not hold, simply because, unlike physics, thin rational choice lacks any means of explaining the discrepancies between its predictions and empirically observed outcomes. Physical theories can be used to explain why, under certain real world circumstances, water boils at a temperature other than 100 degrees centigrade; but proponents of thin rational choice cannot use their theory to tell us why real people vote when agents of the theory do not.

Thick or wide versions of rational choice weaken some, or indeed all, of the assumptions that thin versions make about agents, and they may also allow more flexibility in the definition of opportunities.[7] They retain the basic premise that agents consciously seek to attain a more

---

[7] It is not my aim to try to give a comprehensive review of the variety of ways in which the restrictions of thin rational choice have been relaxed: Opp (1999) and

preferred outcome, but, typically, they allow preferences to be shaped by non-materialistic factors, such as internalized values or norms, or a desire for the approval of others, and to be driven by more than self-interest. They may also permit agents to have information about the world which is imperfect and less than complete; and they usually recognise the limited computational skills that real agents possess. These latter adjustments are often linked with the idea of 'bounded rationality' which Herbert Simon (1979: 502) defines as follows:

> Rationality is bounded when it falls short of omniscience. And the failures of omniscience are largely failures of knowing all the alternatives, uncertainty about relevant exogenous events, and inability to calculate consequences.

Another important distinction among rational choice approaches, aside from the nature of the assumptions that are made about agents, concerns whether or not explanations of aggregate differences in the choice of action on the part of members of different groups (where the groups are, for example, sexes or social classes or age groups and such-like) rest only on differences in their circumstances (that is, constraints and opportunities) or also involve differences in the agents themselves. Rational choice explanations are based on the premise that an agent undertook an action because she believed that that action would yield the best outcome under the circumstances. So when it comes to explaining why different agents choose different actions, all the work normally goes into specifying the circumstances that make one particular action the rational choice for the members of one group, but another action the rational choice for members of a different group.[8] This was the position advanced by Karl Popper (1945, chapter 14) and captured in his idea of the 'logic of the situation': "our actions are to a very large extent explicable in terms of the situation in which they occur [...] when we speak of 'rational behaviour' or of 'irrational behaviour' then we mean behaviour which is, or which is not, in accordance with the logic of the situation" (Popper 1945: 97). Many subsequent sociologists have argued similarly: we should simplify the depiction of agents in our models but we should pay close attention to the institutional setting in

---

Goldthorpe (1998), among others, have usefully sought to systematize the variation in rational choice approaches, albeit in somewhat different ways.

[8] If we have temporal data, these 'groups' might be the same people at different times: why did the working class in Britain vote for the Labour Party in the early 1970s but for the Conservatives in the late 1970s and 1980s?

which action takes place (for example, Lindenberg 1985). Popper, and many sociologists who took this view, did so in an explicit rejection of psychological reductionism; that is the idea that sociological phenomena can be explained by reference to individual psychology. In recent years, however, many proponents of rational choice have argued for more psychologically accurate depictions of agents: in economics this school is usually termed 'behavioural economics.' But even those who do not go so far are often willing to allow explanations of variations in behaviour to include more than differences in circumstances: agents are allowed to differ in their preferences, in their beliefs, in how they discount the future, and so on, depending on their group membership. However, when explanations are based on differences in the characteristics of agents it is then usually necessary to explain why they differ in this way. For example, if someone argues that working class children perform less well in school because they discount the future more heavily than their middle class counterparts, the explanation will not be complete unless we are told why the classes differ in how they discount the future. And this second explanation invariably involves only circumstantial factors.[9] In that sense, all rational choice explanations rest, ultimately, on differences in constraints and opportunities,[10] though they may operate with models of agents which have more or less psychological accuracy.

Measuring Subjective States

Opp (1999) notes several criticisms levelled against more elaborated versions of rational choice, one of which is that they are circular: that is to say, the same piece of evidence that constitutes the *explanandum* is used to infer the existence of some part of the *explanans*. For example, we might argue that people vote out of a sense of civic duty: but if our evidence for their having a sense of civic duty is the fact that they vote, our argument is going nowhere except round in circles. One attraction

---

[9] An exception is found in rational choice explanations influenced by evolutionary psychology which posit genetic differences in psychological functioning, particularly between men and women.

[10] Popper recognized that what he termed 'psychological factors' may be required as part of the explanation, but 'they are not ultimate data of human nature, and [...] they are, in their turn, explicable in terms of the *social situation*' (Popper 1945: 96, italics in original).

of a thin model of rational choice is that it is relatively straightforward to stipulate what constitutes an agent in the narrowly rational sense, whereas, once we move to broader conceptions of rational choice, we have available to us a very wide range of possible preferences, beliefs and competencies, with the attendant danger of simply tailoring the depiction of the agent to fit the explanatory task at hand. One check on this is to have evidence, independent of what we want to explain, about the nature of the agents. In the past economists were resistant to the idea that it might be possible to gain empirical evidence about the nature of agents, and their scepticism was shared by some other social scientists. My opinion is that finding out about internal states of agents, such as their preferences and beliefs, is indeed a difficult task but should rarely be impossible, and nowadays the view that it is feasible to measure at least some subjective phenomena is common among social scientists. Sociologists have a long track record in this area and some economists have lately begun to develop methods for measuring such phenomena using survey data (Dominitz and Manski 1997). The whole field of behavioural economics is based in an attempt to incorporate, into the agents of rational choice models, characteristics of human judgement and decision-making that have been discovered in psychology and in other experimental settings.

From Actors to Interactors

A notable aspect of what we might term conventional rational choice models of the kinds I have been discussing is that, for the most part, agents act independently and so the interactional nature of social life is underplayed. But this changes when we move to game theory, which is the application of rational choice to the analysis of strategic interaction among two or more players; and more recently there has been a growth in the popularity of social interaction models. Here mutual interaction among agents is allowed to influence their actions through its effect on one or more of preferences, beliefs and opportunities. This can lead to a negative or positive feedback: in the latter case this amplifies or sustains some patterns of action above and beyond what would have occurred in the absence of such social interaction. For example, suppose that on Saturday evenings I have the choice of doing the garden or going to the pub. While gardening is a pleasant but solitary activity, the pleasure I get from going to the pub depends on how many of my neighbours I meet there—and the same goes for them. What my neighbours do thus influences my behaviour by changing the relative attractiveness of gardening and going to the pub, and the same is true for my neighbours. One consequence of this, provided these effects are strong enough, is that otherwise identical neighbourhoods might end up looking very different. In one case all the gardens are well tended because no-one goes to the pub, and because no-one goes, no-one wants to; in another all the neighbours go to the pub and no-one wants to stay at home and do the garden.

Social interaction models have become popular in the last decade, and have been used to explain a wide range of empirical phenomena from the distribution of poverty to neighbourhood variations in crime rates, although it is widely agreed that the identification and estimation of such effects is far from straightforward. A particular difficulty arises because of the possible endogeneity of the choice of neighbourhood: that is to say, it is difficult to assess the causal effect of belonging to particular neighbourhoods if the people living in them have cho-sen those neighbourhoods because of the outcomes associated with them—as would be the case, for example, if the people in my village had chosen to live there precisely because everyone spends Saturday evenings in the pub.

Game theory and social interaction models follow the rational choice model, but there is another approach to modelling the way in which context influences aggregate outcomes which has not developed from, nor necessarily makes use of, rational choice: this is agent based modelling. Agent based models (or ABMs) are simulations, usually computer based, of the interactions of agents. These simulations are used to generate aggregate properties of the agent population using very simple characterisations of the agents themselves. As Macy and Willer (2002: 146) put it in their review of the field: 'ABMs explore the simplest set of behavioural assumptions required to generate a macro pattern of explanatory interest'. The roots of this approach are deep, but it is only within the past 15 years or thereabouts that agent based models have become popular. Nevertheless, one of the most influential pieces of agent based modelling predates the availability of powerful computers: this is Schelling's (1971) model of residential segregation. The Schelling model consists of a set of agents, each of which is of one of two types—call them red and blue—arrayed on a network structure such as points on a circle or a lattice. These agents have a preference for a balance of neighbours of each type and in each round of the simulation those agents who are dissatisfied in this respect are allowed to move to any other available location. The strength of preference can be varied in the Schelling model, reflecting the extent to which agents want to be with a majority of their own type or are willing to be in a minority. It transpires that, even if agents' preferences for neighbours of their own type are very weak, after several rounds of the simulation there is complete segregation, so that the network consists of areas that are completely red or completely blue but lacks any mixed areas. This outcome is a stylized version of residential segregation by race in the United States, but the model suggests that a strong desire for such segregation on the part of the agents is not necessary to generate segregation: it can arise from only weak preferences for residing with one's own type. The Schelling model nicely illustrates the characteristic feature of agent based models: namely that a complex social outcome is generated as an emergent property of the interaction of agents who follow very simple rules of behaviour. A more recent and almost equally well known, but much more elaborate, example of an agent based model is the Sugarscape model of Epstein and Axtell (1996) in which a population of agents, again following simple rules, exploits the natural resource of a landscape and in so doing generates social outcomes, such as a distribution of wealth and cultural distinctions which, according to the authors, closely resemble their real world counterparts.

In obvious contrast to the agents of rational choice models, those of agent based models of the sort I have referred to follow simple rules of the kind 'if X then do Y'—so, in the Schelling model, the rule is: if your preferences are not met move; if your preferences are met, stay where you are. To the extent that agents change their behaviour they are adaptive, rather than forward looking. If we take the agents of thin rational choice models as our point of comparison, then thick rational choice (or behavioural) models reflect a desire to make agents more like real human beings, endowed with a more complex psychology, but rather weaker computational powers and restricted knowledge, while, in agent based models, the agents are, if anything, less realistic but much simpler.

Explanation

All explanatory models involve a trade-off between realism, understood as the extent to which the model accurately captures the details of the real world, and parsimony—that is to say, the economy that comes from explaining complex phenomena through less complex mechanisms. Arguments that say that a model ignores the full complexity of what it is trying to explain, or that the agents of a model are lacking some feature of human agents, or that the model is 'unrealistic', are not in themselves useful kinds of criticism: to paraphrase Sen (1986: 11), although all models distort reality and their assumptions lead to mistakes, the goal is to find a model that leads to fewer mistakes than others. And we usually seek to establish this by comparing what the model says should be the case in the real world with how the real world really is. In other words we ask how well the hypothetical or toy world generated by our model corresponds to the true world. This criterion for assessing models is sometimes referred to as 'goodness of fit',[11] but I shall call it 'empirical adequacy'. The criterion is relative: one model is preferred not because it provides a perfect fit to the data but because it is the best among a set of possible alternative models. Models might be thought of as being in competition with one another, with (at least in theory) the competition leading to better and better (in terms of how well they reproduce the real world) models.

If this is going to be a usable criterion it follows that explanatory models must be capable of being tested empirically: there must be some important part of the explanation which we can evaluate by reference to something observable in the real world. An explanation which says that a mass suicide happened because unseen forces were controlling the minds of the people involved is not a testable explanation unless some way can be found of showing the existence of those forces. This may involve directly measuring them, but it might also be done by showing that their existence carried some other empirical implications which we could then test. In many of the natural sciences the obvious empirical criterion is predictive accuracy. This largely follows from the fact that many natural science theories (with physical theories being the clearest example) have the status of general laws. But many other explanations in the natural sciences, and probably all explanations in the social sciences, are not like this: they hold only under certain conditions, called 'scope conditions' (Kiser 1996; Kiser and Hechter 1998). These

---

[11] Among economists, credit for advancing goodness of fit as the criterion by which models should be judged is given to Milton Friedman (1953): for him the question was not whether the assumptions made in a model were accurate or not but whether the model yielded good predictions.

scope conditions lie outside the model because the model itself does not tell us when or where they will hold. Testing the model by using its predictions will only be a valid test if the scope conditions hold and so this limits the usefulness of prediction for testing theory.[12] But this is not to say that the predictive criterion is never used or that social scientists never try to make predictions. After all, any policy recommendation that follows from an explanation of a social phenomenon entails a prediction.

Another way of deriving testable implications of a theory is to ask whether the theory provides an adequate explanation for other similar or closely related phenomena which it might be reasonable to expect it to explain. For example, does a theory that explains why something varies over time also yield a good account of geographical variation? Another is to look for some important element of the theory which, if true, would have some testable empirical consequences. Matters become more difficult when we consider deriving testable hypothesis that will allow us to adjudicate between the claims of two or more competing explanations. Here the task is to find some testable implication which is true if one theory is correct but false if the other is correct. Sometimes it can be difficult to find these crucial tests, or, if found, they may require data that we do not have or which cannot easily be collected. Sometimes, subtle logical deductions are needed to draw out the testable implications, and imprecision in theories may mean that these deductions themselves, and the tests to which they lead, are subject to dispute. Nevertheless, the goal is clear: theories should be capable of being tested empirically.

---

[12] Scope conditions may be more or less general. A very concrete set of scope conditions would say that, for example, a particular theory holds only for Prussia in the early 18th century. But, as Kiser (1996) points out, these conditions might be made more general by asking what features of 18th century Prussia make the theory applicable here. They might be the existence of an absolutist monarchy combined with a rapid militarisation of society. If that is so, then the scope of the theory is in fact wider than 18th century Prussia, since it should apply to any society undergoing rapid militarisation and which had an absolute monarch. But we would need to be sure that these two characteristics were an exhaustive depiction of the relevant scope conditions.

Assumptions About Agents

One difficulty with this is that all explanations include certain assumptions which are not directly tested. The greater the range of possible assumptions that could be made in explaining something, the more important it is to gauge the degree to which the results of the model depend on the particular ones that were chosen. This strategy is sometimes called 'robustness analysis' or 'sensitivity analysis'. If our model fits the data well under one set of untested assumptions (for example, that agents had one particular kind of utility function), but fits the data very poorly under an alternative, but also plausible, set of untested assumptions (a different kind of utility function), we would need to devote much more attention to determining which set of assumptions was correct. Conversely if our results were robust to any choice of plausible assumptions, we would have good grounds for having confidence in our model.

The premise of rational choice explanations is that individuals choose those actions that they believe will lead to the outcome they most prefer, given their circumstances. A rational choice explanation instantiates this premise: through our depiction of the agents and their circumstances we render the choice of action rational. Put another way, the agent in a rational choice explanation is what makes the observed actions rational consequences of the circumstances. In the Popperian idea of the 'logic of the situation' all the effort goes into correctly identifying the objective circumstances of action. In an economic model these objective circumstances would be the relative prices that the agents faced and their budget constraints. The rational agent is, in this account, something rather unproblematic—in fact, just a way of linking the inputs (circumstances) to the outputs (actions). But although this approach has proved influential with some sociologists it cannot, at least in this form, be correct, because the depiction of the agent in rational choice always involves some assumptions that cannot be deduced from rationality alone. This is most obviously true of agents' preferences. For example, the model of educational decision making developed by Breen and Goldthorpe (1997) rests on the assumption that students' and their families' first priority is to secure a level of education that avoids downward class mobility. No matter how accurately we specified the circumstances in which educational decisions are made, without this assumption the model would not work.

Likewise, rival explanations of a particular social outcome are likely to differ mainly in how they depict agents.[13] As an example consider models that try to explain the problem of collective action. The issue here is that, because an individual's actions can make little difference to whether a collective action succeeds or not, participation in the collective action is not rational, even for those who have a strong preference for its success, if it entails any cost. Two main solutions to this have been proposed. In the first, a non-standard assumption is made about preferences: people are not motivated by material incentives (or not by these alone) but by a sense of duty, or something similar, which may lead them to participate despite the costs.[14] In the second an assumption is made about agents' beliefs: they believe that their actions carry more weight than they really do (e.g., Müller and Opp 1986). Once again there is no disagreement between these two explanations on the objective circumstances facing agents or on the action to be explained: they differ only in the assumptions they make about agents' internal states.

The case for realism in the way agents are depicted in social science explanations is put by Searle (1991: 337), who writes:

> The propositional content given by the theorists in the explanation of [...] behaviour must be identical with the propositional content in the actual mind of the agent or agents whose behaviour is being explained; otherwise, the behaviour is not properly explained.

One response to Searle, by, for instance, the proponents of methodological individualistic explanations in the social sciences, might be to argue that this would be all well and good if we were indeed trying to explain the behaviour of an individual agent (and it is noticeable that all the examples with which Searle illustrates his argument are of this kind) but that, since we are in the business of explaining aggregate phenomena, the agents of our models should be such as to produce social outcomes that match those produced by real agents. The distinctions

---

[13] The description of the circumstances of action may also differ depending on the way that agents are depicted because the latter will help to determine which aspects of the circumstances are relevant.

[14] This is a common argument in purported solutions to the paradox of voting. Imagine that a sense of civic duty imposed a utility cost of $-d(i)$ on the ith agent if he failed to vote, and that the utility equivalent cost of voting is $-c(i)$. Then all agents for whom $d(i) > c(i)$ would vote even when $c(i) > 0$.

in the way in which agents are depicted in the three approaches I have
discussed might thus be seen as reflecting disagreements about what
features are necessary for explanatory adequacy. As far as agent based
models are concerned, this can be achieved with very simple agents
and writers like Epstein and Axtell, the inventors of Sugarscape, are at
pains to point out the unexpected power of such simulations to produce
realistic outcomes: as they put it (1996: 52): 'It is not the emergent mac-
roscopic object per se that is surprising, but the generative sufficiency
of the simple local rules.'

The problem, however, lies in the ontological status of these simple
local rules. If we know that people do not in reality follow them, what
are we to make of the fact that the rules nevertheless generate realistic
social outcomes? Or, more generally, in any model, whether rational
choice or agent based model or something else, in which agents doing
X generate an outcome Y which is also observed in reality, we need
to ask whether the observed Y occurred because people really did X
or whether Y occurred as if they did X. If the latter is the case then
more is needed before we can be said to have explained the occurrence
of Y.[15] In an ideal world, an empirical test, or set of tests, could be
constructed that would be sufficiently discriminating so as to support
only the one true model of the process generating Y. The problematic
issue is the extent to which this ideal can be approximated. Manski
(2000: 117) has written that 'the observed outcomes of the population
can usually be generated by many different interaction processes [...]
Hence the findings of empirical studies are often open to an uncomfort-
ably wide range of interpretations'. When we are comparing competing
explanations it may be extremely difficult to find empirical tests that
discriminate between them. Frequently empirical tests can be found,
but they are not powerful enough to rule out all but one of the competing models. Certainly we should reasonably expect that the range
of possible interpretations will be reduced the greater the number of
outcomes on which we focus, because some will be shown to lack the
adequacy of others. But to the extent that this does not rule out all
competing theories, the criterion of explanatory adequacy needs to

---

[15] An example can be found in explanations for the existence of equilibrium asset
prices. While the assumptions that underlie the derivation of competitive equilibrium
prices may be implausible, it turns out that in some circumstances the weaker assumption that agents seek to exploit opportunities for arbitrage can give rise to the same
equilibrium prices.

be augmented by something like, but not identical to, the criterion set out by Searle. We require plausibility: which means that the agents in our models have characteristics and behave in ways that make them at least a plausible approximation to real human agents. As the German psychologist Gerd Gigerenzer (2001: 38) expresses it: '[t]he challenge is to base models [...] on the cognitive, emotional, social and behavioral repertoire that a species actually has.'[16]

Assessing the plausibility of assumptions is itself a kind of goodness of fit test in which we compare characteristics of the agents with what we believe (particularly on the basis of psychological research) that real people are like. But, in invoking plausibility as a criterion, we need to be careful to specify correctly what the characterization of agents in a particular model implies about real people. On the one hand, we do not want to model agents in their full complexity: what we require is accurate simplification, so that, to use Sen's (1980: 358) terms, how we depict agents is true but is not necessarily the whole truth. And how closely we need to come to the whole truth in modelling agents will depend on the purposes of our analysis. On the other hand, because our goal is to explain aggregate actions, the agents of the model and real human beings may differ in legitimate ways. Plausible agents in a model should have all those characteristics on which the aggregate outcome depends—so idiosyncracies of behaviour, for example, insofar as they cancel each other when we move to aggregate outcomes, would not be part of how we model the agents (Stinchcombe 1991; Hernes 1992). Furthermore, the impact of real psychological processes might be adequately captured by assuming somewhat different processes in our agents. For example, to explain some aggregate outcome the assumption that agents know a particular probability could be justified if we had grounds to believe that real people's guesses about the probability were unbiased. In general, the criterion of plausibility does not say that the agents of explanatory models should be identical to real people (since this would be both impossible and pointless) nor even that they should, in all the characteristics they possess, be identical with real

---

[16] Searle's concentration on the propositional content in the mind of the actor is too limited. If we want to know why an agent did A rather than B we need to know not only the propositional content but also the mechanisms that led the agent to do the action that followed from that propositional content. These mechanisms—such as the heuristics that we use in decision making—are part of human psychology and their operation is something that agents themselves are usually not conscious of.

people: rather they should be characterized in a way that implies, or is consistent with, accurate assumptions about real human beings for the purpose of explaining aggregate outcomes.

Theories and Data

I have suggested two criteria by which explanatory models should be judged, but how well we can assess adequacy and plausibility depends on the quality and extent of the data that we have, and so, in this final section of my article, I want to make some remarks about the dependence of theory development on techniques of data collection and analysis.

Consider the case of agent based models. Two of the most appealing things about them are their flexibility and generality. Insofar as one is at liberty to specify the agents in an agent based model in any way one wishes, there is no reason why they should only follow simple local rules: in principle one could go to the other extreme and embed the kind of agents one finds in thin models of rational choice in an agent based model. Likewise for the question of whether we restrict attention to rational action or cast our net more widely: in principle agent based models can accommodate either option. These—and other—kinds of elaboration are indeed found in some of the recent literature in this area. But flexibility comes at a price: we are required to specify not only the nature of the agents and the choices that they can make but also the details of the interactions among them. This involves defining the social network in which each agent is embedded and how it evolves, and the way in which one agent affects another. As far as the structure and evolution of social networks of interacting agents is concerned, this is often not explicitly measured, and so the set of others who influence the actions of each agent is assumed; and the same can be said for the mechanisms by which links between agents are made and broken. Furthermore, even less attention has been given to the exact way in which agents affect each other. Suppose, for example, that the attractiveness to each agent of doing A depends on whether other agents in her network do A. Here the crucial word is *depends*: what, we would like to know, is the exact form of this dependency? Is it the total number who do A? Is it whether more than one does A? Normally we do not know, so we make an assumption. The general difficulty here is that, unless we have empirical data that will allow us to specify all these elements of the model, or unless we can show that the results we get are robust to the assumptions we make about these elements, we will simply be left with too many freely varying parameters and, as a result, the explanation we provide will be rather less than compelling.[17]

The criterion of plausibility should apply to the specification of what we might call the interaction structure of agent based models (that is, the structure of the network and the way in which agents interact) as well as the specification of the agents themselves. There are various sources to which we might turn to achieve this. We might follow the lead of behavioural economics and specify agents in accordance with the findings of experimental psychology. But experiments are not the only source: the linking of the results of systematic empirical analyses—whether these are quantitative or qualitative—would seem to be a promising way of calibrating agent based models such that their agents and the structure of their interactions more closely match those of real agents (Bruch and Mare 2006).

Turning to explanatory adequacy, the usefulness of this criterion depends on the extent to which empirical tests can discriminate between rival theories. One way of increasing discriminatory power is through repetition. If, to explain a given phenomenon, we model our agents in a particular way, we should then ask whether agents, conceptualized in the same way, can also explain other similar or related phenomena. This would guard against the tendency to calibrate agents not in the light of knowledge of how agents empirically are but in the light of the social outcome that is to be explained. Discrimination can also be improved by constructing more demanding tests. We might want to be less concerned with whether or not an agent based model can generate something that looks roughly like, let us say, the wealth distribution of contemporary societies, and more interested in whether an agent based model can be used to explain why wealth distributions differ between societies. A useful question is whether the set of simple rules that agents follow is the only set that would generate the social outcome of interest. We should expect that, if the outcome is specified in very general terms,

---

[17] Bruch and Mare (2006) show that the results of the Schelling model of residential segregation depend on the detailed specification of the ABM itself, so that segregation need not always arise as a consequence of the decision rules that Schelling's agents follow. More simply, the result depends on the assumptions made in constructing the model. Using empirical data they also demonstrate that the real causes of segregation do not lie in the mechanism that Schelling proposes.

then a variety of definitions of agent rules will do the job, whereas the more closely specified is the social outcome the smaller the set of depictions of agents that will be compatible with it.

Taken together, the criteria of adequacy and plausibility imply a search for models that contain realistic agents (in the sense explained earlier) and which can accurately generate sharply defined social outcomes. But our ability to specify such models and the stringency of the tests that we can apply to them will depend on the data at our disposal and on the analytical techniques available to us. Developments in methods of data collection, particularly in research design, and in data analysis, have a crucial role to play in facilitating the development of formal theory in the social sciences. Indeed, one might argue that, to a greater or lesser extent they always have, though, for the most part, the relationship between theory and data has not been close. The great majority of social science data have been collected without reference to theory. Take the data that sociologists use as a case in point. We rely heavily on large scale surveys whose rationale is empirical rather than theoretical and which provide valuable information about things like patterns of social mobility, rates of crime victimization and ethnic differences in educational attainment. But the data that are good for establishing the phenomenon are seldom good for testing explanations of it and so, in many areas—including my own field of social mobility research—explanation lags well behind the accumulation of empirical results. A remedy for this is data collection designed for the purpose of testing theory. So, the data we might collect to test theories about social mobility may not necessarily be data about social mobility itself. To design research, particularly non-experimental research, for the purpose of testing theory, is a challenging task: nevertheless, the one single thing that would do most to improve the development and testing of formal theory in the social sciences is a greater concern with the design of research.

References

Breen, R. and J. H. Goldthorpe. 1997. "Explaining educational differentials: Towards a formal rational action theory" in *Rationality and Society*, 9: 275–305. Reprinted in D. B. Grusky (ed.). 2001. *Social Stratification: Class, Race and Gender in Sociological Perspective*, Second edition, Boulder: Westview Press and also published as Chapter 9 in J. H. Goldthorpe. 2001. *On Sociology: Numbers, Narratives and the Integration of Research and Theory*, Oxford: Oxford University Press.

Bruch, E. E. and R. D. Mare. 2006. "Neighborhood choice and neighborhood change" in *American Journal of Sociology*, 112(3): 667–709.

Cameron, S. V. and J. J. Heckman. 1998. "Life cycle schooling and dynamic selection bias: Models and evidence for five cohorts of American males" in *Journal of Political Economy*, 106: 262–333.

Coase, R. H. 1988. *The Firm, the Market and the Law*, Chicago: University of Chicago Press.

Dominitz, J. and C. Manski. 1997. "Using expectations data to study subjective income expectations" in *Journal of the American Statistical Association*, 92: 855–867.

Epstein, J. M. and R. L. Axtell. 1996. *Growing Artificial Societies: Social Science From the Bottom Up*, Washington DC: Brookings Institution Press, MIT Press.

Ferejohn, J. 1991. "Rationality and interpretation: Parliamentary elections in early Stuart England" in K. Renwick Monroe (ed.), *The Economic Approach to Politics: A Critical Reassessment of the Theory of Rational Action*, New York: Harper-Collins, 279–305.

Friedman, M. 1953. *Essays in Positive Economics*, Chicago: University of Chicago Press.

Gigerenzer, G. 2001. "The adaptive toolbox" in G. Gigerenze and R. Selten (eds.), *Bounded Rationality: The Adaptive Toolbox*, Cambridge, MA and London: MIT Press, 37–50.

Goldthorpe, John H. 1998. "Rational action theory for sociology" in *The British Journal of Sociology*, 49: 167–192.

Green, D. and I. Shapiro. 1994. *Pathologies of Rational Choice*, New Haven: Yale University Press.

Hechter, M. and S. Kanazawa. 1997. "Sociological rational choice theory" in *Annual Review of Sociology*, 23: 191–214.

Hernes, G. 1992. "We are smarter than we think" in *Rationality and Society*, 4: 421–436.

Kiser, E. 1996. "The revival of narrative in Historical Sociology: What rational choice theory can contribute" in *Politics and Society*, 24: 249–271.

Kiser, E. and M. Hechter. 1998. "The debate on Historical Sociology: Rational choice theory and its critics" in *American Journal of Sociology*, 104(3): 785–816.

Lindenberg, S. 1985. "An assessment of the new political economy: Its potential for the social sciences and for sociology in particular" in *Sociological Theory*, 3(1): 99–114.

Macy, M. and R. Willer. 2002. "From factors to actors: Computational sociology and agent based modeling" in *Annual Review of Sociology*, 28: 143–166.

Manski, C. 1993. "Adolescent econometricians: How do youth infer the returns to schooling?" in C. T. Clotfelter and M. Rothschild (eds.), *Studies of Supply and Demand in Higher Education*, Chicago: University of Chicago Press, 57–60.

———. 2000. "Economic analysis of social interactions" in *The Journal of Economic Perspectives*, 14: 115–136.

Müller, E. N. and K.-D. Opp. 1986. "Rational choice and rebellious collective action" in *American Political Science Review*, 80: 471–489.

Opp, K.-D. 1999. "Contending conceptions of the theory of rational action" in *Journal of Theoretical Politics*, 11: 171–202.

Popper, K. R. 1945. *The Open Society and Its Enemies* (vol. 2, Hegel and Marx), London: Routledge.

Schelling, T. C. 1971. "Dynamic models of segregation" in *Journal of Mathematical Sociology*, 1: 143–186.

Searle, J. R. 1991. "Intentionalistic explanations in the social sciences" in *Philosophy of the Social Sciences*, 21: 332–344.

Sen, A. 1980. "Description as choice" in *Oxford Economic Papers*, 32: 353–369.

———. 1986. "Prediction and economic theory" in *Proceedings of the Royal Society of London*, 407: 3–23.

Simon, H. 1979. "Rational decision making in business organizations" in *American Economic Review*, 69: 493–513.

Stinchcombe, A. L. 1991. "The conditions of fruitfulness of theorizing about mechanisms in social science" in *Philosophy of the Social Sciences*, 21: 367–388.

BOURDIEU'S CONTRIBUTION TO ECONOMIC SOCIOLOGY

Richard Swedberg

This brief article has two purposes. The first is to indicate what constitutes the most important contribution to economic sociology that can be found in the work of Pierre Bourdieu (1930–2002). The reason for wanting to establish this is that when a social scientist dies there is always a danger that his or her work will be pushed to the side and forgotten. This makes it important to try to sort out what his or her contribution is—so that it can become part of the tradition, in this case the tradition of economic sociology.

The second and less direct purpose of this article is to raise the question if Bourdieu can contribute to the current dialogue between economics and sociology, which seems to have stalled. This dialogue began, from the perspective of sociology, around 1990 when it for a few years seemed as if sociology and economics were moving towards each other and possibly even could meet (e.g. Swedberg 1990). Today, however, this hope seems vain; and the situation is different. Today, we have instead, on the one hand, a fully developed subfield of economic sociology and, on the other hand, a science of economics that has begun to develop its own concepts of social interaction, norms, institutions and so on (e.g. Manski 2000; Greif 2006). I will return to how Bourdieu may be of help in getting this dialogue going at the end of this article.

Let me now return to the first and main purpose of this article, namely to present and discuss what I consider to be Bourdieu's most important and enduring contributions to economic sociology. The three contributions I have selected are his early studies of Algeria; his attempt to bring a normative dimension into the discussion of economic sociology; and his attempt to develop a sociological concept of interest.

It is true that one might add a few other topics. There is, for example, Bourdieu's interesting attempt to develop a general paradigm for how to go about studies in economic sociology which represents an alternative to the dominant paradigm of embeddedness in contemporary economic sociology. It can be found in an article called "Principles of an Economic

Anthropology", a translation of which has been included in the second edition of *The Handbook of Economic Sociology* (Bourdieu 2004).

There is of course also Bourdieu's classical study of consumption, *Distinction* (Bourdieu 1986). The reason why I will not discuss it here is that it has already found a safe place in the tradition of general sociology as one of the most outstanding studies in the 20th century. A mention should also be made of Bourdieu's study of the private construction and home industry in *The Social Structures of the Economy* (Bourdieu 2005). And finally, Bourdieu has over the years skilfully chosen some themes for his journal *Actes de la Recherche* that are of much relevance to economic sociology, such as "social capital" (no. 31, 1980), "the social construction of the economy" (no. 65, 1986) and "the economy and the economists" (no. 119, 1997).

From this wealth of work from Bourdieu's side in economic sociology I have, to repeat, settled on a few that I consider extra interesting. So let me begin with the first of these by saying a few words about his studies of Algeria and what I consider to be his most important study in economic sociology, namely *Travail et Travailleurs en Algérie* (*Work and Workers in Algeria*). This work was published in 1963 and only exists in a shortened version in English translation (under the title *Algeria 1960*; see Bourdieu 1963, 1979).

Work and Workers in Algeria can be described as an extraordinarily rich and imaginative ethnographic study (Bourdieu 1963). Some of the strength of the analysis in this work, it may be added, also comes from the author's skilful juxtaposition of the traditionalistic habitus or disposition of the Algerian peasants to the rational habitus of people who live in modern capitalist society. Now, Bourdieu's concept of habitus has often been criticized as being too diffuse or too broad to be really helpful. This is true up to a point, as I see it. One should, however, also remember what the alternative usually is in the analysis of the economy: the infamous economic man. *Homo economicus* has no past or a habitus; everything he does is eternally new. *Homo economicus* is, as Bourdieu once famously put it, "*a kind of anthropological monster*" (Bourdieu 1997: 61; emphasis added).

In *Algeria 1960* economic habitus is described as a "disposition [that] orients and organizes the economic practices of daily life—purchases, saving, and credit—and also political representations, whether resigned or revolutionary" (Bourdieu 1979: vii–viii). The key theme in Bourdieu's work on Algeria is that the habitus of the local population is still pre-capitalist and out of joint with the capitalist reality that the colonizing powers have introduced. The result of this conflict, Bourdieu argues, has been extremely painful and disorganizing for the Algerians.

The pre-capitalist habitus of the Algerians is portrayed by Bourdieu as qualitatively different from the capitalist habitus in several ways. In pre-capitalist Algeria the basic economic unit was the kinship group, not the nuclear family as in capitalist society. Property was often owned collectively, and how much each individual contributed to the income of the household was not known. To meld into the group and to *not* stand out, was a norm as in many peasant societies.

In general, Bourdieu argues, much took place in this type of economy as if to *disguise* the fact that economic interests were at stake. The relationship of work to productivity was, for example, not known nor was it looked into. Gifts were common—and "gift exchange is an exchange by which the agents strive to conceal the objective truth of the exchange, i.e. the calculation which guarantees the equity of the exchange" (Bourdieu 1979: 22).

One important difference between the economic habitus of the Algerians and the rational habitus of people who live in a capitalist society, Bourdieu argues, has to do with the concept of *time*. One example of this is that of work; and according to tradition in Algeria a man with self-respect should always keep busy ("at least he can carve a spoon"—Bourdieu 1979: 24).

Another example of the pre-capitalist attitude to time comes out in Bourdieu's discussion of money. Money was seen in Algeria as something that is very abstract and also inferior to what it can buy. According to an Algerian saying, "a product is worth more than its equivalent [in money]" (Bourdieu 1979: 11). When the harvest has been good, Bourdieu also notes, the peasant will typically hoard the surplus for future consumption rather than invest it. As to credit, one only lends to friends or relatives; the time for repayment is left vague; and the idea of interest on a loan is *not* acknowledged (meaning by this that one must pay for the use of resources during so and so many time units, according to some exact scale).

One reason why it was so enormously painful and difficult for the Algerians with their pre-capitalist habitus to adjust to the new, capitalist conditions has to do with the fact that capitalism did not develop organically in Algerian society, from within—but was instead imposed from the outside, by colonial powers.

Another reason has to do with the economic conditions of the Algerian population; and at this point of his argument Bourdieu criticizes the tendency in social science to see cultural change in much too abstract terms and to disregard that it is always anchored in economic reality. If one, for example, looks at the economic situation of the Algerian population, it soon becomes clear that until the workers reach a certain limit of income, according to Bourdieu, they are unable to think and calculate in rational terms, along the lines of people who live in a capitalist society.

At a certain income level—when the Algerian workers feel secure and are able to take a calm and rational look at the future—they typically decide to have fewer children and develop a more realistic view of the future. The Algerians who are poor, on the other hand, continue to have large families and are very unrealistic when it comes to the future. Their social and economic reality, Bourdieu says, push them into a "forced traditionalism" (Bourdieu 1979: 23).

Let me now turn to topic number two that I have selected from Bourdieu's economic sociology, namely his attempt to raise a discussion of the normative dimension of economic sociology, a topic—to repeat—that has *not* had the discussion it deserves in contemporary economic sociology. Whether the reason for this omission is a sense that strict adherence to the Weberian notion of objectivity is in place, or simply a lack of interest in politics among today's economic sociologists, is not clear (though I suspect the latter—perhaps in combination with some influence from the business schools).

In any case, Bourdieu's viewpoint on this topic can be illustrated by *Acts of Resistance: Against the Tyranny of the Market*, a small book which mainly consists of lectures and speeches given at various public and political occasions, including strike meetings (Bourdieu 1998b; a much fuller volume with similar political articles and speeches exists—but unfortunately still only in French [Bourdieu 2002]). The major theme in this work is that the welfare state is under heavy attack from neo-liberalism, and that this attack has to be countered since the welfare state protects people from the ravages of the market. Neo-liberalism advocates individualism and fights every kind of collectivism, especially trade unions. In the developing world the IMF and the World Bank are busy imposing neo-liberal reforms, with the most dismal results.

And in the West people's sense of security is being undermined by dismissals in the private sector as well as in the public sector. Thanks to the success of neo-liberal politics since the 1980s, Bourdieu says, this is just as true for the middle classes as for the workers. "The American middle classes, exposed to the threat of suddenly losing their jobs, are feeling a terrible insecurity (which shows that what is important in a job is not only the activity and the income it provides, but also the sense of security it gives)" (Bourdieu 1998b: 36–7).

A true economic science, according to Bourdieu, would look at *all* the costs of the economy—not only at the costs that corporations are concerned with, but also at the crimes, suicides and so on which are the result of misguided economic policies. What such an "economics of happiness" (as Bourdieu calls it) would look like is described as follows:

> Against this narrow, short-term economics [which is dominant today], we need to put forward an *economics of happiness*, which would take note of all the *profits*, individual and collective, material and symbolic, associated with activity (such as security), and also all the material and symbolic *costs* associated with inactivity or precarious employment (for example, consumption of medicines: France holds the world record for use of tranquilizers). You cannot cheat with *the law of the conservation of violence*: all violence has to be paid for, and, for example, the structural violence exerted by the financial markets, in the form of layoffs, loss of security, etc., is matched sooner or later in the form of suicides, crime and delinquency, drug addiction, alcoholism, a whole host of minor and major everyday acts of violence (Bourdieu 1998a: 40).

It is clear that Bourdieu's attack on neo-liberalism is not very different from what one can find elsewhere among social scientists who define themselves as progressive and anti-liberal. One part of Bourdieu's criticism, however, is definitely *unique* and of special interest to economic sociology, as I see it. This is the part that has to do with Bourdieu's attempt to introduce a new set of concepts to criticize neo-liberalism and capitalism more generally and which serve *both* as political concepts *and* as sociological ones. These are centered around the idea of theodicy and include concepts such as "sociodicy", "social suffering", and "economic violence" (e.g. Bourdieu 1977, 1979, 1991, 1998a). This strand of Bourdieu's thought goes back to his early studies of Algeria but has also come to an expression in some other works by Bourdieu, especially his huge study of social suffering in *The Weight of the World* (Bourdieu et al. 1999).

Theodicy—and this is what I find so valuable in Bourdieu's argument—tries to answer questions such as the following: *Why is there suffering in the world, and why do some people suffer more than others?* Bourdieu's position is that the organization of society has much to do with the creation of suffering, and he therefore speaks of "sociodicy" or "social suffering" (e.g. Bourdieu 1998a: 35, 43). Neo-liberalism, for example, is characterized by Bourdieu as a "conservative sociodicy" since it justifies suffering on the ground that it is necessary for economic progress (Bourdieu 1998a: 35). Unemployment, from this perspective, represents a form of "economic violence" (e.g. Bourdieu 1977: 191–192).

Bourdieu also refers several times to Weber's argument that people who are successful invariably feel that they deserve their good fortune, while in reality their success is primarily due to good luck (*"theodicy of good fortune"* in Weber's terminology; cf. Weber 1946: 271). In modern capitalist society the educational system operates as such a theodicy of good fortune, according to Bourdieu, since it justifies the existence of inequality on the ground that those who are successful are more competent and educated than the rest (Bourdieu 1990: 133). A corollary of the theodicy of good fortune is the belief that the poor deserve to be poor because they are ignorant, lack education and so on (*"theodicy of misfortune"*—Weber 1946: 276).

Let me now proceed to the third main contribution of Bourdieu to economic sociology. By way of introducing it, I also would like to say something about Bourdieu's general economic sociology. In 1997 Bourdieu published an article entitled "The Economic Field", which was revised a few years later and given the title "Principles of an Economic Anthropology" (Bourdieu 1997, 2000). This is the article that I referred to above as having just been translated and made available in the second edition of *The Handbook of Economic Sociology* (Bourdieu 2004).

According to this article then, the economy can be conceptualized as *a field*, that is, as a structure of actual and potential relations (see also Bourdieu and Wacquant 1992: 94–120). But not only a whole economy, also an industry, a firm and many other economic phenomena can be conceptualized as a field. Each field has its own logic and interest. The structure of a field can also be understood in terms of its distribution of various types of capital. In addition to financial capital, the following three famous forms of capital are especially important: social capital, cultural capital and symbolic capital. Social capital in this context is defined by one's connections that are relevant to economic outcomes; cultural capital, one's education and family background; and symbolic capital, by various items with a cognitive basis, such as goodwill and brand loyalty in the economy.

According to Bourdieu, economic sociology, just as any subfield in sociology, should draw on *four* key concepts in order to make a solid analysis. *Three* of these are well known, and I have already mentioned all of them: *habitus, field* and different types of *capital*. The fourth concept, in contrast, is rarely discussed and often not even mentioned. This is: *interest*—and that is also why I want to draw attention to it here.

According to Bourdieu, "*interest* is (as he puts it) 'to be there', to participate, to admit that the game is worth playing and that the stakes created in and through the fact are worth pursuing; it is to recognize the game and to recognize its stakes" (Bourdieu 1998b: 77; cf. Bourdieu 1990, Bourdieu and Wacquant 1992: 115–117). The opposite of interest (or "*illusio*") is indifference (or "*ataraxia*"). Each field has its own interest, even if its masquerades as disinterestedness. Bourdieu criticizes the economists' version of interest for being ahistorical—"far from being an anthropological invariant, interest is a *historical arbitrary*" (Bourdieu and Wacquant 1992: 116). The economists are also in his opinion wrong in thinking that "economic interest" is what drives everything; "anthropology and comparative history show that the properly social magic of institutions can constitute just about anything as an interest" (Bourdieu and Wacquant 1992: 117).

I would now like to make an argument that the concept of interest—conceptualized along the lines of Bourdieu—ought to be *central* to economic sociology, and must not be neglected in this type of sociology, as it is today. I will make references to Bourdieu's concept of interest throughout my argument, but I shall also mention a few other authors since interest analysis goes far back in social thought and exists in many different versions.

So let me start out by saying something in general about the concept of interest in order to bring out Bourdieu's contribution a bit better. While the dominant approach in current economic sociology emphasizes the importance of *social relations* for a proper understanding of the economy, one can argue—with Bourdieu—that while this is obviously important, interests should also be an integral part of the analysis.

Institutions can, for example, be conceptualized as distinct constellations of interests *and* social relations. An economic sociology that ignores the role of interests, I argue, runs the risk of becoming trivial. The reason for this is that interests, much more so than social relations, is what drives economic action. This is by no means a novel insight, as not only Bourdieu shows, but also Weber and Marx. It is, however, a position that has been forgotten in much of modern economic sociology.

It is clear that this argument for an economic sociology, centered around the concept of interest, needs to be discussed. I will therefore first quickly summarize the case for an economic sociology which (like Bourdieu suggests) assigns a key role to the concept of interest, and then indicate some issues that need to be addressed. There is also the questions of circularity and reductionism. It is sometimes argued, for example, that an analysis which draws on interests runs the risk of being tautological: it tries to explain everything as the result of some interest. Interest analysis, it is also argued, has a tendency to reduce everything in a mechanical way to some interest. Finally, a few words must also be said about the relationship between interest and motivation, its equivalent in psychology.

The idea that the concept of interest should be central can be found in many of the classical social theorists as well as the founding fathers of sociology. Among the former are David Hume, Adam Smith and Alexis de Tocqueville; and among the latter Max Weber, Emile Durkheim and Georg Simmel. Also some of the major sociologists of modern times have assigned an important part to the concept of interest in their analyses.

Much more could be said about the general history of the concept of interest, but I do not have the ambition (or the space) to improve on the fine works of Albert O. Hirschman (1977, 1986), Stephen Holmes (1990), Johan Heilbron (2001) and others. There is one exception to this however; and I want to emphasize strongly that there also exists *a sociological concept of interest*, which was developed around 1900. The basic idea of Weber, Simmel and a few other thinkers is that interests can only be realized within the framework of society, and that the role of social relations always has to be taken into account in an analysis of interests (see Swedberg 2005). Bourdieu, of course, is close to this tradition and to some extent also comes out of it.

As opposed to some of the writers who have discussed the concept of interest I am favorably disposed to this concept and advocate its use. I generally think that it should be regarded as a major concept in the social sciences, and that it is absolutely indispensable to economic sociology. If sociologists use the concept of interest in their analyses today, it should be noticed, they tend to do so in a casual and unreflected manner, which differs from the way that they deal with other important concepts. Pierre Demeulenaere writes that "throughout the tradition of sociological analysis it [that is, the concept of interest] is often referred to without further specification" (Demeulenaere 2001: 7715). Key concepts, in contrast, are typically discussed and defined in standard works; they are consciously improved upon; and they are taught to students in introductory courses and texts—all of which is currently *not* the case with the concept of interest in sociology, including economic sociology.

I would also argue that a watershed took place in the history of the concept of interest when the economists, towards the end of the 19th century, gave up on the more complex and many facetted type of interest analysis that can be found in the work of such thinkers as Tocqueville and John Stuart Mill. It is from this point onwards that the concept of interest begins to be reduced to, and exclusively equated with, *economic self-interest*. It is precisely also at this point that interests became the beginning, so to speak, as well as the end of the analysis. That is, instead of using interests *to suggest plausible hypotheses*, to be tested empirically, they were used to logically reason your way to the solution of some problem.

This strategy may well have its advantages—but it has also impoverished the analysis of economic and other phenomena. It has, among other things, eliminated the concern with non-economic interests and other economic interests than self-interest. And this way of using the notion of interest cannot handle the situation that people often do not know what their interests are; and when they do, they do not necessarily know what they should do in order to realize them. When economic analysis is applied to non-economic activities, it also tends to recast these exclusively in economic terms, such as competition, monopoly, trade and so on. It furthermore typically fails to take social relations into account. This whole set of problems is what Bourdieu has in mind when he states that "the word *interest* [...] is also very dangerous because it is liable to suggest a utilitarianism that is the degree zero of sociology" (Bourdieu 1993: 76).

Let me now say something why interest is a very useful concept. For one thing, it imparts a distinct dynamic to the analysis because it is mainly interest which makes people take action. It supplies the force which makes people get up at dawn and work hard throughout the day. Combined with the interests of others, it is a force which can move mountains and create new societies.

A corollary of this is that interest—the sociological concept of interest—helps to explain conflict, which takes place when interests clash. This is true for what happens in a person's mind as well as between individuals, groups and societies. But interests do not only clash and energize the actors; they can also block each other, reinforce each other or immobilize an actor by making her back some religion or politics that supports tradition. The concept of interest, in brief, is a flexible tool of analysis.

Taking interests seriously also means shifting the center of the analysis from the surface of things to what has an important impact on social action. Weber's analysis in *The Protestant Ethic* is paradigmatic in this respect, that is, in its attempt to analyze what made people change their behavior in such a fundamental way that a whole new rationalistic mentality was created. This aspect of *The Protestant Ethic* may in the long run prove as important as its wellknown thesis about the importance of ascetic Protestantism for modern life.

Taking interests seriously can also help to give a balanced place to the role of subjectivity and culture in the analysis of economic behavior. These two types must indeed not be ignored—interests are to some extent always subjective as well as shaped by culture—but interests are also "objective" in the sense that they often constitute an uncommonly stable and stubborn part of social reality. The state or public morality may e.g. forbid a certain economic activity—but it will take place anyway.

Utopian thinkers, from this perspective, can be defined as thinkers who disregard interest. Actors without official interests (say, students) are ignored by those in power and are also prone to utopianism in their actions and thoughts. Being a "free-floating intellectual" is by no means as positive as Karl Mannheim believed. Having an established interest may tie you to the order of things and tempt you to "sell out"—but it also makes you a contender and anchors you in reality.

As noted earlier, there exists an attempt by sociologists in Weber's generation as well as today to integrate interests into the sociological type of analysis; and this approach (as opposed to the non-sociological and non-empirical interest theory of mainstream economics) is what is most congenial to economic sociology. One can summarize this approach as one that takes *both* interests *and* social relations into account—as long as it is clear that interests are defined and expressed through social relations. "Far from being an anthropological invariant," as Bourdieu warns, "interest is *a historical arbitrary*" (Bourdieu and Wacquant 1992: 116). Also the following statement by Bourdieu is relevant in this context: "anthropology and comparative history show that the properly social magic of institutions can constitute just about anything as an interest" (Bourdieu 1998: 83).

But even if there exist a number of positive qualities to the concept of interest, it also raises some problems that need to be discussed. One of these is the issue of tautology. One of Albert O. Hirschman's articles is entitled "The Concept of Interest: From Euphemism to Tautology", and it contains the argument that the economists' concept of interest tends to be tautological since it is used to explain everything (Hirschman 1986). What is at issue here is that if the concept of interest is treated as if it constitutes the philosopher's stone, something which it certainly isn't, it will loose its power to explain. If too much weight is put on the concept of interest, it will brake. Sociologists (as opposed to economists) have, however, not used interest in this way; and the danger of tautology is therefore much less in sociology, including economic sociology, than in economics.

A related topic is the question if the concept of interest is reductionistic in nature, that is, if it reduces everything to some interest and thereby impoverishes the analysis. This critique has recently been made by Frank Dobbin, who argues that in contemporary Western society people tend to explain practically everything in terms of interest (*"the interest frame"*). This, however, is no reason for social scientists to do the same, according to Dobbin, who adds that

> when anthropologists observe totemic societies in which local lore has it that frog spirits rule the universe, they do not conclude that frogs are inscribed in plows and circumcision mats because frogs indeed rule this domain. They conclude that the locals have developed a system of meaning that locates authority over social practices in the frog totem. Likewise, when we study modern social practices, we must do what we can to step outside of the frame of reference of the locals [that is, the interest frame] (Dobbin 2001: 78).

But Dobbin's argument in this quote is not, as I see it, directed at the sociological concept of interest. What he aims his critique at is the concept of self-interest in economics, which is a very different story.

As earlier mentioned, motivation is the equivalent concept in psychology to interest in the other social sciences. The parallels between these two concepts come out well in the following quote:

> Psychologists favor the term *motivation* to describe the wants, needs, and preferences that guide behavior. Without motivation, there would be few conflicts or problems in human life, especially not between people, because no one would care about anything. Then again, without motivation hardly anything would get done. In fact, without motivation, the human race would not even reproduce itself. Motivation is vital for life to continue (Baumeister forthcoming).

Since there exists a body of research on motivation, why not simply discard an old-fashioned and "literary" term such as interest and replace it with a more modern and scientific one, such as motivation?

One reason for *not* doing so, however, is that this would turn the whole analysis into a study in psychology, as opposed to one in sociology. This is a point that both Weber and Parsons have repeatedly made. To this can be added that interests are not exclusively internal; they are at times also located outside of the individual. What makes interest into such a flexible and evocative concept is actually that it often *spans* the individual and the group; the internal and the external; the biological and the social.

A final issue to be discussed is perhaps the most important of all; and it has to do with the way that the notion of interest can be used in concrete analyses. My own stance is that the concept of interest should primarily be seen as a conceptual tool and as part of middle-range sociology. It should definitely *not* be elevated into some kind of general theory. The idea of creating a "sociological interest analysis" makes no more sense than having a conflict sociology. The concept of interest should be one of the key concepts in sociology—as Bourdieu teaches us.

Concluding Remarks

One way of showing how valuable Bourdieu's key contributions to economic sociology are, is to indicate how they may be of assistance in further developing some core concern in economic sociology. In my discussion of the concept of interest I tried to show how this can be done. I began with Bourdieu and then continued to other thinkers and their take on the notion of interest. I distanced myself a bit from Bourdieu in order to exploit the full potential of his ideas. I think that one could also do something similar with his other key contributions, namely his work on Algeria and his attempt to bring in a normative dimension in economic sociology.

Before ending, I would also like to return to the question I mentioned at the outset of this article, namely what can Bourdieu contribute to renewing the current dialogue between sociology and economics? The reader may recall that I think that this dialogue has largely stalled at the moment, with sociologists happily analyzing the economy at one part in the social science universe, and the economists broadening their analysis to include the social, at another.

My general sense is that some ideas in Bourdieus's work might be used to bridge the distance between sociologists and economists or to start off a dialogue. The first of this is his concept of interest. Bourdieu's general formula of *interests + social relations = adequate analysis of economic phenomena*, is something that sociologists as well as economists should be able to subscribe to. One might even say that this formula would maximize the contributions from each side, since sociologists by tradition only analyze social relations (but do this well) and economists only interests (but do this well).

While there is some truth to this argument, it is not the whole truth, and this brings us to Bourdieu's second potential contribution. Charles Manski, for example, has diagnosed the problem of sociology-economics as being something else than sociologists neglecting interests and economists neglecting interests (Manski 2000). Sociologists, Manski instead argues, lack clear concepts, while economists make such strong assumptions that it is hard for them to produce solid empirical analyses. Sociologists, he suggests, should therefore try to develop sharper concepts, and economists try to find a better balance between "strength of assumptions and credibility of findings" (Manski 2000: 125).

Part of this latter enterprise, Manski argues, is for economists to change their attitude to what he calls "subjective data", and to realize that this type of data is not only helpful but indispensable to economic analysis. This brings us to what may be Bourdieu's second contribution to the resumption of a dialogue between economists and sociologists. This is the skill with which he handles subjective data—from his first beautiful ethnographic studies of Algeria to his last study in economic sociology, *The Social Structures of the Economy.*

References

Baumeister, R. Forthcoming. "What do people want?" in *Human Nature in Social Context.*
Bourdieu, P. 1963. "Travail et travailleurs en Algérie: Etude sociologique" in P. Bourdieu et al. *Travail et Travailleurs en Algérie*, Paris: Mouton & Co, 257–389.
——. 1977. *Outline of A Theory of Practice*, Cambridge: Cambridge University Press.
——. 1979. *Algeria 1960: The Disenchantment of the World*, Cambridge: Cambridge University Press.
——. 1986. *Distinction: A Social Critique of the Judgment of Taste*, London: Routledge.
——. 1990. "The interest of the sociologist" in *In Other Words: Essays Towards a Reflexive Sociology*, Stanford: Stanford University Press, 87–93.
——. 1993. *Sociology in Question*, London: SAGE.
——. 1997. "Le champ économique" in *Actes de la Recherche en Sciences Sociales*, 119: 48–66.
——. 1998a. *Acts of Resistance: Against the Tyranny of the Market*, New York: New Press.
——. 1998b. "Is a disinterested act possible?" in *Practical Reason: On the Theory of Action*, Stanford: Stanford University Press, 75–91.

——. 2000. "Principes d'une anthropologie économique" in *Les Structures Sociales de l'Economie*, Paris: Seuil, 233–270.

——. 2002. *Interventions, 1961–2001: Science Sociale & Action Politique*, Marseille: Agone.

——. 2004. "Principles of an economic anthropology" in N. Smelser and R. Swedberg (eds.), *The Handbook of Economic Sociology*, New York and Princeton: Russell Sage Foundation and Princeton University Press, 75–89.

——. 2005. *The Social Structures of the Economy*, Cambridge: Polity Press.

Bourdieu, P. and L. Wacquant. 1992. *An Invitation to Reflexive Sociology*, Chicago: University of Chicago Press.

Bourdieu et al. 1999. *The Weight of the World: Social Suffering in Contemporary Society*, Stanford: Stanford University Press.

Demeulenaere, P. 2001. "Interests, sociological analysis of" in vol. 6 of N. Smelser and P. Baltes (eds.), *International Encyclopaedia of the Social and Behavioral Sciences*, Amsterdam: Elsevier, 7715–7718.

Dobbin, F. 2001. "The business of social movements" in J. Goodwin et al (eds.), *Passionate Politics: Emotions and Social Movements*, Chicago: University of Chicago Press, 74–80.

Greif, A. 2006. *Institutions and the Path to the Modern Economy: Lessons from Medieval Trade*, Cambridge: Cambridge University Press.

Heilbron, J. 2001. "Interest: History of a concept" in N. Smelser and P. Baltes (eds.), *International Encyclopaedia of the Social and Behavioral Sciences*, Amsterdam: Elsevier, vol. 11, 7708–7712.

Hirschman, A. O. 1977. *The Passions and the Interests: Arguments for Capitalism Before Its Triumph*, Princeton: Princeton University Press.

——. 1986. "The concept of interest: From euphemism to tautology" in *Rival Views of Market Society and Other Recent Essays*, New York: Viking, 35–55.

Holmes, S. 1990. "The secret history of self-interest" in Jane Mansbridge (ed.), *Beyond Self-Interest*, Chicago: University of Chicago Press, 267–286.

Manski, C. 2000. "Economic analysis of social interactions" in *Journal of Economic Perspectives*, 14(3): 115–136.

Swedberg, R. 1990. *Economics and Sociology: On Redefining Their Boundaries. Conversations with Economists and Sociologists*, Princeton: Princeton University Press.

——. 2005. *Interest*, Berkshire: Open University Press.

Weber, M. 1946. "The social psychology of the world religions" in H. Gerth and C. Wright Mills (eds.), *From Max Weber*, New York: Oxford University Press, 267–301.

SOCIOLOGY AND THE CULTURAL SCIENCES

MODERNITY AS EXPERIENCE AND AS INTERPRETATION: TOWARDS SOMETHING LIKE A CULTURAL TURN IN THE SOCIOLOGY OF "MODERN SOCIETY"

Peter Wagner

Modernity: Beyond Institutional Analysis

The Current State of Debate

The social sciences of the early post-Second World War decades worked with the assumption that contemporary Western societies, called 'modern societies', had emerged from earlier social configurations by way of a profound rupture. This rupture, although it could stretch over long periods and occur in different societies at different points in time, regularly brought about a new set of *institutions*, most importantly a market-based industrial economy, a democratic polity, based on an idea of national belonging plus rational administration, and autonomous knowledge-producing institutions developing empirical-analytical sciences. Modernity, thus, was located in space, that is: in 'the West', meaning Western Europe and North America, but it tended to get diffused from there and gain global significance. Once such 'modern society' was established, namely, a superior form of social organization was reached that contained all it needed to adapt successfully to changing circumstances. There would, thus, be no further major social transformation. Once it had emerged, modernity stepped out of cultural context and historical time, so to say.

During the 1980s, it was exactly this key conviction of the modern social sciences that was challenged by the idea of 'post-modernity', often understood as the assertion that Western societies had transformed into an entirely new form of social configuration, based on novel forms of social bond. As such, the assertion was most prominently made in Jean-François Lyotard's 'report on knowledge' of 1979, titled *The Postmodern Condition*, but as a hypothesis of an ongoing major social transformation it has guided much sociological research since. At roughly the same time, the spatial connotation of the term was also challenged. The rise of Japan, and other East Asian economies somewhat later, to compete with Western economies in global markets suggested that non-Western forms of modernity could exist. The Iranian Revolution, in turn, inaugurated the idea that modernity could be successfully challenged in societies that had appeared to have safely embarked on the long process of 'modernization'.

This is the context in which the term 'modernity' came into use in sociology. The ideas that modernity was neither established in its final form once and for all nor immune to radical reinterpretations outside of its space of origins was now more readily accepted. Nevertheless, conceptual change in much of sociology remained rather limited. The term 'modernity' tended to replace the earlier concept of 'modern society', but it often simply continued to refer to the history of Western societies since the industrial and market revolutions, and since the democratic revolutions and the building of 'modern', rational-bureaucratic nation-states. In the work of Anthony Giddens, to cite one major example, modernity kept being addressed from the angle of 'institutional analysis', and these institutions are those that arose in the West over the past two centuries. All that happens today is that they undergo an internal transformation towards what Giddens calls 'institutional reflexivity' (Giddens 1990, 1994). This is not a major step beyond Weber's assertion 'that in Western civilization, and in Western civilization only, cultural phenomena have appeared which [...] lie in a line of development having *universal* significance and value' (Weber 1920/1930: 13). The reader may note that I omitted Weber's insert 'as we like to think'; I will come back to this.

With 'modernity', thus, sociology proposes a key concept for understanding socio-historical development, but oddly makes this concept refer to only a single and unique experience. 'Modernity' is one large-scale occurrence the origins of which can be traced in space and time, but which tends to transcend historical time and cover all socio-cultural space. By identifying a concept with a historical social configuration, sociologists conflate theoretical and historical modes of interrogation in a way that is devastating for their whole project. Fortunately, at some point philosophy, anthropology and postcolonial studies tried to come to the rescue of the (other) social sciences. (Rather unfortunate, in turn, was the fact that many of those in peril did not see any danger and did not want to be rescued.)

From the angle of philosophy, with support from the historiography of concepts, the question of concept-formation in the social sciences came under scrutiny. Questioning the facile presupposition that phenomena in the world can always be constructed as empirical 'cases' that are to be subsumed under 'concepts', attention was redirected to the actual 'work' of the concepts, to that which concepts are employed to perform, in social-scientific inquiry. Concepts are proposed not least with the purpose of relating experiences to each other that are otherwise simply separate and different. Particular emphasis was given to the suppression of time in such conceptual labour, by virtue of postulating the timeless validity of concepts. From the angle of anthropology and postcolonial studies, related issues were raised with specific regard to the, so to say, conceptual relation between 'modern' and 'traditional' societies, between colonizers and colonized. While maintaining the suppression of historical temporality, so the critical argument goes, time was here re-instituted into concepts in the mode of a 'denial of co-evalness' (Johannes Fabian). The degree to which a mere application of concepts that were generated in and for a specific context, most often a European one, to other socio-historical situations could be problematic, was often underestimated (Derrida 1978; Lyotard 1979; Koselleck 1979; Fabian 1983; Asad 1995).

Until now, however, it is quite open how such critiques of the conventional social and historical sciences relate to the task of analysing entire social configurations over large stretches of time. Much of the critical work operated in the mode of denunciation and thus tended to discard rather than aim to rethink key concepts of the social sciences. Many of those established concepts, however, do address actual problématiques of human social life, even if they may do so in an overspecific or unreflective way. Thus, work at conceptual *criticism* would also always need to be work at conceptual *retrieval*, i.e. an attempt to understand both the limits and the potential of those concepts. What follows should be seen as a contribution towards a rethinking of the concept 'modernity' in the light of such conceptual retrieval. Starting out from some observations about an existing variety of conceptualizations of 'modernity' in the social sciences, I will claim the need for a spatio-temporally contextualized use of the concept, to then see whether on such a basis something that, with some qualification, one can call European modernity exists and what it looks like.

Varieties of Conceptualizing Modernity

As we have seen, the sociology of modernity operates mostly by means of a distinction between historical eras, by some assumption of a rupture, a major social transformation. Such distinction, however, also demands specification as to how these eras differ, i.e., a conceptualization of what is modern. In other words, the term 'modernity' inevitably carries a double connotation; it is always both philosophical and empirical, or both substantive and temporal, or both conceptual and historical (Yack 1997; Wagner 2001). The conceptual imagery of a 'modern society' as developed in mainstream sociology, characterized by a market-based economy and a nation-based democratic polity, aims to reconcile the historical view of modernity, as the history of Europe, and later the West, with a conceptual view of modernity, namely a social configuration composed of sets of functionally differentiated institutions. It provides the master-case for what I will present here as the first of a variety of possible ways of conceptualizing modernity, namely *modernity as an era and as a set of institutions*.

At a closer look, this imagery sits in an uneasy relation to any array of dates in European history against which one may want to test it. Were one to insist that a full set of functionally differentiated institutions needs to exist before a society can be called modern, socio-political modernity would be limited to a relatively small part of the globe during only a part of the twentieth century. This tension between conceptuality and historicity was resolved by introducing an evolutionary logic in societal development. Based on the assumption of a societally effective voluntarism of human action, realms of social life were considered to have gradually separated from one another according to social functions. Religion, politics, the economy, the arts all emerged as separate spheres in a series of historical breaks—known as the scientific, industrial, democratic revolutions etc.—that follows a logic of differentiation (Parsons 1964; Alexander 1978). A sequence of otherwise contingent ruptures can thus be read as a history of progress, and the era of modernity emerges through an unfolding from very incomplete beginnings. In this view, indeed, modern society came to full fruition only in the US of the post-Second World War era, but 'modernization' processes were moving towards that *telos* for a long time, and have continued to do so in other parts of the world.

In conceptual terms, this perspective on modern social life aimed at combining an emphasis on free human action with the achievement of greater mastery over the natural and social world. The differentiation of functions and their separate institutionalization was seen as both enhancing human freedom and as increasing the range of human action. Thus, it provided a sociologized version of the Enlightenment combination of freedom and reason, or of autonomy and mastery, or of subjectivity and rationality (e.g., Touraine 1992).

In direct contrast to this affirmative, even self-congratulatory conceptualization of modernity, major critical inquiries into the dynamics of modernity were elaborated successively from the middle of the nineteenth century up until the 1930s. This is what I call the *grand critiques of modernity*, the second major mode of conceptualizing modernity. They were grand critiques by virtue of the fact that they identified basic problems in the practices of modernity, but did not on those grounds abandon the commitment to modernity. They all problematized, although in very different ways, the tension between the unleashing of the modern dynamics of freedom and rational mastery, on the one hand, and its, often unintended, collective outcome in the form of major societal institutions, on the other. As such, they provided critical interpretations of the self-understanding of European modernity.

The first such critique was the critique of political economy as developed mainly by Karl Marx. The second grand critique was the critique of large-scale organization and bureaucracy, as analyzed most prominently by Robert Michels and Max Weber. A variant of a critique of conceptions of rationality is the critique of modern philosophy and science, the third grand critique. Weber, too, was aware of the great loss the 'disenchantment of the world' in rational domination entailed, but radical and explicit critiques of science were put forward by others in very different forms. In idealist *Lebensphilosophie* the elaboration of a non-scientistic approach to science was attempted as well as, differently, in early twentieth-century 'Western' Marxism, i.e. by Max Horkheimer and the early Frankfurt School. Synthetically, then, an argumentative figure emerged as follows: In the historical development of modernity as 'liberal' society, the self-produced emergence of overarching structures, such as capitalism and the market, organization and bureaucracy, and modern philosophy and science, is identified. These structures work on the individual subjects and their possibilities for self-realization—up to the threat of self-cancellation of modernity. The more generalized modern practices will become, the more they themselves may undermine the realizability of modernity as a historical project.

This alternative view of modernity, in all its variety, did not really challenge the idea that there is one single form of modernity, emerging in Europe and showing the tendency to transcend time and space. It is thus, despite its critical edge, more a mirror-image than a full alternative to the mainstream sociological view of modernity as the era of functional differentiation. While the critiques of modernity suggested that modernity could not fulfil its promise of increasing both autonomy and rationality in human social life, but tended to undermine both of these commitments, a third, and rather more recent conceptualization of modernity addresses these basic modern commitments from a yet different angle.

Following Cornelius Castoriadis, modernity can be considered as a situation in which the reference to autonomy and mastery provides for a double 'imaginary signification' of social life (Castoriadis 1990; Arnason 1989; Wagner 1994). By this term, Castoriadis refers to what more conventionally would be called a generally held belief or an 'interpretative pattern' (Arnason). More precisely, the two components of this signification are the idea of the autonomy of the human being as the knowing and acting subject, on the one hand, and on the other, the idea of the rationality of the world, i.e. its principled intelligibility. This interpretive approach to modernity, we could say, underlines the importance of the parenthesis 'as we like to think' in Weber's definition of Western rationalism.

With this view, thus, the emphasis shifts from institutions to *interpretations*. Equally starting out from the double concept of autonomy and mastery, even though not in precisely these terms, the sociology of modern society had thought to derive a particular institutional structure from this double imaginary signification. Sociology, for instance, tended to conflate the specific historical form of the European nation-state with the general solution to, as it was often called, the problem of social order, which was expressed in the concept 'society' (Smelser 1997: chapter 3). When assuming, however, that a modern set of institutions can be derived from the imaginary signification of modernity, it is overlooked that the two elements of this signification are ambivalent each one on its own and that the relation between them is ridden with tensions. Therefore, the recent rethinking takes such tensions to open an interpretative space that is consistent with a variety of institutional forms. The relation between autonomy and mastery institutes an interpretative space that is to be specifically filled in each socio-historic situation through struggles over the situation-grounded appropriate meaning. Theoretically, at least, there is always a plurality and diversity of interpretations within this space.[1]

This interpretative approach has, among other features, the merit of having brought the question of autonomy back to the centre of the analysis of modernity, where it had been almost absent during the long period when concerns for functionality, rationalization and, in the critical views, alienation reigned supreme. This leads to the fourth and final conceptualization of modernity that needs to be briefly discussed. A common view of the history of social life in Europe holds that a 'culture of modernity' spread gradually over the past five centuries. This 'is a culture which is individualist [...]: it prizes autonomy; it gives an important place to self-exploration; and its visions of the good life involve personal commitment' (Taylor 1989: 305). Such an emphasis on individuality and individualization is equally alien to the functionalist praise of modern society as to the totalizing critiques of modernity, but it is even quite distant from the more formalized 'modern' discourses of the individual as in rational choice theory or in liberal political philosophy. In literature and the arts, the *experience of modernity* was in the centre of attention and, as an experience, it concerned in the first place the human being in her or his singularity, not an exchangeable atom of social life (Berman 1982). Michel Foucault's lecture 'What is Enlightenment?' very succinctly distinguished between those two readings of modernity. Modernity as an attitude and experience demands the exploration of one's self, the task of separating out, 'from the contingency that has made us what we are, the possibility of no longer being, doing, or thinking what we are, do or think' (Foucault 1984: 46). This view is counter-posed to the one that sees modernity as an epoch and a set of institutions, which demand obedience to agreed-upon rules.

Modernity in Time and Space

In sum, the social sciences have long theorized 'modernity', as the attempt to grasp the specificity of the present, even though the term 'modernity' has been used only rather recently. The dominant strand

---

[1] See Skirbekk 1993. One may argue that the historical critiques of the self-understanding of modernity, as discussed above, can also be regarded as parts of such interpretative struggle over modernity. However, the proponents mostly saw themselves as offering a superior analysis, not one of a possible variety of interpretations.

in the social sciences has aimed at capturing this specificity by struc-
tural-institutional analysis. The modern institutions are here seen as
the embodiments of the promise of freedom and reason. Against and
beyond this dominant strand, three different conceptualizations of
modernity have been proposed. In parallel to the history of the 'modern
social sciences', the critiques of modernity have provided an alternative
institutional analysis, emphasizing the undermining of the promise of
autonomy in and through the workings of the modern institutions.
Both of these views have recently been considered too limited in their
approach, namely in committing themselves to an overly specific understanding of modernity. The research and theory during the past quarter
of a century that explicitly uses the term 'modernity' is by and large
characterized by this insight. The interpretative approach to modernity
has demonstrated the breadth of possible interpretations of what is
commonly understood as the basic self-understanding, or imaginary
signification, of modernity. The conception of modernity as an ethos
and an experience has underlined the normative and agential features
of modernity. In the former sense, it emphasizes the lack of any given
foundations and the possibility to push the 'project of modernity' ever
further. In the latter sense, it accentuates creativity and openness.

Not being able to go here into a full assessment of the conclusions
from this fourfold variety of conceptualizions of modernity, for the
purpose of this article only the following needs to be noted: While we
cannot entirely do without the former two approaches, the institutional
and the critical one, a significant potential to further develop the thinking about modernity lies today with the latter two, the interpretative
and the experiental one. While the interpretive approach provides the
ground for an understanding of the variety of possible forms of modernity, the experiential approach helps to understand why a particular
interpretation may come about in any given setting (for more detail
see now Wagner 2008).

In attempts to combine these insights without abandoning the objective of analyzing spatio-temporally extended configurations, research
interest in what may be called the cultures of modernity has increased
(Friese and Wagner 2000). Such research on the 'varieties of modernity'
or 'multiple modernities' aims at analyzing such wider, present and past,
plurality of interpretations of the modern signification (Eisenstadt 1998).
Despite all accomplishments, however, this novel perspective risks to
merely multiply the forms of modernity by inscribing them into cultural
containers that are coherent and bounded and reproduce themselves

over time. It is overall too strongly shaped by the idea that modernity has a specific and constant basic structure, formed in Europe, but can express itself culturally in different ways, on the basis of older value configurations (see, for example, Eisenstadt 1999: 198). To take the modern commitment to autonomy seriously, however, requires a more open conceptualization of the contexts of modernity, namely as spaces of experience and interpretation, or as 'spatio-temporal envelopes'.[2] In the remainder of this article, I want to illustrate how such an approach could look when applied to the case of Europe.

European Modernity Reconsidered

Thus, Europe will here not be identified with the origin of modernity, but will be regarded as a region of the world—as one among many, but with specificities, which would need to be analysed in terms of spaces of experience and interpretation.[3] Five aspects of the European experience that are significant when aiming to grasp any contemporary specificity of European modernity will be singled out for this purpose. It was possible to arrange them basically chronologically, i.e. roughly and loosely in the order of their emergence and their rise to significance. But these observations are always also of a conceptual nature. Thus, ideally, the following should be an account of modernity that provides a linkage between history and philosophy, though without conflating the two dimensions. It is a historico-philosophical account broadly in the tradition of Jan Patočka's and, more recently, Massimo Cacciari's 'geo-philosophy'.

Europe as a Colonial Power

The reference-point in European history that is the usual starting-point for any sociological narrative of Europe as modernity, namely the

---

[2] Latour 2000. Such a view entails not only that cultures are no longer seen as bounded entities, as populations held together by coherent sets of shared values and beliefs, stable over time, but it also regards culture no longer as a relatively insignificant addendum to structures, functions and institutions, but as a key to understanding modernity, the latter term namely seen as referring to the interpretative and normative ways in which human beings engage their lives with others and the world.

[3] As a region rather than province, even though otherwise the approach followed here is close to Chakrabarty's (2000).

post-revolutionary era from the late-eighteenth century to almost the end of the nineteenth century, will only play a minor role in the following account. This view was historicist (in Dipesh Chakrabarty's sense) and portrayed European history as the history of the realization of freedom and reason. It led from Hegel to Weber, but it keeps serving for self-description and self-understanding up to the present day. The doubts that can be found in Weber are then conveniently overlooked, and later re-elaborations, such as Husserl's attempt at reflection in crisis, entirely ignored. This narrative is too well known to be repeated here.

One aspect of nineteenth-century Europe that was a constitutive component of the identification of Europe with modernity was rarely given central place in accounts of this modernity: Europe as colonial power. The history of colonialism sees Europe certainly as its subject and as the master of the world; it thus emphasizes the modernity of Europe. European history as colonial history establishes precisely the relation between Europe and other parts of the world as relations between 'modernity' and 'tradition', of rupture in temporality and the 'denial of co-evalness'. At the same time, it invited the conceptual distinctions between the 'rational' and the 'cultural', and between the universal and the particular.

However, in terms of an account of modernity as interpretation and experience, one important qualification needs to be made: it was not Europe, but it was the European nation-states that were colonial powers.[4] There is a remark in Edward Said's *Orientalism* about the figure of Mr. Casaubon in George Eliot's *Middlemarch*, which is more significant than the author may have thought: 'One reason Casaubon cannot finish his Key to All Mythologies is [...] that he is unacquainted with German scholarship' (Said 1978: 19). After this unnecessary remark—he did not need to excuse himself—Said embarked on a more complex and hardly sustainable reasoning. On the one hand, he claimed that German scholarship on the East was not in partnership with 'a protracted, sustained *national* interest in the Orient'; thus, it was secondary and not very significant. On the other hand, though, he saw it as sharing with 'Anglo-French and later American Orientalism [...] a kind of intellectual *authority* over the Orient within Western culture.' This statement suggests not only a somewhat off-the-cuff sociology of knowledge; it also

---

[4] For a more detailed and long-term analysis of the changing forms of European political modernity, see Wagner 2005.

compresses intellectual history over quite some space and time into a straight-jacket. It underestimates the variety of 'European' relations to other parts of the world during the nineteenth century and the variety of forms of knowledge that were produced about these other parts, and it suggests too smooth a move, in both respects, to US dominance in the twentieth century, which then just looks like 'more of the same'.

No comment on the contemporary relation between the 'West' and the 'Orient' shall be added here, tempting as it may be, and the nineteenth century will not be discussed further either. At this point, it should just be underlined that the history of the construction of Europe as a region of the world—under its proper name—is a process of, by and large, the last half century only. Possibly, one can say that there was an earlier European history, from at least the Renaissance onwards (some would say from the declining period of the Western Christian Roman Empire) up to the Enlightenment. But as a space of common experience Europe hardly existed during the nineteenth and the first half of the twentieth century, if not as one of the experience of power rivalry between the nation-states. And it did not exist as a space of common interpretation either, given that the national, and often nationalist, view of the world dominated self-interpretation and collective memory. The attempts at creating a space of common interpretation after Nazism and the Second World War were at least in part a response to, and a consequence of, the 'decentering of Europe' in the course of the disastrous first half of the twentieth century. Such decentering was prepared by what has been called a 'break with tradition' in Europe.

The 'Break with Tradition' in Europe

Studies of the 'colonial encounter' (to use Talal Asad's term) often stress the destruction or dissolution of forms of knowledge, of means of interpretation, of situating oneself in the world, as the result of an occurrence. In postcolonial studies, such an encounter is seen as a confrontation with something that comes from the outside. When modernity was thought of in terms of a break with tradition, as it mostly was, that break was seen as an accomplishment, not without frictions certainly, but achieved from within European society and leading to a superior way of engaging with others and the world. There is, thus, in theorizing modernity, at least a dual meaning of the idea of a 'break with tradition', an enabling one if the break comes from within, and a disabling one if the break is imposed, to speak loosely. In this light, I now want to suggest that Europe has undergone, in addition to that break that allegedly set it onto the route of modernity, a second 'break with tradition' that resembles more the breaks that result from a sudden, shock-like encounter with the unknown.

This latter break was in Europe most strongly marked by the experience of the First World War, but in a broader sense its experience stretched from the late nineteenth century to the end of the Second World War. This experience led first of all to the questioning of the concept of the 'rupture' itself as it was constitutive for thinking of the advent of modernity. Rather than using such a notion as an explanatory tool to conceptualise the difference between 'modernity' and 'tradition', it will be taken now as opening the space for a variety of ways to conceive of that relation.

Arguably, this mode of thinking was inaugurated with Friedrich Nietzsche's (1874/1990) 'untimely meditation' on the 'use and disadvantage of history for life'. By distinguishing a multiplicity of ways of relating to the past, Nietzsche opened up this relation to indeterminacy. This step was recognised as well as considerably sharpened and accentuated between the two world wars by thinkers such as Martin Heidegger, Walter Benjamin and later Hannah Arendt. In early writings, already during the First World War, both Heidegger and Benjamin radically questioned the accessibility of the past. Heidegger (1916/1978: 427) emphasised the 'qualitative otherness of past times', which entailed that the past was never available to the present as such, but only through a relation of present valuation. Drawing on Heidegger, Benjamin developed then the ideas about the course of history that he last expressed in the theses 'on the concept of history'. In the essay on the work of art in the age of its technical reproducibility he spoke about 'the shattering of tradition' (1934/1978: 439). Reading Kafka and reflecting about the politico-philosophical choices during the inter-war period, Hannah Arendt later described the present as a 'gap between the past and the future'.

Those interpretations can be related, even though all-too-briefly here, to the experiences of the first half of the twentieth century, especially since the end of the First World War. Already as it was waging, the War meant to many observers the abandonment of any hope that 'modernity' was on an essentially peaceful and progressive path and, with this, it conveyed the undeniable insight that 'modernity' included the possibility of unprecedented horrors. The inter-war years—with hindsight nothing more than an extended cease-fire—witnessed the increasing confrontation between opposed proposals to organise a modernity that had proven more shaky and crisis-prone than its proponents had expected. Then, the Nazi government reopened the War and led it recklessly against the populations of Europe including a major part of its own and the entire European Jewry. When this war was over at mid-century, Continental Europe was emptied of any possibility to resort to tradition. The accumulated experiences of this whole period provide the historical background to the emergence of the philosophical debate about the shattering of tradition.

In the light of these observations, a step towards a reinterpretation of European societal developments during the second half of the twentieth century can be taken. The predominant view sees the social world gradually take its modern organised form during the second half of the nineteenth century up to the First World War in parallel processes of industrialisation, urbanisation, rationalisation (through the modern sciences, but also though bureaucracy) and democratisation in the framework of the nation-state. While some of these processes advance faster than others and in some societies more than in others, everything accelerates after the end of the Second World War, and by the 1960s socio-political modernity is in full place in Northwest Europe and North America. Western modernity seemed to have re-embarked on its successful historical trajectory, if we are willing to believe the standard view. In contrast to this view, I propose to see the struggles over modernity during the first half of the twentieth century and, to speak again loosely, the damages it has inflicted as the major reason for the shaping of European societies after the Second World War. Thus, there was no continuation on a path of modernisation, but conclusions drawn collectively, although with their specific results not necessarily mirroring the intentions, from a historical experience.

This view underlines an overlooked feature of post-war European societies, namely the perceived loss of origins that has now moved far from the philosophical or religious-cosmological issue towards the general impossibility of making actual reference to any 'morality of custom' in everyday social life. The break with all established ways of judging the good, the true and the beautiful was imposed twice—first by the political and military mass mobilisations of the early century and then by the destruction through totalitarianism, war and genocide. And this break was imposed in such a way that large segments of society could not escape the reach of that destruction. The massive material need for reconstruction after the war as well as the re-education programmes in the defeated societies, and the silencing of the rift between resisters and collaborators in the liberated societies, assured the presence of that experience until far into the post-war period.[5]

The Rise of 'Other Modernities'

These observations lead directly to the third aspect of European modernity: During the same period, the early twentieth century, Europeans did not only witness the crisis of their own self-understanding, but at the same time the rise of the US, an occurrence that made it impossible for them to see themselves any longer as the vanguard of modernity, but rather, at best, as one among several modernities. In their relation to the US as a different socio-political configuration, Europeans saw their own modernity as in many respects inferior, especially with regard to technology, economy, organization, and social life, including importantly gender relations, and politics. In significant respects, however, they also saw themselves as still superior, with regard namely to morality and philosophy, thus giving a strong normative tone to many of the writings about America during the interwar period.

Overall, an image of America as 'the other' of Europe emerged (for more detail on the below see Wagner 1999). In brief: 'America' in this view is what we may call *presentist*, that is, without history and tradition. As Ferdinand Tönnies (1922: 356) wrote in 1922 about public opinion in America: 'Its knowledge of the old world, thus of the foundations of its own culture, is rather deficient; it thus lives much more in the present and in representations of the future which are exclusively determined by the present'. America is also *individualist*, that is, there are no ties between the human beings except for those that they themselves create. And it is *rationalist*, that is, it knows no common norms and values except the increase of instrumental mastery, the striving to efficiently use whatever is at hand to reach one's purposes. Again Tönnies (1922:

---

[5] In *A sociology of modernity* (Wagner 1994, chap. 4) I have discussed the tendency of modernity towards self-cancellation as inherent in certain societal implications of the liberal notion of self-regulation; thus, the focus was on self-cancellation of liberal varieties of modernity. Continuing on that train of thought, one might say that the accumulated experiences of the first half of the twentieth century bear witness to a related tendency towards self-cancellation in organised modernity (see for the above reasoning also Wagner 2001, chap. 4).

357), here using Weber's concept of rationality, expresses succinctly his view on American public opinion as 'the essential expression of the spirit of a nation': it is "'rationalistic' [...] in the sense of a reason which prefers to be occupied with the means for external purposes". And, finally, America is what we may call *immanentist*, that is, it rejects the notion of any common higher purpose, anything that transcends the individual lives and may give orientation and direction.

Rather than an enumeration of distinct features, this is a cascade of characteristics where each single one refers to all the other ones. Individualism is directly related to the absence of history, which namely could have been a source of commonalities; and instrumental rationalism may be seen to follow from the absence of any common higher orientation. Trying to condense the imagery even further, we can say that the 'America' the Europeans perceived was the uncontaminated realisation of the modernist principles of *autonomy* and *rationality*. America was *pure modernity*. The significance of this view does not lie in the degree of correspondence to any American reality, and no such claim is intended here, but in the possibility of thinking about modernity in terms of a variety of different socio-political instantiations.

The European experience of a different American modernity, thus, opens the space for an understanding of 'varieties of modernity'. But any such conceptualization advanced but little at this time, because this thinking takes place under the threat of losing all that is important. A highly asymmetrical relation between these two modernities is assumed; and European modernity is no longer the spearhead of progressive history, but becomes a 'tradition of modernity' (Derrida 1989). If we consider the earlier observation of a 'break with tradition' in European modernity together with the one about the rise of 'other modernities', we see how Europe moves closer to the colonized world. A 'decentering of Europe' takes place in the self-awareness of Europeans. It opens a way for, within certain limits, pursuing European studies as subaltern studies.

The Rise of a Self-Critical Attitude to Collective Memory

The final two observations about European specificities refer to the post-Second World War period, and these orientations are in many respects consequences from the insights into the former experiences, i.e. a re-interpretation of the experiences from the first half of the twentieth century. The first of these concern the 'internal' self-understanding of modernity in Europe, the second one its relation to the world, its position in it.

European history between 1800 and 1950, as briefly discussed above, and maybe even too much accepted in the historical and social sciences, is predominantly a history of nation-states. Collective memory during this period gains ever more the form of national memory—across a historical trajectory that reaches from cultural-linguistic theories of the polity in romanticism to national-liberal movements to the so-called national unifications, e.g. of Italy and Germany, to the increasingly aggressive nationalism of the early twentieth century. In this light, the current process of European integration is a quite exceptional occurrence. If conflicts between West European nations are today utterly inconceivable, this is so because of an effective overcoming of the idea of an absolute tie to the national form in the wake of the preceding historical experience.

In terms of political theory, Jean-Marc Ferry (2000) has recently claimed that a 'self-critical attitude towards national historical memory' has become part of the 'ethical substance' of the European polity. There is likely to be too much of an evolutionary understanding in this view, leading straight from Hegel's 'ethical substance' to Habermas' hope for 'expanding normative-political horizons', but nevertheless Ferry captures an important aspect of recent European developments. There is one main addition that needs to be made to this observation; and this addition changes the picture entirely. It needs emphasizing, namely, that this evolution, if it is one, has occurred not in any process of societal rationalization, as modernists including Habermas would prefer, but through the experience of failure, and through the insight into such failure. It takes place against the background of the experience of a break with tradition and of the rise of other modernities. As far as I can see, and obviously without ruling out the possibility of similar developments elsewhere in the world, this pronounced self-critical attitude to collective memory is indeed a specificity of contemporary European modernity. It supports the repositioning of the nations within European history, in terms of what one may call an internal decentering of Europe. This leads me to the final aspect of European modernity that I want to discuss.

European Responsibility in the Current Global Context

The question is whether there is a similar, or at least related, repositioning of Europe within the world, or in other words, whether the combined effect of de-colonization and the rise of a postcolonial intellectual perspective has made a difference for the self-understanding of European modernity. A recent analysis of the transformations of the European development policy discourse towards the African, Caribbean and Pacific countries reveals significant shifts in the self-understanding of European development policy over the past three decades (for details on the below see Karagiannis 2004). In particular, shifts in the use of the term 'responsibility' signal changes in the European attitude to the presence of the colonial past. Responsibility, which was once understood hierarchically, as a responsibility of the Europeans for their colonial past and its consequences, is increasingly understood in an egalitarian way, as a mutual responsibility of European and ACP countries for sustainable development. Parallel shifts in the use of 'efficiency', both in terms of a generally increased importance and in terms of a re-interpretation, appear to reflect experiences in the post-colonial interaction. Efficiency, which was once understood in an 'industrial' sense, that is as using scarce means rationally towards a pre-conceived purpose, namely development, is increasingly used rather in a 'market' sense, that is, in terms of removing obstacles to free exchange, which as such will guarantee a rational outcome.[6]

The analysis in question remains far from any mere denunciation of those shifts—e.g., in terms of an attempt at liberation from historical guilt or of full subordination to a 'pensée unique' of market efficiency—but insists instead on the plurality of possibilities of justification and their ambivalence in any complex constellation such as the one between the EU and the ACP countries. Conversely, such analysis is obviously also far from suggesting that European development policy stands on normatively sound foundations or that it is in any way to be considered adequate to the situation. But it does underline that there has been an ongoing debate about the meaning of European modernity in relation to Europe's former colonies, a debate with a certain degree of sophistication and, more importantly, one that explicitly employs repertoires of moral-political evaluation with a variety of possible outcomes and, indeed, undergoes change over time.

---

[6] The use of the terms 'industry' and 'market' in this sense is borrowed from Boltanski and Thévenot 1991.

Beyond the Modernist Regression

The above attempt at providing a short narrative on a spatio-temporally specific experience and interpretation of European modernity cannot be 'concluded' in a standard way. Suffice it to re-state that recent work on the conceptualization of modernity has demonstrated that modernity is not fruitfully understood as either the superior—more rational—solution to the problem of organizing social life or as an ideology in need of critique or deconstruction. Rather, it should be conceptualized as an interpretive relation to the world that lays bare, or maybe better: brings about, a range of problématiques to which a variety of responses are possible. These responses are then always determined in a situation, defined by its space and its time, that is interpreted as problematic and in which various cultural resources are available for the solution of that which is problematic. Such a view of modernity, even though certainly not uncontested, is philosophically more or less established. However, it still needs to face its 'épreuve de réalité', to use an expression employed by Luc Boltanski and Laurent Thévenot in their political and moral sociology. It yet needs to be shown that it can be translated into a comparative-historical sociology and anthropology, with politico-philosophical sensitivity, of Western and non-Western societies. The preceding reflections were meant to be a small theoretical and historical contribution towards such contextualization of modernity as always specific in space and in time.

References

Alexander, J. C. 1978. "Formal and substantive voluntarism in the work of Talcott Parsons: A theoretical and ideological reinterpretation" in *American Sociological Review*, 43: 177–198.

Arnason, J. P. 1989. "The imaginary constitution of modernity" in G. Busino et al. (eds.), *Autonomie et Autotransformation de la Société: La Philosophie Militante de Cornelius Castoriadis*, Geneva: Droz, 323–337.

Asad, T. 1995. *Anthropology and the Colonial Encounter*, New York: Prometheus Books.

Benjamin, W. 1934/1978. "Das Kunstwerk im Zeitalter seiner technischen Reproduzierbarkeit" in R. Tiedemann and H. Schweppenhäuser, *Gesammelte Schriften*, vol. 1 and 2, Frankfurt/M: Suhrkamp, 431–469.

Berman, M. 1982. *All That is Solid Melts into Air: The Experience of Modernity*, New York: Simon and Schuster.

Boltanski, L. and L. Thévenot. 1991. *De la Justification: Les Économies de la Grandeur*, Paris: Gallimard.

Castoriadis, C. 1990. *Le Monde Morcelé: Les Carrefours du Labyrinthe III*, Paris: Seuil.

Chakrabarty, D. 2000. *Provincializing Europe*, Princeton: Princeton University Press.

Derrida, J. 1978. "Structure, sign and play in the discourse of the human sciences" in *Writing and Difference*, London: Routledge, 280–293.

——. 1989. *Of Spirit: Heidegger and the Question*, Chicago: University of Chicago Press.

Eisenstadt, S. N. 1998. *Antinomien der Moderne*, Frankfurt/M: Suhrkamp.

——. 1999. *Paradoxes of Democracy*, Washington and Baltimore: Woodrow Wilson Center and Johns Hopkins University Press.

Fabian, J. 1983. *Time and the Other*, New York: Columbia University Press.

Ferry, J.-M. 2000. *La Question de l'État Européen*, Paris: Gallimard.

Foucault, M. 1984. "What is enlightenment?" in Paul Rabinow (ed.), *The Foucault Reader*, London: Penguin, 32–50.

Friese, H. and P. Wagner 2000. "When the light of the great cultural problems moves on: On the possibility of a cultural theory of modernity" in *Thesis Eleven*, 61: 25–40.

Giddens, A. 1990. *The Consequences of Modernity*, Cambridge: Polity.

——. 1994. "Living in a post-traditional society" in U. Beck, A. Giddens and S. Lash (eds.), *Reflexive Modernization*, Cambridge: Polity, 59–109.

Heidegger, M. 1916/1978. "Der Zeitbegriff in der Geschichtswissenschft" in *Frühe Schriften*, Frankfurt/M: Klostermann, 413–433.

Karagiannis, N. 2004. *Avoiding Responsibility*, London: Pluto.

Koselleck, R. 1979. *Vergangene Zukunft: Zur Semantik geschichtlicher Zeiten*, Frankfurt/M: Suhrkamp.

Latour, B. 2000. "On the partial existence of existing and non-existing objects" in L. Daston (ed.), *Biographies of Scientific Objects*, Chicago: University of Chicago Press, 247–269.

Lyotard, J.-F. 1979. *La Condition Postmoderne*, Paris: Minuit.

Nietzsche, F. 1874/1990. *Unmodern Observations Unzeitgemäße Betrachtungen*, New Haven: Yale University Press.

Parsons, T. 1964. "Evolutionary universals in society" in *American Sociological Review*, 29 (June).

Said, E. 1978. *Orientalism*, New York: Vintage.

Skirbekk, G. 1993. *Rationality and Modernity: Essays in Philosophical Pragmatics*, Oslo: Scandinavian University Press.

Smelser, N. 1997. *Problematics of Sociology*, Berkeley: University of California Press.

Taylor, C. 1989. *Sources of the Self*, Cambridge, MA: Harvard University Press.

Tönnies, F. 1922. *Kritik der Öffentlichen Meinung*, Berlin: Springer.

Touraine, A. 1992. *Critique de la Modernité*, Paris: Fayard.

Wagner, P. 1994. *A Sociology of Modernity: Liberty and Discipline*, London: Routledge.

——. 1999. "The resistance that modernity constantly provokes: Europe, America and social theory" in *Thesis Eleven*, 58: 35–58.

——. 2001. *Theorizing Modernity: Inescapability and Attainability in Social Theory*, London: Sage.

——. 2005. "The political form of Europe—Europe as a political form" in *Thesis Eleven*, 80: 47–73.

——. 2008. *Modernity as Experience and Interpretation: A New Sociology of Modernity*, Cambridge: Polity.

Weber, M. 1930. *The Protestant Ethic and the Spirit of Capitalism*, London: Allen and Unwin. German original, 1904/1920.

Yack, B. 1997. *The Fetishism of Modernities*, Notre Dame: The University of Notre Dame Press.

GEOCULTURAL SCENARIOS*

Ulf Hannerz

Frontiers can be the zones where cultivated lands shift into wilderness, whether threatening or promising; or they can be borders, more or less contested, between areas under the more or less established control of different parties. As a frontier of sociology, "culture" is of the latter kind. Here is a concept that many disciplines engage with, in the social sciences and in the humanities—some more centrally and perhaps even pedantically, others more occasionally and a bit haphazardly. It is also one that more strictly academic arenas share with public life, in ways which are not entirely simple.

One noteworthy thing about the culture concept is that it is very flexible with reference to scale. In many disciplines the study of culture has thus tended to deal with more circumscribed entities: the cultures of communities, groups or other collectivities, or particular practices, performances, or textual corpuses. Anthropology, my own discipline, too, has tended to take pride in its capacity to understand the local and intimate. There is nothing in principle, however, that prevents us from attempting to take a bird's-eye view, a macroview toward cultural organization and cultural processes.

* The first version of this chapter was written when I was a Sackler Scholar at the Mortimer and Raymond Sackler Institute of Advanced Studies, Tel Aviv University, January–March 2005. I am grateful to the Institute and to the Department of Sociology and Anthropology for excellent working facilities, and to colleagues at the Department for warm friendship, enjoyable exchanges of ideas, and thoughtful hospitality. I have drawn on it for another book chapter in Swedish (Hannerz 2007), in part for a brief intellectual autobiography on the occasion of my receiving an honorary doctorate at the University of Oslo (Hannerz 2006), in an Emeriti Lecture in honor of Gerald D. Berreman at the University of California, Berkeley, in April 2006, and in seminar presentations in the Department of Anthropology, University of St. Andrews, the Department of Social Anthropology, Stockholm University, and the Department of Human Geography, Uppsala University. I am pleased to thank readers and participants for constructive comments. The research is part of my efforts within the interdisciplinary project "Kosmopolit: Culture and Politics in Global Society", based at the Department of Social Anthropology, Stockholm University, and supported by the Bank of Sweden Tercentenary Foundation.

In what follows I will attend to some of the ways that notions of culture have recently figured in the big picture, in scholarship and public argument. I am concerned with varieties of the geocultural imagination. "Geocultural" is probably a somewhat unfamiliar term, although not entirely new.[1] One may say it is a matter of fairly large-scale mapmaking. I will draw on the earthly sense of "geo" to make it refer to the distribution of things cultural, somehow cultural, over territories and their human populations. And the notion of a "geocultural imagination" should suggest that I am really focusing on the way we *think* geoculturally, about the world and its parts, and the main features of those parts.

Some geocultural thinking is indeed very entrenched, taken for granted, and hardly very imaginative. If it used to be true that nation entities seemed to be part of the natural order of things, the upheavals of the latter decades of the twentieth century have perhaps shaken our faith in these at least a little. By now even larger-scale entities such as continents may seem most enduringly given, yet we are at least vaguely aware that these, too, are notions which made their appearance at some point in history, and which may change with time. "Europe" may have emerged perhaps some thirteen hundred years ago, as the Carolingian empire defended itself against the expanding Arabs; now, with the shifting boundaries and two-steps-forward, one-step-backward integration of the European Union, we are again not quite sure what sort of entity it is. The West Indies was fairly quickly discovered to be a misnomer; the Near East, Middle East and Far East are obviously Eurocentric categories; and "the Pacific Rim" emerged as a prominent geocultural category in the late twentieth century. For a period, too—largely the Cold War period—we distinguished between the First, Second and Third Worlds. And most coarsely, we have contrasted "the West and the rest".

Such categories seem to remain basic ingredients in the way we organize our understandings of the world. Having some grasp of them is part of what it means, if not to be human, then to be an at least minimally informed citizen. But then again these are constructs; we realize

---

[1] Immanuel Wallerstein's (1991: 11) use of "geoculture" to refer to "the cultural framework within which the world-system operates" does not seem very clear, and seems too narrowly tied to a mostly present-day global order. Inoguchi (1999) has little in the way of an explanation of his use of a concept of "geocultural networks", but includes Wallerstein among his references; see also note 12.

that in some of this mapmaking there may even be certain identifiable geocultural entrepreneurship involved, and that terms, delineations and characterizations can be vulnerable to critique in one way or other. The late twentieth-century controversy over Orientalism was one conspicuous example of received geocultural thought coming under scrutiny. (Inevitably, perhaps, critical delineations of Occidentalism followed soon after.)[2] We are intrigued, too, by alternative, utopian or dystopian mapmaking fictions. George Orwell's *1984* may be remembered particularly for Big Brother and newspeak, but the global setting was one of three superstates at war: Oceania, Eurasia and Eastasia.

In anthropology, geocultural construction work and critique were early ingredients of the discipline in Europe as well as in North America, in continental *Kulturkreislehre* as well as in the careful mapping of trait distributions to establish the culture areas of Native Americans.

Yet in those days, a century or so ago, these were mostly activities of the ivory tower, where scholars would argue over matters of conceptualization and categorization mostly with their peers. In more recent times, it seems to me that the geocultural imagination has become more volatile, occurring in both academic and public arenas and also crossing the boundaries between them more readily, and more ambiguously.[3] And that may provide reasons to renew our attention to matters geocultural—I would suggest at two levels.

Waves of World Scenarios

What more acutely stimulated my own interest in geocultural ideas (or perhaps "provoked" would be the more appropriate word) was Samuel Huntington's first article about "the clash of civilizations", in the journal *Foreign Affairs* 1993. Here was a very established, prominent international relations theorist retooling for a preoccupation with culture and cultural differences—but then, unfortunately, his understanding of culture turned out to be of a kind that many anthropologists, myself included, were at the same time busily criticizing and rejecting. In Huntington's view

---

[2] For views on Occidentalism see Carrier (1995) and Buruma and Margalit (2004).

[3] For recent concern with what may be described as geocultural conceptions in other disciplines, see e.g. Lewis and Wigen (1997) on "metageography", and Manning (2003) on world history.

of civilizations as timeless, sharply bounded, and mostly hostile to one another, we had a striking example of what we were beginning to refer to as "cultural fundamentalism" (Stolcke 1995).

It was also clear, however, that at the time, in the 1990s, the efforts of Samuel Huntington belonged with a number of other contemporary writings. Briefly, after the end of the Cold War, people habituated for more than a generation to the metaphor of the Iron Curtain and the reality of the Wall could imagine their world anew. A small but lively intellectual industry rose to the challenge, and soon one would learn that this could be the end of history; but then if it was not, the next thing to attend to might be that clash of civilizations, or perhaps jihad versus McWorld, or the electronic herd stampeding through the global market place, or the coming anarchy. The kind of authors I have in mind—apart from Huntington, Francis Fukuyama (1992), Paul Kennedy (1987, 1993), Benjamin Barber (1996), Thomas Friedman (1999), Robert Kaplan (1996, 2000)—should be readily recognizable. Acknowledging that these writings belonged together, Friedman (1999: xviii), the *New York Times* foreign affairs columnist, identified the genre as "The One Big Thing". These were macro-scenarios for a born-again world. I think "scenarios" is the right term because it refers to something rather inclusive, and not least because it points toward the future. More than in much earlier futurist thinking, which had been implicitly inclined to be ethnocentrically Western, there was also a fairly explicit sense of the world as a single place, interconnected but internally diverse.

The 1990s onrush of new (or new-old) interpretive schemes may have slowed down a bit by the time that the decade and the millennium came to an end, but then there was 9–11. Another kind of war was proclaimed, and so there was another wave of global commentary. Perhaps that clash of civilizations was really here now, or maybe anarchy had arrived? Yet if the clashes identified in the 1990s would be further east, there was now possibly also one across the Atlantic, between Europe and America, as the West seemingly fell apart. Americans were now from Mars, and Europeans from Venus (Kagan 2003). And if "civilization" was one old idea coming in for recycling, by the beginning of the new century, "Empire" was also back as a keyword, promoted for one thing by a British star historian (Ferguson 2003) as well as through a noteworthy alliance between the Italian Red Brigades and the Duke University Department of English (Hardt and Negri 2000). Yet someone would still speak up for Atlanticism (Ash 2004), and another Harvard political scientist advised the Empire to use more soft power than hard (Nye, e.g. 2002). Moreover, a centrally placed British diplomat would again propose a "three worlds" scheme, but one of the coexistence and entanglements of premodern, modern and postmodern worlds (Cooper 2003).

In addition, some of the early contributors to the corpus of works I have in mind returned with further writings. He who had identified the adversary relationship between Jihad and McWorld now portrayed a new empire of fear (Barber 2003); he who had seen the rush of the electronic herd in the marketplace now observed that, for reasons of commerce as well as technology, the world had become flat, by which he somehow meant that distances no longer mattered (Friedman 2005); and Samuel Huntington came back home, with a question for his countrymen: *Who Are We?* (2004). In his "clash of civilizations" thesis, a sort of large-scale identity politics, he had argued that it was important for the West to stick together; hence no multiculturalism. Now this theme reappeared, as Huntington dwelt on the lack of patriotism among the elites, and the insufficient assimilation of the Mexican-Americans.

The Geopolitical and the Geocultural: Borders and Flows

The number of writers I have alluded to may be about ten or fifteen, and their relevant writings, in the form of books, would be a somewhat larger number. Again, then, what they have produced we may call scenarios; are they also "geocultural"?

Perhaps some more, some less. With regard to Hardt's and Negri's (2000) vision of Empire, and the "multitude" which would eventually rise against it, commentators have noted that it seldom touches ground anywhere in particular, so there is nothing very "geo" about it, and culture does not get much explicit attention either. Although Fukuyama looked toward "the end of history" from a different location on the political scale, one could say something similar about his work. So these writers are perhaps not so directly relevant to our interest here, although they belong with the other scenario writers in certain ways. Obviously, too, those various gazes into possible futures are in large part primarily about the distribution of power in world space: about geopolitics, to use the much more well-established concept apparently set in circulation some ninety years ago by Rudolf Kjellén (1916). Yet in different ways, many of these scenarios do somehow bring culture in, more centrally than works of geopolitics have usually done. This may entail a change in geopolitical thought, in the disciplines and professions normally occupied with it, but it seems also to reflect changes in the world that such thought has to deal with.

For Samuel Huntington, there is an expansion of the arena of world politics—or in a way a return to an older sense of divisions—as the clash of civilizations follows after the past clash of ideologies. Robert Cooper, the British diplomat, recurrently described as Tony Blair's foreign policy guru, is equally clear on this. "Foreign policy would be easy if it weren't for the foreigners", writes Cooper (2003: 88), and it is important to realize that the end of the Cold War brought a new situation. Until then, Western policy had mostly dealt with countries and people from cultural traditions likewise more or less Western. In the new era problems will come from cultures little understood in the West. Cooper commends the wisdom, on the part of the Pentagon, of commissioning "one of America's greatest anthropologists" to write a study of Japanese society at the end of World War II.[4] Yet Cooper and Huntington are not altogether in agreement. Where Huntington sees a frozen *longue durée* of global identity politics, Cooper is more open to process and change, looking toward diplomatic work to increase order and trust in a varied but fluid environment.

But it is not only the cultural differences conventionally identified at such levels as nations, regions or civilizations that may increasingly lead geopolitical thought toward taking culture into account. Inter-national relations in the literal sense seem no longer to have the autonomy they used to have. There is a degree of embedding of geopolitics in some more complex whole which may also make the, if not holistic, let us at least say contextualizing tendency of cultural imagery attractive. Border-crossing politics is increasingly conducted by other actors than states, with different understandings, different motives. Among the actors are also transnational business conglomerates, NGOs, diasporas, and for that matter crime syndicates. In addition, there is the debated issue of what impact the media, as cultural technologies, with peculiar capacities and biases of representation, now have on the conduct of politics, both domestic and across borders.

So much for the cultural in geocultural, in its obvious affinity to the geopolitical. As to the "geo", my sense is that two key terms sum up

---

[4] The anthropologist in question, of course, was Ruth Benedict, and the resulting book *The Chrysanthemum and the Sword* (1946).

many of the scenario preoccupations. Broadly it is a matter of flows and borders. Borders are sites of difference, of discontinuity in cultural distributions. Flows involve diffusion, redistributions, passages of culture in space, not least across borders; the new appearance of ideas, symbols and practices identified with one territory in another territory.

Samuel Huntington thus wants to draw new attention to some very old cultural borders. These are the fault lines between civilizations, where, in his view, battles are fought—an oft-quoted formulation from his *Foreign Affairs* article is that "Islam has bloody borders". For Robert Cooper, the British diplomat, in contrast, it is a maxim of foreign policy that not only interests but also identities can be negotiated. Borders can go away. Creating a Europe that learns to disregard old battlefields is his obvious example. But then when Robert Kagan turns Americans into Martians and Europeans into Venusians, on the basis of a difference in "strategic cultures", he discovers a new border, emergent in recent times. This, however, is a border that an Atlanticist such as Timothy Garton Ash (2004) refuses to accept, so borders are also contestable. A controversial new geocultural entity, Eurabia, begins to show up here and there, also in the writings of the historian Niall Ferguson (2004b:36, 2004c), otherwise most prominent for his celebration of empires. Eurabia emerges as rapid population growth in North Africa and the Middle East spills over into European cities. ("Londonistan" is a similar construct; see Phillips 2006.) One may see a parallel between this notion and Huntington's recent view of Mexican-Americans in the United States.

Benjamin Barber's book title, as alluded to before, *Jihad vs. McWorld: How Globalism and Tribalism are Reshaping the World*, includes both flow and borders, and opposes them to one another. For a further prominent example of flow-thinking I would point to another Harvard political scientist, Joseph Nye, and his numerous writings on "soft power" (e.g. 1991, 2002, 2004). "Hard power" in Nye's terminology is political power in a narrower sense, not least military power, as well as economic power; all command power. At first glance perhaps a somewhat para-doxical notion, "soft power", in contrast, is said to co-opt rather than coerce people; "if I can get you to *want* to do what I want, then I do not have to force you to do what you do *not* want to do" (Nye 2002: 9). This sounds much like a certain older concept—soft power seems to have a great deal to do with hegemony.

In large part, soft power involves culture, and what Nye is concerned with is primarily American soft power. Nye sees American values as projected in a multiplicity of ways, through higher education or through foreign policy, but not least through popular culture. With time, however, Nye (2004b) has been disturbed by a decline in American soft power, as the increasing use of hard power has subverted the credibility of soft cultural assets. Perhaps Nye does not offer an explicit map of the world and its current divisions, but the German publicist Joseph Joffe, whom he quotes, concludes that American soft power at present "rules over an empire on which the sun never sets". That certainly is a geocultural conception.

Scenarios Under Scrutiny

Now how might we approach these recent waves of products of the geocultural imagination? One important way, certainly, is to scrutinize them as texts, according to scholarly criteria, evaluating their handling of concepts and facts, coming to a judgment on their credibility, at times offering alternatives, in a sort of peer-review fashion. Generally, the academic response to the "One Big Thing" cluster of writings has not been overly enthusiastic. Huntington's "clash of civilizations" scenario has probably received more attention than most of the others.

In the *American Journal of Sociology*, Edward Tiryakian (1997) was mostly favorable, concluding that the study "draws on a large literature and utilizes important empirical documentation", and that it is "a major launching pad for reconceptualizing the world order and its major units of analysis." As far as I know, no major anthropological journal reviewed Huntington's book at the time of its publication, but later on, in a book with the title *Why America's Top Pundits are Wrong*, a group of mostly American anthropologists have somewhat polemically discussed the writings by Samuel Huntington, Thomas Friedman, and Robert Kaplan, as well as a number of commentators on quite other topics (Besteman och Gusterson 2005).[5] One historian reviewer (Marks 2000) has described the clash of civilizations argument as "bad history in at least five ways", which he proceeds to identify—showing, perhaps, that disciplines can have bloody borders, too.

---

[5] I have also dwelt on several of the scenario writings elsewhere (Hannerz 2003, 2004: 226–233). For other anthropological comments see e.g. Herzfeld (1997a) on Huntington's "clash of civilizations", Lomnitz (2005) on Huntington's *Who Are We?*, and Richards (1999) on Kaplan's "coming anarchy".

At a most general level, scholarly inspection may be directed to the uses and misuses of notions of culture. We certainly knew from before that a rhetoric of culture—"the culture of" this, "a culture of" that—is often employed merely to suggest something pervasive, enduring, and rather fuzzy. When newcomers, perhaps with considerable accumulated academic power but in this context usually dilettantes, engage in culturespeak, they often still do not get much further. In anthropology, as certain dangers connected with the culture concept have been identified and as uses exemplifying such dangers have diffused in public discourse, some commentators have proposed that the concept should be discarded altogether. Elsewhere I have argued that we should indeed pay attention to such uses, but that we may more constructively be whistleblowers rather than abolitionists (Hannerz 1996: 30–43, 1999). In the current context, this is certainly not to insist on the superiority of some purely cultural interpretation of the world, its divisions and alignments (and thus to provoke the further spread of "culturalism" and "culture talk" as derogatory labels for certain kinds of imprecise or exaggerated claims).[6] It is rather to suggest, on the basis of the kind of more subtle understandings of culture and cultural processes we possibly have now, what geocultural scenarios are more or less intellectually viable, and also to identify what may be their limitations, what qualifications need to be made, what we see as the interplay between the cultural and whatever may be noncultural. We may find it instructive here to try and figure out what sort of assumptions about cultural processes and mechanisms could possibly underlie the kinds of formulations we find in scenarios, even as their authors do very little to make them explicit. How would Huntington's civilizations achieve their extreme *longue durée*, and how—and among whom—have Kagan's different American and European "strategic cultures" presumably evolved?

Then the scholarly scrutiny of geocultural scenarios could also turn to the specifics of proposed borders and flows. It is worth noting that Alfred Kroeber (1952: 154), an ancestral figure of American anthropology (also active in conceptualizing culture areas), already more than a half-century ago emphasized "the interflow of cultural material between civilizations." Furthermore, he cautioned that one should examine

---

[6] For one example of such critique of "culture talk", see the political scientist Mamdani (2005: 148), criticizing Samuel Huntington's perspective toward Islamist politics.

civilizations "not as static objects but as limited processes of flow in time" (Kroeber 1952: 404). Both points could stand as central criticisms of Huntington's view today. By now, too, when so much ethnographic activity focuses on deterritorialization, virtuality, diasporas, hybridity, creolization and commodity chains, a great deal more could no doubt be said about views of well-bounded, clashing civilizations as well as about overly homogenizing views of McWorld.

A Transnational Collective Consciousness

Yet as I said before, the geocultural scenarios are a genre which has come to interest me at more than one level. Increasingly I have come to view them not only as a certain number of texts on a library shelf, but as significant components in a transnational collective consciousness, a set of representations of the world which are circulated, received and debated in a world-wide web of social relationships, and which again stimulate further cultural production. It is not that I take the question of the truth claims of these texts lightly, but that seeing them as cultural artifacts, I become curious as well about their style and patterning. It becomes a matter, too, of seeing the geocultural imagination as orga-nized through communities and networks, and through what already C. Wright Mills (1963: 406) termed a "cultural apparatus". I will offer only some preliminary observations here.

I was perhaps first drawn in this direction toward the end of the 1990s, when I could find piles of the Huntington book on clashing civilizations in bookstores not only in New York but also in Frankfurt, or Florence, or Tokyo, either in the original or in translation. By now a number of the scenario authors seem to have taken the step into airport literature, the titles we find in the bookstalls at Stockholm-Arlanda or London-Heathrow or Changi Airport, Singapore. This cultural complex is apparently no longer only a matter of books and journal articles either—"the clash of civilizations", I have been told, is now available as computer game.

Let us give some thought to the people who produce scenarios. We have here a rather mixed group of authors: political scientists, histori-ans, diplomats, journalists. Mostly, they are American (I might even say northeastern seaboard). A few are British, although they may then well be transatlantic commuters: Timothy Garton Ash and Niall Ferguson, both historians, have recently had academic appointments on both sides. On a right-left political scale, one would probably place them in somewhat different positions, some perhaps more neoliberal, others neoconservative, perhaps someone identifiable as center or vaguely center-left. At least those I have in mind are all men.

It is probably fair to say that the circle of scenarists shows a certain network density. These commentators on the world and its future quite often refer to each other, comment on each other, review each other, debate with one another, occasionally interview one another and write blurbs for the back covers of each other's books. I also note with some interest that when *Prospect*, the British journal of opinion, identified one hundred leading global public intellectuals in its October, 2005, issue, the list included nine of the scenario authors.[7] That seems to say something about the current prominence of their line of work. But if the notion of "public intellectuals" has recently reached a new level of popularity, another label would likewise be relevant for the scenario writers. They tend to be also "organic intellectuals", the kind of people who refine and explicate the perspectives of a certain political class of which they are in some way members. Several of them—Huntington, Kagan, Nye, Fukuyama—have served in Washington in one administration or the other. The acknowledgements of Robert Cooper's book *The Breaking of Nations* inform us that its second part was "originally intended to be a short note for the Prime Minister to read at Christmas" (Cooper 2003: vi). Those who have not been so directly involved in government may at least have become accustomed to being read and listened to there. Rumor has it that Robert Kaplan's earlier book on the Balkans was read in the White House and played a fateful role in the American reluctance to intervene in the early 1990s conflicts in the region; that his "coming anarchy" article from *The Atlantic Monthly* circulated quickly by fax among ministries and embassies across the world; and also that the more recent book *Imperial Grunts* (2005) became presidential reading during the Christmas holiday.

If it does not seem too difficult to identify the central circle of scenario producers, however, it is also clear that it is surrounded, not just by lay audiences, but by other people who have a special interest

---

[7] Robert Cooper, Niall Ferguson, Thomas Friedman, Francis Fukuyama, Timothy Garton Ash, Samuel Huntington, Robert Kagan, Paul Kennedy and Antonio Negri are on the *Prospect* list. There is one anthropologist, Clifford Geertz, and three who are identified as wholly or partly sociologists: Anthony Giddens, Fernando Henrique Cardoso, and Slavoj Zizek.

in the products, consuming them, commenting on them, and doing somewhat parallel work. At about the time when I started becoming interested in these scenarios, I was engaged in a study of the work of newsmedia foreign correspondents (Hannerz 2004). And I could note that in shaping the geocultural imagination, the correspondents and their editors, on the one hand, and the scenario writers, on the other, faced some of the same challenges, and could become entangled with one another as they sought solutions. Foreign news writing needed story lines, reasonably enduring major interpretive frameworks. For several decades in foreign news, then, the Cold War had been a global story line. When it was gone, the foreign correspondents and their editors faced more or less the same kind of challenge which had provoked Huntington, Friedman, Kaplan and others to look for the next "One Big Thing".

In a conversation I had in the late 1990s with Bill Keller, who was then the foreign editor of the *New York Times*—he is now the executive editor—he mentioned that he had recently for the first time posted a correspondent in Istanbul. Turkey was an increasingly interesting meeting point between East and West, he said, although "you don't have to believe this stuff about a clash of civilizations." And then later on, even though this scenario has been heavily criticized and frequently rejected, the "clash of civilizations" in fact seems to have turned into a substitute for the Cold War as a major story line. It came up quickly and widely again after 9–11, and in 2006 at least in Scandinavian media, after the Danish newspaper *Jyllandsposten* had commissioned a set of caricatures of the Prophet Muhammad, and crowds protested in Palestine, Syria, Lebanon, Pakistan and elsewhere, burning an embassy in one city and a consulate in another, in a rather improbable *jihad* against Denmark.

One could speculate again on the impact of one scenario bestseller as the dominant story line in reporting on India has recently seemed to change, from a theme of grinding poverty to one of industrial and service outsourcing, with Bangalore perhaps replacing Calcutta as favorite dateline for feature stories. Thomas Friedman, with his *The World is Flat* (2005) book, may at least have hurried that shift along. But then here categories become particularly blurred, as Friedman is also a regular foreign affairs columnist, and moreover hosted a series of television reports with the same message.

Among the more thoughtful of the foreign correspondents—and there are many of them—how story lines work, and their limits, and their consequences, are a topic of enduring concern. Perhaps on the whole, in the marketplace of news, the story lines of journalists and the book-length scenarios operate according to complementary logics: the story lines allow audiences to come back to the next instalment in a series of sufficiently familiar products, the scenarios offer a more self-contained and complete vision of proclaimed change and discontinuity. But there are interactions between scenarios and storylines; and it should be clear that the relationship is hardly one-way, but more symbiotic. As you check the footnotes of the scenarios, you find that their empirical evidence is often from journalism—the *New York Times*, the *Washington Post*, the *Boston Globe* (home town newspaper of Harvard faculty), *Wall Street Journal*, *Financial Times*, *The Economist*. Story lines may already be at work here.

Articles, Books, Soundbites

On the basis of even the rough sketch of the background and positioning of the authors I have given, we can perhaps gain a sharper sense of the scenarios as something like a genre of writing. We may be inclined to scrutinize them critically from a scholarly standpoint, but they are really in the borderlands of academia, politics and the marketplace. The authors may be political animals, with agendas, but this is also geocultural imagination in commodity form. Perhaps we could think of it as a sort of hybrid genre, where academics can act like journalists, and journalists are treated as gurus. Intriguingly, two of the political science professors in the circle, Benjamin Barber and Joseph Nye, have also written novels—possibly a sign of a personal inclination toward genre experimentation.

As often noted, in a typical trajectory a scenario enters public life in a brief version in some more or less authoritative American journal of opinion—*Foreign Affairs*, *Foreign Policy*, *The National Interest*, *The Atlantic Monthly*—and then soon enough grows into a book, which may or may not appear to add much to the first conceptualization. And even when the authors are academics, they publish these books mostly with trade presses, not university presses.[8]

---

[8] Hardt and Negri published *Empire* (2000) with Harvard University Press; four years later, when *Multitude* (2004) appeared, it was with Penguin Press.

While articles grow into books, however, it is at least as important that on the other hand, the original also frequently offers the message encapsulated in some even briefer formulation. Again, what above all enters the popular geocultural imagination are those seductive sound-bites: "the end of history", "clash of civilizations", "Americans are from Mars, Europeans are from Venus", "the world is flat", "soft power". Newly discovered territories, and newly imagined borders, also have news value: Eurabia.

As the authors comment on one another, or as other thinkers and writers comment on them, their conceptions and key terms are taken apart and put into play in further multiplying forms and combinations. Niall Ferguson (2004a: 106) describes the Middle East as a "civilization of clashes". Another historian, Timothy Mitchell (2002: 3), describes the involvement of transnational capitalism with conservative Islam as—"if one wants to use these unfortunate labels"—McJihad. Timothy Garton Ash's (2004: 218) label for a certain kind of cultural relativism is "vulgar Huntingtonism".

The capsule formulations may not always be understood precisely in the way their authors had in mind, however, so the game can be a little treacherous. Repeatedly the authors complain that they have been misunderstood. Fukuyama (1995), looking back at the reception of his "end of history" argument, lists Margaret Thatcher, Mikhail Gorbachev, the first President Bush, and Hosni Mubarak among the persons who, noting in their speeches that history still goes on, had rejected what they had thought was his thesis. And a friend had sent him a cutting from a newspaper in Dhaka, Bangladesh, where a columnist had noted that a Bangladeshi had been bumped from a British Airways flight; thus there was still racism in the world, and history had not ended. Joseph Nye (2003) starts out from an exchange between George Carey, ex-archbishop of Canterbury, and Colin Powell, US Secretary of State, at the World Economic Forum, Davos, about the uses of soft power, to try and explain his concept once more.

The Present, the Near Future, and the World

In the introduction to my study of foreign correspondents, I described it as a case of "studying sideways": a case of an anthropologist engaging with a craft in some ways parallel to his own, reporting, representing, interpreting across distances, from one part of the world to another.[9] Approaching the people in the scenario trade is surely another case of studying sideways. As I also noted in the earlier context, there is a certain tension in such study. We may be a little too inclined to judge them entirely by our own standards, instead of accepting that they are a tribe not quite like our own. Certainly there can be nothing wrong in evaluating their truth claims, but beyond that, perhaps there could be room for a certain charity, and even some occasional humility, normally a part of the way an anthropologist does ethnography. I believe I learned some of that as I talked, for example, to "Africa correspondents", with the impossible task of covering a continent. There may be times when the scenario writers, be they academics or journalists, have unusual access to people and events, and put things together in innovative ways which suggest lines of further inquiry to anthropologists, or sociologists, as well.

Perhaps points of view toward time are among those areas where scenario writers, journalists and anthropologists have related interests. It used to be that anthropologists, to the extent that they did not self-consciously stay in the present, mostly looked back to the past, to ethnographic salvage and reconstruction. But we now also turn increasingly to the future, to people's hopes and fears, and to the emergent.[10] So how are we to understand forward views?

In another review of Huntington's scenario, one commentator suggests that it shows a streak of fatalism: "His argument that wars in the future will be conflicts of civilization shifts the responsibility for those wars from the realm of human volition and political decision to that of cultural predestination." (Pfaff 1997: 96) Little room for agency, then; but also in response to Huntington, a fear has been expressed that if enough people take this scenario seriously, it could turn into a self-fulfilling prophecy. Yet the opposite is likewise possible. If scenarios credibly depict tendencies which we find unattractive and even dangerous, we may do something about it—and then they become self-destructing

---

[9] "Studying sideways" is of course a notion related to Nader's (1972) conception, well-known in anthropology, of "studying up".

[10] For recent considerations of the future in anthropological study, see Malkki (2001), Fischer (2003: 37–58), Miyazaki (2003) and Appadurai (2004).

prophecies. Of course, the chances of the scenarios becoming self-fulfilling or self-destructing may to a degree depend on who the scenarists are. The kind of authors we have identified, organic intellectuals again, could possibly exercise some influence of their own.

Anyhow, with regard to the question what this image-making is for, we should hardly see it as a matter of forecasts, as attempts to really predict. We know that the human sciences tend not to do very well in predictive exercises. We would be better off viewing the scenarios rather as somewhat elaborate conversation pieces. The scenario writers surely have their own particular agendas, but together their claims and visions become instruments of debate and deliberation, form part of the self-monitoring of a reflexive society.

But then whose conversation, whose debate and deliberation, in what society? It is obvious enough why American critics may describe Thomas Friedman, Samuel Huntington, Robert Kaplan and others as "America's top pundits". Their texts often show that they are primarily intended for American readers. These are stories that Americans tell themselves about themselves and their own place in the world. Even so, the rest of us do read them, too, if only over the natives' shoulders. I am interested here, consequently, in a double passage of concepts and conceptualizations: to a degree between academic and public discourse, but also within global society.

In the occasional instance a geocultural innovation may move in another direction. The origins of the notion of "Eurabia" are still a bit obscure to me. I have said that it appears in the writings of Niall Ferguson, the British historian. One less-known British-based writer, originally from the Jewish community in Egypt and writing mostly under the name Bat Ye'or (e.g. 2005), has promoted it particularly energetically, but without so much visibility. The recently deceased Italian journalist Oriana Fallaci (2006) clearly played a part in spreading it. But then in the next move it has been picked up not least by what I gather are right-wing web sites in the USA. By the summer of 2006, it was also the rubric of a cover story of *The Economist*, the newsweekly, with a British base but with a wide transatlantic circulation, and perhaps that will turn out to be important in its further diffusion. On the whole, nevertheless, passages have mostly been from the United States outwards. The dominance of American scenarios can itself be seen as an instance of cultural flows. Yet I think some of the more interesting questions about them begin there, because their reception elsewhere does not seem entirely passive, smooth, and altogether predictable.

I am struck again and again by the fact that language diversity remains a very effective obstacle to the global flow of knowledge and ideas. Only the Anglophone language area is now really wide-open at least to informed citizens of the world.[11] Beyond it, the world as a space of intellectual activity remains remarkably opaque, not only to Anglophones but to all others as well. Compared to all that gets said and written in its languages, translations remain scarce. As far as the scenarios are concerned, they certainly find readers the world over in the original, but then at least some of them are translated, sooner or later, into other languages. The translation of Huntington's 1996 book into Swedish appeared ten years later—obviously its thesis has long been reasonably well-known to most members of the Swedish book-reading public that would care, and one might wonder what finally made this an attractive publishing project.

Yet what happens in the next step? What have been the responses to the scenarios as they enter other milieux? That is hardly so clear to us, insofar as this work of interpretation, commentary and critique proceeds in a number of other languages. Occasionally we can catch a glimpse of how, through acts of intellectual brokerage, the scenarios pass into regional or national debates, and how in the latter debates they can get entangled with local arguments and divides. Tsygankov (2003), an international relations scholar based in the United States, reports on the Russian reception of "the end of history" and "the clash of civilizations" that Fukuyama's perspective was initially viewed more favorably among Russian liberals, in the final period of Soviet decline. With its emphasis on deep-lying differences and on conflict, the Huntington scenario, arriving on the scene a little later, could meet a certain understanding among those intellectuals and politicians still preoccupied with the centrality of the state, and not least among remaining national communists. Yet in the end neither view was acceptable to Russians, Tsygankov argues, due to their ethnocentrism; and so he concludes that those theorists who wish to be influential across borders which are both political and cultural need to take some responsibility for framing their ideas so as to make them more fit to travel.

Recently when I spent a few months as an academic visitor in Tokyo, I had some opportunity to learn of Japanese responses to some of the

---

[11] On the global sociology of language, and the current preeminence of English, see de Swaan (1993).

geocultural scenarios. Much of the local comment and debate was obviously carried out in Japanese, and consequently hidden to me.[12] But through English-language journals or journals of translation, and through conversations with colleagues, I could at least get some idea of what was thought and said also behind what has been referred to as the "*kanji* curtain" (Arnason 2002).

In certain Japanese circles, colleagues would suggest, there had been a measure of sympathy with Huntington's "clash of civilizations" argument because of his anti-multiculturalism stance; this resonated with fairly widespread preferences for a homogeneous society in the Japanese context. Otherwise, however, there were various more critical views. In this country which had been involved in what Huntington might see as two major civilizational clashes, in the Russo-Japanese War a hundred years ago, and then in World War II, there were still those commentators who preferred to see civilizational encounters as culturally productive. Someone following debates in contemporary international politics would point out with a measure of irony that Huntington, who a few years earlier had depicted Japan as an adversary, now wanted this civilization as an American ally in the coming conflict with China. And generally, the geocultural and geopolitical perspectives seemed to be from Japan westwards, toward East and Southeast Asia, or eastwards, across the Pacific toward the United States. From this vantage point, Islamic civilization was not really in the neighborhood.

By the time I was in Tokyo, however, the Huntington scenario was no longer so much in the news among Japanese academics or other

---

[12] A major exception is the work of Takashi Inoguchi (e.g. 1999), University of Tokyo political scientist, who is unusual both in creating his own synthesis of Occidental scenarios and in feeding it back into transnational discussions. I could hardly do justice to his perspective here, but he boldly identifies three major paradigms in global politics, "Westphalian", "Philadelphian" and "Anti-Utopian", and proceeds to link the geopolitical dimensions of these to geoeconomic and geocultural dimensions. If Henry Kissinger stands for Westphalian geopolitics, Fukuyama is Philadelphian and Huntington Anti-Utopian. Along the geocultural dimension Benedict Anderson is Westphalian, Benjamin Barber is in the Philadelphian column with McWorld and in the Anti-Utopian with Jihad, and he shares the latter place with Robert Kaplan and the approach of anarchy. Inoguchi's favored sources for the geoeconomic dimension of his paradigms are Alexander Gershenkron for the Westphalian, Robert Reich for the Philadelphian, and David Landes for the Anti-Utopian. The labels for two of the paradigms are obvious enough; the choice of "Philadelphian" is based on the American historical connection between that city and the concept of popular sovereignty.

Inoguchi's point of view and terminology may not be altogether in line with what has been said here, but his work clearly exemplifies how the scenarios can serve as transnational intellectual currency.

commentators. Instead, it appeared that the notion of soft power was one with a certain appeal. And just as Huntington's critique of multi-culturalism had to a degree been domesticated, one could discern that soft power could become "made in Japan". The part played by popular culture was again central. Japanese popular culture has recently dif-fused widely in East Asia; and as far as the relationship between culture and politics is concerned, the point was made that especially members of the younger generation in other parts of the region, enthusiastic about new tunes and new idols out of Tokyo and Osaka, are after all less inclined to take over those anti-Japanese sentiments which among older people still go with memories of conquest and occupation from the earlier decades of the twentieth century.

This Japanese experience made me a little curious about the contin-ued career of the concept of soft power, so to learn something about this I tried it out on Google. There were a great many hits, most of them certainly relating to Joseph Nye and the American sources. I found it interesting, however, to see how commentators in the media in varied parts of the world have now made use of the idea in their own ways.

On the eve of an annual gathering of China and Southeast Asian nations in Beijing, the venerable Communist party organ the *People's Daily* (2004) notes the rise of China's soft power. Among the youth of the region there is a fascination with Chinese popular culture, even as it is true that some of it does not come from the mainland but from Hong Kong and Taiwan. In *The Hindu*, the quality daily newspaper out of Chennai (previously Madras), another columnist notes that India has Bollywood which makes Syrian and Senegalese movie goers look at the country with stars in their eyes. And India has fashion designers, and Misses World and Universe, and software developers; and above all it has free media, energetic human rights groups, and the recurrent spectacle of remarkable general elections which make it an example of the successful management of diversity—so "let us not allow the spectre of religious intolerance and political opportunism to undermine the soft power which is India's greatest asset in the world of the 21st century" (Tharoor 2003). Elsewhere again, the *Mail & Guardian*, a South African weekly of news and commentary, reports on the show of two South African artists at a New York gallery. Although they may not know it, the writer points out, by communicating the values of diversity, open-ness and tolerance, they represent the soft power of South Africa to the world (Barns 2003).

The arts correspondent for the *Mail & Guardian* indeed identifies Joseph Nye as the originator of the term. The *People's Daily* does not. It seems the term is just passing into the global collective consciousness, and that moreover soft power is no longer entirely US property. Generally it seems understood that it is something nations (or possibly regions, such as Europe) can have, and that it is something they should be aware of and carefully cultivate. Moreover, they should avoid exhibiting undesirable characteristics that would detract from the buildup of such power. The concept thus comes to work as a new tool of self-reflexivity—what are we in our country good at, how do we want to be perceived by others? It is the opposite, it seems, of what Michael Herzfeld (1997b) has referred to as "cultural intimacy", those characteristics which may be recognized at home, but which become a bit embarrassing when noticed by the outside world.

Soft power, clashing civilizations, flat earth—by way of conclusion, let me first note that probably few ways of writing culture have recently been so effective on a worldwide basis in reaching wider publics, and provoking conversations and debates about the actual present, and desirable and undesirable futures, as some of these exercises in the geocultural imagination. We can respond to them in different ways. We can and should scrutinize them as representations of the world. We should also try to understand how they work. As things are now, they move within the global center-periphery structure, as instances of American soft power. So there we are—we may much prefer soft power to hard power, but then again, if not spread out among India, China, Japan, South Africa or wherever, soft power has much to do with hegemony, and we may not be entirely enthusiastic about that either. If the global conversation about the future could be less one-sided, allow more voices, people from all corners talking back, could that also point to a way out of an empire of fear?

References

Appadurai, A. 2004. "The capacity to aspire: Culture and the terms of recognition" in V. Rao and M. Walton (eds.), *Culture and Public Action*, Stanford, CA: Stanford University Press.
Arnason, J. P. 2002. *The Peripheral Centre*, Melbourne: Trans Pacific Press.
Ash, T. G. 2004. *Free World*, New York: Random House.
Barber, B. 1996. *Jihad vs. McWorld*, New York: Ballantine.
———. 2003. *Fear's Empire*, New York: Norton.
Barns, G. 2003. "Soft power" in *Mail and Guardian Online*, July 18.

Benedict, R. 1946. *The Chrysanthemum and the Sword*, Boston: Houghton Mifflin.

Besteman, C. and H. Gusterson (eds.). 2005. *Why America's Top Pundits Are Wrong*, Berkeley, CA: University of California Press.

Buruma, I. and A. Margalit. 2004. *Occidentalism*, New York: Penguin Press.

Carrier, J. (ed.). 1995. *Occidentalism*, Oxford: Oxford University Press.

Cooper, R. 2003. *The Breaking of Nations: Order and Chaos in the Twenty-first Century*, London: Atlantic Books.

Economist. 2006. "Tales from Eurabia", June 24, p. 11.

Fallaci, O. 2004. *The Force of Reason*, New York: Rizzoli International.

Ferguson, N. 2003. *Empire*, New York: Allen Lane.

——. 2004a. *Colossus*, New York: Penguin Press.

——. 2004b. "A world without power" in *Foreign Policy*, 143: 32–39.

——. 2004c. "Eurabia?" in *New York Times*, April 4.

Fischer, M. M. J. 2003. *Emergent Forms of Life and the Anthropological Voice*, Durham, NC: Duke University Press.

Friedman, T. 1999. *The Lexus and the Olive Tree*, London: HarperCollins.

——. 2005. *The World is Flat*, New York: Farrar, Straus & Giroux.

Fukuyama, F. 1992. *The End of History and the Last Man*, New York: Free Press.

——. 1995. "Reflections on the end of history, five years later" in *History and Theory*, 34(2): 27–43.

Hannerz, U. 1996. *Transnational Connections*, London: Routledge.

——. 1999. "Reflections on varieties of culturespeak" in *European Journal of Cultural Studies*, 2: 393–407.

——. 2003. "Macro-scenarios: Anthropology and the debate over contemporary and future worlds" in *Social Anthropology*, 11: 169–187.

——. 2004. *Foreign News*, Chicago: University of Chicago Press.

——. 2006. "Minnen och scenarier: Om vägar genom antropologins historia till framtiden" in *Norsk Antropologisk Tidsskrift*, 17: 7–21.

——. 2007. "Geokulturella scenarier" in B. Axelsson and J. Fornäs (eds.), *Kulturstudier i Sverige*, Lund: Studentlitteratur.

Hardt, M. and A. Negri. 2000. *Empire*, Cambridge, MA: Harvard University Press.

——. 2004. *Multitude*, New York: Penguin Press.

Herzfeld, M. 1997a. "Anthropology and the politics of significance" in *Social Analysis*, 41: 107–138.

——. 1997b. *Cultural Intimacy*, London: Routledge.

Huntington, S. P. 1996. *The Clash of Civilizations and the Remaking of World Order*, New York: Simon and Schuster.

——. 2004. *Who Are We?*, New York: Simon and Schuster.

Inoguchi, T. 1999. "Peering into the future by looking back: The westphalian, philadelphian, and anti-utopian paradigms" in *International Studies Review*, 1(2): 173–191.

Kagan, R. 2003. *Paradise and Power*, New York: Alfred A. Knopf.

Kaplan, R. D. 1996. *The Ends of the Earth*, New York: Random House.

——. 2000. *The Coming Anarchy*, New York: Random House.

——. 2005. *Imperial Grunts*, New York: Random House.

Kennedy, P. 1987. *The Rise and Fall of the Great Powers*, New York: Random House.

——. 1993. *Preparing for the Twenty-first Century*, New York: Random House.

Kjellén, R. 1916. *The state as a Form of Life*, Stockholm: Gebers.

Kroeber, A. L. 1952. *The nature of Culture*, Chicago: University of Chicago Press.

Lewis, M. W. and K. E. Wigen. 1997. *The Myth of Continents*, Berkeley: University of California Press.

Lomnitz, C. 2005. "American soup: Are we all anglo-protestants?" in *Boston Review*, February/March.

Malkki, L. H. 2001. "Figures of the future: Dystopia and subjectivity in the social imagination of the future" in D. Holland and J. Lave (eds.), *History in Person*, Santa Fe, NM: School of American Research Press.

Mamdani, M. 2005. "Whither political islam? Understanding the modern jihad" in *Foreign Affairs*, 84(1): 148–155.

Manning, P. 2003. *Navigating World History*, New York: Palgrave Macmillan.

Marks, R. 2000. Review of S. P. Huntington, "The Clash of Civilizations and the Remaking of World Order" in *Journal of World History*, 11(1): 101–104.

Miyazaki, H. 2003. "The temporalities of the market" in *American Anthropologist*, 105(2): 255–265.

Mills, C. W. 1963. *Power, Politics, and People*, New York: Ballantine.

Mitchell, T. 2002. "McJihad: Islam in the U.S. global order" in *Social Text*, 20(4): 1–18.

Nader, L. 1972. "Up the anthropologist: Perspectives gained from studying up" in D. Hymes (ed.), *Reinventing Anthropology*, New York: Pantheon.

Nye, J. S. Jr. 1991. *Bound to Lead*, New York: Basic Books.

——. 2002. *The Paradox of American Power*, New York: Oxford University Press.

——. 2003. "The velvet hegemon: How soft power can help defeat terrorism" in *Foreign Policy*, 136: 74–75.

——. 2004a. *Soft Power*, New York: Public Affairs.

——. 2004b. "The decline of America's soft power: Why Washington should worry" in *Foreign Affairs*, 83(3): 16–20.

People's Daily. 2004. "Solidifying China's regional partnerships" in *People's Daily Online*, May 17. http://english.peopledaily.com.cn/.

Pfaff, W. 1997. "The reality of human affairs" in *World Policy Journal*, 14(2): 89–96.

Phillips, M. 2006. *Londonistan*, London: Gibson Square.

Richards, P. 1999. "Out of the wilderness? Escaping Robert Kaplan's dystopia" in *Anthropology Today*, 15(6): 16–18.

Stolcke, V. 1995. "Talking culture: New boundaries, new rhetorics of exclusion in Europe" in *Current Anthropology*, 36: 1–13.

De Swaan, A. 1993. "The emergent world language system: An introduction" in *International Political Science Review*, 14: 219–226.

Tharoor, S. 2003. "The new global mantra" in *The Hindu*, September 28.

Tiryakian, E. 1997. Review of S. P. Huntington, "The clash of civilizations and the remaking of world order" in *American Journal of Sociology*, 103: 475–477.

Tsygankov, A. P. 2003. "The irony of western ideas in a multicultural world: Russians' intellectual engagement with the 'end of history' and 'clash of civilizations'" in *International Studies Review*, 5: 53–76.

Wallerstein, I. 1991. *Geopolitics and Geoculture*, Cambridge University Press.

Ye'or, B. 2005. *Eurabia*, Madision, NJ: Fairleigh Dickinsion University Press.

SOCIOLOGY AND THE COGNITIVE SCIENCES

THE SOCIAL STANCE AND ITS RELATION TO INTERSUBJECTIVITY

Peter Gärdenfors

1. *Program*

In this paper, I shall argue that it is sometimes necessary to go one step beyond Dennett's (1978) three different stances and adopt a *social stance* to certain phenomena. I shall argue that this stance is necessary for *social intentions*, which are intentions that cannot be replaced by individual intentions. Social intentions function as causal factors and they are thereby helpful for understanding language and other conventions. I shall then argue that the social stance can only be attained with advanced forms of intersubjectivity (theory of mind) involving social intentions and common beliefs. Among other things, this will explain why humans are the only species to which the social stance applies. Finally, I will argue that there is an interesting mapping between Peirce's (1932) three kinds of signs and different stances.

2. *Dennett's Three Stances*

My first aim is to specify what I mean by the social stance.[1] To do this, I will briefly present the three stances from Dennett's *Brainstorms* (1978). The starting point is that a particular thing or system can be described only in relation to the *perspective* of someone trying to explain or predict its operation. I will illustrate the stances by Dennett's example of a chess-playing computer. First, there is the *physical stance*, which considers the computer as a physical object, constructed by various semi-conductors, metal wires, etc. Unless it is malfunctioning, one seldom adopts the physical stance in dealing with a computer, since it would be too complicated to use the physical structure to determine its behaviour. Instead one adopts the *design stance*, or the *functional stance* as I prefer to call it. If one knows exactly how the computer is programmed, one can

---

[1] Sections 2–3 of this article are adapted from Gärdenfors (1994).

predict its response to any move one makes by following the instructions of the program step by step. The prediction will come true provided only that the computer functions as it has been designed; we need not know its physical constitution.

However, the chess-playing computers today have such complicated programs that it is practically impossible to make any predictions about their behaviour from either the physical or the functional stance. Instead, one must base the predictions or explanations on the assumption that the design is close to optimum so that the computer will choose the most *rational* move. This means that we adopt the *intentional stance* when thinking about the computer's performance and treat it as being rational and having *goals* and *beliefs*. The goals we ascribe to the computer include not only winning the game, but also things like "by moving the bishop to QB4, the computer wants to hinder me from castling." Similarly, the beliefs ascribed are not only beliefs about the position on the board, but also things like "the program believes that in this end game two pawns are stronger than a knight, since it sacrificed its knight." We adopt the intentional stance as long as the program selects rational moves; it is only when it plays badly that we return to the design stance and say things like "the program very often uses too few pieces in an attack." We can also apply Dennett's concepts to humans: When adopting the physical or functional stance we see a human as a biological organism. When adopting the intentional stance we see a human as a rational agent.

One aspect of the three stances that has not been discussed in the literature is their relation to *causal thinking*. If one takes a Kantian, or rather a neo-Kantian, view on causality, so that causal relations are seen as mental constructions, then the question becomes what kinds of causal relations occur in a particular mind. Taking the physical stance would involve only allowing physical causality in the classical sense. Taking the design stance means that also *functions* are allowed to be causes. This distinction can shed new light on the debate concerning covering-law explanations versus functional explanations. For example, blood flows in an animal because the heart has the function to pump blood. Of course, one can also adopt the physical stance to the heart and explain what physical and physiological features of the heart make it fulfil the functions. However, in many cases, we allow ourselves to let functions serve as causes in order to avoid descriptions that are too complicated.

Finally, adopting the intentional stance means that *desires, beliefs* and *goals* are allowed as causes. By ascribing these entities as causal factors to other individuals, we explain their behaviour. In other words, taking the intentional stance means acting *as if* the folk psychological concepts stand for entities that have causal powers.

3. *Why a Social Stance is Necessary*

In addition to the three stances considered by Dennett, I will propose that for some systems we sometimes have to adopt a *social stance*. This stance applies to all situations that involve the ascription of social intentions or joint beliefs as causal factors. Its role can perhaps be highlighted by considering the role of language in a community. The physical aspect of (spoken) language is just sound waves with certain frequency patterns. The functional role of language is to communicate information to other members of the society. But also a bird's warning call conveys information to other birds, without being intentional or part of a language. When we adopt the intentional stance to language we ascribe meanings to the linguistic utterances and don't simply view them as signs. We also interpret the speaker as having a specific purpose in making the utterance (cf. Grice 1969).[2]

However, even if the purpose of the utterance is an individual intention, there is a very clear sense in which the meaning of the utterance is not individual but *social* (cf. Putnam 1975; Gärdenfors 1993; Gärdenfors and Warglien 2006). In order to successfully use a particular language, the speaker must accept the grammatical and semantic *conventions* inherent in the language. These conventions play a crucial role when we try to explain or predict the linguistic behaviour of a particular individual: if we only rely on the lower stances, we cannot explain why a particular sequence of sounds were uttered or how a speaker succeeded to convey the meaning of what he intended to say. "La langue" in Saussure's distinction is a social convention that exists "above" individual intentions. As Taylor (1990: 53) puts it: "Acknowledging the independent place of the dimension of langue means accepting something into one's social ontology which can't be decomposed into individual occurrences." To this I would add that "accepting something into one's social ontology" means allowing it to have causal powers.

---

[2] In Zlatev, Persson and Gärdenfors (2005) what is meant by the *communicative sign function* is that the subject intends for the act to stand for some action, object or event for an addressee, and for the addressee to appreciate this.

In general, all conventions, not only linguistic, must be viewed as social intentions, since an individual cannot, by himself, establish a new convention without having it accepted by a majority of the society.[3] Linguistic conventions depend on joint beliefs. This is why Humpty Dumpty fails to use a language when he says that "When I use a word it means just what I choose it to mean."[4] The same argument also seems to apply to other forms of social ontology such as social roles.

The main reason why conventions and other social intentions must be viewed from a social stance and not as simple aggregates of individual intentions is that they are necessary for *causal explanations*. It is, for example, the existence of certain conventions that I recognize as social intentions that explain why I speak English and drive on the left hand side of the road while I am in Australia. These aspects of my behaviour are not explained by the intentions of any individual Australians.

By acknowledging the causal explanatory efficacy of social intentions I do not think methodological individualism has to be sacrificed, since the social intentions are *supervenient* on the individual intentions in the sense that without the individual intentions there would be no social intentions.[5] The situation is parallel to what happens on lower stances: for example, the functioning of programming instructions is supervenient on the physical structure of the computer.

On the other hand, recognizing social intentions involves a form of contextualism in the sense that "the individual person depends for certain of his significant features on the social relations that bind him to other members of his community; those relations are internal or intrinsic to what makes him, as it is often put, a full person" (Pettit 1986: 19). Or, in other words, certain features of an individual's behaviour can only be explained in terms of his social context. Contextualism can naturally be contrasted with atomism or "isolationism" which, in the present terminology, claims that reference to social intentions is never required when explaining or predicting individual behaviour.

In philosophy, the topic of *social intentions* (or *collective intentions* or *we-intentions* or *joint intentions*) is currently much in focus (e.g. Gilbert 1989; Searle 1990 and 1995; Bratman 1993; Tuomela 1995). Searle (1990)

---

[3] For an early analysis of the complexities of individual intentions and beliefs that are presupposed for the existence of a convention, see Lewis (1969).

[4] This argument is developed in a model theoretic context in Gärdenfors (1993) and Gärdenfors and Warglien (2006).

[5] In the terminology of Pettit (1986), I am a methodological individualist at least to the second degree.

gives an American football team executing a pass play or an orchestra playing a piece of music as examples of collective intentions. In section 5, I shall apply a theory of intersubjectivity (to be presented in Section 4) to further motivate that all phenomena that involve causally efficacious collective intentions or joint beliefs require the social stance.

Of course, the existence of social intentions does not entail that there are any social *agents* like the Hegelian Volksgeist, which have these intentions. On the contrary, I claim that the social intentions derive ultimately from a system of individual intentions. The crucial point is that the system of individual intentions forming a language, for example, is so complicated that we have to adopt the social stance and view the social intention as an *emergent property* of the system of individual intentions in order to understand, explain and predict the causal effects of the system. This is parallel, but on a higher level, to the situation where we adopt the intentional stance in relation to the chess-playing computer since the system of programming instructions on the functional level is too complicated to be effective when attempting to explain the behaviour of the computer.

The concept of an emergent property of a system is a fairly old idea within cybernetics which is perhaps best illustrated by Wiener's (1961) famous example of the "virtual governor": Consider a system that consists of a network of AC generators. Each generator has built into it a regulator that controls its speed so that it deviates very little from 60 Hz at any time. However, a generator in isolation does not give a very steady 60 Hz output. In remarkable contrast, when a large number of such generators are interconnected, they behave much more stably. This "mutual entrainment" of the generators is an example of self-organization. Out of the mutual entrainment emerges what Wiener calls a "virtual governor" which is an equilibrium property of the entire system that is viewed as having causal effects on the individual generators in the system. If a new generator is added to the system, this is best explained by saying that the virtual governor causes it to "get into step" by pumping energy into it, if it lags in phase, or by absorbing energy, if it runs too fast.[6] It should be noted that the notion of emergence introduced here, apart from properties normally ascribed to physical systems, involves no further mystical properties.

---

[6] For an elaboration of this example and a discussion of "consciousness" as a virtual governor of the brain, see Dewan (1976).

4. Different Kinds of Intersubjectivity

The available empirical evidence supports that the social stance is only necessary for understanding certain human activities. Even though some collective behaviour among animals, such as the collective hunting of wolves, lions and chimpanzees, is often described in term of collective intentions, it seems possible to describe this behaviour without invoking such intentions or joint beliefs. To understand why the social stance applies only to us, we must consider what is unique about human cognition. My thesis is that the unique forms of human intersubjectivity are what form the basis for the social stance.

In this context, intersubjectivity means *the sharing and understanding of others' mentality*. The term "mentality" is taken here to involve not only beliefs and other proposition-like entities, but all sorts of forms of consciousness such as emotions, desires, attentional foci and intentions. In the philosophical debate, intersubjectivity is commonly called having a "theory of mind" (see e.g. Premack and Woodruff 1978; Tomasello 1999; Gärdenfors 2003). I want to avoid this term since it often presumes that one can understand the beliefs of others, something which, on the account presented here, is but one aspect of intersubjectivity.

The question of whether an animal or a child exhibits intersubjectivity does not have a simple yes or no answer. For this purpose, intersubjectivity will here be decomposed into five capacities. In Gärdenfors (2001, 2003), I discussed four: representing the emotions of others (empathy), representing the attention of others, representing the intentions of others and representing the beliefs and knowledge of others (theory of mind). To these I now want to add one more: representing the desires of others. From the analysis of these five factors it will be clear that humans exhibit more kinds of intersubjectivity than other animals. In particular, we have a well-developed competence for representing the beliefs of others, but we also excel at forming joint intentions (Tomasello et al. 2005) and joint beliefs. As I shall argue, these differences are crucial for the emergence of a social stance.

A prerequisite for an animal (or a human) to entertain any form of intersubjectivity is that it has an *inner world*. The crucial issue is whether an individual has any representation of other individuals' inner worlds. To achieve sufficient precision in the analysis of the cognitive abilities of animals and humans, intersubjectivity will be split into the following five competencies:

(a) Representing the *emotions* of others. At this level one can, for example, understand that someone else is in pain. This is what is usually meant by *empathy*. Even though one can understand others' emotions, it does not mean that one understands what they believe or want.

Bodily expressions of emotions have a communicative purpose. The expressions are most obvious among social animals. The evolutionary explanation for this seems to be that a capacity for *empathy* leads to greater solidarity within the group. This reduces the risk of violent conflicts in which individuals injure one another.

(b) Representing the *desires* of others. This involves understanding that the other may not like the same things as you do.

Emotions concern the inner state of an individual, without reference to an external object. A desire is a positive attitude towards some external object or event. Understanding that somebody has a desire for something therefore involves more than understanding emotions. Results from child development studies (e.g. Repacholi and Gopnik 1997, Wellman and Liu 2004) suggest that 18-month-olds can understand that others have different desires than they have themselves. As we shall see below, this occurs earlier in children's development than understanding the beliefs of others.

(c) Representing the *attention* of others. This means that one can understand, for example, what someone else is looking at. However, this ability does not presuppose any conception of other parts of their inner world. Humans, other primates, and some other mammals are good at following the *direction* of other individuals' gazes. Even very young children can understand where other people are looking. A more sophisticated form of attention is to succeed in drawing *joint attention* to an object. If I see that you are looking at an object and you see that I see the same object, we have established joint attention. This presupposes that both you and I can achieve second-order attention.

(d) Representing the *intentions* of others. This capacity means, above all, being able to understand the objective that may lie behind another individual's behaviour.

As Kant and others have argued, humans have a powerful inclination to look for *causes* in the world. By reasoning about causes and effects, we become better at predicting the future. The ability to distinguish phenomena caused by other agents (animals or humans), is fundamental for the capacity of understanding intentionality in other individuals' behaviour. When we see that something is caused by an agent, our cognitive system presumes that there is some purpose for the act, in other words, that it is intentional. Humans thus find it very easy to create a representation of the objective of an action—we see other people's behaviour as being goal-directed. This involves adopting the intentional stance. Mostly, the intentional stance is successful, but it happens that people do things unintentionally.

It is important to notice that, even though one can interpret some-one else's behaviour as goal-directed, this does not necessarily mean that one has any conception of the other's beliefs. It is sufficient that one creates for oneself a representation of the *goal* of the action. The ability to see objectives thus requires a less advanced inner world than the ability to have representations of others' beliefs. The intentional stance belongs to the one who interprets the behaviour, and it is far from certain that it agrees with the objective of the person who actually performs the act.

Of course, both participants in an interaction can adopt the intentional stance. Tomasello et al. (2005) strongly emphasize the role of *sharing intentions*. They write that "the crucial difference between human cognition and that of other species is the ability to participate with others in collaborative activities with shared goals and intentions: shared intentionality" (2005: 675). At nine to twelve months of age, infants begin to understand other individuals as intentional and then they can begin to interact with them in activities with shared goals. For example, an adult and an infant can create a shared goal to build a tower of blocks together.

An even stronger form of intersubjectivity is to achieve *joint intention*. This involves that a child can understand the plans of somebody else and coordinate its own intention with the goals of the other. This involves that "I intend that you intend" and that "you intend that I intend" and that both are aware of these second-order intentions. When one can coordinate roles in working towards a goal, then joint intention is achieved. For example, in building the tower of blocks the child may understand that the adult holds the tower steady while the child places new blocks. In human children, joint intentions seem to develop between twelve and fifteen months of age. Once we have accepted joint intentions as causal factors in interaction, we have adopted the social stance.

(e) Representing the *beliefs* and *knowledge* of others. This ability involves, among other things, understanding that others don't know the same things as you do.

Several experiments have been performed to test whether apes and monkeys can represent the beliefs of others. Most experiments focus on whether they understand that "seeing is knowing." So far the outcomes are negative and therefore there is nothing to suggest that primates have representations of others' beliefs and knowledge.

It is easier to test whether young children can understand that "seeing is knowing", since one can communicate with them through language from a fairly early age. A common type of tests of children's under-standing of other people's beliefs concern whether they can understand that someone else has a *false* belief about what the world is like (see e.g. Perner, Leekam and Wimmer 1987; Gopnik and Astington 1988; Mitchell 1997). The best known of these experiments is about an oblong Smarties tube. The test is carried out on children aged between three and five. The children are first shown the tube and then asked what they think is in it. All the children reply "Smarties" (or "sweets"). When the tube is opened it is found to contain a pencil. Then the tube is closed. The children are now asked what a friend, who has not yet seen what is in the tube, will say that it contains. The three-year-olds generally answer "pencil" whereas most of the older children say "Smarties". The older children understand that the friend does not have the same knowledge as they do. They thus realize that the friend has a false belief about what is in the tube. This is a clear example that they represent the belief of others. The younger children, on the other hand, do not appear to be able to distinguish between their own beliefs and other people's (Perner, Leekam and Wimmer 1987). This is one of several experiments, which suggest that a representation of others' beliefs and knowledge develops in humans at the age of about four. Variations of the false belief tasks have also been performed with chimpanzees, but so far there is no indication that they understand the beliefs of others.

Humans cannot only know that someone else knows, that is have second-order knowledge, but they can also have higher orders of knowledge and belief, such as "I know that you know that I believe that there will be frost tonight." This capacity forms the basis for *joint beliefs*, which is often called *common knowledge*. Again, reasoning about joint beliefs requires the social stance.

The upshot is that when reasoning about joint (social) intentions or joint beliefs (common knowledge) of a group of individuals, it is necessary to adopt the social stance. The crucial factor is that joint intentions and joint beliefs are seen as causes regulating the behaviour of the individuals. Since the current evidence concerning the intersubjectivity of other animals does not indicate that they can achieve joint intentions or joint beliefs, this explains why the social stance is only successful when applied to human activities.

5. *Conventions Require the Social Stance*

In many of the cases where the social stance is required, the phenomenon is a result of cooperation between two or more individuals. Joint intentions and joint beliefs open up for many new forms of collaboration that do not seem to be possible outside the human species (Gärdenfors 2007).

For example, in human societies many forms of cooperation are based on *conventions*. The important point here is that conventions presume joint beliefs. For example, if two cars meet on a gravel road in Australia, then both drivers know that this co-ordination problem has been solved by driving on the left hand side numerous times before, both know that both know this, both know that both know that both know this, etc., and they then both drive on their left without any hesitation (Lewis 1969).

In a sense, conventions function as virtual governors in a society. Successful conventions create equilibrium points, which, once established, tend to be stable. The convention of driving on the left hand side of the road will force me to "get into step" and drive on the left. The same applies to language: A new member of a society will have to adjust to the language adopted by the community. The meaning of the linguistic utterances emerges from the individuals' meanings. Language, in the sense of "la langue," thus has no existence independently of the individual "generators." This form of emergence of a social meaning of language is modelled in Gärdenfors (1993) and Gärdenfors and Warglien (2006). There are, of course, an infinite number of possible "equilibrium" languages in a society, but the point is that once a language has developed it will have strong causal effects on the behaviour of the individuals in the society.

I have been using language as a paradigmatic example of social intentions, but let me also give a simple economic example: I suggest that the concept of "money" requires the social stance, which involves a particular social intention emerging out of a system of individual beliefs and values. We can, of course, adopt different stances towards money. On the physical level, money is just pieces of metal or paper. On the functional level, money is an exchange commodity: I can exchange my metal coin for an apple or a cup of coffee. By adopting the intentional stance, I can view money as something I can use to buy and sell other things ("buy" and "sell" are obviously intentional notions). But it is only by adopting the social stance that we can explain why we have paper money: This depends on a *mutual agreement* to accept certain decorated pieces of paper as a medium of exchange. The agreement normally has legal status within a nation. And being a member of a monetary society, or just visiting one, I must "get into step" and accept the conventional medium of exchange as legal tender.

Actually, there are many similarities between language and money as tools for cooperation. Humans have been trading goods as long as they have existed. But when a monetary system does emerge, it makes economic transactions more efficient. The same applies to language: Hominids have been communicating long before they had a language, but language makes the exchange of information more efficient. The analogy carries further: When money is introduced in a society, a relatively stable system of *prices* emerges. Similarly, when linguistic communication develops individuals will come to share a relatively stable system of *meanings*, that is, components in their inner worlds that communicators can exchange between each other. In this way, language fosters a *common structure* of the inner worlds of the individuals in a society (see Gärdenfors and Warglien 2006).

Money is an example of "social software" (Parikh 2002) that improves the cooperation within a society. In general, the social ontology that we construct increases the possibilities of establishing contracts, conventions and other social goods.

In order to function at all, most conventions presume that certain *applicability conditions* are fulfilled (for a general analysis of such conditions, see Lewis (1969)). For example, using a language presumes quite a lot concerning the intersubjectivity of the members of the linguistic community. As regards paper money, or more generally, media of exchange, the convention presumes, among other things, a functioning legal system which can enforce sanctions on individuals who misuse the medium. The legal system cannot exist without a complicated network of joint beliefs.

When a society breaks down, the applicability conditions of some of its conventions may not be fulfilled any longer, and thus the convention ceases to function, that is, the virtual governor disappears. I take it that this is what happened in Germany during the end of the Second World War, when German bank notes become worthless: The economic value of paper money depends on the *support* from the underlying convention and the validity of its applicability conditions. For a fascinating account of how a monetary system develops and breaks down in a Prisoners of War Camp, cf. Radford (1945). He also presents an analysis of the conditions under which the necessary conventions may function.

6. *A Connection to Peirce's Three Kinds of Signs*

In this final section I shall make some brief comments on how the different stances correspond to different modes of communication and the relevance of this for the evolution of communication. It seems that there is an interesting mapping between the stances and the three kinds of signs proposed by Peirce, that is, signals (indices), icons and symbols. Signals are signs that refer to something in the current environment. Smoke is a signal for fire. A pigeon can learn that when the green light is on in its cage, it is a signal that food will appear if it pecks on the lever. An *icon* is a sign that resembles the representation denoted by the sign.[7] A silhouette of a woman on the door to the ladies' room is an icon for those persons who are expected to enter. A white arrow to the right on a round blue road sign in a traffic circle is an icon for which direction one is supposed to take. In distinction to symbols, the choice of icons is not arbitrary, but dependent on the resemblance between the sign and what it denotes. Finally, Peirce's use of the concept "symbol" corresponds quite well with the meaning I have discussed elsewhere (Gärdenfors 2003): A conventional arbitrary sign primarily used for communication about non-present objects and events.

Barber and Peters (1992) describe the difference between signals, icons and symbols in the following way:

> An icon can be interpreted without previous agreement, through general knowledge of the world, and an index [i.e., a signal] through either knowledge of the world or pre-wired instinct. But an arbitrary symbol can only be interpreted through the direct process of agreeing on a convention and then learning it. That is, some preliminary mode of com-

---

[7] This is only marginally related to the religious uses of the notion of an icon. However, the concept is nowadays used in Peirce's way in connection with the design of computer interfaces.

munication is needed to begin making the conventional agreements that underlie arbitrary systems. Icons and indices can serve this bootstrapping function because they can exist without conventional agreement. Thus spoken communication, like writing and sign, had to have begun iconically and/or indexically, and gradually shifted to arbitrariness.

The mapping between Peirce's signs and different stances I put forward is the following:

(1) Using an index requires the physical or functional stance.
(2) Using an icon requires the intentional stance.
(3) Using a symbol requires the social stance.

Almost all known natural animal communication systems involve signalling. The function of a signal is to *draw attention* to something in the environment or to the emotional state of the signaller. The reference of the signal is something that is present (or was recently present) in the nearby environment. Animal signals, be they the dancing of bees, the quacking of frogs or the play-face of chimpanzees, are by and large innate rather than learned. Signalling can be explained in behaviourist terms and need not involve any intentionality or other forms of intersubjectivity. Hence, the physical or functional stance is sufficient.

Using icons in communication involves that the sender intends the communicative act to represent something for the addressee and that the addressee understands this (Zlatev, Persson and Gärdenfors 2005). In the literature on the evolution of language, it has been proposed that there is a stage of *miming* that is intermediate between mere signalling and symbolic communication (Donald 1991; Corballis 2002). Among the great apes one finds some examples of inventions of iconic signs (Patterson 1980; Miles 1990; Tanner and Byrne 1996; Pika and Mitani 2006), not to mention the "encultured" apes that have been taught sign language. This form of communication at least involves that the addressee understands that the sender intends something by the sign and hence presumes that the addressee adopts the intentional stance. Achieving joint intentions requires an even more advanced form of communication where the participants all adopt the social stance.

The important difference between symbols and icons is that symbols are *conventional*. Icons can be understood without learning, if the addressee just understands the similarity expressed in the iconic sign. But arbitrary conventional symbols must be learned. As we have seen linguistic conventions involve joint beliefs about the use of symbols and hence they presume the social stance.

From an evolutionary perspective, it is implicit in this analysis that using signals, icons and symbols involve narrowing down the species that manage the different kinds of signs: Signals are used by most animal species, icons only by some of the apes and symbols only by Homo sapiens.

In conclusion, I claim that the evolution of communication involves adopting more and more advanced stances. By triangulating types of communication, types of intersubjectivity and different stances, I believe we can achieve a better understanding of the mechanisms behind the evolution of communication.

References

Barber, E. and A. M. Peters. 1992. "Ontogeny and phylogeny: What child language and archeology have to say to each other" in J. A. Hawkins and M. Gell-Mann (eds.), *The Evolution of Human Languages*, Redwood City, CA: Addison Wesley, 305–351.

Bratman, M. 1993. "Shared intention" in *Ethics*, 103: 97–103.

Corballis, M. 2002. *From Hand to Mouth*, Princeton, NJ: Princeton University Press.

Dennett, D. C. 1978. *Brainstorms*, Cambridge, MA: Bradford Books, MIT Press.

Dewan, E. M. 1976. "Consciousness as an emergent causal agent in the context of control system theory" in G. Globus, G. Maxwell and I. Savodnik, (eds.), *Consciousness and the Brain*, New York, NY: Plenum Press.

Donald, M. 1991. *Origins of the Modern Mind*, Cambridge, MA: Harvard University Press.

Gärdenfors, P. 1993. "The emergence of meaning" in *Linguistics and Philosophy*, 16: 285–309.

———. 1994. "The social stance" in *Protosoziologie*, Heft 6: 91–94.

———. 2001. "Slicing the theory of mind" in *Danish Yearbook for Philosophy*, 36: 7–34.

———. 2003. *How Homo Became Sapiens*, Oxford: Oxford University Press.

———. 2007. "The cognitive and communicative demands of cooperation" in the electronic Festschrift *Hommage à Wlodek: Philosophical Papers Dedicated to Wlodek Rabinowicz* (http://www.fil.lu.se/hommageawlodek/).

Gärdenfors, P. and M. Warglien. 2006. "Cooperation, conceptual spaces and the evolution of semantics" in P. Vogt, Y. Sugita, E. Tuci and C. Nehaniv (eds.), *Symbol Grounding and Beyond*, Berlin: Springer, 16–30.

Gilbert, M. 1989. *On Social Facts*, Princeton: Princeton University Press.

Grice, H. P. 1969. "Utterer's meaning and intentions" in *The Philosophical Review*, 78: 147–177.

Gopnik, A. and J. W. Astington. 1988. "Children's understanding of representational change, and its relation to the understanding of false belief and the appearance-reality distinction" in *Child Development*, 59: 26–37.

Lewis, D. K. 1969. *Convention*, Boston: Harvard University Press.

Miles, L. 1990. "The cognitive foundations for reference in a signing orangutan" in S. T. Parker and K. R. Gibson (eds.), *"Language" and Intelligence in Monkeys and Apes*, Cambridge: Cambridge University Press, 511–539.

Mitchell, P. 1997. *Introduction to Theory of Mind: Children, Autism and Apes*, London: Arnold.

Parikh, R. 2002. "Social software" in *Synthese*, 132: 187–211.

Patterson, F. G. 1980. "Innovative uses of language by a gorilla: A case study" in K. E. Nelson, (ed.), *Children's Language*, vol. 2, New York, NY: Gardner Press.

Peirce, C. S. 1932. *Collected Papers of Charles Sanders Peirce*, vol. 2, *Elements of Logic*, Hart-shorne and P. Weiss (eds.), Cambridge, MA: Harvard University Press.

Perner, J., S. Leekam and H. Wimmer. 1987. "Three-year-old's difficulty with false belief: The case for a conceptual deficit" in *British Journal of Developmental Psychology*, 5: 125–137.

Pettit, P. 1986. "Social holism without collectivism" in E. Ullman-Margalit (ed.), *The Prism of Science: The Israel Colloquium; Studies in History, Philosophy and Sociology of Science*, Dordrecht: Reidel.

Pika, S. and J. Mitani. 2006. "Referential gesturing in wild chimpanzees (Pan troglodytes)" in *Current Biology*, 16(6): 191–192.

Premack, D. and G. Woodruff. 1978. "Does the chimpanzee have a theory of mind?" in *Behavioral and Brain Sciences*, 4: 515–526.

Putnam, H. 1975. "The meaning of 'meaning'" in *Mind, Language and Reality*, Cambridge: Cambridge University Press, 215–271.

Radford, R. A. 1945. "The economic organisation of a P.O.W. camp" in *Economica*, 12: 189–201.

Repacholi, B. and A. Gopnik 1997. "Early understanding of desires: Evidence from 14- and 18-month-olds" in *Developmental Psychology*, 33: 12–21.

Searle, J. R. 1990. "Collective intentions and actions" in P. R. Cohen, J. Morgan and M. E. Pollack (eds.), *Intentions in Communication*. Cambridge, MA: MIT Press.

———. 1995. *The Construction of Social Reality*, New York, NY: Free Press.

Tanner, J. E. and R. W. Byrne. 1996. "Representation of action through iconic gesture in a captive lowland gorilla" in *Current Anthropology*, 37(1): 162–73.

Taylor, C. 1990. "Irreducibly social goods" in G. Brennan and C. Walsh (eds.), *Rationality, Individualism and Public Policy*, Canberra: Centre for Research on Federal Financial Relations.

Tomasello, M. 1999. *The Cultural Origins of Human Cognition*, Cambridge, MA: Harvard University Press.

Tomasello, M., M. Carpenter, J. Call, T. Behne and H. Moll. 2005. "Understanding and sharing intentions: The origins of cultural cognition" in *Behavioral and Brain Sciences*, 28: 675–691.

Tuomela, R. 1995. *The Importance of Us*, Stanford, CA: Stanford University Press.

Wellman, H. M. and D. Liu. 2004. "Scaling of theory-of-mind tasks" in *Child Development*, 75: 523–541.

Wiener, N. 1961. *Cybernetics*, Cambridge, MA: MIT Press.

Zlatev, J., T. Persson and P. Gärdenfors. 2005. "Bodily mimesis as 'the missing link' in Human Cognitive Evolution" in *Lund University Cognitive Studies*, 121, Lund.

SHARED BELIEFS ABOUT THE PAST: A COGNITIVE SOCIOLOGY OF INTERSUBJECTIVE MEMORY

Jens Rydgren

Introduction

Together with desires and opportunities, beliefs are fundamental to explaining action (Hedström 2005). In order to assess people's reasons for why they act the way they do, we have to take their beliefs (i.e., their 'knowledge about the world') into account. If these beliefs were always congruent with reality, that is, if beliefs could be inferred from people's structural situation in a perfect way, belief formation processes would be transparent and of little interest to explanatory sociology. On the other hand, if beliefs were always incorrect and flawed in a uniquely idiosyncratic way, beliefs would also be of little interest to analytical sociology because what needs to be explained is not the concrete actions of single individuals but rather the typical actions of typical individuals. This fact points to the need to identify patterns in belief formation processes because although beliefs, as we will see below, are often biased and flawed, these biases are not always random and unpredictable. It moreover points to the usefulness of staking out a middle ground between subjectivist approaches and universalistic ambitions. Although few beliefs are unique to a specific person, most beliefs are not shared by everyone else. A more reasonable assumption is that most beliefs are, to a varying extent, intersubjective, and it is important for sociologists to identify the boundaries of this intersubjectivity. In this paper, culture, structural equivalence, social category belonging, and social network belonging will be discussed as important parameters of such boundaries. It is important—both for consensus-oriented sociology and conflict-oriented sociology—to understand the reasons for intersubjective uniformities in beliefs: shared beliefs are one important mechanism holding together social entities (e.g., societies, organizations, groups) (Bar-Tal 2000), and differences in beliefs between social entities are an equally important reason for conflict (e.g., Rydgren 2007).

This paper will in particular focus on the importance of beliefs about the past, and *shared* beliefs about the past in particular. People's predictions about future events, and their strategies for dealing with new situations, are often based on beliefs about similar events and situations in the past. As will be discussed below, analogism plays a crucial role in these processes.

In contemporary sociology, shared beliefs about the past is often, in my view rather unfortunately, discussed in terms of collective memory. In this literature, *autobiographical memory, social memory*, and *collective memory* are often confused. First, the concept collective memory is misleading; it is important to emphasize that only individuals, and not collectives, do the remembering. However, this does not mean that memory is "completely personal" and non-social, as Gedi and Elam (1996: 34) have suggested. There is a common misapprehension in the literature that memory is either individual or social (see, e.g., Schudson 1995: 346). This is a false distinction; the real distinction is between individual and collective memory, on the one hand, and between social and anti-social (atomistic) memory, on the other. In my view memory—as other beliefs about the past—is individual *and* social. More specifically, the position taken in this paper is that we all have some autobiographical memories that we do not share with others (which nonetheless may be social in some sense, not the least because they are mediated through language) but that we also have many memories that we share with some people but not with others (see Zerubavel 1996: 284). In this sense, it is more appropriate to talk about *intersubjective* rather than collective memories (cf. Misztal 2003: 11). What we do find are collective *sites* of memory (archives, history books, commemorative rituals, etc.), which people draw upon, and which direct people's memory in certain directions by indicating which past events are considered important. Susan Sontag (2003) calls this collective *instruction*. However, there are no analytical reasons for calling such collective sites or instructions collective memories. Second, the literature on collective memory not only treats autobiographical memories as memories, but also other kinds of beliefs about the past—such as popular conceptions of the French revolution and other historical events of which people lack living memory.[1] This is untenable from an analytical perspective. In this paper popular conceptions about history and autobiographical memories will be treated as distinct subcategories of the wider category of beliefs about the past. The reason for treating autobiographical memories as beliefs

---

[1] In this context we may define autobiographical memory as 'knowledge', subjectively held to be true, about events that individuals 'know' they have experienced personally.

is analytical as well as ontological in that it emphasizes that memories should not be treated as something distinct from beliefs but can be understood by largely the same mechanisms. It is a popular misconception that memory works like a camera, inscribing snapshots of lived reality. However, research in the cognitive sciences, psychology, and sociology shows that this is a false conception of how memory works. Like beliefs, memories are often biased and distorted—indeed, they are often even erroneous—and they are influenced by a large number of social factors (see, e.g., Schacter 1995), including those that will be discussed in this paper.

This paper will be structured as follows: First, I will present the socio-cognitive approach, which constitutes the theoretical point of departure for the following discussion on memories and other beliefs about the past. Second, I will discuss analogism and other mechanisms for explaining the ways in which beliefs about the past matter for action in the present. Together the two first sections discuss typical ways in which beliefs about the past become biased and distorted. In the four last sections of the paper, I will discuss how and in what ways memories and other beliefs about the past become intersubjective: *culture* (collective memory sites as a factor creating intersubjective uniformities in memories and other beliefs about the past), *structural equivalence* (similar experiences as well as interest-driven distortions as factors creating intersubjective uniformities in memories and other beliefs about the past), *social network belonging* (symmetries and asymmetries in information as a factor creating intersubjective uniformities in memories and other beliefs about the past), and *social category belonging* (identity-driven distortions as a factor creating intersubjective uniformities in memories and other beliefs about the past).

The Socio-cognitive Approach

In contrast to rationalistic micro theories, the socio-cognitive framework does not assume rational actors, but is based on the assumption that individuals are motivated by an "effort after meaning" (Bartlett 1995: 44), or that they strive to obtain cognitive closure by imposing order upon what William James (1890) called the "blooming, buzzing confusion" of raw experience.[2] Not being able to understand what is

---

[2] Pages 4–9 are largely based on Rydgren (2004) and Rydgren (2007).

happening in ones surround, including what is likely to happen in the immediate future, results in negative emotions such as stress and frustration, something which most people try to avoid. This attempt to create meaning is mostly unconscious in that adults almost never approach objects and events as if they were *sui generis* configurations, but rather perceive and conceive of them through the lens of pre-existing systems of schematized knowledge (i.e., beliefs, theories, propositions, and schemas) (Tversky and Kahneman 1982a: 117).

Categorization is one important part of this system of schematized knowledge. A category could, in this context, be defined as the "totality of information that perceivers have in mind about particular classes of individuals" (Macrea and Bodenhausen 2000: 96). Once such a particular category has been mobilized in meeting an object, event, situation, or person, further perception of the object will partly be dictated by the characteristics of the category (Kahneman and Tversky 1982).

Moreover, pre-existing systems of schematized knowledge not only influence the ways in which people categorize, but also the ways in which they make inferences. This will be discussed in greater detail below. What has been called *logical a priori* (Rydgren 2004)—especially people's inclination toward simplified and/or invalid (but often useful) inductive reasoning in the form of analogism will be a particular focus of this article. This mechanism is commonly used by people to understand the present and often to predict the future.

These beliefs, theories, and schemas are acquired through a range of different channels such as socialization in childhood, education, the media, and all kinds of social interactions in everyday-life (Nisbett and Ross 1980: 119). Although some schematic cognitive structures are fairly universal, and others are highly personal and thus idiosyncratic, many emanate from group cultures, which to a significant degree make them intersubjective (see DiMaggio 1997: 273). I will come back to this below, in discussing how collective memory sites influence people's belief-formation processes.

At the same time, individuals are assumed to be cognitive misers, that is, motivated by a drive to save time and cognitive energy. This often leads them to use cognitive strategies without much reflection, very often strategies that are readily available and that have proved useful in the past. This more or less unconscious reliance on different cognitive strategies generally serves people well in everyday life—when they typically confront situations that are repetitive, and thus have the chance to continuously adjust their pre-existing systems of schematized knowledge. Confusion and breakdown in the effort after meaning are most likely to occur in so-called black-box situations, that is, in situations of uncertainty (Boudon 1989) when people face new situations which their standard cognitive strategies fail to handle (whether understanding present situations or predicting future ones). In such black-box situations people are likely either to use schematized knowledge structures that have proved valid in other situations, or to rely on others. As a result, dubious knowledge structures, including myths and rumors, are more likely to become activated in black-box situations.

However, people not only try to grasp what is going on around them, but also to understand the own self: who am I, where do I come from, and what will happen to me in the future, are all crucial questions. As will be further discussed below, much research suggests that cognitive strategies for understanding the social surround are strongly influenced by these particular questions. We may, for example, assume that individuals are motivated to think well of themselves. This may make them update and modify their autobiographical memories in order to make them congruent with the selves they have become in the present (Berger 1963; Rubin 1986), partly as a way of reducing cognitive dissonance (cf. Festinger 1957). Schacter (2001: 9) terms *consistency bias* the tendency to bring memories and other beliefs about the past in line with what one believes in the present, while *egocentric bias* is the tendency to modify memories about the past in a self-enhancing manner. As will be further discussed below, the egocentric bias may also have a group dimension, which we may call the *ethnocentric bias*.

Analogism

Analogism is a fundamental mechanism for understanding how beliefs about the past matter for action in the present. We have an analogism when we draw the conclusion from

1. the fact that Object A (or Event A, Situation A, etc.) has the Properties p and q
2. and the observation that Object B has the Property p
3. that object B also has Property q.

Although it is obvious that this type of reasoning can never be valid from a logical point of view, it is one of the most important and common mechanisms underpinning beliefs, and it can, moreover, be a useful one (Holyoak and Thagard 1999: 7). The psychological power of analogism is its ability to reduce felt uncertainty in black-box situations by helping individuals make apparent sense of what is going on—and what to expect in the near future—but often also by pointing out solutions for dealing with specific problems. Hence, analogism has both a diagnostic and a prognostic function (cf. Benford and Snow 2000).

One can easily think of numerous examples of how this mechanism works in everyday-life. If one does not know much about wine, for example, and is going to have some friends over for dinner, it is likely that one follows the line of reasoning that

1. since the bottle I bought last time (A) was a Bordeaux (p) and tasted good (q)
2. among all the possible alternatives in the store, bottle B which also is a Bordeaux (p)
3. ought to taste good as well (q).

Although this decision-making mechanism is error prone, the likelihood of making sound predictions is likely to be higher than when no heuristic is used in such black-box situations. Moreover, this likelihood grows with increases in relevant knowledge. If one learns to discern other properties of the wine (through practical experience or theoretical learning), the chances of finding a wine one likes when using this heuristic mechanism will increase.

Yet, the psychological power of analogism may make it a threat both to logic and to empiricism. Indeed, as Fischer (1970: 259) has demonstrated, many "bad ideas have had a long life because of a good (effective) analogy." There are a variety of fallacies associated with analogism, of which only a few will be mentioned here.

First, we have the problem of selection bias. For the first step of the analogism, that is, historical events with which to compare the present, people tend to select events that are easily accessible to memory (cf. Khong 1992: 35). In the terminology of Tversky and Kahneman (1982b), people use the *availability heuristic*, which is often useful because people tend to remember significant events better than insignificant ones. However, there are a variety of factors affecting availability that may lead to bias. For one thing, studies have shown that vivid information is better remembered and is more accessible than pallid information (Nisbett and Ross 1980: 44–45). Events that are unique and unexpected and that provoke emotional reactions are more easily remembered than other events (Paez et al. 1997: 150). A particular type of pallid information, which people consequently tend to overlook, is null information about potential events that did not occur. For most of us, events that take place are more concrete and immediately real than the nonoccurrence of potential events. This type of memory bias may, for example, be one reason why a history of intergroup conflict may make conflicts more likely in the present (or future). Because people are more likely to recall instances of conflict than instances of peace, as the former are more salient than the latter, they may overestimate the likelihood of future conflict, which may lead them to mobilize in order to defend themselves and/or to take preemptive actions in ways that actually foment conflict (Rydgren, 2007).

Second, memories or other beliefs about the past that are selected for analogism tend to be highly simplified and sometimes inaccurate. To begin with, the very fact that memories are stored in some conceptual form implies a simplification compared to the full representation of the event that actually occurred (Fentress and Wickham 1992: 32). Like other cognitive schemas, analogism imposes itself upon the new information, and often fills in missing data, while ambiguous and discrepant information is denigrated or ignored (see Khong 1992: 38). Over time, memories and other beliefs about the past are likely to become simplified and condensed, as details—in particular subtle connections—are reduced or lost (Bartlett 1995; Belli and Schuman 1996: 423). In Maurice Halbwachs's (1992: 183) words, "we distort the past, because we wish to introduce greater coherence." Moreover, it has often been observed that because they are intrinsically social in character, memories and other beliefs about the past adapt to socially shared stereotypes and conventions within the group, that is, memories tend to converge to "what is common in the group" (Allport and Postman 1947: 60). Finally, psychological and social psychological research has convincingly shown that memories are often inaccurate, often grossly so, and that this is also the case for vivid, "subjectively compelling memories" (Schacter 1995: 22), including emotionally traumatic ones (Schacter 1995: 27).

Third, analogical inferences are at best probabilistic and always unacceptable from a logical point of view. Because analogism is often applied to non-repetitive events, which makes it difficult for people to falsify them within the realms of everyday epistemology, people tend to rely on analogisms more uncritically than they should.

Fourth, as a result of people's innate tendency to evaluate their in-group membership positively as a way to enhance their self-esteem, they tend to select analogies that absolve the in-group from any responsibility for negative events (often by attributing blame to the out-group), while taking credit for positive ones (e.g., Tajfel 1981). We may call this the *ethnocentric bias*. It is also common to underestimate the influence of situational or structural factors, and to overestimate the influence of actors and their intentions. This tendency is commonly referred to as the *fundamental attribution error* (Ross 1977). Taken together, therefore, analogism may promote scapegoating and underpin inter-group conflicts (see Rydgren 2007).

Mapping the Boundaries of Intersubjectivity

Above I have outlined the ways in which memories and other beliefs about the past matter for action in the present. Such beliefs, activated by the availability heuristic and inferences based on analogism, are often of fundamental importance. However, as should be evident from the discussion above, memories and other beliefs about the past are often flawed. Most events never enter into people's memory, and the details of events that are remembered are often lost or distorted over time. There is a tendency to forget events that are seen as insignificant, or that are less flattering for one's self-esteem. As was argued in the Introduction, moreover, there are good reasons to assume that various social factors create systematic uniformities in people's memories and other beliefs about the past. I will below argue that culture, structural equivalence, social network belonging, and social category belonging are important social factors in creating intersubjective uniformities in people's memories and other beliefs about the past. As a result, they also create some uniformity in present action. These factors should not be viewed in isolation, however, as they overlap in important ways. As shown in Figure 1, some people share both culture and social cat-egory belonging (or network belonging or structural equivalence, etc.). We may assume that the more these four categories overlap the more intersubjective will people's memories and other beliefs about the past be—and the more likely they will be to act in similar ways and, indeed, to engage in collective action. In Figure 1, this is illustrated by color: the darker the shade of gray the stronger the intersubjectivity.

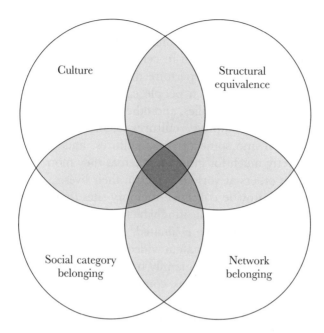

Figure 1. Intersubjectivity.

Culture

As stressed above, a position that holds that cognition plays an important role in the understanding of social action should not be seen as a plea for an atomistic approach. Individuals are socially situated, thinking and feeling beings with personal biographies who live embedded in certain material and historical conditions. The conceptual schemes, knowledge, and information that shape our view of the world are socially mediated and always shared to some extent. As Mannheim (1936: 3) noted, growing up in a society provides "preformed patterns of thought and of conduct" that profoundly influence our thinking. With language, for instance, various interpretive schemes are internalized and institutionally defined (Berger and Luckmann 1966). Hence, it should be noted that beliefs, categories, and schemas are essentially social and always culturally shared to some extent.

I will in this paper follow Swidler's (1986: 273) well-known definition of culture as "the publicly available symbolic forms through which people experience meaning." Such symbolic forms include language, rituals, ceremonies, stories, art forms, various informal practices, and so on. Culture, so conceived, should not be understood as "a unified system" that determines action in certain directions once and for all, but rather as a tool-kit or repertoire that offers a variety of relatively fixed alternatives from which people can chose (Swidler 1986: 277). Nations, organizations, families, and other kinds of groups may espouse distinct—albeit overlapping—cultures according to this definition. People are born into some of these cultures, and are thus likely to take them pretty much for granted, whereas they more or less actively choose to join others at various stages in their lives.

Cultures also provide collective memory sites that instruct people's beliefs about the past by indicating which events are worth remembering and how they should be evaluated. For families, for instance, the family photo album and amateur video archive constitute important collective memory sites, as do family traditions, anniversaries, etc. (see Zerubavel 1996: 293). In nations, commemorations (including national holidays), school curricula, museums, and archives, play the same role. To commemorate a particular event is to constitute it as "an objective fact of the world," to mark it out as a true historical event; as a significant event (Frijda 1997: 111; Schwartz et al. 1986: 148). Commemoration also serves a legitimizing function by signaling to people that it is legitimate to remember and express this memory in certain fashions. Cultures may also have established taboos, which pattern the avoidance practice of group members by influencing which events one should not discuss (Olick and Levy 1997). Also the mass media, television in particular, instruct people's beliefs about the past in patterned ways. Events that are given extensive media coverage are more easily remembered than those that do not pass the news hole. In the logic of the mass media, this implies that events that contain a certain degree of drama (Schudson 1992: 56), get more immediate notice, and are more easily remembered, than other events.

Aside from television, the educational system offers the only information most people have about historical events (Irwin-Zarecka 1994: 155). This gives the state great influence over how people's beliefs about the past are shaped (Wertsch 2002: 10), and one would expect stronger and more far-reaching intersubjective uniformities (i.e., more homogeneous beliefs) in societies in which the state has a monopoly over the production of knowledge, including over the mass media.

Symbolic forms that influence people's beliefs about the past are occasionally created purposefully, and in fact sometimes also destroyed purposefully. As Baumeister and Hastings (1997: 280) have noted, the "easiest and most obvious way to distort collective memory involves the selective omission of disagreeable facts" (see also Devine-Wright 2003: 12). This implies that elites may play important roles in shaping people's beliefs about the past, and not least in influencing the selection of what historic events will enter into analogical reasoning. As Schuman and Reiger (1992: 316) have argued, most "people do not spontaneously dwell on historical analogies when attempting to understand a present problem. Instead analogies to past events are often made salient by those who attempt to shape support for a particular policy." After the Iraqi occupation of Kuwait in 1990, for instance, both leading advocates for and against sending American troops to the Gulf used analogism to win over public support. Those who advocated sending troops relied on the World War II analogism, comparing Saddam Hussein to Hitler and arguing against "appeasement" (comparing war opponents to Chamberlain and others during the 1930s, who refused to act against Hitler up until the invasion of Poland). Those who were against sending troops to the Gulf, on the other hand, relied on the Vietnam War analogy (Schuman and Rieger 1992).

It could thus be argued that people's beliefs are not always fully articulated until they are confronted with the ready-made explicit lines of thought presented by elites (cf. Bourdieu 1984: 459–460). Yet, in order to be successful such elite propaganda must be sufficiently attuned to people's preconceptions, and be in line with their emotional disposition and/or interests (Merton 1968: 572–573). It must resonate (see also Schwartz 1991: 222; Irwin-Zarecka 1994: 71). In the example above, both analogisms were highly resonant; however, the former resonated more strongly among the older generations, whereas the latter more among the younger generations.

Nonetheless, elites and other key actors tend to have a stronger influence than others on people's belief formation process. This is not only because people receive most of their information from these sources, but also that information from certain key actors is seen as more authoritative. We not only see this phenomenon within national cultures, but within other group cultures as well. Kruglanski (1989) has termed these actors *epistemic authorities*. People have greater confidence in information coming from epistemic authorities. They also consider beliefs espoused by these actors as truth; they rely on them and tend to adopt these beliefs as part of their own repertoires. The authority of epistemic authorities often derives from the social role the actor

occupies, a social role often associated with a position of power. Political, intellectual, and religious leaders are typical examples of epistemic
authorities (see Bar-Tal 1990: 71). However, epistemic authorities may
also be more local, such as the family eldest. There will be reasons to
come back to the concept epistemic authority below when discussing
social category belonging and catnets.

Structural Equivalence

There has been an almost single-minded focus on culture in the sociological literature on memory. As implied above, culture is an important
factor in creating intersubjective uniformities in memories and other
beliefs about the past, but far from the only one. The fact that some
people have similar memories and form similar beliefs about the past
that are distinct from those formed by certain other individuals can
also be the result of structural equivalence. We may say that two
persons are structurally equivalent when they occupy the same social
position. We may also assume that individuals in a similar position will
have similar experiences and form similar conceptions around those
experiences (Lorrain and White 1971). People may occupy the same
social position in different ways. They may share institutionalized roles
(e.g., fathers), which means that they "do similar things in relation to
similar others," or by occupying equivalent positions in the distribution
of resources, which results in similar opportunities and interests (e.g.,
blue collar workers) (see e.g., Scott 2000: 124). Structural equivalence
thus captures the phenomenon that Marx talked about in terms of
"class-in-itself" (see also Bearman 1993: 79). In this respect it should be
noted that structural equivalence is a relational concept: people share
social positions vis-à-vis others.

Structural equivalence may create intersubjective uniformities in
memories and other beliefs about the past for two reasons: because of
shared experiences and because of interest-driven distortions. Let us
start with the former. Although shared experiences result in intersubjective patterns in belief formation, they do not, per se, lead to biased
beliefs. However, many people are largely unaware that they engage
with specific but limited slices of reality because of their location in the
social structure. As Nisbett and Ross (1980: 262–263) put it, people
tend to be insensitive to the fact that "their particular niches in the
universe may funnel unrepresentative evidence or information to them

in a thousand different domains." This leads to biases when using the availability heuristic (see above) and, thus, to biased inferences when using analogism as a guiding principle. Currently unemployed workers, for example, tend to overestimate the rate of unemployment, while currently employed workers tend to underestimate it (Nisbett and Ross 1980: 19).

Structural equivalence also yields shared interests. Shared interests, in turn, are an important reason for uniformities in social action. As Weber (1978: 30) noted, "[m]any of the especially notable uniformities in the course of social action [...] [depend] entirely on the fact that the corresponding type of social action is in the nature of the case best adapted to the normal interests of the actors as they themselves are aware of them." Interests, of course, often determine action more directly by influencing people's desires; but they also determine action more indirectly by influencing people's beliefs. This also holds true for people's beliefs about the past. As Bartlett (1995: 256) demonstrated in his pioneering work on memory, interests, which "very often have a direct social origin [...] may decide what it is that a person remember." As was discussed above, at an individual level interests may lead to egocentric biases, and to ethnocentric biases at a group level.

Social Networks, Social Categories, and Catnets

I have so far discussed how culture and structural equivalence, and therefore interests, create intersubjective patterns in memories and other beliefs about the past. In the last section, I will discuss two factors that are of even greater importance: social network belonging and social category belonging. The former is important primarily because it structures people's information; the latter because it is a vector for social identity and because it influences the ways in which information is validated. The reason for bringing social network belonging and social category belonging together in this section rather than giving them separate sections is that they sometimes give rise to emerging properties when they are brought together. So called *catnets*, that is, networks that are homogeneous in terms of social category belonging, are likely to cause far stronger and more extensive intersubjective uniformities in beliefs about the past than are both social network belonging that is heterogeneous in terms of social category belonging and social category belonging among people who are not interlinked in a social network. In fact, one definition of a *social group*, in the strong sense, is that it constitutes a catnet (Tilly 1978: 63). If structural equivalence, as discussed above, comes close to Marx's class-in-itself, the connectivity and identity provided by catnets potentially yield class-for-itself (cf. Bearman 1993: 79).[3]

The social network approach is a way of conceptualizing interpersonal relations. The focus is on relations that link individuals. Such a connection can be directed or undirected, and direct or indirect—that is, individuals A and C can be linked directly or indirectly through individual B (Scott 2000). Such interpersonal relations, in turn, are important as they are simultaneously channels of information, sources of social pressure, and sources of social support, and are thus likely to influence people's beliefs—including their beliefs about the past—and actions in fundamental ways (see Katz 1957). Information is particularly important for understanding intersubjective patterns in memories and other beliefs about the past. Information is not only diffused by mass media, nor does it emanate solely from the tool-kit offered by culture. People also receive much information from persons with whom they interact. People interlinked in a network, and in particular those who find themselves in close-knit networks, are thus likely to share information about various domains. This may, in turn, promote intersubjective beliefs (see Bar-Tal 1990: 9), in particular in black-box situations when people are more likely to rely on information received from others. However, uniformities in memories may be created not only in the process of *receiving* information, but also in *sharing* it. With whom you talk about your experiences is important. Most experiences that enter into working memory are forgotten within a few seconds; they never enter into long-time memory. Cognitive research has shown that experiences that one not only shares with others but also *talks* about with others are less likely to be forgotten—they are partly protected from this kind of transience (Schacter 2001: 31).

A *social category* may be defined as a group of people who recognize their own common characteristics, while other people recognize these

---

[3] As a result, a group of people who constitute a catnet is more likely to engage in collective action—because the chances are greater that its members share a social identity—than is a group of people who only comprise a network *or* a social category (cf. Tilly 1978). This likelihood, of course, will increase to the extent that catnet-members are also in structurally equivalent positions in which they are more likely to mobilize around common goals because they are more likely to share or believe they share interests.

specific shared characteristics as well (Tilly 1978: 62; White 1965: 4). A social category is thus both ascribed and self-understood, and although its distinguishing characteristics can be real enough, social categorization ultimately depends on people's perceptions, interpretations, and cognition (cf. Brubaker et al. 2004). In addition, social category is a relational concept; social categories do not exist in isolation but are social categories in relation to other social categories (e.g., Hogg and Abrams 1988: 14). We all belong to a multitude of different social categories (based on gender, occupation, class, religion, ethnicity, life styles, etc.). The extent to which social category belonging promotes intersubjective uniformities in beliefs about the past depends on two main factors: first, the extent to which social category members belong to crosscutting social categories or overlapping social categories (cf. Simmel 1955). In the first case—when two people are similar across one or two social categories but dissimilar across several others—the intersubjectivity will presumably be rather limited and weak, whereas it will be strong and extensive when two people are similar across a large variety of social categories. As Bar-Tal (1990) has argued, only in really strong cases of overlapping social category belonging—such as in traditional tribal societies—does it make some sense to talk about *collective* beliefs and *collective* memory. However, because of increasing role differentiation, such strong cases of overlapping social category belonging are extremely rare in modern societies (cf. Durkheim 1984; Simmel 1971). Second, the extent to which social category belonging promotes intersubjective beliefs about the past depends on how salient the social category is for the people involved. Salient social categories are likely to yield stronger identity and therefore stronger and more extensive intersubjectivity. Although the salience of social categories is always bound to vary according to context (being Swedish is likely to be a more salient social category when traveling abroad than when staying in Sweden, for instance), two things in particular are likely to influence the salience of a social category: First, social categories that have crystallized "around markers that have systematic implication for people's welfare" (Hechter 2000: 98), or are at least believed to have such implications, can be assumed to be of higher salience than other social categories. Second, social categories that are difficult to wish away—mostly *ascribed* rather than *achieved* social categories, that is, social categories one was born into, such as ethnic or racial belonging—are likely to be more salient, and thus yield stronger social identity and intersubjectivity.

Social category belonging is important for many reasons, one of them being identity-driven distortions that create intersubjective patterns in memories and other beliefs about the past. As discussed above, because people's social identities largely derive from their social category membership, people tend to evaluate such membership positively to enhance their self-esteem (Tajfel 1981). One important strategy is to glorify the history of one's social category by selecting the events that are remembered (or commemorated) and/or by embellishing the memories of these events (see Baumeister and Hastings 1997: 283).

A catnet, finally, can be defined as "a set of individuals comprising both a [social] category and a network" (Tilly 1978: 62; cf. White 1965, 1992). Catnets are common because of the tendency to homophily. People tend to develop relationships with people who belong to the same social category (e.g., Blau 1994; Marsden 1987; McPherson et al. 2001). This has several causes. First, socially similar people may share similar interests. Second, even when they do not share common interests, they tend to spend time in the same place (housing area, clubs, work place, etc.). Third, most people tend to find people with similar tastes to be attractive (Burt 1992: 12). Finally, there are sometimes taboos against intimacy with people of other groups (Zerubavel 1991).

As was discussed above, people tend to rely strongly on information received from epistemic authorities. Social psychological research has demonstrated that information is ascribed stronger epistemic authority when it comes from in-group members than when it comes from out-group members: people are more likely to view somebody belonging to the same social category as themselves as an epistemic authority (Hardin and Higgins 1996: 65; Raviv et al. 1993: 132). This strongly suggests that information within catnets is more likely to yield intersubjective beliefs than does information within ordinary networks.

It should be emphasized that catnets can be of different degree of closure, that is, to varying extents connected to individuals belonging to other social categories. Catnets that are effectively decoupled from others are isolated from information from the outside. This will increase their intersubjective uniformity in beliefs. One reason for such decoupling is physical, geographical distance—either self-selected (such as religious sects that choose physical isolation from non-believers) or not (such as people born on small islands). Another reason for decoupling is insulation, that is, isolation as a result of shared beliefs that nothing good comes from outsiders (e.g., 'infidels') and that interaction with out-group members should be kept at a minimum. Sometimes organizations may also actively try to create overlapping social category belonging in order to reinforce homogeneity of belief. Church groups, for instance, may try to involve their members in various time-consuming voluntary organizations in which they are unlikely to form network ties with people not belonging to the same church. Because it is time-consuming, participation in these organizations "precludes participation in associations that transmit other beliefs" (Borhek and Curtis 1983: 106–107).

The degree of closure of catnets has important implications for the intersubjectivity of memories and other beliefs of the past because it structures social reality testing (Festinger 1950) or social comparisons (Festinger 1954). As discussed above, information from other persons is likely to influence people's beliefs much more strongly in black-box situations—in situations of subjective uncertainty—and in particular when people lack objective reference points for their beliefs and cannot directly check their beliefs against physical reality, or when they lack confidence in such objective reference points (Hogg and Abrams 1988: 167). In such situations of uncertainty, people tend to compare their beliefs to those of significant others, that is, to those of fellow catnet members. The more their beliefs harmonize with those of significant others, the more valid the beliefs are judged to be. In fact, in cases in which people discover that their beliefs harmonize with those held by most others in the group, they tend to become confident in their rightness and they seldom change their opinion (Bar-Tal 2000; Hogg and Abrams 1988). However, situations in which people's beliefs harmonize poorly with those held by significant others—that is, with the general opinion within the catnet—tend to aggravate the feeling of subjective uncertainty. In order to remedy this situation of acute uncertainty, people may either try to change the beliefs held by the others in the group or change their own beliefs "so as to move closer to the group" (Festinger 1954: 126), which is far easier. Processes of social comparison or social reality testing thus often follow catnet-boundaries and are likely to lead to increased belief conformity as a result of a convergence of subjective beliefs toward the general opinion within the group. There are good reasons to assume that such tendencies toward convergence and conformity are particularly strong in the case of memories and other beliefs about the past. For such beliefs there are seldom objective referents with which to verify the beliefs directly, which is why we may assume that social comparison and reality testing become even more common in these cases. Although people are always more likely to compare themselves to similar than to dissimilar persons in social reality testing, an effective decoupling of catnets makes it more difficult—or even impossible—to check ones memories and other beliefs about the past against the opinions of network contacts across social category belonging. This is likely to increase intersubjective uniformities.

As social psychological research in the tradition of Sherif (1936) and Asch (1952, 1956; 1958) has indicated, people are particularly likely to conform to the beliefs held by fellow catnet members when they are faced by a unanimous majority of significant others. As a result, once shared beliefs have been established within catnets, they are rather difficult to change (cf. Hardin and Higgins 1996: 33). Given the strong influence of majorities on individuals' beliefs and action, it is crucial to discuss how likely different forms of ego networks are to produce situations in which persons are faced with unanimous majorities of significant others. One way of doing this is to distinguish between interlocking and radial ego networks (see Figure 2).

In an interlocking network, Egos B and C are not only related to Ego A but also to each other. This is not the case in a radial network. As a consequence, in interlocking networks, Ego A must confront at least two significant others "who are likely to be in communication with one another concerning his manifest behavior and attitudes" (Laumann 1973: 115), and who thus are in a position to form majority coalitions against Ego A. In radial networks, on the other hand, the potential for such coalition building is practically nonexistent, because the relevant others (Egos B and C) lack direct ties to each other. We may as a consequence of this fact assume that beliefs about the past will show stronger intersubjectivity among persons who are interconnected in interlocking than in radial networks, and in particular among those interconnected in interlocking catnets.

There are good reasons to assume that structural situations characterized by decoupled *and* interlocking catnets are more common in rural areas, especially in traditional societies, whereas integrated *and*

Interlocking ego-network   Radial ego-network

Figure 2. Network forms.

radial catnets are more common in urban areas, in particular in the big cities of modern societies—and that the intersubjective uniformities in beliefs about the past therefore tend to be stronger in rural than in urban areas. There are several reasons for this. First, multiform heterogeneity, that is, heterogeneity that penetrates more deeply into substructures (Blau 1977), is more common in urban areas. Second, organizational brokers with the capacity to bridge catnets, that is, organizations that are heterogeneous across a large variety of social categories, are more common in urban areas because the division of labor is more developed and because there is a greater variety of civil society organizations. In rural areas, kin—which tends to be strongly homophile—is more likely to be the dominant organizational principle. Third, geographically and socially mobile persons are more common in urban than in rural areas, and such persons are more likely to be embedded in radial networks, whereas interlocking networks are more common in rural areas where "everyone knows everyone else" (see Laumann 1973: 115–116; cf. Coser 1991).

Conclusion

In order to explain action we have to take people's beliefs, not the least their beliefs about past events, into account. As sociologists, however, we are not primarily interested in explaining the concrete actions of single individuals, but in explaining the typical actions of typical individuals. Weber (2001), for instance, was not interested in explaining why any particular Calvinist or Capitalist believed in what they believed, but why typical beliefs common among, or even constitutive of, Calvinists prepared the ground for the ethos or spirit of capitalism. Hence, most of the time, we are interested in finding patterns in beliefs and actions: why are certain persons (sometimes constituting a group, social class, nation, etc.) more likely to act in a specific way and/or to share specific beliefs? In approaching such questions, I have in this paper argued that culture, structural equivalence, social category belonging, and social network belonging promote intersubjective uniformities in memories and other beliefs about the past.

Culture provides symbolic forms which may direct people's memories and other beliefs about the past in certain directions by indicating which events are considered important and legitimate. To name but a few, archives, educational systems, history books, commemorative rituals play this role. Structural equivalence implies that persons in similar positions will share experiences and will form similar memories and beliefs around these experiences. These persons are also likely to share interests, which may distort their beliefs in important ways. Social networks may create intersubjective uniformities in beliefs about the past because they structure the information that people receive, and also because they channel the social pressure and social support that people feel from significant others. Social networks tend toward social homophily, and also social category belonging may contribute to intersubjective patterns in memories and beliefs about past events. This is primarily because they constitute a basis for social identity, but also because they influence the ways in which information is validated. People are more likely to trust and rely on information received from people belonging to the same social category. It should be emphasized, moreover, that these four factors overlap, and that memories and other beliefs about the past are more likely to be shared when several of these factors overlap.

References

Allport, G. W. and L. J. Postman. 1947. *The Psychology of Rumor*, New York: Holt, Rinehart and Winston.

Asch, S. E. 1952. *Social Psychology*, New York: Prentice-Hall.

——. 1956. "Studies of independence and conformity: A minority of one against a unanimous majority" in *Psychological Monographs*, 70.

——. 1958. "Effects of group pressure upon the modification and distortion of judgments" in E. E. Macoby, T. M. Newcombe and E. L. Hartley (eds.), *Readings in Social Psychology*, New York: Holt, Rinehart and Winston.

Bar-Tal, D. 1990. *Group Beliefs: A Conception for Analyzing Group Structure, Processes, and Behavior*, New York: Springer.

——. 2000. *Shared Beliefs in a Society: Social Psychological Analysis*, London: Sage.

Bartlett, F. C. 1995. *Remembering: A Study in Experimental Social Psychology*, Cambridge: Cambridge University Press.

Baumeister, R. F. and S. Hastings. 1997. "Distortions of collective memory: How groups flatter and deceive themselves" in J. W. Pennebaker, et al. (eds.), *Collective Memory of Political Events: Social Psychological Perspectives*, Mahwah, NJ: Lawrence Erlbaum.

Bearman, P. S. 1993. *Relations into Rhetorics: Local Elite Social Structures in Norfolk, England, 1540–1640*, New Brunswick, NJ: Rutgers University Press.

Belli, R. E. and H. Schuman. 1996. "The complexity of ignorance" in *Qualitative Sociology*, 19(3): 423–430.

Benford, R. D. and D. A. Snow. 2000. "Framing processes and social movements: An overview and assessment" in *Annual Review of Sociology*, 26: 611–639.

Berger, P. L. 1963. *Invitation to Sociology: A Humanistic Perspective*, Garden City, NY: Doubleday Anchor.

Berger, P. and T. Luckmann. 1966. *The Social Construction of Reality: A Treatise in the Sociology of Knowledge*, London: Penguin.

Blau, P. M. 1977. *Inequality and Heterogeneity: A Primitive Theory of Social Structure*, New York: Free Press.

———. 1994. *Structural Contexts of Opportunities*, Chicago: University of Chicago Press.

Borhek, J. T. and R. F. Curtis. 1983. *A Sociology of Belief*, Malabar, FL: Krieger.

Boudon, R. 1989. *The Analysis of Ideology*, Oxford: Polity.

Bourdieu, P. 1984. *Distinction: A Social Critique of the Judgment of Taste*, London: Routledge.

Brubaker, R., M. Loveman and P. Stamatov. 2004. "Ethnicity as cognition" in *Theory and Society*, 33: 31–64.

Burt, R. S. 1992. *Structural Holes: The Social Structure of Competition*, Cambridge, MA: Harvard University Press.

Coser, R. L. 1991. *In Defense of Modernity: Role Complexity and Individual Autonomy*, Stanford: Stanford University Press.

Devine-Wright, P. 2003. "A theoretical overview of memory and conflict" in E. Cairns and M. Roe (eds.), *The Role of Memory in Ethnic Conflict*, Basingstoke: Palgrave.

DiMaggio, P. 1997. "Culture and cognition" in *Annual Review of Sociology*, 23: 263–287.

Durkheim, E. 1984. *The Division of Labor in Society*, New York: The Free Press.

Fentress, J. and C. Wickham. 1992. *Social Memory*, Oxford: Blackwell.

Festinger, L. 1950. "Informal social communication" in *Psychological Review*, 57: 271–282.

———. 1954. "A theory of social comparison processes" in *Human Relations*, 7: 117–140.

———. 1957. *A Theory of Cognitive Dissonance*, Stanford, CA: Stanford University Press.

Fischer, D. H. 1970. *Historians' Fallacies: Toward a Logic of Historical Thought*, New York: Harper Perennial.

Frijda, N. H. 1997. "Commemorating" in J. W. Pennebaker, D. Paez, and B. Rime (eds.), *Collective Memory of Political Events: Social Psychological Perspectives*, Mahwah, NJ: Lawrence Erlbaum.

Gedi, N. and Y. Elam. 1996. "Collective memory: What is it?" in *History and Memory*, 8: 30–50.

Halbwachs, M. 1992. *On Collective Memory*, Chicago: University of Chicago Press.

Hardin, C. D. and E. T. Higgins. 1996. "Shared reality: How social verification makes the subjective objective" in R. M. Sorrentino and E. T. Higgins (eds.), *Handbook of Motivation and Cognition*, vol. 3, New York: Guildford.

Hechter, M. 2000. *Containing Nationalism*, Oxford: Oxford University Press.

Hedström, P. 2005. *Dissecting the Social: On the Principles of Analytical Sociology*, Cambridge: Cambridge University Press.

Hogg, M. A. and D. Abrams. 1988. *Social Identifications: A Social Psychology of Intergroup Relations and Group Processes*, London: Routledge.

Holyoak, K. J. and P. Thagard. 1999. *Mental Leaps: Analogy in Creative Thought*, Cambridge, MA: MIT Press.

Irwin-Zarecka, I. 1994. *Frames of Remembrance: The Dynamics of Collective Memory*, London: Transaction Publishers.

James, W. 1890. *The Principles of Psychology*, New York: Holt, Rinehart and Winston.

Kahneman, D. and A. Tversky. 1982. "Subjective probability: A judgment of representativeness" in D. Kahneman, P. Slovic, and A. Tversky (eds.), *Judgment under Uncertainty: Heuristics and Biases*, Cambridge: Cambridge University Press.

Katz, E. 1957. "The two-step flow of communication: An up-to-date report on a hypothesis" in *Public Opinion Quarterly*, 21: 61–78.

Khong, Y. F. 1992. *Analogies at War: Korea, Munich, Dien Bien Phu, and the Vietnam Decisions of 1965*, Princeton: Princeton University Press.

Kruglanski, A. W. 1989. *Lay Epistemics and Human Knowledge: Cognitive and Motivational Bases*, New York: Plenum.

Laumann, E. O. 1973. *Bonds of Pluralism*, New York: Wiley.

Lorrain, F. and H. C. White 1971. "Structural equivalence of individuals in social networks" in *Journal of Mathematical Sociology*, 1: 49–80.

Macrae, C. N. and G. V. Bodenhausen 2000. "Social cognition: Thinking categorically about others" in *Annual Review of Psychology*, 51: 93–120.

McPherson, M., L. Smith-Lovin and J. C. Cook. 2001. "Birds of a feather: Homophily in social networks" in *Annual Review of Sociology*, 27: 415–444.

Mannheim, K. 1936. *Ideology and Utopia: An Introduction to the Sociology of Knowledge*, New York: Harcourt Brace.

Marsden, P. V. 1987. "Core discussion networks of Americans" in *American Sociological Review*, 52: 122–131.

Merton, R. K. 1968. *Social Theory and Social Structure*, New York: Free Press.

Misztal, B. A. 2003. *Theories of Social Remembering*, Maidenhead: Open University Press.

Nisbett, R. and L. Ross. 1980. *Human Inference: Strategies and Shortcomings of Social Judgement*, Englewood Cliffs NJ: Prentice-Hall.

Olick, J. K. and D. Levy. 1997. "Collective memory and cultural constraints: Holocaust myth and rationality in German politics" in *American Sociological Review*, 62: 921–936.

Paez, D., N. Basabe and J. L. Gonzalez. 1997. "Social processes and collective memory: A cross-cultural approach to remembering political events" in J. W. Pennebaker, D. Paez and B. Rime (eds.), *Collective Memory of Political Events: Social Psychological Perspectives*, Mahwah, NJ: Lawrence Erlbaum.

Raviv, A., D. Bar-Tal and R. Albin. 1993. "Measuring epistemic authority: Studies of politicians and professors" in *European Journal of Personality*, 7: 119–138.

Ross, L. 1977. "The intuitive psychologist and his shortcomings" in L. Berkowitz (ed.), *Advances in experimental social psychology*, vol. 10, New York: Academic Press.

Rubin, D. C. (ed.). 1986. *Autobiographical Memory*, Cambridge: Cambridge University Press.

Rydgren, J. 2004. "The logic of xenophobia" in *Rationality and Society*, 16(2): 123–148.

——. 2007. "The Power of the Past" in *Sociological Theory*, 25: 225–244.

Schacter, D. L. 1995. "Memory distortion: History and current status" in D. L. Schacter (ed.), *Memory Distortion: How Minds, Brains, and Societies Reconstruct their Past*, Cambridge, MA: Harvard University Press.

——. 2001. *The Seven Sins of Memory: How Mind Forgets and Remembers*, New York: Houghton Mifflin.

Schudson, M. 1992. *Watergate in American Memory: How We Remember, Forget and Reconstruct the Past*, New York: Basic Books.

——. 1995. "Dynamics of distortion in collective memory" in D. L. Schacter (ed.), *Memory Distortion: How Minds, Brains, and Societies Reconstruct their Past*, Cambridge, MA: Harvard University Press.

Schuman, H. and C. Rieger. 1992. "Historical analogies, generational effects, and attitudes toward war" in *American Sociological Review*, 57(3): 315–326.

Schwartz, B. 1991. "Social change and collective memory: The democratisation of George Washington" in *American Sociological Review*, 56: 221–236.

Schwartz, B., Y. Zeruvavel and B. Barnett, 1986. "The recovery of Masada: A study in collective memory" in *Sociological Quarterly*, 27(2): 147–164.

Scott, J. 2000. *Social Network Analysis: A Handbook*, London: Sage Publications.

Sherif, M. 1936. *The Psychology of Social Norms*, New York: Harper.

Simmel, G. 1955. *Conflict and The Web of Group-Affiliations*, New York: The Free Press.

——. 1971. "The metropolis and mental life" in D. N. Levine (ed.), *Georg Simmel on Individuality and Social Forms*, Chicago: The University of Chicago Press.

Sontag, S. 2003. *Representing the Pain of Others*, New York: Farrar, Strauss and Giroux.

Swidler, A. 1986. "Culture in action: Symbols and strategies" in *American Sociological Review*, 51: 273–286.

Tajfel, H. 1981. *Human Groups and Social Categories: Studies in Social Psychology*, Cambridge: Cambridge University Press.

Tilly, C. 1978. *From Mobilization to Revolution*, New York: McGraw-Hill.

Tversky, A. and D. Kahneman. 1982a. "Causal schemas in judgments under uncertainty" in D. Kahneman, P. Slovic and A. Tversky (eds.), *Judgment Under Uncertainty: Heuristics and Biases*, Cambridge: Cambridge University Press.

——. 1982b. "Judgment under uncertainty: Heuristics and biases" in D. Kahneman, P. Slovic and A. Tversky (eds.), *Judgment Under Uncertainty: Heuristics and Biases*, Cambridge: Cambridge University Press.

Weber, M. 1978. *Economy and Society: An Outline of Interpretive Sociology*, Los Angeles: University of California Press.

——. 2001. *The Protestant Ethic and the Spirit of Capitalism*, London: Routledge.

Wertsch, J. 2002. *Voices of Collective Remembering*, Cambridge: Cambridge University Press.

White, H. C. 1965. "Notes on the constituents of social structure", *Mimeo*, Department of Sociology, Harvard University.

——. 1992. *Identity and Control: A Structural Theory of Social Action*, Princeton, NJ: Princeton University Press.

Zerubavel, E. 1991. *The Fine Line: Making Distinctions in Everyday Life*, Chicago: University of Chicago Press.

——. 1996. "Social memories: Steps to a sociology of the past" in *Qualitative Sociology*, 19(3): 283–300.

THE ANALYTICAL TURN IN SOCIOLOGY

Peter Hedström

In his highly readable book, *Dreams of a Final Theory* (1993), the Nobel laureate in physics, Steven Weinberg, discusses the role philosophy has played in the development of physics. According to Weinberg little of value has been gained by interacting with philosophers: "I know of *no one* who has participated actively in the advance of physics in the post-war period whose research has been significantly helped by the work of philosophers." Instead he gives a range of examples that show how various philosophical dogmas, such as the positivistic one that theories always must refer to observable entities, have hindered the development of physics. The only somewhat positive influence he can discern is that one philosophical doctrine sometimes has protected from the influence of even more harmful ones: "The insights of philosophers have occasionally benefited physicists, but generally in a negative fashion—by protecting them from the preconceptions of other philosophers".

Despite the fact that one could easily find examples of philosophical ideas and philosophers that have negatively influenced the development of sociology as a scientific discipline, I do not share Weinberg's pessimistic view. In fact, I believe that something which can be described as an analytical turn in sociological theorizing is making certain branches of analytical philosophy increasingly important for sociology.

Analytical philosophy is a rather heterogeneous field but a common theme in most branches of analytical philosophy is the conviction that many of the intellectual puzzles and problems we face are due to ambiguities in our language. Once we express them with sufficient clarity, they will become soluble or cease to exist. Hence most analytical philosophers are interested in various forms of formal logic as a more precise language than our natural languages.

Although the use of formal logic would seem to be of considerable importance for sociology, it is rarely used. One important exception is the ambitious book by Michael Hannan, Laszlo Polos, and Glenn Carroll (2007) which uses logic to formalize various aspects of organizational ecology. An important reason why they have turned to logic is their belief that natural languages are not well suited for theoretical integration, and, one of the major goals of their book is to show the power of formal logic for theory integration in the social sciences.

Important as this may prove to be, logic is neither the area of analytical philosophy that excites me the most, nor is it the area of analytical philosophy that I believe to be the most important for the development of an analytically oriented sociology. In my view, other formalisms such as mathematics and computational modeling appear to be more important for sociology than formal logic (see the chapters by Breen and Edling for discussions about the role of mathematics and computer simulation in sociological theory and research). What I find particularly attractive in analytical philosophy is rather the general style of scholarship as well as a number of specific conceptual clarifications that are of considerable importance for sociological theory.

The style of scholarship one finds in analytical philosophy can be concisely characterized as follows:

- An emphasis on the importance of clarity: If it is not perfectly clear what someone is trying to say, confusion is likely to arise, and this will hamper our understanding.
- An emphasis on the importance of analysis in terms of breaking something down to its basic constituents in order to better understand it.
- An academic style of writing that does not shy away from abstraction and formalization when this is deemed necessary.

By adopting principles such as these, it is possible to devise a more analytically oriented sociology that seeks to explain complex social processes by carefully dissecting them, bringing into focus their most important constituent components, and then to construct appropriate models which help us to understand why we observe what we observe. Let me try to briefly indicate what I have in mind, starting with analysis in terms of dissection and abstraction.

Dissection, Action, and Interaction

To dissect, as I use the term, is to decompose a complex process into its constituent entities and activities in order to bring into focus what is believed to be its most essential elements. It is through dissection and abstraction that the important cogs and wheels of social processes are made visible and intelligible.

When a complex process is decomposed into its constituent components, the type of problem being analyzed will obviously dictate which entities and activities are considered important. In most sociological inquiries, however, the core entities tend to be actors, and the core activities tend to be the actions of these actors. Through their actions actors make society 'tick', and without their actions social processes would come to a halt. Theories of action are therefore of fundamental importance for explanatory sociological theories.

This is an area in which philosophers of mind and action, such as George Henrik von Wright (1971) and Donald Davidson (1980), have made important contributions. They have clarified many of the issues involved and thereby enhanced sociological theory. What I have in mind is their analyses of action-explanations and of the notion to causally explain an action by referring to the reasons—desires and beliefs—that motivated it.

As suggested by von Wright, a particular combination of desires and beliefs constitutes a 'compelling reason' for performing an action. Desires and beliefs have a motivational force that allows us to understand and, in this respect, explain the action. The cause of an action therefore is a constellation of desires and beliefs in the light of which the action appears reasonable.

In most of the philosophy of action literature, the focus is on the action of a single actor. For sociologists, however, the focus typically is on social (as distinct from psychological) explananda. That is, sociology is not a science which seeks to explain why single individuals do what they do or feel the way they do. The focus on actions is merely an intermediate step in an explanatory strategy that seeks to understand change at a social level.

As I use the term, the 'social' refers to collective properties that are not definable for a single member of the collectivity. Important examples of such phenomena include:

- typical actions, beliefs, desires etc. among the members of the collectivity;
- distributions and aggregate patterns such as spatial distributions and inequalities;
- topologies of networks that describe relationships between the members of the collectivity; and
- informal rules or social norms that constrain the actions of the members of the collectivity.

It is important to recognize that social outcomes like these are *emergent* phenomena. With emergent phenomena I am not referring to mystic holistic entities with their own causal powers, but to social phenomena like these that are brought about usually as unintended by-products of the actions of interacting individuals.

Once we shift the focus from that of a single actor to that of a collectivity of actors, two additional types of explanandum are involved. Not only must we focus on reasons as causes, as Davidson and others did, we must also consider the causes of reasons, as well as the effects of the actions that these reasons cause. We can express these ideas with a slightly modified version of James Coleman's (1986) so-called micro-macro graph.

The philosophy of action literature is mainly concerned with the link between B and C, reasons or other orientations to action, on the one hand, and actions, on the other, and to some extent with the internal relations within B, such as Davidson's analyses of wishful thinking. For social scientists the links between A and B, and between C and D can be said to be even more crucial since we primarily want to understand why we observe whatever we observe at the macro level.

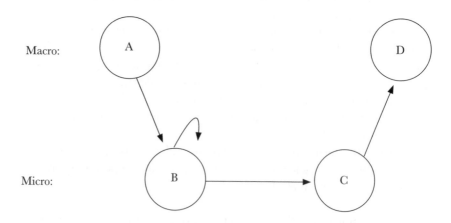

Macro: A   D

Micro: B ——————————▶ C

A: Actions of others or other relevant environmental conditions

B: Individual beliefs, desires, opportunities, etc.

C: Individual action

D: Emergent social outcomes, e.g., extent of action, inequalities, and networks.

Figure 1. Micro-macro relations typically involved in sociological explanations.

In making these sort of transitions between different levels of analysis, social interactions come to the fore. That is, in order to explain an actor's reasons, desires, beliefs, etc., the A-to-B link, we must relate them to the actions, desires, beliefs, etc of those with whom the actor interacts. Similarly, and as will be illustrated in the next section, when we seek to make the transition from micro to macro and explain the macro-level outcomes that actors bring about, the C-to-D link, interactions are crucial.

Clarity, Precision, and the Micro-Macro Link

If it is not perfectly clear what a given theory or theorist is trying to say, it is impossible to assess the potential merits of the theory being proposed. The purpose of theorizing should always be to clarify matters, to make the complex and seemingly obscure clear and understandable. But if the theory itself lacks clarity, this goal cannot be attained.

One example of a mystifying statement is the following, in which Bourdieu tries explicitly to define his master concept of habitus. According to Bourdieu (1990: 53), habitus should be understood as

> [...] systems of durable, transposable dispositions, structured structures predisposed to function as structuring structures, that is, as principles which generate and organize practices and representations that can be objectively adapted to their outcomes without presupposing a conscious aiming at ends or an express mastery of the operations necessary in order to attain them. Objectively 'regulated' and 'regular' without being in any way the product of obedience to rules, they can be collectively orchestrated without being the product of the organizing action of a conductor.

Ambiguous definitions like this one are like mental clouds that mystify rather than clarify, and from the perspective of explanatory theory they are clearly unsatisfactory. Not only is it unclear what habitus more precisely refers to and how it differs from habits, traditions, conventions, etc., it is also unclear why he believes that habitus, whatever it is, operates the way it does. If we want to propose that one phenomenon partly or fully explains another, it must at least be perfectly clear what phenomena we are referring to and why and how we believe they are interrelated. That is to say, definitions of the key terms must be clear and precise, and we must specify in great detail the causal mechanisms believed to be at work.

Clarity, in the sense of precision, is important for a slightly different reason as well. If, for example, a theory states that 'agency' and 'structure' are important for explaining a particular social outcome, most likely this would not be incorrect, but it would be too blunt and imprecise to be of much use. As perhaps most vividly demonstrated in Thomas Schelling's work (e.g., Schelling 1978), small and seemingly insignificant differences or events can sometimes set in motion social processes that make a huge difference for the outcomes we are trying to explain. If our concepts and theories are not sufficiently precise to pick up on such differences, they are not capable of explaining why we observe what we observe.

Schelling was interested in the link between micro-motives and actions, on the one hand, and the oftentimes unexpected and unintended macro-behavior these actions bring about, on the other. His most famous example concerns residential segregation and his core ideas can be summarized as follows. We have two types of individuals, let us call them White and Black, who individually decide where to live, but these decisions are influenced by the decisions of others. The Blacks and the Whites are not necessarily prejudiced against one another, but they prefer to live near at least some of 'their own' kind. That is, each White wants to live near at least some Whites, and each Black wants to live near at least some Blacks.

Let us start with a 'state of nature' in which the Whites and the Blacks are randomly distributed in the city, society, or social space represented by a large lattice like the one in Figure 2.[1]

When distributed randomly like this, many will be "unhappy" since they do not have enough neighbors of their own color. The unhappy therefore move to new locations, but in the new locations, they might tip the balance of the local population, prompting others to leave. If a few Whites move into an area, the local Blacks might leave, and when they arrive to their new area, they might prompt Whites to leave, and so on.

Let us start with assuming that these agents indeed are somewhat prejudiced and want at least 60 percent of their own kind in their neighborhood to be satisfied (a 'neighborhood' here is defined as the eight squares surrounding an individual). Not surprisingly, the pattern

---

[1] The segregation model in NetLogo version 3.1.4 has been used for these simulations. See Wilensky (1998) for details.

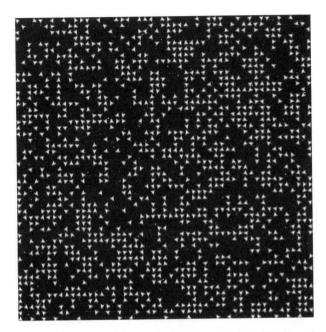

Figure 2. Random spatial distribution of 1,250 Black and
1,250 White agents.

that then emerges is segregated, but possibly more segregated than
one would expect given the desires of the individual agents. A typical
pattern looks like the one in Figure 3, i.e., the agents sort themselves
into highly segregated clusters.

The most interesting aspect of Schelling's analysis is that is shows
that even if individual agents are almost 'color blind', segregation often
arises. The pattern in Figure 4, for example, is a typical pattern brought
about when individuals tolerate up to 74 percent of the other kind in
their neighborhood before they want to leave.

There are more white and black 'islands' in Figure 4 than in Figure 3,
but the segregation still is highly pronounced. There is also a considerable difference between the collective outcome the individuals bring
about and their individual desires. Although each individual was willing to accept up to 74 percent of the other kind in the neighborhood,
the social dynamics led to a situation where the average neighborhood
consisted of only 30 percent of the other kind. Thus, although the individuals do not mind that three out of four neighbors are of the other
kind, as an unintended by-product of their behavior they bring about
a much more segregated outcome.

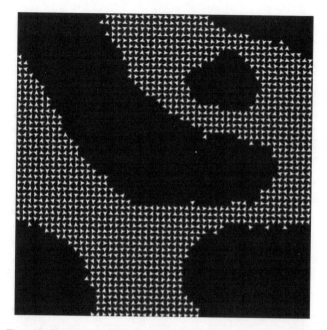

Figure 3. Typical segregation pattern emerging when agents accept up to 60 percent of the other kind in their neighborhood.

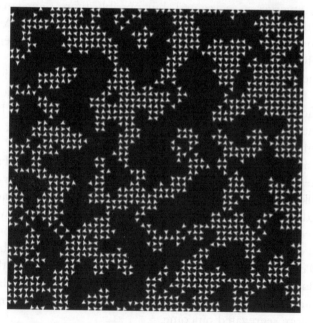

Figure 4. Typical segregation pattern emerging when agents accept up to 74 percent of the other kind in their neighborhood.

The reason why I find Schelling's analyses so important is not because they always say much about why real-world societies are highly segregated. As we know, such processes are also influenced by a host of other factors.[2] Its importance lies in the purely theoretical aspects: the fact that it, better that any other analysis or argument that I know of, brings home the point about the privileged status of micro-level interactions in explaining macro-level outcomes. The difficulties of trying to use macro patterns to infer something about the micro-motives that brought them about is even more striking if we compare the "74%-society" in Figure 4 to the "75%-society" in Figure 5.

While segregation was clearly discernable in Figure 4, the pattern in Figure 5 is barely distinguishable from the random allocation of Figure 2. The difference between Figure 4 and Figure 5 illustrates a so-called tipping point. A small difference at the micro-level makes a considerable difference at the macro-level. If we were presented with

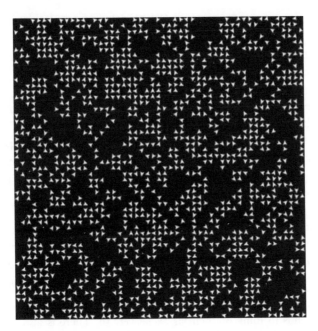

Figure 5. Typical segregation pattern emerging when agents accept up to 75 percent of the other kind in their neighborhood.

---

[2] See Bruch and Mare (2006) for an interesting attempt to empirically test Schelling's model.

the macro-level patterns only, it is very likely that we would draw the conclusion that because the society pictured in Figure 4 is so segregated, those who generated its pattern must be much more prejudiced than those who generated the pattern in Figure 5 even though the individual-level differences between the individuals in the two societies are in fact negligible.

This is a very important result that extends far beyond these stylized examples: *Macro-level outcomes and relationships tell us very little about why we observe the macro-level outcomes and relationships we observe.* Trying to make causal inferences on the basis of macro-level data is highly error prone. The reason for this is that the mechanisms that bring about macro-level outcomes and relationships are not found at this aggregate level. We must instead seek to make the transitions between micro and macro levels as indicated in Figure 1 and as illustrated by the Schelling-type of simulations.

Concluding Remarks

At least three important lessons can be learned from the stylized analyses presented in the previous section:

1. There is no necessary proportionality between the size of a cause and the size of its effect.
2. The structure of social interaction is of considerable explanatory importance in its own right for the social outcomes that emerge.
3. Aggregate patterns say very little about the micro-level processes that brought them about.

The relationship between micro and macro is far from transparent. If we fail to take these complexities into account by properly explicating the type of process likely to have been at work, we are easily led astray. Half a century ago, Leon Festinger (1957: 233) made a similar point:

> Mass phenomena are frequently so striking and dramatic in quality that one tends to think of them as exclusively so. There is also a tendency to seek explanations of these striking phenomena which match them in dramatic quality; that is, one looks for something unusual to explain the unusual result. It may be, however, that there is nothing more unusual about these phenomena than the relative rarity of the specific combination of ordinary circumstances that brings about their occurrence.

As the existence of notions such as Matthew effects (Merton 1968), threshold effects (Granovetter 1978), tipping points (Schelling 1978), cumulative causality (Myrdal 1944), and path dependency (Arthur 1994) suggests, the interactive and endogenous nature of social processes has been a key concern of some of the very best social scientists. Nevertheless, I think it is fair to say that the insights of these writers have not fully penetrated the discipline, and that many sociologists still commit to the type of linear exogeneity fallacy that Festinger referred to.

The prevalence of this fallacy can, at least in part, be attributed to the informal character of most sociological theories. As discussed above, the social processes linking micro and macro are usually so complex that they are virtually incomprehensible without the aid of some formal analytical tools like the agent-based simulation models used above. Without such tools it is difficult to recognize, and even more difficult to convince others, that the large-scale phenomena that are observed may simply be due to an uncommon combination of common events and circumstances, or to small and seemingly unimportant changes at the micro level. Sociology focuses on complex and difficult subject matters and, if the discipline is to be a rigorous science of the social, formal analytical tools is simply a necessity.

As I have argued at great length in Hedström (2005), in order to further the development of explanatory sociological theory, our theories need to be based on clearly defined action- and interaction-related mechanisms. By piecing together the relevant set of mechanisms, we can construct explanatory models applicable to the particular problem at hand. The mechanisms to be used should be compatible with each other and with what is known in other disciplines, but like in the case of Merton's (1967) notion of middle-range theory, there is no attempt to unify all mechanisms under one general theory.

As argued in Hedström and Ylikoski (2009), the structure of theoretical knowledge is better understood as a theoretical toolbox than as a deductively organized axiomatic system. Sociological theory is constituted by a set of semi-general explanatory tools that can be used in a range of different domains. A fully developed mechanism-oriented sociology differs from many other types of sociology that tend to be organized around specific 'social domains' such as work, family, or organizations, leading to sub-fields such as the sociology of work, family sociology, and organizational sociology. If the traditional domain-based organization of the discipline is thought of as being vertical, the mechanism-oriented approach is horizontal. Instead of specializing in the study of some specific vertical slice, the family, for example, such an approach would slice the discipline horizontally and study mechanisms that cut across different domains. It seeks to identify semi-general mechanisms which are as relevant in the organizational domain as in the family or the work domain, for example.

References

Arthur, W. B. 1994. "Path dependence, self-reinforcement, and human learning" in W. B. Arthur (ed.), *Increasing Returns and Path Dependency in the Economy*, Ann Arbor: University of Michigan Press.
Bourdieu, P. 1990. *The Logic of Practice*, Cambridge: Polity Press.
Bruch, E. E. and R. D. Mare. 2006. "Neighborhood choice and neighborhood change" in *American Journal of Sociology*, 112: 667–709.
Coleman, J. S. 1986. "Social theory, social research, and a theory of action" in *American Journal of Sociology*, 91: 1309–1335.
Davidson, D. 1980. *Essays on Actions and Events*, Oxford: Clarendon Press.
Festinger, L. 1957. *A Theory of Cognitive Dissonance*, Stanford, CA: Stanford University Press.
Granovetter, M. S. 1978. "Threshold models of collective behavior" in *American Journal of Sociology*, 83: 1420–1443.
Hannan, M. T., L. Polos, and G. R. Carroll. 2007. *Logics of Organization Theory: Audiences, Codes, and Ecologies*, Princeton: Princeton University Press.
Hedström, P. 2005. *Dissecting the Social: On the Principles of Analytical Sociology*, Cambridge: Cambridge University Press.
Hedström, P. and P. Ylikoski. 2009. "Analytical sociology" in I. Jarvie and J. Zamora-Bonilla (eds.), *The SAGE Handbook of the Philosophy of the Social Sciences*, Sage Publications Ltd.
Merton, R. K. 1967. "On sociological theories of the middle range" in R. K. Merton (ed.), *On Theoretical Sociology*, New York: The Free Press, 39–72.
———. 1968. "The Matthew effect in science" in *Science*, 159: 56–63.
Myrdal, G. 1944. *An American Dilemma: The Negro Problem and Modern Democracy*, New York: Harper & Brothers Publishers.
Schelling, T. C. 1978. *Micromotives and Macrobehavior*, New York: W.W. Norton.
von Wright, G. H. 1971. *Explanation and Understanding*, Ithaca, NY: Cornell University Press.
Weinberg, S. 1993. *Dreams of a Final Theory*, London: Vintage.
Wilensky, U. 1998. "NetLogo segregation model", see http://ccl.northwestern.edu/netlogo/models/Segregation.

SOCIOLOGY AND THE MATHEMATICAL AND
STATISTICAL SCIENCES

WE ALWAYS KNOW MORE THAN WE CAN SAY: MATHEMATICAL SOCIOLOGISTS ON MATHEMATICAL SOCIOLOGY

Christofer Edling

Introduction

It is hard to exaggerate the role of mathematical tools for the advances of science.[1] Indeed one needs only to pick up a copy of a science journal such as *Nature* or *Science* to realize that a good deal of technical skill is needed to follow the frontiers of science. The same can hardly be said about the frontiers of sociology and many other social sciences. Because of the tension between science and literature, a defining characteristic of sociology throughout its history, the role of mathematics in the advancement of sociology has always been, and still is an issue. In this chapter I once more revisit the question of the possibility of a mathematical sociology through a set of interviews with mathematical sociologists.

There are many examples of sociology trying to take advantage of mathematics to solve problems (Coleman 1964; Edling 2002; Fararo 1997; Heckathorn 1984). However it is less easy to find examples where sociological problems, broadly defined, have stimulated mathematical work. Still, we have two powerful examples where it is easy to see how mathematics has contributed to the development of the social sciences.

First there is the well-known example of the development of game theory by the mathematicians von Neumann (von Neumann and Morgenstern 1944) and Nash (1951) that effectively re-draw the map of

---

[1] I wish to thank the scholars who accepted not only to be interviewed by me, but who also shared valuable experiences and suggestions; Peter Abell, Philip Bonacich, Kathleen Carley, Patrick Doreian, Thomas Fararo, and Harrison White. I owe the late Aage Sørensen for his enthusiasm in this project and for sharing many thoughts in extended discussions. Part of this work has been presented at Utrecht University and at Swedish Collegium for Advanced Study (SCAS) and I thank participants in those seminars for useful remarks and suggestions. In addition, I wish to thank Peter Hedström, Fredrik Liljeros, Werner Raub, and Richard Swedberg for very helpful suggestions.

neoclassical economics, and eventually also spilled over to the biological sciences (Maynard Smith 1982). Game theory builds on the simple idea that the action of ego is strategically dependent on the action of alter; a Weberian idea that sociologists should indeed find attractive. But however dramatic the effect on economics, game theory has had very little impact on the other social sciences save perhaps for political science (but see Swedberg 2001 for a discussion on game theory in sociology).

Second, and highly relevant for sociology, there is the less well-known example of social network analysis. Network analysis has grown tremendously during the last 30 years or so into a very vigorous research tradition, spanning so many disciplines (Carrington, Scott and Wasserman 2005; Newman, Barabási and Watts 2006) that by some even referred to as a Kuhnian paradigm. Although social network ideas can be traced further back, contemporary network analysis was developed at Harvard in the early 1970s under leadership of Harrison White (Freeman 2004; Wellman 1988) with a great deal of inspiration and motivation from development in graph theory (Harary, Norman and Cartwright 1965). Due to the complexity in analyzing even a small structure of social entities and their interrelations, mathematical tools are at the core of both theoretical and empirical network analysis. Indeed, social network analysis is a prime example of sociology "turning a profit from mathematics" (Freeman 1984). And the most remarkable fact is that while the general experience is that use of mathematics tends to scare sociologists off, network analysis is the home to scholars whose diverse research interests span from personal identity construction to epidemiology, from ethnography to analyzing the structure of Internet communication.

Before turning to the interviews, I wish to highlight a few of the utilities that arise from using mathematics as a tool for social science. These will be touched upon also in the remainder of the chapter. First of all mathematics is a much more exact language than the written or spoken word, which brings clarification and coherence to theoretical arguments and help eliminate ambiguous interpretation. Thus it is a very powerful tool. Second, mathematics is a unifying language that promotes communication and problem solving among otherwise conceptually separate scientific communities. In his book on the transdisciplinary Santa Fe Institute, Waldrop quotes a discussion with Eugenia Singer claiming that "it was mathematics that provided the common language" and "if they had gotten a lot of social scientists in there with no technical background, I'm not sure the gulf could have been crossed" (Waldrop 1992: 195). Thirdly, because it is a unifying language, mathematics provides a way to learn from other scientific domains that struggle with structurally similar properties. Mathematics can bring our attention both to the isomorphism between sociology and other sciences and by way of example suggest possible ways to apply mathematics in sociology (Coleman 1964; White 1997).

From social network analysis we learn that mathematics can serve the social sciences in just the same way as it serves the natural sciences. In the development of social network analysis mathematics has provided a tool to tackle complexity, a language to ease communication, and a way to bridge theoretical concepts in sociology, mathematics, anthropology, computer science, physics, etc. So we do know that mathematics can help us make considerable scientific progress. However, the rest of the chapter takes as a point of departure the fact that by and large, mathematics is rarely put to work in sociology and when it is, it is done by a small number of sociologists.

Interviews

My interest in mathematical sociology deals both with the possibility of applying some mathematics in my own work as well as with the tradition in itself and the biographies of mathematical sociologists. The first admittedly remains an ongoing struggle. But as a consequence of the latter—and by inspiration from Swedberg's (1990) book of interviews with economists and sociologists on the interface between economics and sociology—I carried out a set of interviews with a small number of influential contemporary mathematical sociologists. In parallel I studied mathematical sociology, trying to get a grip on what type of work mathematical sociologists really did. While that effort was published in a review article some years ago (Edling 2002) I would like to take this opportunity to present some more of the interview material.

I conducted six interviews in the late 1990s. Chronologically, the interviews were done in the following order: Patrick Doreian (May 29, 1998), Harrison White (May 29, 1998), Philip Bonacich (August 22, 1998), Kathleen Carley (February 20, 1999), Peter Abell (May 3, 1999), and Thomas Fararo (August 9, 1999). The interviews did not focus primarily on the substantial sociological contributions of these scholars. Rather I used the interviews in order to find out how they turned to mathematical sociology, and from what background they came. And my prime interest was to get their view on the role of mathematics in sociology at large. I also wanted to hear what they had to say on the evolution, status, and future promises of the field in a broad perspective. I selected my victims on an ad hoc basis, formed by my own readings in mathematical sociology. I wanted to meet with people who had long experience from mathematical sociology and who were still contemporary leaders in the field. Obviously there are several biases in my selection and I wish to stress that even given my selection criteria, the list of people that would have been perfect to interview is quite long. One striking selection bias is my preponderance towards sociologists active in the US Another apparent bias is that there is only one woman in my sample. An obvious reason is that there are not many women actively pursuing mathematical sociology. However, a few additional women could easily be included if the set of interviews were to be extended or revised.

A special characteristic of the mathematical approach to sociological problems is that it involves many scholars from outside academic sociology, something that was clearly brought out in some of the interviews. Therefore it might seem awkward that I concentrate only on sociologists. Several persons of the past and present that are not sociologists have made substantial contributions to mathematical sociology. Names that spring to mind are Herbert Simon, Garry Becker, Dirk Helbing, and Robert Axelrod. But there are many others. However, I wanted to make sure that I talked to people who strongly identified both with sociology in itself and with mathematical sociology.

As it turned out, Peter Abell only hesitantly agreed to the label while others did with some qualifications. This is Abell's frank answer to my opening question on how he got into mathematical sociology:

> Let me say first that I do not regard myself as a mathematical sociologist. I regard myself as a sociologist who is often led to try and use mathematics because it is the only way of really being clear about complex phenomena. So I am not a mathematical sociologist, and I do not really regard myself as a good enough mathematician to so describe myself (Peter Abell).

While both Patrik Doreian and Harrison White did identify stronger with the label mathematical sociologist they too did throw in caveats. Doreian, long term and highly dedicated editor of *Journal of Mathematical Sociology* and since recently the editor of *Social Networks* said that,

> Given that I work in a lot of different substantive areas, and that I always use some mathematics at some point, I would have to say it is mathematical sociology. When I describe what I do, often I use mathematical sociology as a description. I have tried using "playing in a mathematical play pen", but that generates a similar response to saying mathematical sociology. Maybe the conjunction of 'play' and 'mathematical' was the problem! (Patrik Doreian)

And White, indeed one of the most prominent mathematical sociologists ever and also a key person in the development of contemporary network analysis said that,

> I would prefer sociologist, and theoretical sociologist. But I am also a mathematical sociologist, and that is a fine thing to be. But I do not want to be just a mathematical sociologist. I think mathematical modeling is an auxiliary; it is not the driving thing. I am a sociologist, and that is the whole point, you want to understand social phenomena, their political and economical aspects, and their anthropological aspects (Harrison White).

These quotations do capture some of the contradictory essence of mathematical sociology. On the one hand, one is hesitant to name oneself a mathematical sociologist and even to claim mathematical sociology as a sub-field in its own because it is the sociological issues that are always at stake, and on the other hand one tends at the same time to value highly mathematical sociology as such. But the driving force is not to carve out a niche space on sociology but to contribute to sociology with a capital s. Rather, one is drawn to applying mathematics out of necessity in the strive for precision, as in Abell's case, or as a means to an end as in White's case, or one is just inclined to do so out of personal preference, as in Doreian's case, just as one might have a personal preference for some method or theory over others. I proceed now by turning first to the mathematical sociology, second to the mathematical sociologists, and finally to some concluding remarks.

What is Mathematical Sociology?

So, what is this thing called mathematical sociology? In a sense the question directly targets the historically ever imminent tension over what is the core of sociology itself. Is sociology a humanist endeavor, the critical and reflexive voice in (post)modern society? Or is sociology a science of the social, similar to the way in which physics is a science of the natural? Is sociology maybe both? It might very well be the case that this tension in itself is really the core of sociology, as some have claimed (Lepenies 1988). Whatever is the case; with some confidence I would say that a mathematical sociologist certainly subscribes to the idea that sociology is a science of the social, possibly to the idea that it can be both. Of course this does not help much as sociology has not decided what it means to be a science of the social. But nor, do I believe, have mathematical sociologists. Just as sociology at large, mathematical sociology is a very heterogeneous field (Freese 1980). What does constitute its borders is a shared conviction that mathematics can bring leverage to sociological analysis. Even though this might be debated, most sociologists, and including the ones I have interviewed, would make a very clear distinction between statistical modeling and mathematical sociology. Indeed, the literature on mathematical sociology and the interviews with mathematical sociologists suggest that mathematical sociology is strictly a theoretical affair. Thus, it is the application of mathematics to sociological theorizing that defines mathematical sociology. And mathematics is used broadly to include also logic and computer models. Formal theory could therefore be an alternative label and is often used as such. However, it would be at fault not to acknowledge that statistical modeling is the area within sociology in which mathematics has the strongest impact on the field as a whole. The statistical tools being put to work in network analysis, event-history analysis, and hierarchical modeling do bring added sophistication to quantitative sociology.

Nevertheless, classifications of mathematical sociology highlight the use of mathematics for constructing *theoretical* models of social phenomena. Even though many mathematical sociologists are using and sometimes even develop quantitative methods, they often point out explicitly that the use of mathematics in sociology should not be equated with statistics. And the people I interviewed all subscribe to the idea that mathematical sociology belongs to theoretical sociology proper. In general there is no agreement on what is theoretical sociology. Many things indeed go into that label. In this respect, mathematical sociologists seem to be a bit more united than the discipline at large.

Many, including myself, take the view that theoretical model building is an act of balancing realism, generality, and precision. In this act of balance, one will have to stand back in favor of the other two simply because all things cannot be achieved (Heckathorn 1984; Levins 1966). If one accepts this premise, one can continue discussing the pros and cons of model building. Mathematical sociology is often accused of sacrificing realism for precision. To some extent this critique is justi-fied, but as was implied by Abell in the opening quotation precision might be what foremost attracts many of the proponents of the field. Moreover the way to manage this balancing act is not agreed upon. And to contrast, Fararo (1989) argues that realism is the driving force in model construction because we build the model only when there is something there to be modeled, and models are deliberately constructed as representations of the real world.

Obviously, model building is about making idealizations of a complex reality by using simplifying, and sometimes false, assumptions. However, few sociologists would base their models on obviously false assumptions if it means distorting the essential feature of the problem. Some of those that I interviewed did express doubts over some scientific endeavors perceived as over-theorized, such as mathematical physics and parts of neo-classical economics. In this respect, mathematical sociologists appear to safe-guard against loosing touch with real sociological issues and are very reluctant to withdraw into pure model development. This, for instance is Peter Abell's reflection on the relationship between mathematical sociology and sociology.

> If I look at contemporary economics, for instance, I am sometimes worried about the extent to which technical facility is so highly rated that people can spend their time immersed in the technical problems and loose sight of the fact that we are really trying to understand a complex world. They have to simplify the world that they want to look at to such a degree that one sometimes wonder whether it is worthwhile. I would *not* like sociology to take that direction. I think the great strength of sociology, if it has any strength, is that it has tried to take empirical complexity seriously, and has not done what some parts of economics have done, and I think we should preserve that (Peter Abell).

Still, the issue is delicate, as it is extremely hard to decide how much complexity and heterogeneity one should account for. I would argue in favor of a sociological model to be general enough to explain social phenomena across time and space, whereas some would claim that sociology is a historical science and as such no model can be applied across time and space. In addition sociological models should be pre-cise, or else they cannot serve as hypothesis generators and consistency checkers in any substantial way; and those are two important functions for theoretical models (Carley 1997). Consequently it can be argued that realism will have to give way to generality and precision. Such a modeling paradigm is characterized by the expectation "that many

of the unrealistic assumptions will cancel each other, that small deviations from realism result in small deviations in the conclusions, and
that, in any case, the way in which nature departs from theory will
suggest where future complications will be useful" (Levins 1966: 422).
To illustrate the balance of realism, generality and precision, I wish to
give two examples of simple mathematical models that successfully walk
the line. Incidentally, both models are submitted by non-sociologists,
although Watts later transferred to a sociology department. Schelling's
model of segregation is a classic example and Watts' and Strogatz's
model of the small world is on its way to becoming one.

The motivation for Thomas Schelling's dynamic models of segregation was the observation that people get segregated across many dimensions and often by discrimatory individual behavior. "By 'discrimatory'
I mean reflecting an awareness, conscious, or unconscious, of sex or age
or religion or color or whatever the basis of segregation is, an awareness that influences decisions on where to live, whom to sit by, what
occupation to join or to avoid, whom to play with or whom to talk to"
(Schelling 1971: 144). But ethnic segregation was the prime concern
at the time when Schelling proposed his model, and it is primarily in
such light that it has been discussed. Yet, Schelling is very clear that
the model as such is abstract enough that results can be generalized to
any preference driven segregation process. Thus following Fararo, the
model is fueled by concern for a real social issue and in that sense it is
a realistic model. But it is also a general model claiming to shed light
on a range of segregation phenomena. However, Schelling remarks
early on that some very important factors that explain segregation are
not included, such as institutionalized segregation (that he calls organizational) and economically driven segregation. In Schelling's models,
the segregation process is driven by individual preferences only. In this
respect they are also fairly precise models. Both initial and boundary
conditions are clearly defined, but because the analysis was made by
hand, agents' movement rules for instance are only loosely defined (but
contemporary computer replications give exactly the same results).

One of Schelling's models is a two dimensional lattice of 13 rows
and 16 columns on which 25 star-chips and 18 zero-chips are distributed randomly. Assuming that both stars and zeros have a preference
for having at least 50 percent neighbors of their own type Schelling
rearranges the chips so that this condition is met for every chip. The
result is a strikingly segregated pattern in which a star have about 80

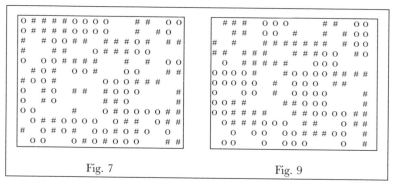

Figure 1. Initial random distribution and final equilibrium distribution in Schelling's dynamic two-dimensional spatial proximity model of segregation (Schelling 1971: 155–157).

percent of her neighbors being stars and a zero has about 83 percent zeros in her neighborhood (in the random initial distribution the corresponding numbers was 46 and 53 percent).

Schelling's dynamic model of segregation is in many ways a role-model in mathematical sociology. Not only does it strike the balance between realism, generality, and precision perfectly but it also generates surprising, and even counterintuitive results. Recall that in the model, segregation emerges solely from the action of uncoordinated individual actors and in that respect this model is a beautiful example of the link between micro-interaction and macro-dynamics.

The rationale for Duncan Watts' and Steven Strogatz's model of small world dynamics (Watts and Strogatz 1998) is not motivated by a pressing social issue such as segregation. Rather it is the answer to a puzzling question of how to understand a particular network structure. For a long time the ideal type networks that mathematical sociologists worked with were either random networks or ordered networks despite the fact that all sociologists knew empirically that social networks are neither random nor ordered. For one, social networks are clustered, that is, people tend to form tight knit groups that are distinguishable from other groups. Trying to capture this intuition mathematically, for instance by modeling biased networks, is hard. A particularly interesting and popularized network communication phenomenon is the so-called small-world effect. This effect was illustrated experimentally in the 1960s with the implication that only six intermediary steps separate any two Americans. A question that had deluded sociologists since these experiments and that captured Watts' imagination was this: what makes a network small? In Watts' model actors are put in an ordered circle and every actor is connected to its four nearest neighbors. One of the actors is selected and at random one of its connections re-connected to another randomly selected actor in the ring. As the process of re-connection is repeated, the ring transforms from an ordered network structure into a random network structure as in Figure 2 (Watts and Strogatz 1998).

Starting from a very simple model of an ordered network structure Watts could demonstrate that what is characteristic of a small-world network is both a high level of clustering and a short average distance between actors in the network. Thus a small-world network seems to capture both the property of random networks, i.e., short path lengths, and ordered networks, i.e., high clustering. What is really interesting with Watt's model is that parameter p, the degree of randomness, need only be very small for the ordered structure to transform into a small-world network.

Watts' small-world model is even simpler than Schelling's model of segregation but still very elegant. In terms of the balance between realism, generality and precision, the judgment is perhaps not as clear cut. The model as such is not particularly realistic in the sense that it does not even abstract from observed social reality. Few sociologists would feel at home at this level of abstraction. On the other hand,

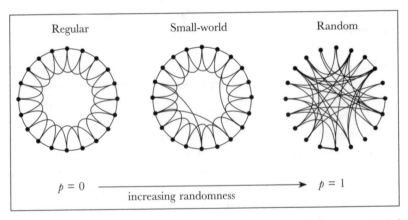

Figure 2. Watts' and Strogatz's small-world model. An ordered network (left) is transformed into a random network (right) by a process of randomly re-connecting actors. The small-world is situated in between these extremes (Watts and Strogatz 1998).

the model is general and has applications way beyond sociology; the network properties under analysis are present in many biological and physical networks, both natural and designed. And it is precise and well-defined. In contrast to Schelling's model this one needs a fair deal of interpretation before it can be mapped onto social reality. But it does highlight important properties in almost all social networks that are now, because of this model, easier to understand and theoretically scrutinize.

These two examples do bring out both the attractions and the potential shortcomings of mathematical sociology that I believe are nicely captured by the balance of realism, generality, and precision. Another way to phrase this problem is in terms of a conflict between sociological intuition and formal theorizing, as Fararo does in this quotation.

> I always think about it, as we always know more than we can say. And we always can say more than we can really formally put down in more exacting terms. So as you go further and further from the fundamental intuitions in the interest of being logical and mathematical, you can potentially loose contact with the governing intuitions. But the main gain would be to try to bring the mathematics back into, and as close as possible to the basic intuitions of the field. Trying to represent those intuitions in some way. It is what Bourdieu calls a habitus. It is a kind of a sociological habitus you acquire by exposing yourself to classical ideas and postclassical ideas and so on. You know, you think sociologically, and then you think mathematically. But these are often hard to fit together. The mathematics enforces a discipline that the other discipline does not really value in the same way. It has it its own forms of rigor but they are not the same. To bring those two into conjunction has always been the sort of thing that I thought of as important. I do not think we've been that successful really, but collectively we are trying (Thomas Fararo).

This challenge might be especially tricky for sociology, a subject that attracts students from a wide population, not seldom driven by strong political and social interests rather than analytical.

> The problem is that many people come into sociology not really seeing it as a hard science. They see it as a sort of spiritual adventure of knowing about society in a qualitative, grounded way, to be able to reflect upon the big political and social policy issues. In a sense, I came to sociology a bit like that, and I have respect for that. I think that if we would loose that, we would loose something important. What we need to do is to add to that the idea that technical grounding is important if you really want to make a contribution. By and large, my generation of sociologists has failed. There are a few pimples on the top that look good: James Coleman, and probably Harrison White. But it is not a story of great success (Peter Abell).

As far as I am aware no extensive piece on the history of mathematical sociology is available. Some notes are spread around in reviews and books (e.g., Fararo 1997) and there seem to be agreement that mathematical sociology as we apply the term today is a child of the 1950s. I believe that the recent revival and interest in mathematical sociology is mainly due to the enormous interest in structural and relation sociology as it is approached by social network analysis. Admittedly, network analysis is both methodology and theory, but its theoretical components have always been mathematically charged (Freeman 2004). Network analysis has been constantly growing within sociology since the late 1970s and with the advent of the "new science of networks" in the early 2000s (Watts 2004) interest has sky-rocketed. Other developments also spur the re-vitalization of mathematical sociology, such as the growing use of computer simulation models across the social sciences (Macy and Willer 2002) and current theoretical debates in European sociology on social mechanisms (Barbera 2004) and analytical sociology (Hedström 2005). In the mid 2000s, mathematical sociology is visible in state of the art journals, and the range of problems approached and the level of sophistication are striking.

In my review of mathematical sociology, following Sørensen (1978) I classified mathematical sociology along three broad strains—process, structure, and action—based partly but not entirely on the different types of mathematics involved (Edling 2002). With models of processes one typically study social change over longer or shorter time-periods using various types of discrete and continuous mathematical models. Mathematically, these models have a lot in common with various system-analyses in other fields, ranging from physics to ecology, and usually they do not allow for much in terms of structural or individual heterogeneity. Diffusion models, such as James Coleman's famous analysis of medical innovation (Coleman, Katz and Menzel 1966), and models of organizational change as developed within organizational ecology (Hannan and Freeman 1989), are typical examples of process models.

If Coleman can be said to be the father of the mathematical sociology of process, then Harrison White would undoubtedly be named the father of mathematical sociology of structure. Models of structure tie directly into social network analysis, their most important field of application in which graph theory and matrix algebra are primarily used. However, as more and more attention is directed towards understanding system dynamics and structural change, it makes little sense to uphold a clear cut distinction between process and structure as research enterprises. Describing a structure without accounting for its emergence and stability is simply not satisfactory. Patrik Doreian expressed this clearly in our interview.

> It is interesting that you have this history of James Coleman coming in from one side with his kind of dynamics models, and Harrison White coming in from another side with his kind of structural models. It would be great if we could synthesize those two traditions and really model social structure and social process in an integrated and coherent fashion. [...] My sense about mathematical social science is this: let us do it. If we are successful great, if we are not successful, then we admit that we failed. I think that if we model successfully the dynamics of structured systems—networks with social objects and relations between them with levels and multiple populations—we will have done very well. Structures evolve through time and we need to be attentive to both the structural characteristics and the social actor characteristics. If we succeed, that is when I think we will really have successful mathematical social science and successful social science. It sounds very methodological and program-matic, but I think that is what we should be aspiring to. And that would be a synthesis of the White and Coleman traditions. The physicists at the Institute for Theoretical Physics in Stuttgart that have contributed to the Journal of Mathematical Sociology (Helbing 1994; Weidlich 1994), for instance, use partial differential equation models that moves us into the whole debate of complexity and chaos. At the moment they seem more like buzzwords. I think that if we can successfully use that kind of modeling and be genuinely concerned with structure, and genuinely concerned with process, then we are going somewhere. Let me add that I am skeptical that the models from physics are useful for sociology in an *unmodified* form. But I think they need to pursue their program—just as mathematical sociologists need to use mathematics. If they succeed then we will have learned much (Patrik Doreian).

Doreian also draws our attention to the third type of models, models of action. Prototypical examples of such models would be those of util-ity maximizing individuals. Indeed, James Coleman proposed that the simple and well defined assumptions about individual rational choice should provide the foundation for social theory (Coleman 1990). This is not yet the case, neither in sociology at large (but see Goldthorpe 2007) nor in mathematical sociology. On the contrary, if there is one thing that my earlier review (Edling 2002) clearly shows it is that mathemati-cal sociology spans across a broad range of phenomena and applies an equally broad set of mathematical tools to try and understand those phenomena.

Who is the Mathematical Sociologist?

The interviews can be summarized along four themes: the scholarly background of the interviewees, their attraction to mathematical sociology, their thoughts on the strengths and weaknesses of mathematical sociology, and their thoughts on institutional problems and limitations.

With respect to their background the six scholars fall nicely into two categories. I realize it is dubious to classify this small a number of observations, but nevertheless I will do so as it serves the purpose of my presentation. Three of the interviewees immigrated to sociology from a, relatively speaking, mathematically strong background. Peter Abell came to sociology at Essex University via philosophy, with a PhD in physical science, and he was hired to do philosophy of sciences. Patrick Doreian earned a Bachelors degree in mathematics before deciding to enter a cross-disciplinary program in mathematical social science, and Harrison White switched to sociology after completing a PhD in physics. The other three came into sociology much earlier in their academic career and mathematical and computational modeling was brought into their thinking parallel to or even after their maturation as social scientists. Philip Bonacich says he was heavily influenced by a strong role model at Harvard, namely Harrison White, Kathleen Carley was early on seduced by the possibility of modeling man, and Thomas Fararo was philosophically committed to axiomatic science. One of the nicest stories about the attraction of mathematical sociology is indeed that of Kathleen Carley:

> [My] interest in modeling started [...] when I was in high school, when I read Isaac Asimov's the *Foundation Trilogy*. I thought this is what I want to do: Build models of people! So then I went to college and tried to take every course I could to make that happen. [...] Actually I was very interested in artificial intelligence; but they did not have a degree in it yet in that point in time. And I did not realize that you could get what would become the degree by going through engineering, so I did not do that. So, I do not have a degree in AI, and I was actively discouraged from going into mathematics because I was female. I was told: "You'll never make it because you're a woman". And I thought, Ok, they must know what they are saying (Kathleen Carley).

Incidentally, Carley shares her fascination with Asimov's novels with Duncan Watts, who used Asimov's *Robot* series as an inspiration for one of his models of emergent system behavior (Watts 2003: 74). But

Carley's account is of course also a sad reminder of the kind of gender stereotyping that helped and still helps pushing male and female students into different college programs.

The difference between a science and a social science background becomes somewhat visible in the view on mathematics in sociology. For example, the three persons with a science/mathematics background are quite pragmatic and non-programmatic in arguing that mathematics has its place but that it is not an end in itself. The three persons with a social science background much more strongly believe that mathematics is intrinsically good and something to generally strive for. One reason the first group has a more relaxed attitude could be that they had an early training in mathematics which they can both easier and more naturally call upon when it seems fit. The other group, on the contrary, had a less thorough and sometimes more shallow training and therefore they had to, and have to, fight harder for the mathematical leverage.

One should of course be cautious with personal accounts of ones own career. It is all too easy to find a pattern in ones personal history, and perhaps even easier to paint this pattern in self-flattering strokes. For instance, how come Abell, Doreian, and White left the hard sciences to go into sociology? Is not the most probable answer that they had failed in these areas, or that they where sensing failure coming? Assuming they wished to pursue an academic career, both physics and mathematics holds much more status and resources than do sociology, so the sensible thing would be not to transfer. Only if failure is certain would it pay off to switch a career in physics for one in sociology. On the other hand, is it so strange that people actually hold a strong interest in the subject matter? Being a sociologist myself, I actually find that quite easy to believe. Sociology is a rich and fascinating discipline and it relates to everyday experiences and intuitions in a myriad of ways. Still, it is probably safe to assume that none of the three immigrants were doing remarkably well in their original fields. If they were, they would not have been allowed to repel but would have been sucked deeper into the attraction of disciplinary, departmental and collegial structures. But, picking up on the rationality once again, the fact that among all alternatives they chose sociology actually strengthens the interest-hypothesis, because if they wanted a trade-off from their training, engineering, business administration, or economics would have been a much more reasonable pick.

In some sense, the social science group is more interesting. People migrating from science and mathematics into sociology do formal theory

because this is how their training wired them to think. But people that
start out in social science and decide to bring in mathematics and other
formal tools actually turn away from the highway and pick the straight
and narrow road. I think Abell is right in his analysis that the rational
choice in contemporary sociology is to not do formal theory.

> I think at some stage sociology just has to face up to that. Sociology is
> so diverse, and because it shades of into history, there will always be this
> other end of things. But it has to change. I am not optimistic about it
> changing in the foreseeable future, because I think the present "social
> construction" of sociology is such that there is a mutual interest between
> teachers, students, publishers, etc. to maintain the present paradigm. In
> my view it is intellectually sub optimal. Nevertheless, it is equilibrium.
> Everybody wants it and everybody in it would be worse off by moving
> away from it. So, you find it very difficult to break that. Human history
> is littered with failed intellectual tradition. Not empirical sociology, but
> social theory is a failed intellectual tradition, and future generations will
> necessarily see it as such. At the moment, though, it is relatively stable
> (Peter Abell).

If Abell is right, one might wonder why mathematical sociologists continue to pursue mathematical sociology. One possible route to answering that question is to look at what these persons see as the strength of
mathematical sociology. Philip Bonacich admits to hold what he calls
a mystical belief saying:

> Well, part of it is kind of a mystical belief. It is a non-rational belief
> that if there is a deep structure in sociology, and deep truths, they will
> only be discovered through mathematics. But then apart from that, in
> a more mundane kind of way, I think that mathematics leads to precise
> thoughts and precise thinking. The concepts, as opposed to English, are
> completely unambiguous. There is tremendously powerful machinery
> developed over hundreds of years to draw implications from. I person-
> ally think that the finest things about western civilization are music and
> mathematics. So I think there is this powerful logical apparatus that we
> should avail ourselves in. [...] I think that if we are going to become a
> science, we have got to use mathematics (Philip Bonacich).

In Bonacich's case it is a firm conviction that sociology will make
progress from the power of mathematics. Thomas Fararo gives a rather
thorough account of how he got into mathematical sociology and what
he sees as the attraction. Mainly it is the power of axiomatic theory
construction and the possibility of theoretical unification. Fararo have
presented arguments for unification both with and without formalization, but really strong axiomatization cannot be achieved without formal

arguments and so, in Fararo's case, mathematics becomes a necessity out of the preferred style of scientific explanation.

> In the summer of 1960 when I was a graduate student, I needed some funding, and I was recommended for a sociological research project that was just beginning. That was the study of community power structure in Syracuse under the direction of Linton Freeman. That for me was really a transformative experience because it was knowledge as a problem of something to be constructed rather than something read in the library. It really put me in touch with the constructive research process. So sociology then became a place for me where knowledge is constructed rather than just read about. [...] But in the context of the community power structure research we were confronted with kind of a structural problem. We had a massive sociogram, as it were, of claims about who was involved in what. We were looking for some kind of mathematical apparatus; we did not even know the name of it, but something to analyze this kind of thing. We did not know of anything, so I undertook that as a direction of my thesis research. I spent a summer reading the *Bulletin of Mathematical Biophysics*, which was a place where people like Anatol Rapaport were writing. In my thesis I really just practice and apply the idea of mathematics and mathematical model building to this community power structure data. Basically, that whole idea of constructing and testing a mathematical model, which was totally new as I did not have any classroom training in it at all. [...] Remember, I came to mathematics from philosophy so I was very interested in things like; what is a mathematical entity, what is the relationship between mathematics and logic? So I read a lot about the philosophy of mathematics too. I taught Patrick Suppes' book, *Introduction to logic* (Suppes 1957). A fabulous book, and I was very attracted to this idea of axiomatization within set theory. So actually, the first two years of my post-doctoral I worked formally under the sponsorship of Patrik Suppes at Stanford (Tomas Fararo).

Indirectly, Kathleen Carley who went to MIT inspired by the vision of modeling man in society, argues that the greatest utility from mathematical sociology arise from the fact that the substantial research funding goes to projects with some mathematical and computational sophistication, and therefore a formal approach increases the survival chances of sociological research (having spent a great deal of her career at Carnegie-Mellon University, Carley is probably affectively colored by this engineering heavy environment). Bonacich, Carley, and Fararo are all convinced, but not at all by the same arguments, that mathematics is necessary.

Neither Patrick Doreian nor Harrison White would go as far as to argue that mathematical sociology is necessary. White admits that he finds it hard to believe that progress will be achieved without mathematics, but Doreian simply rests his case, does his thing, and leaves it for others to decide on the utility of what he is doing. Peter Abell, who also came from science to sociology, shares with the social science group a strong belief in the value of mathematics. He actually argues that social scientists are morally obliged to be "clear and precise" in their thinking, and that mathematics is needed to guarantee this.

Some of the interviewees also commented specifically on weaknesses and potential risks of mathematical sociology. Peter Abell for instance, compares sociology to economics and warns that in economics the mathematics is sometimes valued so highly that it overshadows the substantial issues. He argues in effect that our curiosity of empirical complexity always should have the upper hand over technical proficiency in defining what problems to study. In the same line of reasoning, Harrison White points out that even if the mathematical approach by itself is praiseworthy we must be aware that the mathematics we need might not actually be the mathematics we have access to at the moment. As a result, sociologists must have a flexible attitude towards mathematics and, which is of course much, much harder, sociologists must keep a constant eye on development in mathematics. Looking at the same issue from another angle, Thomas Fararo sees a problem in bringing mathematics and sociology together. To his mind they represent two different modes of thinking, two intuitions, which are not always easy to link. The risk arises when one continues to construct mathematical models even when the mathematical and the sociological intuitions are not in touch with each other. This leads to the same problem that Abell identified in economics, the problem which arises when the models no longer represent the sociological intuitions.

Concluding Remarks

Obviously, a very positive impression of applying mathematical models to sociology emerges from these interviews. All six scholars I talked to share the view that perhaps the most prime benefit of a formal approach is to achieve coherence and logical consistency in theory construction. Also, there are several signs that mathematical sociology in the beginning of the new millennium is stronger than it has been since the late 1960s. New publication outlets, a section in the American Sociological Association, and an increased exposure of mathematical and computational models in general sociology journals serve to prove this point. My interviews bear witness that there are positive adherents of mathematical sociology, and my literature review (Edling 2002) provides references to impressing work on many timely problems. At the same time, it is obvious that mathematics has not established itself as a general tool in the discipline.

Several people interested in mathematical sociology testify to the institutional fragility of mathematical sociology, evident in many ways, and most likely derived from the small number of adherents of this sub-discipline. For example, both Peter Abell and Patrick Doreian got into mathematical sociology through a program at University of Essex. This led me to believe that there was actually something exciting going on in mathematical sociology in England in the late 1960s. Apparently, this was not the case. Apart from these two, no lasting contribution to the field evolved out of Essex. Doreian's unconcerned and laconic observation that the program "died" leads me to conclude that although there where certainly an inter-personal xenogamy of ideas going on (Abell 1971; Doreian 1970) the program in itself is not much to be spoken of. Indeed, Doreian left for a position in US in the early 1970s and Abell, who remained in England, become devoutly disillusioned of the future of any version of mathematical application in sociology.

Patrick Doriean was the editor of the *Journal of Mathematical Sociology* between 1982 and 2005. It is beyond doubt that the journal has survived until this day much through his hard work. While this has saved the journal from going under, it is possible that, by attaching survival chances to the energy and professional contact network of one single individual, its vulnerability has also increased. Again, this is the problem of a small field. A parallel case is the International Network for Social Network Analysts (INSNA). With the growing popularity of network analysis, INSNA has become a firmly established organization and is no longer dependent on one dedicated person, but for a long time it almost was. But, according to Doreian's account, even after over 30 years since its inception the *Journal of Mathematical Sociology* struggles to stay alive. A small field simply cannot support a specialist journal, and especially so at times when institutional subscription rates are sky-high and academic libraries experience budget shrinkages year after year. It is not the case that there are no outlets for mathematical sociology, several papers in general sociology journals draw on mathematical or computational modeling. Indeed, this is a very positive thing for mathematical sociology.

Another example of institutional fragility surfaces most clearly in the interview with Phil Bonacich in the discussion about the section for mathematical sociology in the American Sociological Association (ASA). This might sound as if a national assemblage, but as several of the other ASA sections, this section is truly international and thus it can be regarded as the international forum for mathematical sociologists. The ASA only saw the formation of this dedicated section for Mathematical Sociology in 1996. The section is still one of the smallest in the ASA and in 2003 the section had just over 160 members (to be compared to the mean of all sections, which is approximately 470 members). However, the bylaws of ASA stipulate that the minimum requirement for holding section status is 300 members, so there is an actual risk that the section will have to shut down. Although in practice, according to Bonacich's experience, this will be highly dependent on section activity. In recent years sessions at the annual ASA meetings have been quite successful, so if this is true perhaps there is no real reason to worry. But still, small is weak when it comes to making lasting contributions in an organizational environment with competition for members.

It might be interesting to compare with other small sections in the ASA. Like most sections of the association many of the small ones define pretty narrow interests. In 2003, the following sections had less than 300 members: Animals and Society, Communication and Information Technology, Ethnomethodology/Conversational Analysis, History of Sociology, Latino/a Sociology, Mathematical Sociology, Peace, War and Social Conflict, Rationality and Society, Sociological Practice, and Sociology of Emotions. Among these, the sections for Ethnomethodology and Animals and Society are new, instituted in the 21st century. The oldest is Peace and War that goes back to the mid 1970s followed by Sociological Practice that got started in the late 1970s. Some of these sections have to be considered to be of minor interest, given the nature of sociology. The interest for Latino Sociology, Ethnomethodology or Animals and Society for example simply isn't that widespread among sociologists. However, all three of these sections had more members that the section for Mathematical Sociology, whose members would claim that they represent broad and general sociological interests. In fact, among the small sections, only Rationality and Society had fewer members than Mathematical Sociology in 2003. Really large sections, with over 900 members are few. Here we find Organizations, Occupations and Work, Sociology of Culture, and Medical Sociology. Largest, with over 1000 members, is the section for Sex and Gender.

But the biggest obstacle to any substantial expansion of mathematical sociology within sociology is firstly the fact that sociology students have very little technical training when they enter sociology, and are given very little further training once they are in. Secondly, and perhaps more surprisingly, in most universities sociology students have no exposure to formal theory construction. And for students with low technical motivation and no training in theory construction mathematical models in sociology are perceived to be so esoteric that nobody needs to care. But the proper use of mathematics is not a question of choice. When the problem is formulated precisely enough the use of mathematics is unavoidable. One should not simply take the mathematics and apply them to a sociological problem. The problem has to be thoroughly worked through and if necessary, then be given a mathematical formulation. The reason we do not see (and perhaps do not need) much mathematical sociology is simply a reflection of the nature of contemporary sociology. A reasonable expectation is that mathematical sociology will be taken care of by other disciplines, and as a consequence it will be difficult to find people in the future who, like the ones I have interviewed, are dedicated both to sociology and to mathematical sociology.

On the other hand, as we have learned from the example of social network analysis, given a dedication to solve a set of real world problems, the turn towards mathematical tools will be unavoidable and come natural if needed. It seems appropriate to end this chapter with the following advisory note from James Coleman's *Introduction to Mathematical Sociology* (1964: 54); "the necessarily difficult task of developing mathematical sociology can best be performed when our concentration remain upon the sociological problem, and the mathematical tools remain means to an end."

References

Abell, P. 1971. *Model Building in Sociology*, London: Weidenfeld and Nicolson.
Barbera, F. 2004. *Meccanisimi Sociali*, Bologna: Il Mulino.
Carley, K. M. 1997. "Computational organization theory: Introduction" in *Journal of Mathematical Sociology*, 22: 91–93.
Carrington, P. J., J. Scott and S. Wasserman. 2005. *Models and Methods in Social Network Analysis*, New York: Cambridge University Press.
Coleman, J. S. 1964. *Introduction to Mathematical Sociology*, New York: Free Press of Glencoe.
———. 1990. *Foundations of Social Theory*, Cambridge, MA: Harvard University Press.
Coleman, J. S., E. Katz and H. Menzel. 1966. *Medical Innovation: A Diffusion Study*, Indianapolis: Bobbs-Merrill.

Doreian, P. 1970. *Mathematics and the Study of Social Relations*, London: Weidenfeld and Nicolson.

Edling, C. R. 2002. "Mathematics in sociology" in *Annual Review of Sociology*, 28: 197–220.

Fararo, T. J. 1989. *The Meaning of General Theoretical Sociology: Tradition and Formalization*, Cambridge: Cambridge University Press.

——. 1997. "Reflections on mathematical sociology" in *Sociological Forum*, 12: 73–101.

Freeman, L. C. 1984. "Turning a profit from mathematics: The case of social networks" in *Journal of Mathematical Sociology*, 10: 343–360.

——. 2004. *The Development of Social Network Analysis: A Study in the Sociology of Science*, Vancouver: Empirical Press.

Freese, L. 1980. "Formal theorizing" in *Annual Review of Sociology*, 6: 187–212.

Goldthorpe, J. H. 2007. *On Sociology*, vol. 1, Second edition, Stanford: Stanford University Press.

Hannan, M. T. and J. Freeman. 1989. *Organizational Ecology*, Cambridge, MA: Harvard University Press.

Harary, F., R. Z. Norman and D. Cartwright. 1965. *Structural Models: An Introduction to the Theory of Directed Graphs*, Wiley: New York.

Heckathorn, D. D. 1984. "Mathematical theory construction in sociology: Analytical power, scope, and descriptive accuracy as trade-off" in *Journal of Mathematical Sociology*, 10: 295–323.

Hedström, P. 2005. *Dissecting the Social: On the Principles of analytical sociology*, Cambridge: Cambridge University Press.

Helbing, D. 1994. "A mathematical model for the behavior of individuals in a social field" in *Journal of Mathematical Sociology*, 19: 189–219.

Lepenies, W. 1988. *Between literature and science: The rise of sociology*, Cambridge: Cambridge University Press.

Levins, R. 1966. "The strategy of model building in population biology" in *American Scientist*, 54: 421–431.

Macy, M. W. and R. Willer. 2002. "From factors to actors: Computational sociology and agent-based modeling" in *Annual Review of Sociology*, 28: 143–166.

Maynard Smith, J. 1982. *Evolution and the theory of games*, Cambridge: Cambridge University Press.

Nash, J. 1951. "Non-cooperative games" in *Annals of Mathematics*, 54: 286–295.

Newman, M. E. J., A. L. Barabási and D. J. Watts. 2006. *The structure and dynamics of networks*, Princeton, NJ: Princeton University Press.

Schelling, T. C. 1971. "Dynamic models of segregation" in *Journal of Mathematical Sociology*, 1: 143–186.

Sørensen, A. B. 1978. "Mathematical-models in sociology" in *Annual Review of Sociology*, 4: 345–371.

Suppes, P. 1957. *Introduction to logic*, Princeton, NJ: D. Van Nostrand Co.

Swedberg, R. 1990. *Economics and sociology*, Princeton, NJ: Princeton University Press.

——. 2001. "Sociology and game theory: Contemporary and historical perspectives" in *Theory and Society*, 30: 301–335.

Waldrop, M. M. 1992. *Complexity: The emerging science at the edge of order and chaos*, New York: Simon & Schuster.

Watts, D. J. 2003. *Six degrees: The science of a connected age*, New York: Norton.

——. 2004. "The 'new' science of networks" in *Annual Review of Sociology*, 30: 243–270.

Watts, D. J. and S. H. Strogatz. 1998. "Collective dynamics of 'small-world' networks" in *Nature*, 393: 440–442.

Weidlich, W. 1994. "Synergetic modeling concepts for sociodynamics with application to collective political opinion formation" in *Journal of Mathematical Sociology*, 18: 267–291.

Wellman, B. 1988. "Structural analysis: From method and metaphor to theory and substance" in B. Wellman and S. D. Berkowitz (eds.), *Social structures*, Cambridge: Cambridge University Press, 19–61.

White, H. C. 1997. "Can mathematics be social? Flexible representations for interaction process and its sociocultural constructions" in *Sociological Forum*, 12: 53–71.

Von Neumann, J. and O. Morgenstern. 1944. *Theory of games and economic behavior*, Princeton: Princeton University Press.

STATISTICAL MODELS AND MECHANISMS
OF SOCIAL PROCESSES[1]

Aage B. Sørensen

Introduction

Not all sociologists adhere to the view that sociology is a science of sorts. The minority believing sociology is a science agrees it is very desirable to reach an integration between social theory and empirical social research. The integration comes about by the two activities, theory development and gathering of evidence, inspiring and reinforcing each other: research improves theory and theory improves research. More precisely, evidence, produced by research using appropriate methodology, somehow speaks to the validity and usefulness of theory, and theory inspires procedures and questions for the research enterprises. The dual nature of the integration has been elegantly discussed by Merton (1957a, b) in two essays that form some of the few enduring classics of sociology published after 1920.

If this happy integration is to be achieved, theory development will be steered by reality rather than fantasy, or ideology. This may make the social world described by theory less strange and quixotic than suggested by post-modernist and similar current versions of contemporary sociological theory. Further, the integration may make sociological research more focused on answering questions about how social processes work rather than focus on interesting phenomena, such as identity formation among ethnic minorities, or the nature of the risk-society. The integration presumably would also make sociologists engage in the same kinds of activities as other scientists—adjudicating theories with observations and designing research to test predictions from theories.

While the goal is agreed upon, the means to reach it are not. The choice of theory is obviously important since not all theories are likely

[1] Paper presented at the Annual Meetings of the Swedish Sociological Association, University of Stockholm, Stockholm, Sweden, January 28, 1999. An earlier version for this paper was presented at the conference on 'Statistical Issues in the Social Sciences,' Swedish Academy of Sciences, Stockholm, Sweden, October 1–3, 1998.

to be amenable to integration with empirical observation. In this article, I will first discuss the requirements of sociological theory for the integration of theory and observation. I will argue that theory that focuses on explaining how change is brought about is most likely to produce a fruitful integration of theory and research. These are then theories that focus on specifying mechanisms for change in social processes. They come in two types, I will argue: push and pull theories, or causal and rational choice theories. Both types of theories can and should be represented in models for how change occurs. These models are differential or difference equations. Their solution gives models that express the relationships or associations between observed variables. These relationships will have a certain functional form, dictated by the proposed mechanisms for how change is brought about.

Understanding the association between observed variables is what most of us believe research is about. However, we rarely worry about the functional form of the relationship. The main reason is that we rarely worry about how we get from our ideas about how change is brought about, or the mechanisms of social processes, to empirical observation. In other words, sociologists rarely model mechanisms explicitly. In the few cases where they do model mechanisms, they are labeled mathematical sociologists, not a very large or important specialty in sociology.

We need to estimate relationship in order to figure out if our theoretical ideas have some support in evidence. For this purpose, we use statistics. Statistics is a branch of mathematics and might seem alien to sociologists for this reason. However, while sociologists are not very eager to formulate their theories as mathematical models, sociologists are very eager to learn statistics, and quite good at it. They therefore use statistical models to estimate the relationships that concern them in research. These statistical models are usually presented by statisticians as default models, to be used when a substantive model is lacking. The models are invariably additive, at least as a point of departure. They have the virtue of being parsimonious. The statistical models have the defect that they sometime are poor theories of the processes under investigation.

My main purpose with this article is to emphasize the importance of modeling theoretical ideas abut how change comes about when studying social processes and the unfortunate consequences of taking ad hoc statistical models as models of substantive processes. There has been much recent discussion of ideas about causality in sociology and about the integration of theory and research, particularly with the use of rational choice theory. Many useful ideas have been presented, but the discussion remains largely dominated by the conventional wisdom that it is the task of the sociologist to choose the variables and design the research while the statistician, who may be a statistician-sociologist, provides the tools and models for estimation. I believe this conventional wisdom harms the progress of the discipline because statistical models often are bad theories and/or make the researcher ignore or unable to answer important substantive questions. I will present examples from two important areas of sociological research to illustrate my point. These areas are research on social mobility and research on school effects on learning.

Theory and Empirical Observation

It seems quite strange, but it is nevertheless true. The most popular sociological theories are those that cannot be linked directly to empirical observations. They are particularly popular among those sociologists identifying themselves as theorists and writing theory texts and teaching courses about post and neo -modernism, -functionalism and -structuralism. Some theorists see theory as world views with almost no empirical reference. Though these grand theories speak about entities that presumably exist, such as society, the empirical references in such theories are global and abstract statements, often about the imagined or desired state of the world, that defy the derivation of testable propositions about how the world works. Others see theory as an exercise in conceptual construction and elaboration in the tradition that originated with Max Weber and continued with Parsons. These approaches pose few, if any, empirically answerable questions, though conceptual elaboration and development of course may be important for what we will be looking for in empirical research.

Not all sociological theory is devoted to conceptual elaboration or to the analysis of imagined or imaginary worlds. The type of theory that lends itself to empirical research makes statements about social processes, for only theories that speak about something that relates to something else can be integrated with evidence. This means that an empirically usable theory will be a set of statements about processes of change. The change process may be the direct focus of the theory, as when we propose a theory of diffusion or job mobility, or the outcome of the change process is the focus. In the latter case the theory is about associations between variables. Since associations among variables are created by change processes, explanations for observed associations are provided by theories of how change comes about. For example, the association between educational attainment and income is created by some process where people are allocated to jobs or wage levels in a manner so that those with higher educational attainment obtain a higher wage. One theory, that is, human capital theory, suggests that this association comes about by people improving their skills to become more productive and therefore command higher earnings in the labor market. Thus change in skills produce change in earnings and hence create the cross-sectional association we observe. This is not the only possible explanation for the association. There are other theories that could explain how education would be associated with a change in income.

The theories, we tend to find helpful for understanding what we observe, all seem to rely on ideas about how change in something comes about. They are theories that specify some mechanisms by which outcomes are produced. The desirability of theories of this nature for empirically oriented social research has been emphasized recently; see the contributions in Hedström and Swedberg (1998). It is not a new idea, much of the best empirically oriented scholarship in sociology is concerned with specifying mechanisms and in this regard Durkheim's study of suicide can be seen as a prominent early example. There is some disagreement about what one should understand by a mechanism. However, I will proceed here using my own concept of a mechanism. It is simply a specification of how change is brought about (Sørensen 1998).

There are basically two types of theories of how change comes about, and thus of mechanisms of social processes. I will call them push and pull theories. Push theories are sometimes (Stinchcombe 1968; Coleman 1990) called causal theories, but it is not altogether clear why the other type, pull theories, do not deserve that name too. Push theories are those that see some force or event outside of an individual, or whatever is the unit of analysis, producing change in this individual. For example, a student receives a good grade and changes her level of aspiration. Or a person discovers that other people act in a certain manner and imitates their action. Or values that families hold create certain levels of educational aspirations (Gambetta 1987). Until recently, that is, until rational action theory became popular among empirically minded sociologists, the push theories were what sociologists thought about when discussing the integration of theory and research and the issues involved in linking theory to data are perhaps a bit simpler with push theories than with pull theories. I shall therefore first discuss the manner in which these theories are linked to data and then later make some remarks about the problems raised by pull theories, especially rational choice theories.

Causal theories of the push type can be confronted with empirical observations and tested by either manipulating the force that causes the change in some type of experiment, or by formulating a model of the process under investigation and validate the properties of that model with data. The former strategy is the simplest and the results of using this strategy are usually less ambiguous to interpret than the result of the model building strategy. The main requirement is that we have confidence that the link between the causal variable and the outcome variable is real. The link is not being produced by something other than the force our theory say is the causal variable. We do not need to specify a theory of how change is actually brought about, let alone a model of the process that produces this change. Seeing what occurs after the manipulation of the causal variable is believing.

It is one of the great illusions of modern social science that the attractive properties of experiments can be approximated in the investigation of processes that do not lend themselves to experimental manipulation through the use of statistical controls in multivariate statistical models. The problem has been ably dissected by Lieberson (1985). There is no justification for the belief, nor for the resulting practice of using long lists of variables in multiple regression models in an attempt to show that a given effect is really there. While more controls are supposed to make us have greater confidence in the existence of an effect, more controls actually often should make us loose confidence because of the reduction in statistical power and the likely meaningless coefficients produced by multi-collinearity. The statistical models we employ to estimate effects are not somehow mirroring an experiment. Whether we recognize it or not, the statistical models are models and therefore theories of the processes being investigated. They are often poor theories, I will argue.

With non-experimental observation schemes, the proper approach is to use the classic strategy in science: to formulate a model for how change is brought about. This is done by formulating differential or difference equation models of change. The differential equation is appropriate, when change is continuous; the difference equation is appropriate, when change is discrete. Differential equation models have infinitesimal quantities as dependent variables and therefore need to be solved to allow for empirical analysis of the properties of the model and estimation of parameters. Calculus was invented to produce these solutions. Difference equation need not be solved to allow for empirical estimation. However, solutions are still useful to assess the properties of the models and the theory behind it.

With push models, the models for change are usually formulated as models for change in an interval of time, or models for the quantity $dy(t)/dt$, where $y(t)$ is the time dependent variable of interest. The differential equation states how the rate of change in $y(t)$ depends on certain causal variables, including often $y(t)$ itself and time. For example, in the well-known logistic diffusion model, the rate of growth in the number having adopted a certain technique or learned a certain piece of news, is assumed to depend on the number who do not yet know and the number who already know. Hence if we take, as our y variable, the quantity $p(t)$ as a measure of the proportion of a population who knows or has adopted something, the theory of the process suggests this defining equation:

$$dp(t)/dt = kp(t) \left[1 - p(t)\right] \tag{1}$$

where k is the rate of contact between the members in a population.

Since we cannot observe $dp(t)/dt$ we need a solution to the differential equation, obtained by integration. Assuming that the process somehow gets going, the solution is:

$$p(t) = ae^{kt}/(ae^{kt} + 1) \tag{2a}$$

where

$$a = p(0) \: / \: \left[1 - p(0)\right] \tag{2b}$$

This is very elementary. Nevertheless, the derivation illustrates important and often neglected ideas in social research. The simple theory specified a certain mechanism for change, here diffusion. This mechanism produced a model that can be used to study the properties of the process proposed by the theory and compare these properties to empirically observed processes (the logistic diffusion model actually is one instance where many empirical processes conform to the s-shaped pattern, suggested by the model) and the parameter k can be estimated, perhaps for different populations or different types of knowledge and we can make comparison of these estimates, to say something about how populations or systems differ in the rate of contact among members, or how different types of messages are likely to spread with unequal speed.

These investigations would be possible using maximum likelihood estimation of equation (2) or even simpler methods (see Coleman, Katz and Menzel (1957) for an exemplary analysis of diffusion processes using simple models and simple methods). However, a quantitative sociologist with average statistical sophistication is unlikely to proceed in this manner. Rather she or he is likely to estimate a linear regression model with the number of adopters as the dependent variables and the various characteristics of those adopting as independent variables along with the population sizes (see Nielsen and Hannan 1977, for an example). I will return to the discussion of this practice below. First, I want to return to a discussion of the manner in which pull theories are translated into models for empirical investigation.

The formulation of a differential equation for change in time conforms to the idea of push theories that see causal forces acting to produce change. Matters are more complicated with the type of theories I have called pull theories. Indeed Coleman (1990) makes a fundamental distinction between push theories, which he calls causal theories, and rational choice or purposive actor theory.

There are two types of pull theories: rational actor theories and functionalist theories. Both types of theories see change brought about by the consequences of the change. In functionalist theories these consequences are at the level of society. Societal needs for survival or integration create institutions and patterns of behavior that contribute to survival and/or integration. The mechanism that achieves this can be conceptualized either as an unspecified causal chain in a kind of feedback mechanism as detailed by Stinchcombe (1968), or as selection mechanisms analogous to evolutionary theory in biology, which seems to have been what Parsons imagined.

In rational choice theory, the consequences are at the individual level. It is the maximization by the individual of utility at the individual or actor level that brings about the action. Empirically oriented sociologists with an interest in theory have lately been quite taken by rational action theory. It is seen the most promising base for the integration of theory and research, see, for example, Goldthorpe (1996), and the contributions to Blossfeld and Prein (1998). The success of economics in the competition for research grants and recognition probably plays a role here, and the best empirical research by economists does indeed avoid the problems that I discuss in this paper. However, the causal arguments of pull theories are much less straightforward than the direct link between change and causal forces suggested by push theories.

The problem with basing causal arguments on pull theories, whether they are functionalist or rational choice theories, reflect that pull theories inevitably can be accused of engaging in teleological reasoning. The teleological reasoning has been used by Elster (1989), and others, to severely criticize functionalist theory, but the situation is not different from rational choice theory and we have continuing debates about whether or not people are altruistic for this reason.

The difference between the two approaches for the formulation of empirically testable models shows up in what is focused upon in the differential or difference equation that defines the model. In push theories the focus is on change over time, as shown above. In pull theories the focus is on a quantity that is being maximized or optimized. In functionalist theory this quantity should be societal integration or survival, but I have never encountered a differential equation model implementing functionalist reasoning. In rational choice models, utility is the quantity focused upon, and rational choice theory, especially in micro-economics, is replete with differential equations in utility, for example as a function of actors' effort and wage. This produces a model in the variables entering the maximization equation, but usually not in time. The resulting model is a model in variables that may be observed. They often have no time path explicitly introduced and the rationale used by economists is to assume equilibrium. In fact, most time series models used by economists assume equilibrium in each period so that the shifts in independent variables account for the changes in the dependent variable over time. This practice has been adopted by sociologists in the analysis of panel data, often without a strong rationale. Most econometric textbooks therefore have much to say about estimation of models assuming equilibrium in each period, and much less to say about so-called dynamic models where processes of time are explicitly focused upon. These models often pose severe estimation problems when applied to single time series with autocorrelation problems.

Distinctions between the two approaches, based on pull and push theories, need not have fundamental consequences for empirical work. It is of course possible to use rational choice theory to justify the specification of how independent variables interrelate and cause change. For example, a career model I have used extensively is based on a simple linear differential equation model:

$$dy(t) \ / \ dt = z + by(t) \tag{3}$$

where $y(t)$ is the level of attainment, income or socioeconomic status, at time t and z is a measure of the resources a person brings to the labor market. The model gives a career curve, with the basic concave shape we observe, and produce reasonable empirical results. It is derived from an elaborate account of the movement of vacancies defining the rate of job shifts in a simple system with an exponential distribution (Sørensen 1977), and b therefore provides a measure of the opportunities for career gains available in the system. The details need not concern us here. In empirical work, I use a linear specification of how z depends on measures of resources, say a person's education, thus $z = c_0 + c_1x$, where x is a measure of educational attainment. Obviously the parameter c1 needs a theoretical interpretation and such an interpretation could be derived from human capital theory or some other theory. It is a second order link between theory and data, so to speak, and I therefore agree with Goldthorpe (1998) that the appropriate causal language to be used in empirical work should be one of causal narrative, accounts of how the causal linkages are created. This is another way of stating that in non-experimental research, the specification of mechanisms is indeed essential. The use of statistical models with elaborate control variables to simulate an experimental situation is indeed inappropriate and misleading.

My main point is that with both types of theories, the link between observable quantities and the theory is produced by a defining model, focusing either on change over time or change in utility. They are indeed the proper basis for empirical work. These defining equations result in models with a particular functional form that can be compared to the behavior of empirical processes and used to estimate the relationship among variables. For this empirical work we need statistics to provide the standards of the comparison, to tell how much confidence we should have in our comparison and estimates, and to provide estimation techniques. The usefulness of statistics has certainly been taken to heart by empirically oriented sociologists. The problem is that sociologists often confuse the models used to illustrate statistical methods with the substantive models. I will discuss this problem in more detail next.

Mechanisms of Social Processes and Statistical Models

Well trained sociologists learn regression tools, not only OLS regression, but often also a variety of regression-like tools for estimating hazard models, count models and log-linear models for tables. They also are taught to carefully consider various assumptions, about bias, heteroscedasticity, serial correlation, and so forth. Computational power is abundant, and we can use powerful statistical software packages to estimate almost anything the textbooks propose. These are very important changes in how we go about conducting empirical research and what we teach our students. Almost all these changes have taken place within the last thirty years, and the enormous technological changes in computing power have spearheaded these developments.

Statistics is a branch of applied mathematics. It provides tools for how to estimate quantities that inform about the state of the world where these estimates have desirable properties. Statistics also provides tools for deciding how confident we should be in our knowledge about the world. These are very important tools and the mathematical models that are used for estimation and inferences are extremely sophisticated and powerful. They represent a major advance for science and society. Just consider how important statistical tools have been for the development of medicine and for agriculture. However, the mathematical tools statisticians use do not represent models of social processes. They are not meant to mirror actual social processes. They may sometime do so because statistics heavily rely on probability theory and probability theory may provide the basic framework for modeling social processes that behave stochastically. Coleman provides numerous examples in his creative applications of simple stochastic process models to model influence processes in groups (Coleman 1964). However, statisticians have no responsibility for providing models of social processes. Sociologists have this responsibility if they want to work with quantitative data.

I believe that statisticians think the relationship between statisticians and other scientists, including sociologists, ought to be one where the scientist comes to the statisticians with a model of something and ask the statistician how to best estimate the model, with the data available. The statistician comes up with an estimation procedure. The scientist goes home and uses the procedure until he develops a new model for which he again needs statistical assistance. Obviously the scientist may not have a model, but just a good idea.[2] Then should the scientist be doing experiments, there is no major problem, for one does not need mathematical models of processes to do research with experiments, as noted above. However, when the scientist is doing non-experimental research, the statistician has a problem. How can he help estimate a model that the scientist has not been able to develop? The scientist will want something for the trouble and possible expense of asking the statistician, and the statistician obviously would like to be helpful. So, rather than sending the scientist back to think more about the matter and come up with the needed model, the statistician proposes to move things along by suggesting the scientist estimate something simple and parsimonious. This is presumably based on the wisdom that whoever designed the process under investigation wanted to make it simple. Why the statistician has privileged information about the design of processes I do not know, but so it is. The simple and parsimonious models are usually additive. This creates the added benefit that the computational effort needed usually is less than for more complicated models, and this used to be important too. The situation described is very much the situation for the sociologist. I never heard about a sociologist asking a statistician for help with a model. When the sociologist can construct a model, he or she usually can also devise a manner of estimating it. However, sociologists very rarely develop models, as I have argued. It has therefore become the general belief among several generations of sociologists that statistical models, satisfying the criteria of simplicity and parsimony, are needed to make good research.

By making statistical models the main tools for analysis, mathematically gifted sociologists have become good statisticians and some have made valuable contributions to the statistical literature and sociological methodology. We are quite sophisticated about estimation methods in a variety of circumstances and about the proper statistical tests to perform. However, we have focused our attention on these efforts rather than on developing theoretically adequate models of the process we are investigating. In fact, some sociologist-statisticians seem to believe that there are facts out there, and relationships that can be adequately

---

[2] I suspect that those sciences with the best models often have the least use for statisticians. Many of the science students I have in my courses, and sometimes use as research assistants, seem ignorant of even simple statistical methods.

captured by statistical models without any need to be concerned about the mechanisms that produce these facts and relationships. They will argue that theories come cheap, but good data and good estimates take effort. Theory has been relegated to the role of justifying the inclusion of variables in the statistical models. We include education in an earnings equation and invoke human capital theory to justify this and we include a class category and invoke class analysis. In sociological labor market research, it is in fact common to see models where different groups of variables invoke different groups of theories that may be analytically wholly incompatible. The statistical model serves to adjudicate among these theories by presumably showing which theory is more important, using variance explained or standardized regression coefficients to decide the matter. The proper question should be which theory is correct, but few seem to worry about such matters.

As noted, the statistical models are almost always additive because this is the most parsimonious specification and the computationally least expensive specification. This may indeed be the proper specification for an experimental design where we have occasion to manipulate the causal variables. However, with non-experimental data it is actually hard to construct a mechanism for change that will result in an additive model. With push theories, where the focus is on the rate of change, one might suggest the model $dy(t)/dt = a$, where a is a constant. However, integration of the equation will produce a model where $y(t)$ grows linearly in time. This is not a model of a process that conforms to what we usually observe.

It is possible to obtain a linear specification from a simple model for change. Consider again, the simple linear growth model:

$$dy(t) \ / \ dt = a + by(t) \tag{4}$$

If here the quantity a is expanded as a linear function of a set of independent variables, so that $a = a_0 + a_1x_1 + a_2x \ldots + a_nx_n$, one obtains after solving the differential equation and letting $t \to \infty$:

$$y(e) = d_0 + d_1x_1 + d_2x_2 \ldots + d_nx_n \tag{5}$$

where $d_i = -a_i \ / \ bx_i$. This is linear, but the linear specification is completely ad hoc. It may be justified by some ad hoc push theory or derived from maximization of utility in a rational choice theory, but clearly the linearity does not follow from a specification of the mechanisms by which the parameter, a, comes to be dependent on the x variables. So, the example proves very little about when a mechanism of change may produce the kind of linear model we usually estimate.

It should be noted that however simple this example may seem, there is still some value in deriving the equilibrium formulation (5). It demonstrates that the simple change process may generate an equilibrium that produces an observed association among variables, measured by the d_i parameters. These are the parameters we estimate in our usual cross-sectional analysis (cf. Coleman 1968). They are seen to be functions of both the contribution of x to a and of the parameter b that governs the shape of the growth process. For the use of (3) as a model of the career process, b is a measure of opportunities for advancements (Sørensen 1977). Hence the observed association between, say, education and socioeconomic attainment is a function of the opportunity structure of the system. If there are few opportunities for advancement, education will have very little to act on after entry into the labor force, and its observed effect will be lower than in a system where there are many opportunities. Similarly, in the simple model for learning I consider below, when there are few opportunities for learning, the family background of students and their ability will have little to act on, and equality of opportunity will result from there being little to learn.

The failure to consider mechanism of change and to try to formulate them in models of the processes we investigate, however primitive the result may be, has important consequences for the state of sociological research. The almost universal use of statistical models and specifications have two sets of important implications. First, we are constrained by the statistical models to not consider whether or not we actually obtain, from our research, a greater understanding of the processes we investigate. In other words, the statistical models give us theoretical blinders. I will use research on social mobility as an example of this problem. Second, we may actually produce results that on closer consideration seems theoretically unfounded and, very likely, misleading. I will use research on school effects as an example of the latter problem.

Loglinear Models and Mechanisms of Mobility Processes

Sociologists have long been interested in the study of social mobility; in particular the type of mobility we call intergenerational mobility, where we study the movement of families in social structure from one generation to another. Data on such moves are available in several forms, early investigations would look at inflow tables for the recruitment to elite positions available from biographies of the occupants of elite positions. These data have clear limitations because they do not inform about the sizes of the origin categories. The preferred source of data is information from surveys about the (usually male) respondents' current occupation and the occupation of their fathers when they grew up. This produces, with a collapsing of the occupation categories into major occupational groups or social classes, a cross-tabulation of father's positions with son's position. Assuming that male respondents' position indicates the family's position, this intergenerational mobility table has been the basic source of data in innumerable investigations of social mobility processes. The link between family position and the male's position has been a source of some controversy, extensively discussed in Erikson and Goldthorpe (1992). I shall not deal with this issue here.

Sorokin (1927) provided early an elaborate conception of mobility processes as movement in social space along what he called channels of mobility that define distances between the various positions in the social space. Conceptions of this kind have been adopted in almost all subsequent mobility research, and I have no quarrel with it.

What is the purpose of this research on social mobility? Early research, that is mobility research until the nineteen seventies, was motivated by the idea that social mobility told us something about the degree of equality of opportunity characterizing a society. Therefore, research should focus on societal comparison of mobility tables and a host of national studies were conducted in the fifties and sixties to achieve this aim. They are still going on and we have now mobility tables for many societies, often many tables for each society, all having basically the same form, presented by the cross-tabulation of fathers' and sons' position.

Anyone who has looked at a mobility table will realize that it is not particularly easy to make sense of such a table and to summarize its content. One feature is apparent. The marginals will usually differ, and despite Duncan (1966)'s warnings, these marginals are usually taken to present social structure in the two generations. The different distributions presumably mean that some families are mobile because they are pushed and pulled by the changes in the distribution of positions, or changes in social structure, while others move net of these changes, what is usually called exchange mobility. It was thought desirable to separate these two types of mobility. Indeed it seems to have been thought that only exchange mobility measures equality of opportunity. Why this idea was developed is unclear. If what is measured by mobility somehow should reflect something that members of society recognize as equality of opportunity, one would think that they pay attention to the absolute magnitude of mobility, regardless of its source. This simple observation has however rarely, if ever, been considered by mobility researchers.

The sociologists turned to the statisticians for help in separating the structural from the exchange mobility. The first solution was a chi-square like measure that compares the actual amount of mobility to the amount of mobility that would have been observed if there was statistical independence between origins and destination (Rogoff 1953). Summarized across the whole table this measure was taken to be a measure of the degree of equality of opportunity; the ratios in each cell were interpreted to suggest the distance between occupational or class categories in the Sorokin conception. As it turned out, many found this mobility measure wanting (e.g. Duncan 1966). Hauser (1978b) states the problem succinctly. The base model used to compare actual to expected mobility does not describe the table. Fortunately there was much more help to be obtained from statisticians. The statistician-sociologist Leo Goodman began already in the late sixties to develop statistical models for mobility tables, with many variants and often with very good statistical properties, meaning that they provide a statistical adequate description of mobility tables. The log-linear models became the tools to use for the analysis of mobility tables. A particularly prominent variant in the Goodman arsenal was proposed by Hauser (1978b) and later modified and applied in what I consider the culmination of the intergenerational mobility research tradition, presented by Erikson and Goldthorpe (1992).

All is well, apparently. There is a very large literature on variants of the log-linear models. There are some acrimonious debates, but they are statistical debates. The literature is almost completely devoid of substantive considerations in terms of whether or not the various variants capture adequately the mechanisms by which mobility occur, and/or whether the parameters of these models have some social significance. However, the good models do describe mobility tables well. There are no statistical issues to be concerned with. But, the plethora of different models that provide equally satisfying descriptions, statistically, suggests that fit is not the only criterion to apply. It may also be useful to consider substantive issues.

First, it seems reasonable to ask, if the preferred log-linear models do indeed inform about the concepts that mobility research would like to measure. Second, we might ask if these statistical models inform about the properties of mobility processes so that we understand better how these processes operate and what governs their outcomes. The answer is no to both these questions, more resounding perhaps to the second than to the first question.

As noted, much mobility research has the objective to measure the degree of inequality of opportunity of a society. The early Rogoff index provided a single measure, presumably providing an overall measure. Its statistical defects have often been discussed and the index has not been used for a very long time. However, the index also has a substantive defect. It measures equality of opportunity as deviation from randomness. This suggests that randomness is equated with perfect equality of opportunity. This is not what most non-statisticians have in mind when thinking of equality of opportunity. There is an early and vivid illustration of the point. Duncan (1968) a long time ago presented intergenerational mobility tables for American Blacks and Whites. They clearly show, also without help from statistics, that there is more randomness for Blacks than for Whites. Specifically, Blacks whatever their origins tend to end up at the bottom of society. Most would reject that this means that there is more equality of opportunity in the Black population than in the White population. Of course, if we insist on taking the statistical measure to mean equality of opportunity then it will be so. However, we need not reify statistics in this manner. The issue is that opportunity means 'favorable occasions.' Equality of opportunity means equal access to these occasions. Clearly Blacks encounter fewer favorable occasions and this is not reflected in the statistical measure. This might be easily remedied by looking at the distribution of chances for upward mobility. However, no statistical measure or model is designed to do that. The modified Rogoff index suggested by Hauser (1978b) emphasizes the randomness interpretation, by measuring the degree of random deviation from a well-fitting model of the table. Hauser (1978b) attempts no substantive interpretation of the model or the proposed overall mobility measure.

There is a solution to this problem, although the solution was not proposed to serve this purpose. Goldthorpe (1984, see also Erikson and Goldthorpe 1992) advocates seeing the exercise of modeling mobility tables as a method for detecting the class structure of society. The rationale comes from a brief remark by Weber (1978) to the effect that social classes are mobility classes. The table reveals barriers to mobility among social classes that determine their demographic stability and therefore the likelihood of class formation. This rationale avoids the problem of measuring equality of opportunity with statistical models designed to provide a log-linear description of the table. Indeed, this rationale seems impeccable. There is the problem that the statistical models measure distances by relative mobility chances since the margins are controlled for in the log linear models. These are perhaps not the distances people experience, though Goldthorpe (1984) suggests that they matter. Further, they only detect distances if the entries in the table can provide information about distances in social structure. I do not believe it can. The table assumes that families remain in the same location in the social structure their whole lives, and that a single move, except for randomness, produces the intergenerational mobility. We know this is not true. People move intragenerationally and the moves have direction, so they cannot be considered random fluctuations around a life-time class location. Therefore the entries in the tables will depend on the age distribution of the population, on the distribution of career trajectories in society, and on other matters irrelevant for the class structure in society. I have elaborated on this elsewhere (Sørensen 1987b) and will not elaborate on it here. The point has inspired some debate about whether life course or intergenerational mobility is more 'important' (Erikson and Goldtorpe 1992), a question that may not have an answer. In any event, the information problem is not the fault of the statistical models.

The main problem I see with the now more than twenty year long fascination with modeling mobility tables using log-linear models is one of missed opportunities. The mobility process is a stochastic process in a discrete state space, as the social structure is usually conceived. It is natural to suggest that this process can be modeled using a discrete time Markov Chain for intergenerational mobility and a continuous time process for career mobility. Before the advent of log-linear models there were several attempts to implement this suggestion, for intergenerational processes by, for example, Lieberson and Fuguitt (1967) and for intragenerational processes by, for example, Blumen, Kogan and McCharthy (1955). Lack of data prevents a test of the intergenerational models, but job mobility data provides an opportunity for assessing the fit of the Markov model to observed processes. They do not fit. A rich literature suggesting numerous modifications of the simple models by incorporating heterogeneity and non-stationarity were suggested and reviewed, for example, in Sørensen (1975). This activity almost completely ceased with the emergence of the log-linear models, for these models provide no manner in which to judge whether we have obtained an adequate model for the mobility process as a time dependent process.

The activity of modeling mobility processes ceased for another reason, again statistical. Those interested in analyzing job mobility processes obtained a set of tools for the use of linear regression type analysis on rates of mobility in the form of event history or hazard rate models (e.g. Sørensen and Tuma 1981, a review is presented by Rosenfeld, 1992). The event history analysis can be seen as a tool for the incorporation of heterogeneity and non-stationarity in Semi-Markovian models of mobility process. This interpretation is rarely used. In any event, the resulting estimates are never used to conduct a test of whether the stochastic process model provides an adequate model for the time dependent stochastic process being observed. Rather, we have obtained another statistical model for regression type analysis.

It is quite possible that incorporating heterogeneity and non-stationarity will improve the fit of a Markovian model to a particular observed mobility process. However, these techniques cannot overcome a fundamental conceptual problem with the Markov models. The model generates distributions over time as a function of the rates of mobility. Indeed, in the long run, these distributions are completely determined by the mobility patterns as expressed in the transition probabilities or transition rates and are independent of the initial distribution. This means that when applied to societal mobility, social structure is generated by mobility patterns. This is an awkward property that seems to fly in the face of how we usually consider the matter. We usually conceive of social structure as something that could be quite stable, in the absence of class conflict and technological change, and not something generated by mobility processes. In fact, this is probably the idea that justifies the wish to control for the marginals in the mobility table in all the statistical efforts at modeling this table.

In a fixed distribution of positions mobility can be seen as generated by a mechanism of vacancy competition as suggested by a simple model for these matters presented in Sørensen (1977). In a system of closed positions, each move is made possible by the creation of a vacancy caused by someone leaving the system, by death or retirement, or by someone moving to a vacancy in a better position. Mobility processes are then generated by vacancy chains (White 1970). White proposed to overcome the fundamental conceptual problem of the Markov model by focusing on the movement of vacancies rather than of people. The proposal requires data rarely available since we usually do not track the movement of vacancies. Harrison (1988) does provide a proposal for the empirical analysis of mobility processes, using panel data, incorporating estimates of the distribution of vacancies, but this effort has not generated a following. There is some work on mobility in organizations using the vacancy chain approach (Stewman 1975). However, for societal processes we are left with approaches that rely on very strong and simplifying assumptions as in Sørensen (1977) or Harrison (1988).

The vacancy competition idea has received no attention by the statistical modelers and little attention overall. This leaves the task of developing theoretically satisfying models for the mobility process very far from completion. The vacancy competition approach is incomplete, for not all mobility is generated by vacancy chains. In fact, the basic view of labor markets adopted in neo-classical labor economics is one where 'positions' that are wage levels, are completely open to anyone requiring the needed skills for generating a certain output. So, social structure is a mixture of open and closed positions presumably with variation over time and across societies (Sørensen 1983). No mobility analysis captures these properties and the different mechanisms associated with them.

The problem outlined here has relevance for our understanding of mobility processes described in the standard intergenerational mobility table. The distribution of vacancies gives a precise meaning to the concept of opportunities, as argued in Sørensen (1983), and therefore to what is meant by equality of opportunity. The class analysis perspective frequently invoked ideas about closure in social structure, meaning class locations far away from other class locations (e.g. Parkin 1979). However, a location can be distant from other locations for two reasons. It may provide access only when a vacancy is created by a retirement from that location. Or, the class location may offer open positions, only getting access to these positions demands hard to get qualifications, for example when access to elite education is severely restricted and class bias in access is strong. These two scenarios give us quite different understanding of what accounts for distances in social structure that should be important for how we conceive of differences among societies and over time in history. The log-linear models of mobility tables provide no information about these fundamental issues.

Lack of interest in modeling mobility processes coincides with the emergence of log-linear models of the mobility table. They have therefore blinded us to the basic issues that needed to be addressed. It is time to move on.

Statistical Models and the Detection of School Effects

My second example shows that the ad hoc use of statistical estimation procedures not only may have blinded research to fundamental theoretical problems, but may actually have produced results, of policy significance, that are not solidly grounded despite huge databases and very competent use of statistics and a strong desire to produce solid evidence.

In 1966, the results of the possibly largest social science survey ever conducted, were published. The study was about equality of educational opportunity in America (Coleman et al. 1966). Coleman and his associates decided to formulate the basic research question as one of assessing the relative importance of measures of the family background of students, the backgrounds of their peers, and measures of school facilities and economic resources. They provided the answer estimating very long regression models and using the relative contribution of the three groups of variables to the variance explained in the academic achievement of students measured by standardized achievement tests.

The main conclusion of what has become known as the (first) Coleman Report is well known and became widely accepted, if also controversial. The results indicated that schools' resources and facilities make little difference for the academic achievement of students. Family background has by far the dominant effect, though peers also make some difference. The later results were used to justify the busing of children among schools to achieve racial integration. The controversy about the results has largely focused on criticizing the causal order among the groups of variables assumed by Coleman et al., since this causal ordering determines the relative explanatory power of the various groups of variables (see Mosteller and Moynihan 1972). The Coleman Report and the controversies about its findings initiated a long research tradition on the effects of schools on learning (for a review see, for example, Sørensen and Morgan 2006). This research has been much occupied with statistical issues. Most of this need however not concern us here.

Later research has, for good reasons, not used variance explained as the measure of effect. Also later research, including the research on public and private schools by Coleman (Coleman and Hoffer 1987) has used gains in achievement over a period (usually two years) as the dependent variable, on the good rationale that while schools may not determine the overall level of academic achievement, they may influence learning, or gains in achievement. However, the additive models remain the favorite models for the learning process that creates the observed gains in achievement. This assumes a peculiar theory of the learning process, as I will show.

Conclusions from school effects research have shifted from the claim that schools make little difference for learning to the alternative claim that organizational features of schools make a lot of difference (e.g. Chubb and Moe 1990). Behind the most recent claims is the relatively uncontroversial finding that the main effects of schools are effects of their academic programs. Differences in teaching programs are also what appear to account for the results of the international comparisons of the performance of US schools with the schools of other nations. In short, schools make a difference by teaching students.

This simple conclusion suggests that research on school effects should pay more attention to variables measuring teaching effort and curricula-variables that measure the opportunities for learning provided by schools. When these variables are added to the plethora of other variables that enter the regression equations typically estimated in school effects research, opportunities for learning should further explain achievement. However, simply adding variables providing measures of opportunities for learning to the standard additive models, as is done in almost all studies, is not necessarily the correct specification. The effects of opportunities for learning do not simply add to the effects of student endowments; they interact with the effects of student endowments.

Suppose, to take an extreme example, that we have a school in which no English is taught. All instruction is in Hungarian and about Hungarian topics. Furthermore, parents who send their children to this school speak Hungarian and nothing but Hungarian. If given the standard English verbal ability test analyzed in educational research, students from this school will all achieve the same score. Students will not have been taught anything relevant for performance on the English test. No effect of family background on learning outcomes in this school will be observed, for no learning relevant for the test has taken place.

Suppose, in contrast, that there is a school with an extremely rich curriculum, say, in mathematics. Students can progress from very simple algebra to very advanced mathematical topics. Every progression in this curriculum depends on how well students learned the previous step. The learning of each sequence depends to some degree on the student's background; say his mental ability that is correlated with his family's socioeconomic status. The cumulative nature of the material, coupled with the relevance of ability for the completion of each stage in the curriculum, implies both that learning increases with the number of stages in the curriculum *and* that the correlation between mental ability and the amount of what is learned increases with the number of stages in the curriculum. The assumption of a correlation between family background and mental ability ensures that, other things equal, the more instructional material that is covered in a period of instruction, the higher the observed effect of family background on academic achievement.

These simple ideas suggest that there are two components to the educational process in schools—what students are taught and how much they learn of what they are taught. Schools, classrooms, and other instructional groups differ in what and how much is taught. Students will differ, by ability and effort, in how much they learn. Students' abilities and efforts can change over time as a result of learning and as a result of motivational processes associated with the social systems to which they belong. Schools can influence how much a student will learn by how much they try to teach and by changing student effort.

A simple formal representation, originally proposed in Sørensen and Hallinan (1977), expresses these ideas. Denote by $y(t)$ the amount a student has learned by time t of material in an instructional period, or course, for which instruction began at time 0. Let $v(t)$ be a measure of how much material has been presented by time t. The amount, $y(t)$, students will have learned of this material in the period from time 0 to time t depends on students' abilities and efforts. Denote jointly ability and effort expended by s, and assume, for now, that s remains constant throughout the learning process. Learning and teaching are related by the simple differential equation:

$$dy(t)/dt = s \, dv(t) \qquad (6)$$

The increase in learned material (or achievement) is a constant function of what has been taught in period dt. This simple equation has the solution:

$$y(t) - y(0) = s[v(t) - v(0)] \qquad (7)$$

In words, the amount learned in period 0 to t depends on the amount taught, $v(t) - v(0)$, and the ability and effort of students. This very simple formulation provides one elementary insight. Opportunities for learning interact with the effort and ability of students in producing learning. If nothing is taught, nothing is learned. The implications of this can be seen by introducing variables that cause s, the ability and effort of students. Assume that we have measures of a student's endowments, such as family background variables and other variables (perhaps school characteristics) that influence the efforts of students. Assume further that we are uninterested in how these variables actually produce ability and effort, so that a linear formulation is adequate. Thus, we specify s as $s = c_0 + c_1 x_1 + c_2 x_2 \ldots + c_n x_n$ and re-express Equation (7) as:

$$y(t) - y(0) = [v(t) - v(0)][c + c_1 x_1 + c_2 x_2 \ldots + c_n x_n]. \qquad (8)$$

In a regression of $y(t) - y(0)$ on the x_i variables, the coefficients of the x_i variables will depend on $v(t) - v(0)$, the amount of instructional material presented in the period over which the gain in achievement is observed. The larger $v(t) - v(0)$, the larger will be the estimates of these coefficients. Schools that cover a lot of material in their instruction, provide many opportunities for learning, and will create more growth in achievement. If opportunities for learning are not measured and included in the model, the estimated coefficients of the x_i variables will be biased.

There are several objections that may be raised against the formulation proposed by Equation (8). First, it assumes that effort and ability are constant over the period 0 to t. This is not a reasonable assumption if students' ability to learn new material depends on what they already know and if their effort depends on how successful they are. These are both reasonable mechanisms. For short periods of time, such as the two year period covered by the panel datasets commonly analyzed in school effects research, the assumptions of stable effort and ability may be reasonable. Second, the model is nonlinear and requires a sophisticated estimation such as maximum-likelihood. These techniques are now widely available.

A much more serious problem is that direct measures of opportunities for learning are usually not available. Data available for research on school effects do not measure what and how much schools teach, making it impossible to estimate Equation (8) directly.[3] The solution to this problem adopted in Sørensen and Hallinan (1977) is to assume a particular dependency of $v(t)$ on time. Assuming that the amount of new material presented, $dv(t)$, declines over time in proportion to what has already been taught, one obtains the expression for $v(t)$:

$$v(t) = (e^{bt} - 1)/b \tag{9}$$

Letting $t \to \infty$, the total amount of material presented in period 0 to t, is $-1/b$, so that b provides a measure of the opportunities for learning. The formulation assumes that $v(0) = 0$, but the specification implies a simple linear differential equation for learning, $dy(t)/dt = s + by(t)$, that can be solved for any period of time. The solution is:

$$y(t_2) = c_0^* + b^* y(t_1) + c_1^* x_1 + c_2^* x_2 \ldots + c_n^* x_n \tag{10}$$

where $b^* = e^{b\Delta t}$, and the c_i^* coefficients have the form, $c_i^* = c_i/b(e^{b\Delta t} - 1)$. Here $\Delta t = t_2 - t_1$, the period of observation (e.g., 10th to 12th grade). From estimates of b^*, one can obtain b as $\ln b^*/\Delta t$. And using this estimate, one can also generate the parameters c_i from measures of the c_i^*s.

Equation (5) is the lagged regression model estimated by Coleman and Hoffer (1987), Chubb and Moe (1990), and many others. However, the derivation proposed here, and the resulting specification, allows for the estimation of the fundamental forces governing learning: the opportunities for learning characterizing schools and the individual endowments of students, perhaps augmented by their schools. Such estimates are presented for various school characteristics in Sørensen and Hallinan (1977), for ability groups in Sørensen and Hallinan (1986), for academic tracks in Sørensen (1987a), and for public versus Catholic schools in Sørensen (1996). All of these applications provide results consistent with the ideas suggested above. In the analysis of the Catholic versus public school differences, estimates for b in different subject areas suggest that

---

[3] An instructive exception is provided by Barr and Dreeben (1983). They obtain measures of the amount of material taught in reading and mathematics, and they obtain very interesting results about the variation in opportunities for learning among schools, classrooms, and ability groups.

Catholic Schools do indeed provide more opportunities for learning, in addition to whatever effects the functional communities have on the efforts of students (Sørensen 1996). This appears to be mainly a result of more students being allocated to academic tracks in Catholic schools, as noted above.

The here proposed conception of how school effects are produced is very different from what Coleman proposed in the additive models used in Coleman et al (1966) and in subsequent school effects research. These additive models assume that schools can shape the minds and motivations of students to possibly override the influence of family background. These models pay no attention to the interaction between the influence on student endowments and what schools put in the minds, or the process of learning modeled above.

Against an early version of the model proposed above, Hauser (1978a) argues that it is unreasonable to assume that school effects are produced primarily by opportunities for learning. He suggests that there may be considerably more learning going on in a boot camp where relative achievement levels are in flux than in a perfunctorily led high school class where relative learning differences persist. Evidently, Hauser conceives of learning as change in student ability and effort only. Furthermore, Hauser seems only to allow school effects that change students relative to each other. This is an unreasonably restrictive definition of school effects: schools only matter if they make the bright dull and the dull brighter. It is, however, part of the effect detected by the variance partitioning in cross-sectional models.[4]

Hauser, Coleman, Chubb and Moe and others conceive of schooling as a process whereby schools somehow add to, or subtract from, the intellectual resources of students. This is an attractive scenario for it implies that schools should be able to produce gifted students and equal educational outcomes for all. At least all students attending the same schools should come out pretty much alike, and all students in America should become equal if schools are equally equipped with the things that mold young minds. This in turn would mean that schools can achieve equality of results, as well as equality of educational opportunity, if those who are in charge of schools think that this is an important goal.

---

[4] A number of implications for policy of the debate between Hauser and me about the nature of school effects are developed by Hoaglin et al. (1982).

This conception of the educational process and of the role of schools is an important one in American culture. The comprehensive system of secondary education, or the "common school" (Cremin 1951), is a unique American institution designed to achieve a basic equality of educational outcomes. The institution has been imitated in a number of European countries, as a replacement for, or alternative to, the very selective and highly differentiated European school systems, designed originally to achieve the opposite of the American schools: maximum feasible inequality of educational outcomes.[5]

The American goal of the "common school" is not an easy one to achieve, at least not if it is taken literally. Presumably, schools would add to the ability and effort of children primarily by teaching and thus by creating opportunities for learning. If equal outcomes are desired, these opportunities should be allocated so that the least able receive the most opportunities and the most able the fewest. This is not what usually goes on in schools. One main reason may be that such an allocation of opportunities is in direct contradiction to another popularly accepted educational goal: the goal of providing each student with the opportunity to achieve to the maximum of his or her potential.

Providing students with more opportunities for learning produces more inequality in academic achievement. This is easily seen from the conception of learning and teaching proposed here. Opportunities for learning determine the parameter of Equation (5) in such a manner that the variance of $y(t)$ in the long run will become $\sigma^2_{y(max)} = (-1/b)^2 \sigma^2_s$. Here $y(max)$ is the eventual academic achievement, and σ^2_s is the variance in student intellectual resources. Clearly, as more opportunities are provided, more variance or inequality in academic achievement will be created, for given inputs. From Equation (5), it can also easily be seen that the variance in achievement will increase over time until it reaches the value $\sigma^2_{y(max)}$. There is empirical support for this prediction about the increase in inequality in achievement in the form of a phenomenon called 'fan spread'. For example, Willms and Jacobsen (1990) report that while students tend to maintain their initial position in the distribution of mathematics achievement from grades 3 to 7, there is an increase in the variance in the scores in later grades that is consistent with the predictions suggested here.

---

[5] Kerckhoff (1993) presents an exemplary illustration of the contrast in an empirical analysis of schooling processes in the U.K., emphasizing the long term consequences of processes creating inequality.

In fact, the goal of providing each student with the opportunities to achieve the maximum of his or her potential has stronger implications. Such a goal implies that those with the greatest intellectual resources should have the most favorable opportunities for learning. For this reason, ability grouping and similar arrangements are often adopted in the lower grades in tandem with elaborate curriculum differentiation in the higher grades. Schools that provide the most opportunities given to the most able students are also schools that maximize differences among students in academic achievement.

The goal of maximizing each student's academic achievement, therefore, implies the maximization of inequality of educational outcomes given individual endowments. It is not easy to reconcile this with the goal of making schools equalizers. This may be well understood by educators and educational policymakers, although it is often hidden behind the rhetoric of schools as equalizers. If policymakers understand the relationship between school performance and inequality, then by equal they presumably mean not equality of outcomes, but equality of opportunities.

Presumably it is possible to maximize outcomes and therefore inequality in outcomes and minimize inequality of opportunity for achieving these outcomes at the same time. However, it is not easy. The problem is that good schools, in terms of providing opportunities for learning, also tend to have higher inequality of opportunity. This follows directly from the relationship between the observed effect of an independent variable and opportunities for learning discussed above. The more opportunities for learning presented to students, the higher the observed effect of an independent variable x_i (including variables that measure ascriptive attributes of students such as race, ethnicity, or family background). In other words, good schools are likely to increase observed inequality of opportunities that magnify inequality of outcomes by further differentiating students along ascriptive characteristics that determine ability and effort. Thus, the simplest way to create both equality of opportunity and equality of outcomes is to teach very little.

If we consider good schools to be schools which try to teach a lot, and if the model proposed above is true, then good schools increase the effect of family background. This is the exact opposite of what Coleman argued in Coleman and Hoffer (1987). His conception of a good school implies that characteristics of good schools reduce the effect of family background. For example, the x_i variables measuring characteristics of Catholic schools reduce the effects of variables measuring family background. This could result from higher effort produced by functional communities, or it could result from selection into Catholic schools producing a correlation between unmeasured variables that determine learning and family background variables. Both these mechanisms may, of course, compensate for the increased inequality caused by more ample opportunities for learning, if such better opportunities indeed are provided by Catholic schools.

While these fundamental relationships between opportunities and equality may be well understood by parents and educators, apparently they are not as well understood by sociologists and other researchers who continue to estimate school effects relying on statistical models that ignore the role of opportunities for learning. James S. Coleman, in exemplary fashion, showed the power of mathematics as a tool for mirroring ideas about mechanisms of social processes (Coleman 1964). It is ironic that he, in his large scale empirical research, invariably used ad hoc statistical models for the estimation of relationships among variables. These models do not implement a simple and reasonable conceptualization of what governs the processes he investigated. Coleman's large scale research on school effects had a stronger impact on policy and on the research of others than most other research by sociologists. I will argue in the conclusion of this paper that his desire for having this impact may, in fact, explain why he chose to forget his own idea about the proper way to link theory and evidence.

Conclusion

I have argued that the integration of theory and evidence in sociology must take place by choosing theories that allow for such integration by producing ideas about what generates change in social processes. In order to be fully successful, this strategy should result in the formulation of mathematical models for change. These ideas are not novel. They form the justification for the creation of a specialty in sociology called mathematical sociology and the power of the ideas is illustrated with numerous examples in Coleman (1964) and related work. Nevertheless, sociologists have largely chosen a different strategy for going about testing their ideas with evidence. They adopt ad hoc statistical models as described in textbooks and they have become quite sophisticated at statistics. I have tried to show that this use of statistical models and the fascination with their elaboration has blinded sociologists to exploring fundamental properties of the processes they investigate, such as social mobility processes. In turn this has sometimes produced quite unreasonable substantive models for the processes being investigated, as in the case of research on schools effects.

There are several reasons for why statistical models came to dominate. I have argued elsewhere that the increase in computing power allowed sociologists to estimate what with less computing power had to be modeled (Sørensen 1998). So instead of formulating stochastic process models for the mechanisms of what we are interested in, we proceed directly to estimate how parameters of these processes depend on independent variables in hazard rate analysis.

Evidently the tendency for mathematically gifted students to choose disciplines other than sociology, economics in particular, also plays a role. Obviously the use of statistical models also demands some mathematical skills. However, much can be done by simply using what is available in the main software packages and explained in their manuals without necessarily understanding the mathematical rationale.

There is an additional reason. Sociologists seem to lack confidence in their own ideas and theories and fear that their research conclusions will not be accepted unless the statistical analysis follows the textbook guidelines. There is a serious dilemma for sociological research here. Sociologists have few well-specified theories translatable into mathematical models for processes, and those theories that do exist, such as the one we outlined above, are unlikely to be agreed upon. This means that sociologists are unlikely to propose a conclusion based on models that deviate from the standard linear statistical models we are taught to use by statisticians. This is an especially important consideration when sociologists conduct research of policy relevance, such as research on school effects. The need to convince others, who believe in numbers produced by good statistical methodology, but who perhaps do not believe in the ideas of sociologists, seems to have been the rationale for Coleman's use of ad hoc statistical models.

References

Barr, R. and R. Dreeben. 1983. *How Schools Work*, Chicago, IL: Chicago University Press.

Blossfeld, H.-P. and G. Prein. 1998. *Rational Choice Theory and Large Scale Data Analysis*, Boulder, CO: Westview Press.

Blumen, I., M. Kogan and P. J. McCharthy. 1955. *The Industrial Mobility of Labor as a Probability Process*, Itacha, NY: Cornell University Press.

Chubb, J. E. and T. M. Moe. 1990. *Politics, Markets, and America's Schools*, Washington, DC: Brookings.

Coleman, J. S. 1964. *Introduction to Mathematical Sociology*, Glencoe, IL: The Free Press.
———. 1968. "The mathematical study of change" in H. M. Blalock and A. Blalock (eds.), *Methodology in Social Research*, New York: McGraw-Hill, 428–478.
———. 1990. *The Foundations of Social Theory*, Cambridge, MA: The Belknap Press of Harvard University Press.
Coleman, J. S., E. Q. Campbell, C. J. Hobson, J. McPartland, A. Mood, F. D. Weinfeld and R. L. York. 1966. *Equality of Educational Opportunity*, Washington, DC: US Government Printing Office.
Coleman, J. S. and T. Hoffer. 1987. *Public and Private Schools: The Impact of Communities*, New York: Basic Books.
Coleman, J. S., E. Katz, and H. Menzel. 1957. "The diffusion of an innovation among physcians" in *Sociometry*, 20(4): 253–270.
Cremin, L. A. 1951. *The American Common School: An Historic conception*, New York: Teachers College, Columbia University.
Duncan, O. D. 1966. "Methodological issues in the analysis of social mobility" in N. J. Smelser and S. M. Lipset (eds.), *Social Structure and Mobility in Economic Development*, Chicago: Aldine, 51–97.
———. 1968. "Pattern of occupational mobility among negro men" in *Demography*, 5(1): 11–22.
Elster, J. 1989. *Nuts and Bolts for Social Sciences*, New York: Cambridge University Press.
Erikson, R. and J. H. Goldthorpe. 1992. *The Constant Flux*, New York: Clarendon.
Gambetta, D. 1987. *Were They Pushed or Did They Jump*, New York: Cambridge University Press.
Goldthorpe, J. H. 1984. Social mobility and class formation: On the renewal of a tradition in sociological inquiry, *Working Paper*. CASMIN-Project, Institut für Sozialwissenschaften. Universität Mannheim, Mannheim.
———. 1996. "The quantitative analysis of large scale data-sets and rational action theory: For a sociological alliance" in *European Sociological Review*, 12: 109–26.
———. 1998. Causation, Statistics and Sociology, *Manuscript*. Nuffield College, Oxford.
Harrison, R. J. 1988. "Opportunity models: An adaption of vacancy models to national occupational structures" in *Research in Social Stratification and Mobility*, 7: 3–33.
Hauser, R. M. 1978a. "On 'A reconceptualization of school effects'" in *Sociology of Education*, 51(1): 86–73.
———. 1978b. "A structural model of the mobility table" in *Social Forces*, 56: 919–953.
Hedström, P. and R. Swedberg. 1998. *Social Mechanisms: An Analytical Approach to Social Theory*, New York: Cambridge University Press.
Hoaglin, D. C., R. J. Light, B. McPeek, F. Mosteller and M. A. Stoto. 1982. *Data for Decisions*, Cambridge, MA: Abt Books.
Kerckhoff, A. C. 1993. *Diverging Pathways: Social Structure and Career Decisions*, New York: Cambridge University Press.
Lieberson, S. 1985. *Making It Count*, Berkeley, CA: University of California Press.
Lieberson, S. and G. V. Fuguitt. 1967. "Negra-white occupational differences in the absence of discrimination" in *American Journal of Sociology*, 73: 188–200.
Merton, R. K. 1957a. "The bearing of empirical research on sociological theory" in R. K. Merton, *Social Theory and Social Structure*, Clencoe, IL: The Free Press, 102–17.
———. 1957b. "The bearing of sociological theory on empirical research" in R. K. Merton, *Social Theory and Social Structure*, Clencoe, IL: The Free Press, 85–101.
Mosteller, F. and D. P. Moynihan (eds.). 1972. *On Equality of Educational Opportunity*, New York: Random House.
Nielsen, F. and M. T. Hannan. 1977. "The expansion of national educational systems: Test of a population ecology model" in *American Sociological Review*, 42: 479–490.
Parkin, F. 1979. *Marxism and Class Theory*, New York: Columbia University.
Rogoff, N. 1953. *Recent Trends in Occupational Mobility*, New York: Free Press.

Rosenfeld, Rachel A. 1992. "Job mobility and career processes" in *Annual Review of Sociology*, 18: 39–61.

Sørensen, A. B. 1975. "Models of social mobility" in *Social Science Research*, 4(2): 65–92.

——. 1977. "The structure of inequality and the process of attainment" in *American Sociological Review*, 42: 965–978.

——. 1983. "Processes of allocation to open and closed positions in social structure" in *Zeitschrift für Soziologie*, 12: 203–224.

——. 1987a. "The organizational differentiation of students in schools as an opportunity structure" in M. T. Hallinan (ed.), *The Social Organization of School: New Conceptualizations of the Learning Process*, New York: Plenum Press, 103–130.

——. 1987b. "Theory and methodology in stratification research" in U. Himmelstrand (ed.), *The Sociology of Structure and Action*, London: Sage.

——. 1996. "Educational opportunities and school effects" in J. Clark (ed.), *James S. Colemam: Consensus and Controversy*, London: Falmer Press, 207–225.

——. 1998. "Theoretical mechanisms and the empirical study of social processes" in P. Hedstrom and R. Swedberg (eds.), *Social Mechanisms: An Analytical Approach to Social Theory*, New York: Cambridge University Press, 238–266.

Sørensen, A. B. and M. T. Hallinan. 1977. "A reconceptualization of school effects" in *Sociology of Education*, 50: 522–535.

——. 1986. "Effects of ability grouping on growth in academic achievement" in *American Educational Research Journal*, 23(4): 519–542.

Sørensen, A. B. and S. L. Morgan. 2006. "School effects: Theoretical and methodological issues" in M. T. Hallinan (ed.), *Handbook of Sociology of Education*, New York: Plenum Publishing Company.

Sørensen, A. B. and N. B. Tuma. 1981. "Labor market structures and rates of job shifts" in *Research in Social Stratification and Mobility*, 1: 67–97.

Sorokin, P. 1927. *Social Mobility*, New York: Harper Brothers.

Stewman, S. 1975. "An application of job vacancy models to a civil service internal labor market" in *Journal of Mathematical Sociology*, 4: 37–59.

Stinchcombe, A. 1968. *Constructing Social Theories*, New York: Harcourt, Brace and World.

Weber, M. 1920/1978. *Economy and Society*, Berkeley, CA: University of California Press.

White, H. 1970. *Chains of Opportunity*, Cambridge, MA: Harvard University Press.

Willms, J. D. and S. Jacobsen. 1990. "Growth in mathematics skills during the intermediate years: Sex differences and school effects" in *International Journal of Educational Research*, 14: 157–174.

CAUSAL INFERENCE AND STATISTICAL MODELS IN MODERN SOCIAL SCIENCES

Hans-Peter Blossfeld

1. *Introduction*

The empirical investigation of causal relationships is an important but difficult scientific endeavor. In the social sciences, two understandings of causation have guided the empirical analysis of causal relationships: (1) "Causation as robust dependence" and (2) "causation as consequential manipulation." Both approaches clearly have strengths and weaknesses for the social sciences which will be described in detail in this chapter. Based on this discussion, a third understanding of "causation as generative process," proposed by David Cox, is then further developed. This idea seems to be particularly valuable for modern social sciences because it can easily be combined with a narrative in terms of actor's objectives, knowledge, reasoning, and decisions (methodological individualism). Using event history models, this approach will then be applied to the causal analysis of an interdependent dynamic social system. In doing so, we first describe parallel processes and time-dependent covariates, the latter of which are often used to include the sample path of parallel processes in transition rate models. The widely used 'system' and 'causal' approach are contrasted, with the latter proposed as a more appropriate method from an analytical point of view and that it provides straightforward solutions to simultaneity problems, time lags and varying temporal shapes of effects. Based on separate applications in West and East Germany, Canada, Latvia, and the Netherlands, the usefulness of the approach of "causation as generative process" is demonstrated by analyzing two highly interdependent family processes: entry into marriage (for individuals in a consensual union) as the dependent process and first pregnancy/childbirth as the explaining one. After potential statistical reasons for the time-dependent effects are described, we move to more substantive explanations, including the importance of actors, probabilistic causal relations, preferences and negotiation, observed and unobserved decisions and the problem of conditioning on future events.

2. Models of Causal Inference

The goal to find scientifically based evidence for causal relationships leads
to design questions, such as which inference model is appropriate to specify
the relationship between cause and effect and which statistical procedures
can be used to determine the strength of that relationship (Schneider
et al. 2007). Two different models of causal inference have dominated
the work of practitioners in the social sciences over the last decades: (1)
"Causation as robust dependence" and (2) "causation as consequential
manipulation." The former approach—which in multiple regression or
path analysis is known as the "control variable" or "partialling" approach
(Duncan 1966; Kerlinger and Pedhazer 1973; Blalock 1970) and in the
econometric analysis of time-series as "Granger causation" (Granger 1969;
Johnston 1972)—starts from the presumption that correlation does not
necessarily imply causation but causation must in some way or the other
imply correlation. In this view, the key problem of causal inference is to
determine whether an observed correlation of variable X with variable
Y, where X is temporally prior to Y, can be established as a "genuine
causal relationship."

The advocates of the "causation as robust dependence" approach
call X a "genuine" cause of Y in so far as the dependence of Y on X
cannot be eliminated through additional variables being introduced
into the statistical analysis. Thus, in this approach causation is established essentially through the elimination of spurious (or non-causal)
influences. Although this approach has dominated the social sciences
for several decades, sociologists consider it as a too limited approach.
First, they think that causal inference should not be limited entirely to
a matter of statistical predictability but should include predictability in
accordance with theory (Goldthorpe 2001: 3). Second, since scientists
rarely know all of the causes of observed effects or how they relate to
one another, it is impossible to be sure that all other important variables have in fact been controlled for (Shadish, Cook and Campbell
2002). A variable X can therefore never be regarded as having causal
significance for Y in anything more than a provisional sense: "At any
point, further information might be produced that would show that the
dependence of Y on X is not robust after all or, in other words, that
the apparent causal force of X is, at least to some extent, spurious."
(Goldthorpe 2001: 5)

The second understanding of "causation as consequential manipulation" seems to have emerged as a reaction to the limitations of "cau-

sation as robust dependence." Instead of "establishing the causes of effects," Holland (1986, 1988) and Rubin (1974, 1978, 1980) are concerned with "establishing the effects of causes." They make clear that it is more to the point to take causes simply as given, and to concentrate on the question of how their effects can be securely measured. According to this approach, causes can only be those factors that could serve as treatments or interventions in well-designed controlled experiments or quasi-experiments. Thus, given appropriate experimental controls, if a causal factor X is manipulated, then a systematic effect is produced on the response variable Y. The particular strength of this design is that "[...] while statements in the form 'Y is a cause of X' are always likely to be proved wrong as knowledge advances, statements in the form 'Y is an effect of X,' once they have been experimentally verified, do not subsequently become false: 'Old, replicable experiments never die, they just get reinterpreted'." (Goldthorpe 2001: 5).

Understood in this way, causation is always relative in the sense that the specific treatment of X_{tr} and its observed outcome Y_{tr} are compared with what would have happened to the same unit if it had not been exposed to this treatment (counterfactual account of causality). Since it is not possible in the same experiment for a unit to be both exposed and not exposed to the treatment, the conception of "causation as consequential manipulation" leads to what Holland (1986) has called the "fundamental problem of causal inference." For example, a student who completes one mathematics program cannot go back in time and complete a different program so that we can compare the two outcomes. Thus, the question arises of how we make sure that one gets convincing measurements for something that is in fact impossible to measure, i.e., the outcome of Y_{con}, if the unit had not been exposed to the treatment (X_{con}) in the same experiment?

In the hard sciences, such as physics or chemistry, it is often relatively easy to conduct strictly controlled experiments and to demonstrate, based on the qualities of the objects under study (e.g., physical entities), what would have happened (Y_{con}) to the same unit (u) of analysis if it had not been exposed to the treatment (X_{con}). In other words, it is often plausible to assume that these objects have a constancy of response over time (temporal stability) and that the effect of the first treatment is transient and does not affect the object's response to the second treatment (causal transience). Or at least, that the physical entities or chemical substances respond similar under certain conditions. In these cases, the causal effect for u, $CauEff_u$, is easily defined as $CauEff_u = Y_{tr} - Y_{con}$.

In fact, the model of "causation as consequential manipulation" based on the well-designed controlled experiment has been quite successful in the hard sciences.

In other disciplines such as biology, medicine or psychology, it is often not possible to assume temporal stability and causal transience at the level of the individual unit and it is normally impossible to eliminate the impact of confounding influences at the individual level. For these sciences, Rubin and Holland suggest a statistical approach to the fundamental problem of causal inference: rather than focusing on specific units, this approach estimates an average causal effect for a population of units: $CauEff = E(Y_{tr}|X_{tr}) - E(Y_{con}|X_{con})$, where $E(Y_{tr}|X_{tr})$ is the expected value for participants in the treatment group, and $E(Y_{con}|X_{con})$ is the expected value for participants in the control group. For this solution to work, however, participants in the treatment and control groups should differ only in terms of treatment group assignment, not on any other variables that might potentially affect their responses. The approach to make sure that this is indeed the case is the randomized experiment, where participants are randomly assigned to the treatment and control conditions, so that one can expect that treatment group assignment would, on average, over repeated experiments, be independent of any measurement or unmeasured pretreatment characteristics (Fisher 1935). In randomized experiments treatment assignment and unit response are therefore statistically independent of each other and any kind of selection bias is eliminated. However, it must be noted that the average causal effect of randomized experiments in populations with different distributions might be quite different, so that the effect of a randomized controlled experiment is strongly context-dependent, too (see Rohwer 2007). For example, when experimenters use convenience samples (e.g. if they use university students as experimental units), the outcome might differ from the outcome of an experiment based on a random sample from the larger population (Agresti and Franklin 2007: 170).

In sociology, economics, and demography, however, the situation under which causal inferences have to be drawn is often even more complex and complicated. In particular, randomization is often practically or socially unacceptable (e.g., it is morally and legally impossible to assign twins at birth randomly to different social classes in order to study the impact of various social environments on school success). In addition, strict experimental controls are hard to apply. Thus, well-designed randomized controlled experiments or quasi-experiments are rarely applied by practitioners in the social sciences and most demographic and sociological causal inference is based on non-experimental observations of social processes.

Since these observational data are often highly selective, Rubin, Holland and others subscribing to the approach of "causation as consequential manipulation" recommend that in their empirical work social scientists should make the process of unit assignment itself a prime concern of the inquiry. In particular, social scientists should attempt to identify, and then to represent through covariates in their data analyses all unobserved and observed influences on the response variable that could conceivable be involved in, or follow from this unit assignment process (Goldthorpe 2001). A difficulty at once obvious here is that of how one demonstrates that given a constellation of covariables, treatment assignment and unit response are indeed independent of each other. Thus the question arises: Have all relevant variables been included and adequately measured and controlled?

A whole battery of statistical techniques has been developed to help to approximate randomized controlled experiments with observational data (Schneider et al. 2007). These methods include fixed effect models (i.e., the adjustment for fixed, unobserved individual characteristics), instrumental variables (i.e., a method to correct for omitted variables bias due to unobserved characteristics), propensity score matching (an approach where individuals are matched on the basis of their observed aggregate characteristics), and regression discontinuity designs (where samples and comparisons between groups be restricted to individuals who fall just above or below a specific cut-off point and, at the same time, are likely to be similar on a set of unobserved variables). Yet, how valuable these techniques might be, "[. . .] it is still difficult to avoid the conclusion that, in non-experimental social research, attempts to determine the effects of causes will lead not to results that 'never die' but only to ones that have differing degrees of plausibility. [. . .] (Or in other words), such results will have to be provisional in just the same way and for just the same reasons as those of attempts to determine the causes of effects via the 'partialling' approach." (Goldthorpe 2001: 6) It therefore seems that the benefits of the approach of "causation as consequential manipulation" in the social sciences is quite limited.

Another and even more serious issue for the social scientists arises from the insistence of the exponents of the "causation as consequential manipulation" approach that causes must be manipulable (by an experimenter or intervener—at least in principle) (e.g., Holland 1986). The idea is that once the treatment or intervention is introduced, it will automatically lead to an outcome: $X_{tr} \rightarrow Y_{tr}$. The units of analysis in the social sciences, the individuals, are therefore assumed to be passive subjects whose behavior is explained only by causal factors and their "[. . .] 'objectives, knowledge, reasoning and decisions' have no further relevance" (Goldthorpe 2001: 8). This understanding of causation clearly reduces the testability of relevant theories and models in the social sciences. In particular, it seems not to be compatible with the micro-foundation of modern sociological theory where actors are considered to have agency, where individuals have objectives and knowledge and, when faced with a choice between different courses of action, will make decisions. Thus, the "causation as consequential manipulation" approach has a limited bearing for social scientists who have conceptionally moved from so-called factor-based to so-called actor-based models (Macy 1991; Macy and Willer 2002).

This limiting understanding of "causation as consequential manipulation" is particularly obvious, if dynamic social systems are studied over longer time-spans. Life course research has demonstrated that by studying lives over substantial periods of time social scientists increase their opportunities to understand and explain the lives within their changing social context, including relationships, workplaces, schools, and communities (Elder, Kirkpatrick Johnson and Crosnoe 2004). Individuals and their purposeful actions are embedded and shaped by the historical times so that the same event may differ in substance and meaning across different birth cohorts. The same events may also affect individuals in different ways depending on when they occur in the life course. Lives are also lived interdependently so that events in one person's life often entail events for other people as well. Thus, lives cannot be adequately represented when removed from relationships with significant others. It is well known that individuals' objectives, knowledge and beliefs are influenced by the interactions with others over time (Hedström 2005). It is therefore theoretically important to study dynamic social systems as processes over substantial periods of time.

These issues lead us to the third understanding of "causation as generative process." According to Cox (1990, 1992) it is crucial to the claim of a causal link that there is an elaboration of an underlying, generative process existing in time and space. A causal association between X and Y must be considered as being produced by a process and is created by some (substantive) mechanism. A major shortcoming of the approaches of "causation as robust dependence" and "causation as consequential manipulation" is that there is no explicit notion of an underlying generative process present in these models. Thus, "causation as generative process" seems to be a necessary expansion of these two understandings of causation (Goldthorpe 2001).

In summary, causal inference clearly should not be limited entirely to a matter of statistical predictability as in the *causation as robust dependence approach*. Well-designed controlled experiments or quasi-experiments would be a great study design for causal inference, but since in the social sciences randomization is often practically or socially unacceptable, they are rarely applied by their practitioners. Thus, most demographic and sociological causal inference has to be based on non-experimental observations of social processes. Under these conditions, both approaches, *causation as consequential manipulation* and *causation as generative process*, need also to eliminate spurious (or non-causal) influences and will therefore never lead to results that 'never die' but only to ones that have differing degrees of plausibility. Finally, the *causation as generative process approach* has the comparative advantage that it focuses our thoughtful consideration on the theoretical and statistical elaboration of an underlying, generative causal process existing in time and space, including also actors who make decisions within social contexts.

In the present contribution I would like to explore what the approach of "causation as generative process" has to offer to empirically working social scientists who wish to engage in the causal analysis of dynamic systems using event history data. Event history models are linked very naturally to an understanding of "causation as generative process" because the transition rate provides a local, time-related description of how the process evolves in time (Blossfeld, Golsch, and Rohwer 2007: 33). For each point in time, these models try to predict future changes of the transition rate of the dependent process on the basis of events of independent processes in the past.

3. *Parallel and Interdependent Processes*

The study of parallel or interdependent processes with transition rate models is one of the most important advances of event history analysis (Willekens 1991; Courgeau and Lelièvre 1992; Blossfeld and Rohwer 2002; Blossfeld, Golsch and Rohwer 2007). Parallel or interdependent processes can operate at a variety of different levels. There may be interdependent or parallel processes at the level of:

- *different domains of an individual's life*. For instance, one may ask how upward and downward moves in an individual's job career influences her/his family trajectory (e.g., Blossfeld and Huinink 1991).
- *individuals interacting with each other*, termed 'interdependent or linked lives' (Elder 1987). One might study the effect of the career of the husband on his wife's labour force participation (Blossfeld and Drobnič 2001) or how the death or migration of the head of the household impacts other family members (Courgeau and Lelièvre 1992).
- *intermediate organizations*, such as how the changing household structure determines women's labour force participation.
- *macro processes*, where the researcher may be interested, for instance, in the effect of changes in the business cycle on family formation (e.g., Blossfeld and Huinink 1991).
- *any combination of the aforementioned processes*. For example, in the study of life course, cohort, and period effects, time-dependent covariates measured at different levels must be included simultaneously (Blossfeld 1986; Mayer and Huinink 1990). Such an analysis combines processes at the individual level (life course change) with two kinds of processes at the macro level: (1) variations in structural conditions across successive (birth, marriage, etc.) cohorts; and, (2) changes in particular historical conditions affecting all cohorts in the same way.

In event history analysis, time-dependent covariates are often used to include the sample path of parallel processes in transition rate models. In the literature, however, only two types of time-dependent covariates have been described as not being subject to reverse causation (see for e.g., Kalbfleisch and Prentice 1980; Tuma and Hannan 1984; Blossfeld, Hamerle and Mayer 1989; Yamaguchi 1991; Courgeau and Lelièvre 1992). The first are *defined* time-dependent covariates whose total time path (or functional form of change over time) is determined in advance in the same way for all subjects under study. For example, process time like age or duration in a state (e.g., duration of marriage in divorce studies), is a defined time-dependent covariate because its values are predetermined for all subjects. It is the predefined onset of the process when the individual becomes 'at risk' in the event history model. Thus, by definition, the values of these time-dependent covariates cannot be affected by the dependent process under study. The second type are *ancillary* time-dependent covariates whose time path is the output of a stochastic process that is external to the units under study. Again, by definition, the values of these time-dependent covariates are not influenced by the dependent process itself. Examples of time-dependent covariates that are approximately external in the analysis of individual life courses are variables that reflect changes at the macro level of society (unemployment rates, occupational structure, etc.) or the population level (composition of the population in terms of age, sex, race, etc.), provided that the contribution of each unit is small and does not really affect the structure in the population (Yamaguchi 1991).

In contrast to defined or ancillary time-dependent covariates are *internal* time-dependent covariates, which are often referred to as being problematic for causal analysis in event history models (e.g., Kalbfleisch and Prentice 1980; Tuma and Hannan 1984; Blossfeld, Hamerle, and Mayer 1989; Yamaguchi 1991; Courgeau and Lelièvre 1992). An internal time-dependent covariate Y_t^B describes a stochastic process, considered in a causal model as being the cause, that in turn is affected by another stochastic process Y_t^A, considered in the causal model as being the effect. Thus, there are direct effects in which the processes autonomously affect each other (Y_t^B affects Y_t^A and Y_t^A affects Y_t^B), and there are 'feedback' effects, in which these processes are affected by themselves via the respective other processes (Y_t^B affects Y_t^B via Y_t^A and Y_t^A affects Y_t^A via Y_t^B). In other words, such processes are interdependent and form what has been called a dynamic system (Tuma and Hannan 1984). Interdependence is typical at the individual level for processes in different domains of life and at the level of a few individuals interacting with each other (e.g., career trajectories of partners) (see Blossfeld and Drobnič 2001). For example, the empirical literature suggests that the employment trajectory of an individual is influenced by his/her marital history and marital history is dependent on the employment trajectory. In the literature, there are two central approaches to modelling these processes, what we term here as the 'system approach' and the 'causal approach,' with the former often used to deal with such dynamic systems.

3.1   *Interdependent Processes: The System Approach*

The system approach in the analysis of interdependent processes (Tuma and Hannan 1984; Courgeau and Lelièvre 1992) defines change in the system of interdependent processes as a new 'dependent variable.' Thus, instead of analyzing one of the interdependent processes with respect to its dependence on the respective others, the focus is on the modelling of a system of state variables. In other words, the interdependence between the various processes is taken into account only implicitly.

Suppose that there are J interrelated qualitative time-dependent variables (i.e., processes): Y_t^A, Y_t^B, Y_t^C, ..., Y_t^C. A new time-dependent variable (or process) Y_t, representing the system of these J variables, is then defined by associating each discrete state of the ordered J-tuple with a particular discrete state of Y_t. As shown by Tuma and Hannan (1984), as long as change in the entire system only depends on the various states of the J qualitative variables and on exogenous variables, this model is identical to modelling change in a single qualitative variable. Thus, the idea of this approach is to simply define a new joint state space, based on the various states spaces of the coupled qualitative processes, and then to proceed as in the case of a single dependent process.

Although the system approach provides insights into the behaviour of the dynamic system as a whole, it has several disadvantages. First, from a causal analytical point of view, the approach presented by Courgeau and Lelièvre (1992) does not provide direct estimates of effects of coupled processes on the process under study. In other words, when using the system approach, one normally does not know to what extent one or more of other coupled processes affect the process of interest, controlling for other exogenous variables and the history of the dependent process. Since the effects can only be identified in simple models via a comparison of the constant terms of hazard rate equations, it is only possible to compare transition rates for general models without covariates (see Courgeau and Lelièvre 1992; Blossfeld and Rohwer 2002). Second, in particular a mixture of qualitative and quantitative processes, in which the transition rate of a qualitative process depends on the levels of one or more metric variables, turns out to be a problem in this approach. Tuma and Hannan (1984) suggest that in these situations it is not very useful. Third, this approach is also unable to handle interdependencies between coupled processes occurring in specific phases of the process (e.g., processes might be interdependent only in specific phases of the life course) or interdependencies that are dynamic over time (e.g., an interdependence might be reversed in later life phases, see Courgeau and Lelièvre, 1992), what Tuma and Hannan (1984) term 'cross-state dependence.' Finally, the number of origin and destination states of the combined process Y_t, representing the system of J variables, may lead to practical problems. Even when the number of variables and their distinct values is small, the state space of the system is large. Therefore, in light of rising parameters, the event history data sets must contain a great number of events, even if only the most general models of change (i.e., models without covariates) are to be estimated.

Considering these limitations, Blossfeld and Rohwer (2002) therefore suggested a different perspective in modelling dynamic systems, which they call the 'causal approach.'

3.2   Interdependent Processes: The Causal Approach

The underlying idea of the causal approach for analyzing interdependent processes can be outlined as follows (Blossfeld and Rohwer 2002). Based on theoretical reasons, the researcher focuses on one of the interdependent processes and considers it as the dependent one. The future changes of this process are linked to the present state and history of the entire dynamic system as well as to other exogenous variables (see Blossfeld 1986; Blossfeld and Huinink 1991). Thus, in this approach the variable Y_t, representing the system of joint processes at time t, is not used as a multivariate dependent variable. Instead, the history and the present state of the system are seen as a condition for change in (any) one of its processes. The question of how to give a more precise formulation for the causal approach remains. The following ideas may be helpful.

Causes and time-dependent covariates. As discussed above, Holland (1986) developed the idea that causal statements imply counterfactual reasoning: If the cause had been different, there would have been another outcome, at least with a certain probability. However, the consequences of conditions that could be different from their actual state are obviously not empirically observable. This means that it is simply impossible to observe the effect that would have happened on the same unit of analysis, if it were exposed to another condition at the same time.

To find an empirical approach to examine longitudinal causal relations, Blossfeld and Rohwer (2002) suggested the examination of conditions which actually do change in time, controlling for other factors. These changes are characterized as events or transitions. More formally, an event is specified as a change in a variable, and this change must happen at a specific point in time. The most obvious empirical representation of causes is therefore in terms of quantitative or qualitative variables that can change their states over time. These kind of variables link very naturally to the concept of time-dependent covariates in event history analysis. The role of a time-dependent covariate in this approach is to indicate that a (qualitative or metric) causal factor has changed its state at a specific time and that the unit under study is exposed to another causal condition. From this point of view, it seems somewhat

misleading to regard whole processes as causes. Rather, only events, or
changes in state space can sensibly be viewed as possible causes.

Time and casual effects. Consequently, we do not suggest that process
Y_t^A is a cause of process $Y_{t'}^B$, but that *a change* in Y_t^A could be a cause
(or provide a new condition) of *a change* in Y_t^B. Or, more formally:
$\Delta Y_t^A \rightarrow \Delta Y_{t'}^B$, t<t', meaning that a change in variable Y_t^A at an earlier
time t is a cause of a change in variable Y_t^B at a later point in time,
t'. Of course, it is not implied that Y_t^A is the only cause which might
affect Y_t^B. We speak of causal conditions to stress that there might be,
and normally is, a quite complex set of causes (see Marini and Singer
1988). Thus, if causal statements are studied empirically, they must
intrinsically be related to time, which relates to three important aspects
of "causation as generative process":

First, to speak of a change in variables necessarily implies reference
to a time axis. We need at least two points in time to observe that
a variable has changed its value. Of course, at least approximately,
we can say that a variable has changed its value *at a specific point in*
time. Therefore, we use the following symbols to refer to changes in
the values of the time-dependent variable ΔY_t^A and the state variable
ΔY_t^B at time t. This leads to the important point that *causal statements*
relate changes in two (or more) variables, if we think in terms of "causation
as generative process."

Second, we must consider *time ordering, time intervals* and *apparent*
simultaneity. Time ordering assumes that cause must precede the effect
in time: t < t', in the formal representation given above, an assumption
which is generally accepted (Eells 1991: Chapter 5). As an implication,
the "causation as generative process" approach must specify a temporal
interval between the change in the variable representing a cause and
the corresponding effect (Kelly and McGrath 1988). The finite time
interval may be very short or very long, but can never be zero or
infinity (Kelly and McGrath 1988). In other words, in time-continu-
ous event history models there can never be simultaneity of the causal
event and its effect event.

Some effects take place almost instantaneously. However, some effects may
occur in a time interval that requires small time units (e.g., microseconds)
or are too small to be measured by any given methods, so that cause and
effect seem to occur at the same point in time. Apparent simultaneity
is often the case where temporal intervals are relatively crude such as,
for example, yearly data. For example, the events 'first marriage' and
'first childbirth' may be interdependent, but whether these two events

are observed simultaneously or successively depends on the degree of temporal refinement of the scale used in making the observations. Other effects need a long time until they start to occur. Marini and Singer (1988), for example, discuss the gap between mental causal priority and observed temporal sequences of behaviour. Thus, there is a *delay or lag between cause and effect* (see Figure 1) that must be specified in an appropriate model of "causation as generative process." Unfortunately, in most of the current social science theories and interpretations of research findings, this interval is left conceptually unspecified.

This leads to the third point of "causation as generative process": *temporal shapes of the unfolding effect.* This means that there might be different shapes of how the causal effect Y_t, unfolds over time (see Figure 1). While the problem of time-lags is widely recognized in the social science literature, only little attention has been given to the temporal shapes of effects in the social sciences (Kelly and McGrath 1988). Researchers (using experimental or observational data) often seem to either ignore or be ignorant about the fact that causal effects could be highly time-dependent, which, of course, is an important aspect of "causation as generative process." For instance in Figure 1a, there may be an immediate impact of change that is then maintained (this obviously is the idea underlying the approaches of "causation as robust dependence" and "causation of consequential manipulation" because there is no explicit notion of an underlying generative process present in these models). Or, the effect could occur with a lengthy time-lag and then become time-invariant (see Figure 1b). The effect could start almost immediately and then gradually increase (see Figure 1c) or there may be an almost all-at-once increase which reaches a maximum after some time and then decreases (see Figure 1d). Finally, there could exist a cyclical effect pattern over time (see Figure 1e). Thus, based on these examples it is clear that we cannot rely on the assumption of eternal, time-less laws but have to recognize that the causal effect may change during the development of social processes. Since the approaches of "causation as robust dependence" and "causation of consequential manipulation" do not have an explicit idea of an underlying generative process in time and space, it might happen, that the timing of observations in observational or experimental studies (see for example the arbitrary chosen observation times p2, p3 or p4 in Figure 1) lead to completely different empirical evidences for causal relationships.

The principle of conditional independence. We consider here only interdependent processes that are not just an expression of another underlying

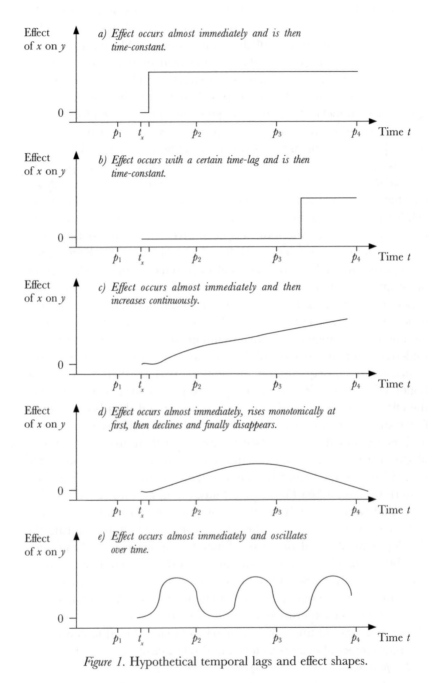

Figure 1. Hypothetical temporal lags and effect shapes.

process so that it is meaningful to assess the properties of the two processes without regarding the underlying one (control variable approach).
This means, for instance, that what happens next to Y_t^A should not be
directly related to what happens to Y_t^B, at the same point in time, and
vice versa. This condition, which we call 'local autonomy' (see Pötter
and Blossfeld 2001), can be formulated in terms of the uncorrelatedness
of the prediction errors of both processes, Y_t^A and Y_t^B, and excludes
stochastic processes that are functionally related.

Combining the ideas above, a causal view of parallel and interdependent processes becomes easy, at least in principle. Given two parallel
processes, Y_t^A and Y_t^B, a change in Y_t^A at any (specific) point in time
t′ may depend on the history of both processes up to, but not including t′. Or stated in another way: what happens with Y_t^A at any point
in time t′ is conditionally independent of what happens with Y_t^B at t′,
conditional on the history of the joint process $Y_t = (Y_t^A, Y_t^B)$ up to, but
not including, t′. Of course, the same reasoning can be applied if one
focuses on Y_t^A instead of Y_t^B as the 'dependent variable.' This is the
principle of conditional independence for parallel and interdependent
processes.

The same idea can be developed more formally. Beginning with a
transition rate model for the joint process, $Y_t = (Y_t^A, Y_t^B)$ and assuming
the principle of conditional independence, the likelihood for this model
can be factorized into a product of the likelihoods for two separate
models: a transition rate model for Y_t^A which is dependent on Y_t^B as
a time-dependent covariate, and a transition rate model for Y_t^B which is
dependent on Y_t^A as a time-dependent covariate. Estimating the effects
of time-dependent (qualitative and metric) processes on the transition
rate can be easily achieved by applying the method of episode-splitting
(Blossfeld, Hamerle, and Mayer 1989; Blossfeld and Rohwer 2002, for
a detailed explanation in relation to this analysis see also Mills 2000).

This result has important implications for the modelling of event
histories. From a technical point of view there is no need to distinguish
between defined, ancillary, and internal covariates because all of these
time-dependent covariate types can be treated equally in the estimation
procedure. A distinction between defined and ancillary covariates on
the one hand and internal covariates on the other is however sensible
from a theoretical perspective, because only in the case of internal
covariates does it make sense to examine whether parallel processes
are independent, whether one of the parallel processes is endogenous

and the other ones are exogenous, or whether parallel processes form an interdependent system (i.e., they are all endogenous).

Joint determination of interdependent processes. The principle of conditional independence implies that the prediction errors (or residuals) of the correlated processes Y_t^A and Y_t^B are uncorrelated, given the history of each process up t and the covariates. In practice, however, there may be time-invariant unmeasured characteristics that affect both Y_t^A and Y_t^B leading to a residual correlation between the processes. In that case, we say that the two processes are jointly determined by some unmeasured influences. Suppose, for example, that we are interested in studying the relationships between employment transitions and fertility among women. We might expect that a woman's chance of making an employment transition at t would depend on her childbearing history up to t (e.g. the presence and age of children), and that her decision on whether to have a(nother) child at t would depend on her employment history up to t. There may be unobserved individual characteristics, fixed over time, that affect the chances of both an employment and a fertility transition at t. For example, more 'career-minded' women may delay childbearing and have fewer children than less 'career-minded' women. In the absence of suitable measures of 'career-mindedness', this variable would be absorbed into the residual terms of both processes, leading to a cross-process residual correlation. If the residual correlation cannot be explained by time-dependent and time-invariant covariates, the two processes should be modelled simultaneously and multiprocess models (Lillard and Waite 1993) have been developed for this purpose.

Unobserved heterogeneity. Unfortunately, we are not always able to include all important factors into the event history analysis. One reason is the limitation of available data; we would like to include some important variables, but we simply do not have the information. Furthermore, we often do not know what is important. So what are the consequences of this situation? Basically, there are two aspects to be taken into consideration. The first one is well-known from "causation as robust dependence." Because our covariates are often correlated, the parameter estimates depend on the specific set of covariates included in the model. Every change in this set is likely to change the parameter estimates of the variables already included in previous models. Thus, as in the "causation as robust dependence" approach the only way to proceed is to estimate a series of models with different specifications and then to check whether the estimation results are stable or not. Since our theoretical models are normally weak, this procedure can provide additional insights into what may be called context sensitivity of causal effects in the social world.

Second, changing the set of covariates in a transition rate model will very often also lead to changes in the time-dependent shape of the transition rate. A similar effect occurs in traditional regression models: Depending on the set of covariates, the empirical distribution of the residuals changes. But, as opposed to regression models, where the residuals are normally only used for checking model assumptions, in transition rate models the residuals become the focus of modelling. In fact, if transition rate models are reformulated as regression models, the transition rate becomes a description of the residuals, and any change in the distribution of the residuals becomes a change in the time-dependent shape of the transition rate (see Blossfeld, Golsch, and Rohwer 2007). Consequently, the empirical insight that a transition rate model provides for the time-dependent shape of the transition rate more or less depends on the set of covariates used to estimate the model. So the question is whether a transition rate model can provide at least some reliable insights into a time-dependent transition rate.

The transition rate that is estimated for a population can be the result (a mixture) of quite different transition rates in the subpopulations. What are the consequences? First, this result means that one can "explain" an observed transition rate at the population level as the result of different transition rates in subpopulations. Of course, this will only be a sensible strategy if we are able to identify important subpopulations. To follow this strategy one obviously needs observable characteristics to partition a population into subpopulations. Although there might be unobserved heterogeneity (and we can usually be sure that we were not able to include all important variables), just to make more or less arbitrary distributional assumptions about unobserved heterogeneity will not lead to better models. On the contrary, the estimation results will be more dependent on assumptions than would be the case otherwise (Lieberson 1985). Therefore, we would like to stress our view that the most important basis for any progress in model building is sufficient and appropriate data.

There remains the problem of how to interpret a time-dependent transition rate from a causal view. The question is: Can time be considered as a proxy for an unmeasured variable producing a time-dependent rate, or is it simply an expression of unobserved heterogeneity, which does not allow for any substantive interpretation? There have been several proposals to deal with unobserved heterogeneity in transition rate models, which cannot be developed here (see, e.g., Tuma and Hannan 1984; Blossfeld, Golsch and Rohwer 2007). Furthermore, fixed-effects methods have become increasingly popular in the analysis of event history data in which repeated events are observed for each individual. They make it possible to control for all stable characteristics of the individual, even if those characteristics cannot be measured (Yamaguchi 1986; Allison 1996; Steele 2003; Zhang and Steele 2004). All these models broadly enrich the spectrum of models and can be quite helpful in separating robust estimation results (i.e., estimation results that are to a large degree independent of a specific model specification) and "spurious" results, which might be defined by the fact that they heavily depend on a specific type of model.

4. *An Application Example*

In order to demonstrate the utility of the "causation as generative process" approach to interdependent dynamic systems, we report the results of three cross-national comparative studies about the effect of first pregnancy/first birth on entry into first marriage for couples living in consensual unions. The earliest investigation was conducted by Blossfeld, Manting, and Rohwer (1993), followed by Blossfeld, Klijzing, Pohl, and Rohwer (1996, 1999) and finally, Mills and Trovato (2001).

The basic research problem underpinning these studies can be defined as follows. Historically, marriage has preceded the birth of a child in many countries. However, in the last two decades, the link between marriage and childbirth has become more complex, a phenomenon that has occurred in conjunction with a rapid rise in consensual unions. The three studies explored this relationship by examining how the experience of a pregnancy within a consensual union conditioned the likelihood of transition to a formal marriage with the same partner. In the later investigations, the process was modeled as explicitly time-dependent, with entry into first marriage as the dependent and first pregnancy/childbirth as the explaining process. The theoretical framework used by the authors to guide a substantive explanation of the time-dependent process was the rational actor model, which proposes that norm-guided and rational self-centered behaviour co-exist.

4.1   *The Blossfeld-Manting-Rohwer Study*

The purpose of the earlier study by Blossfeld, Manting, and Rohwer (1993) was to gain insight into the process of how consensual unions were transformed into marriages in the former West Germany and the Netherlands. It focused on the effect of fertility on the rate of entry into marriage, controlling for other important covariates in a transition rate model. Nationally representative longitudinal data were used: the German Socioeconomic Panel (West Germany) and the Fertility Survey (Netherlands) were applied. Both data sets provide information about the dynamics of consensual unions in the 1980s. Attention was limited to cohorts born between 1950–1969 that started a consensual union between 1984–1989 (West Germany) and 1980–1988 (Netherlands).

Recall that a change in the marriage process at any point in time during a consensual union may depend on the history of both processes up to, but not including t'.[1] Thus, a change in the marriage process at time t' is conditionally independent of what happens with the fertility process at t', conditional on the history of the joint process up to, but not including t'. The likelihood for the joint process of first marriage and birth can therefore be factorized into a product of the likelihoods for two separate transition rate models for: (1) first pregnancy/first birth, dependent on first marriage as a time-dependent covariate; and, (2) first marriage, dependent on first pregnancy/first birth as a time-dependent covariate.

We will discuss only the fertility effects of one transition model from this study, which utilized a piecewise constant exponential model to estimate transitions from consensual unions to both marriage and dissolution (results not shown here, see Blossfeld et al. 1993). The change in the fertility process was included as a series of time-dependent dummy variables with the states: 'not pregnant,' 'pregnant,' 'first childbirth,' and '6 months after birth.' The effects of the fertility variables on the marriage rate were significant for both countries and worked in the same direction. As long as women were not pregnant, they observed a significant and comparatively low rate of entry into marriage. But, as soon as a woman in both countries became pregnant (and in West

---

[1] We are viewing each of these two processes as having various states in their histories. For example, the partnership process could consist of the states of never married, consensual union, married and the pregnancy/birth process may consist of the states of not pregnant, pregnant and first child.

Germany also around the time when the woman gets her child), the rate of entry into marriage increased strongly. If the couple did not get married within six months after the child was born, the rate of entry into marriage again dropped to a comparatively low level in West Germany. In the Netherlands, this level is even below the 'not pregnant' level (see Manting 1994).

4.2   *The Blossfeld-Klijzing-Pohl-Rohwer Study*

About a year after this comparative study was conducted, Blossfeld et al. (1996, 1999) wanted to examine whether these results could be replicated with other data from the German Fertility and Family Survey. These data were collected retrospectively from respondents aged 20–39 years in West and East Germany in 1992. They started with a simple model of the process of entry into first marriage for couples living in consensual unions using only one time-dependent dummy variable for the event of first birth. However, the effect of this covariate was—surprisingly—not significant. What happened to the fertility effect? After much theoretical discussion, a hypothesis was put forward that could explain the seemingly contradictory results of the estimated models: the effect of changes in fertility on entry into marriage *must be strongly time-dependent in a very specific way*. According to the first study, the rate is low as long as women are not pregnant, then starts to rise at some time shortly after conception, increases during pregnancy to a maximum and finally drops again a few months after birth has taken place. Thus, when a time-dependent covariate was switched at the time of childbirth, a period with a low marriage rate up to the time of discovery of conception and a period with a high marriage rate during pregnancy was confounded and compared with a relatively low rate after the birth had taken place. Thus, the aggregated average tendency to marry before the child is born could equal the aggregate average tendency to marry after the child is born, therefore making the estimated coefficient of the time-dependent covariate 'childbirth' not significantly different from zero.

To deal with this problem, a series of 14 time-dependent pregnancy/birth binary variables were created using information from the reported date of first birth (see Table 1). These variables were grouped into categories ranging from 'marriage before the month of pregnancy,' 'month of the pregnancy,' 'one month since pregnancy,' and so on, to 'more than seven months after birth'. To be clear, since no information

Table 1. Partial likelihood estimates of the transition from consensual union to marriage (final model), West and East Germany, Canada, Latvia, the Netherlands

Covariates	Final model results by country				
	West Germany	East Germany	Canada	Latvia	the Netherlands
Pregnancy/birth process (1)					
[time before pregnancy]	−1.2595	−0.6179	−1.0768	−1.3918	−1.0909
month of pregnancy	0.1131	0.1729	−0.1157	0.3822	−0.2217
month since pregnancy	0.4783	0.2715	0.7107	0.2009	0.3769
months since pregnancy	0.8837*	0.4225	1.0851*	1.0109*	0.9374*
months since pregnancy	1.0260*	0.7723*	0.5849	1.2959*	1.3229*
months since pregnancy	0.8578*	1.3903*	0.6563	1.0817*	1.5587*
months since pregnancy	0.9905*	0.7938*	0.2480	0.9328*	1.0743*
months since pregnancy	0.8701*	0.1510	−0.8948	0.7525*	0.0227
months since pregnancy	0.8158*	−0.5166	−0.0365	0.4793	0.1028
months since pregnancy	−0.8121*	−2.5449*	−0.5693	−0.4727	−0.2350
Month of birth	−1.4709	−0.6254	−0.1115	−1.6669	−1.2711
−3 months after birth	−0.7513	0.2875	0.0096	−0.0136	−0.4595
−6 months after birth	−0.7638	0.1351	0.0363	−1.3576*	−0.4404
More than 7 months after birth	−0.9877*	−0.0921	−0.5263*	−1.2336*	−1.6771*
Birth cohort (2)					
965–69	−0.3094	−0.6001*	−0.4341*	−1.3096*	−2.2829*
960–64	−0.1700	−0.0536	−0.3589*	−0.8563*	−1.4258*
955–59	−0.1486	0.0920	−0.4324*	−0.6154	−0.8228*
1950–54]	0.0	0.0	0.0	0.0	0.0
Historical period					
[Before 1974]	0.0	0.0	0.0	0.0	0.0
974–83	0.0882	0.3521	−0.3027	0.0010	−0.2488
After 1983	−0.1554	0.0363	−0.2905	−0.3164	−1.7642*
Highest education level					
Low	0.1722*	−0.0189	0.1563	−0.0164	0.2490*
Medium]	0.0	0.0	0.0	0.0	0.0
High	−0.0354	0.0941	−0.1092	−0.0763	−0.1962*
Educational enrollment					
In school	−0.3575*	0.0061	−0.3187	0.2700	−0.1856
[Out of school]	0.0	0.0	0.0	0.0	0.0

* = significant at the 0.05 level. Results are shown for the final model. (1) First covariate coded as centered effects, all others as cornered effects. Reference groups denoted by brackets. (2) Birth cohorts for West and East Germany are represented by 1968–72, 1963–67, 1958–62 and 1953–57. *Source:* Blossfeld et al. (1999) for West and East Germany and Mills and Trovato (2001) for Canada, Latvia and the Netherlands. Both the pregnancy/birth and educational enrollment variables are time-dependent.

on the timing of pregnancy and only on the timing of successful births was available, we were looking backward in time from the first birth and thus estimated the date of pregnancy as nine months before the date of birth. As we discuss in greater detail shortly, this presents two potential problems: neglecting abortions and miscarriages, and conditioning past on future events.

4.3   *The Mills-Trovato Study*

Building on the previous two studies, Mills and Trovato (2001) wanted to see if the findings would hold in other diverse contexts such as North America or Eastern Europe or during a more recent time period within Western Europe. For this reason, they selected Canada and Latvia and more recent data from the Netherlands. Replication using diverse contexts provides a harsher and more useful validation than statistical testing of many models on only one data set. Normally, there is less chance of an artefact, more kinds of variation can be explored, and alternative explanations can be ruled out (Freedman 1991). A further impetus for this study centered on the fact that consensual unions and non-marital births in Eastern Europe and the Baltic States have skyrocketed since the 1980s (Katus 1992). Yet, these countries are rarely included in comparative analyses. Similarly, Mills and Trovato (2001) questioned whether this type of behaviour would still hold in the North American context in a country such as Canada. Using data from the Fertility and Family Surveys (FFS) for Canada (1995), Latvia (1995) and the Netherlands (1993), Mills and Trovato (2001) selected a comparative sample of women born between 1950 and 1969.

Table 1 summarizes the results of the partial likelihood estimates from the Cox models for the transition from consensual union to marriage and for the final models from the Blossfeld et al. (1999) and Mills and Trovato (2001) studies. Figure 1 plots the final partial likelihood estimates (coefficients) for the time-dependent pregnancy/birth process variable. Overall, the findings suggest a high degree of uniformity, though the levels and significance of effects tend to vary slightly across countries. Notwithstanding these similarities, we acknowledge that the Canadian and East German case show a few unexpected effects on the transition rate. In Canada, the likelihood appears to drop earlier, at approximately three months before birth, with fluctuations after that point. We attribute this largely to methodological factors since some of the monthly data had to be partially estimated (see Mills and Trovato

2001). In East Germany, there is a large drop one month before birth as opposed to the month of birth. Difference in the significance level of results by country (especially Canada and East Germany) may also be related to smaller sample sizes and less events. The theoretical reasons behind the generally comparable effects that we observe across the five areas are central to understanding these investigations.

5. *Substantive Explanations*

We just speculated about these time-dependent fertility effects in *statistical* terms, which does not, however, explain why we should expect these time-dependent effects in *substantive* terms at all. How can this effect found across a variety of countries be explained? Before we give a more detailed answer to this question, some more general remarks about actors and probabilistic causal relations in the "causation as generative process" approach are in order.

5.1   *Actors, Probabilistic Causal Relations and the Hazard Rate*

"When an analysis becomes causal, social regularities represent the effects for which causes have to be discovered. And this task, contrary to what proponents of the idea of causation as robust dependence would seem to have supposed, cannot be a purely statistical one but requires a crucial subject-matter input" (Goldthorpe 2001: 11). Today, there is a general consensus that demographic and sociological phenomena are always directly or indirectly based on actions and interactions of individuals (methodological individualism). We do not deal with associations among variables per se, but with variables that are associated via acting people (see Blossfeld and Prein 1998; Blossfeld, Golsch, and Rowher 2007).

There are at least three consequences for explanations of causal relations. First, if individuals relate causes and effects through actions and interactions, then explanation of demographic processes should be related to *individuals*. This is why life history data on individuals, and not aggregated longitudinal data, provide the most appropriate empirical evidence for causal relationships. Second, explaining or understanding of demographic processes requires: (1) a *time-related* specification of structural constraints which cut down the set of abstractly possible courses of action to a vastly smaller subset of feasible actions; and, (2) a *mechanism* that singles out which of the feasible courses of action shall be realized (see Elster 1979). Because this is done by individuals, this mechanism must rest on the beliefs, expectations, and motivations of the agents. (3) Since individuals are the actors, causal inference must also take into account their *free will*.

This introduces an essential element of indeterminacy into causal inferences. Hence, in demography and sociology we can only reasonably account for and model the generality but not the determinacy of behaviour. The aim of substantive (and statistical) causal models in the social sciences must therefore be to capture common elements in the behaviour of people, or patterns of action that recur in many cases (Goldthorpe 1998, 2000). A narrative of action must be provided that captures the main tendencies that arise in similar situations. This theoretical model must not seek to explain the behaviour of single individuals, but abstract ideal-typical actors (Hedström 2005: 38). As Stinchcombe (1968) has shown, the behaviour of large aggregates can be reasonably well comprehended, even when the individual components of the aggregate are poorly understood. Given this macro-level focus, small idiosyncratic deviations from the postulated model are not damaging (Hedström 1995). The consequence, however, is that in demographic applications, randomness has to enter as a defining characteristic of causal models.

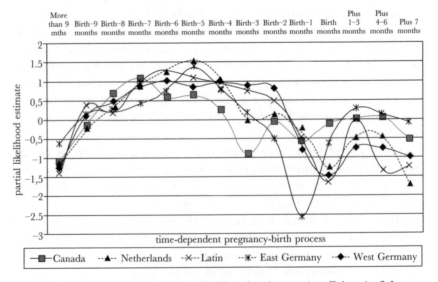

Figure 2. Comparison of partial likelihood estimates (coefficients) of the transition from consensual union to marriage, West and East Germany, Canada, Latvia and the Netherlands.

We can only hope to make sensible causal statements about how a given or (hypothesized) change in variable Y_t^A (e.g., pregnancy/birth) in the past affects the probability of a change in variable Y_t^B (e.g., marriage) in the future. Correspondingly, the basic causal relation becomes:

$\Delta Y_t^A \rightarrow \Delta \Pr(\Delta Y_{t'}^B)$, $t < t'$. In other words, a change in the time-dependent covariate Y_t^A will change the probability that the dependent variable $Y_{t'}^B$ will change in the future ($t < t'$).

In demography and sociology, this interpretation seems more appropriate than the traditional deterministic approach. The essential difference is not that our knowledge about causes is insufficient allowing only probabilistic statements, but that the causal effect to be explained is a probability. Thus, probability in this context is not just a technical term anymore, but is considered a theoretical one: it is the propensity of social agents to change their behaviour intentionally.

Using continuous event history data and hazard rate models, the causal reasoning underlying our approach can therefore be restated in a somewhat more precise form as: $\Delta Y_t^A \rightarrow \Delta r(t')$, $t < t'$. As a causal effect, the changes in covariates Y_t^A in the past may lead to changes in the time-dependent transition rate $r(t')$ in the future, which in turn describes the propensity that the actors under study will change their course of action. This causal interpretation requires that we take the temporal order in which structural constraints and the actors' beliefs and motivations evolve in time very seriously.

5.2   *Diffuse Marriage Preferences and the Negotiation Process*

With regard to the marriage decision in our example study, it seems important to distinguish two completely different situations at the time of the discovery of the pregnancy: (1) the preferences of the partners to marry are vague and diffuse; and, (2) the couple has already reached a decision to marry or not to marry in the case of child. In the first instance, the occurrence of a pregnancy may initiate a process of preference formation and persuasion. *Formation* means that initially rather vague preferences with regard to marriage are formed, resulting in more clear-cut preferences in a step-wise negotiation process. *Persuasion* means that an individual is led by a sequence of short-term improvements into preferring marriage over non-marriage, even if he or she has initially vaguely preferred non-marriage over marriage. In such cases the discovery of a pregnancy engenders a time-structured process of reasoning and interactions which results in a change in preferences. On the one hand, the opportunity to legalize the birth of the child tends to decrease with the duration of pregnancy. At the same time, the likelihood of possible medical complications connected with the pregnancy and the visibility of pregnancy to others increases.

With these contradicting factors in mind, the optimal time for marriage is at a relatively early pregnancy phase. On the other hand, the optimum in the sense of a safe, well thought-out decision based on a negotiation process between the partners, is often at a relatively later phase of the pregnancy. Thus, there is constant tension between these opposing forces that may often (but not necessarily) be connected to a considerable shift in preferences with regard to marriage. Based on these contradictory forces, one would expect that the rate of entry into marriage after the discovery of pregnancy at first increases with the duration of pregnancy and then, after reaching some maximum, decreases again as the time of birth comes closer. Shortly before and after the birth, one would expect a very low marriage rate. Finally, after the birth has already taken place out of wedlock, the decision of whether or not to marry has a different social meaning. The child is then already 'illegitimate,' and the normative time pressure to marry has disappeared, thus resulting in a relatively low marriage rate after some time since the birth of the child.

Table 1 and Figure 2 illustrate that after controlling for several important covariates, women in consensual unions do indeed seem to follow this pattern with respect to the rate of entry into marriage: the marriage rate is very low before pregnancy across all countries; it generally increases strongly up to about 5 months before birth, then falls deeply around the time of birth, and is finally at a relatively low level than 7 months after the birth. Therefore, our substantive interpretation of the time-dependence in Table 1 is derived from a theoretically supposed underlying negotiation process with the time-dependent dummy-variables serving as proxies for a theoretically important process that is hard (or even impossible) to measure.

5.3 *Unobserved Marriage Decisions and the Observed Rate of Entry into Marriage*

Of course, one could also argue that many couples have already reached a decision to marry or not to marry in the case of a child at the time of the discovery of the pregnancy. Thus, couples are in fact extremely

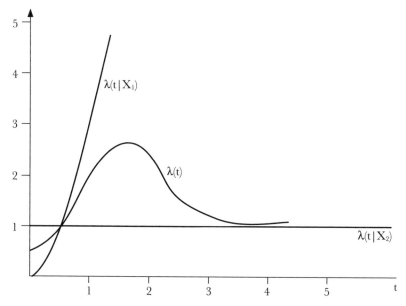

Figure 3. Marriage rate for couples who had already decided to marry before the event of pregnancy $\lambda(t \mid x_1)$, marriage rate for couples who had decided that they would never marry before the event of pregnancy $\lambda(t \mid x_2)$, and observed marriage rate $\lambda(t)$, if these two subpopulations are not controlled for in the model.

heterogeneous with regard to their baseline rate to enter into marriage when the pregnancy is observed. Consider the example where the consensual union population consists of two groups—one with a constantly low marriage rate $\lambda(t \mid x_2)$ and the other with an increasing rate as pregnancy progresses $\lambda(t \mid x_1)$ (see Figure 3). This neglected heterogeneity would result in a bell-shaped marriage rate $\lambda(t)$ (see Figure 3). This is due to the fact that when pregnancy progresses, the composition of the unmarried couples shifts towards couples being 'less' or 'not' ready for marriage which, at first, increases and then decreases the observed effect pattern. Thus, if we do not know whether the couples have already reached a decision to marry in the case of a child at the time of pregnancy, we are unable to say whether the effects of the dummy variables must be considered as proxies for the formation of couples' decisions during pregnancy, or for the heterogeneity of couples' marriage decisions at the beginning of pregnancy. Obviously, in reality both interpretations may be valid. The important conclusion is, however, that the discovery of a pregnancy leads to a changing marriage rate for most couples.

5.4   *Abortion, Miscarriage and the Problem of Conditioning on Future Events*

Another methodological problem is that we have not considered abortion and miscarriage. Couples can avoid the birth of children (and therefore marriage) by abortion, and they can experience a miscarriage. Both groups present a problem for our causal analysis because we do not have any information about abortion and miscarriages in our data sets and have constructed the fertility variables on the basis of successful births. In other words, there is the danger that we have committed one of the most serious methodological errors in causal analysis: We have conditioned past events on future events, reversing the temporal order of cause and effect. As long as conditions are random and concern only a small proportion of couples, as is the case with miscarriages, this objection is not exceedingly important. We get biased estimates only if specific couples sort themselves out by choice in greater numbers, as is probably the case with abortion. In particular, we overestimate the size of the pregnancy/birth effect because we systematically under-represented pregnant couples that would not have wanted to marry because of a child in our 'risk set of pregnant couples' (i.e., if we over-estimate, then the effect is negative on the rate which gives a downward bias). In former East Germany and Latvia, abortion was easier and more socially accepted than in the other countries. In Latvia, abortion is a widespread method of fertility control with 111 terminated pregnancies per 100 live births and stillbirths in 1991 (Government of Latvia 1999: 125).

6. *Summary and Concluding Remarks*

Two understandings of causation have guided the empirical analysis of causal relationships in the social sciences: (1) "Causation as robust dependence" and (2) "causation as consequential manipulation." On the one hand, our discussion of both approaches made clear, that the idea of "causation as robust dependence" is too limited because causal inference cannot be a purely statistical consideration. Rather it requires a crucial subject-matter input. On the other hand, the idea of "causation as consequential manipulation" requires well-designed randomized controlled experiments or quasi-experiments. Since such designs can only rarely be applied in the social sciences, most demographic and sociological causal inference is based on non-experimental observations of social processes—these data are often highly selective. A whole battery of statistical techniques has therefore been developed to help to approximate randomized controlled experiments with observational data. However, it is still difficult to avoid the conclusion that, non-experimental social research, will lead to results that 'never die' but only to ones that have differing degrees of plausibility. Thus such results will have to be provisional in just the same sense and for just the same reasons as those of attempts to determine the causes of effects via the "causation as robust dependence" approach. Furthermore, the approach of "causation as consequential manipulation" is still too restrictive for modern social sciences because the idea is that once the treatment or intervention is introduced, it will automatically lead to an outcome. The units of analysis in the social sciences, the individuals, are therefore assumed to be passive subjects whose behavior is explained only by causal factors. This restricted understanding of "causation as consequential manipulation" is particularly problematic, if dynamic social systems are studied over longer time-spans. A necessary augmentation of the two understandings of causation is therefore the idea of "causation as generative process", proposed by David Cox. According to this view, it is crucial to the claim of a causal link that there is an elaboration of an underlying (substantive) generative process existing in time and space.

The main aim of this paper was to further develop the idea of "causation as generative process" and to demonstrate the viability of this understanding in a cross-national empirical investigation of interrelated family events. The story these empirical studies tell is persuasive. In substantive terms, the investigations confirm the existence of a highly time-dependent causal process between pregnancy and marriage for individuals in consensual unions across five different national contexts. In particular, it shows that the force of an empirical analysis results from the clarity of the prior substantive reasoning and the bringing together of seemingly contradictory evidence. All studies have been instructive in methodological terms because: (1) they *analyzed two highly interdependent processes* from a causal point of view, (2) the interdependence occurs mainly in a very *specific phase of individuals' lives* (i.e., family formation), (3) the relationship between cause and its effect involves *time lags* (e.g., time until detection of pregnancy); and, (4) the unfolding *effect is highly dynamic over time.*

These applications illustrate the substantive importance and methodological pitfalls of the identification of time-dependent causes and their time-dependent effect patterns. A central contribution is that we have been able to demonstrate that one process is influencing or causing a change in the other—even if they are interdependent. In cross-sectional data, we often have interdependent systems with feedback mechanisms, but are unable to discern how one process influences the other. We witness associations that describe what has happened, but cannot separate the effect. Associations are quite different from causal statements designed to say something about how events are produced or conditioned by other events. With the event history approach, however, it becomes possible to separate correlation and causation (Blossfeld and Rohwer 2002).

One shortcoming is that our applications are only based on observed behaviour. It could happen that a couple first decides to marry, the woman becomes pregnant, and then the couple marries. In this case, we would observe only pregnancy occurring before marriage and assume that it increases the likelihood of marriage. Yet, the time order is exactly the other way around. Courgeau and Lelièvre (1992) have introduced the notion of 'fuzzy time' to represent this time span between decisions and behaviour. Since the time between decisions and behaviour is probably not random and differs per couple, examining observed behaviour could lead to false causal inferences. This does not alter the key temporal issues embedded within the causal logic. However, we must admit that using the time order of only behavioural events without taking into account the timing of decisions could lead to serious misspecification. Thus, for studies aiming to model "causation as a generative process" through the relationship between individuals' objectives, knowledge, reasoning and decisions over time, prospective panel observations of objectives and decisions and retrospective information on behavioural events appear to be a very desirable design.

References

Agresti, A. and Ch. Franklin. 2007. *Statistics: The Art and Science of Learning from Data*, Upper Saddle River, NJ: Person Prentice Hall.

Allison, P. D. 1996. "Fixed-effects partial likelihood for repeated events" in *Sociological Methods & Research*, 25: 207–222.

Blalock, H. M. (ed.). 1970. *Causal Models in the Social Sciences*, Chicago, IL: Aldine.

Blossfeld, H.-P. 1986. "Career opportunities in the Federal Republic of Germany: A dynamic approach to the study of life-course, cohort, and period effects" in *European Sociological Review*, 2: 208–225.

Blossfeld, H.-P. and S. Drobnič (eds.). 2001. *Careers of Couples in Contemporary Societies*, Oxford: Oxford University Press.

Blossfeld, H.-P. and J. Huinink. 1991. "Human capital investments or norms of role transition? How women's schooling and career affect the process of family formation" in *American Journal of Sociology*, 97: 143–168.

Blossfeld, H.-P. and G. Prein (eds.). 1998. *Rational Choice Theory and Large-scale Data Analysis*, Boulder: Westview Press.

Blossfeld, H.-P. and G. Rohwer. 2002. *Techniques of Event History Modeling*, Mahwah: Erlbaum.

Blossfeld, H.-P., K. Golsch, and G. Rohwer. 2007. *Event History Analysis with Stata*, Mahwah: Erlbaum.

Blossfeld, H.-P., A. Hamerle and K. U. Mayer. 1989. *Event History Analysis*, Hillsdale: Erlbaum.

Blossfeld, H.-P., E. Klijzing, K. Pohl and G. Rohwer. 1996. "Die Modellierung interdependenter Prozesse in der demographischen forschung: Konzepte, methoden und anwendung auf nichteheliche Lebensgemeinschaften" in *Zeitschrift für Bevölkerungswissenschaft*, 22: 29–56.

———. 1999. "Why do cohabiting couples marry? An example of a causal event history approach to interdependent systems" in *Quality and Quantity*, 33(3): 229–42.

Blossfeld, H-P., D. Manting and G. Rohwer 1993. "Patterns of change in family formation in the Federal Republic of Germany and the Netherlands: Some consequences for the solidarity between generations" in H. A. Becker and P. L. J. Hermkens (eds.), *Solidarity of Generations*, Amsterdam: Thesis Publishers, 75–196.

Courgeau, D. and E. Lelièvre. 1992. *Event History Analysis in Demography*, Oxford: Clarendon Press.

Cox, D. R. 1990. "Role of models in statistical analysis" in *Statistical science*, 5: 169–174.

———. 1992. "Causality: Some statistical aspects" in *Journal of the Royal Statistical Society*, Series A, 155: 291–301.

Duncan, O. D. 1966. "Path analysis: Sociological examples" in *American Journal of Sociology*, 72: 1–16.

Eells, E. 1991. *Probabilistic Causality*, Cambridge: Cambridge University Press.

Elder, G. H. Jr. 1987. "Families and lives: Some developments in life-course studies" in *Journal of Family History*, 12(1–3): 179–199.

Elder, G. H. Jr., M. Kirkpatrick Johnson and R. Crosnoe. 2004. "The emergence and development of life course theory" in J. T. Mortimer and M. J. Shanahan (eds.), *Handbook of the Life Course*, New York, NY: Springer, 3–19.

Elster, J. 1979. *Ulysses and the Sirens*, Cambridge: Cambridge University Press.

Fisher, R. A. 1935. *The Design of Experiments*, Edinburgh, UK: Oliver & Boyd.

Freedman, R. A. 1991. "Statistical analysis and shoe leather" in *Sociological Methodology*, 21: 291–313.

Goldthorpe, J. H. 1998. "The quantitative analysis of large-scale data-sets and rational action theory: For a sociological alliance" in H.-P. Blossfeld and G. Prein (eds.), *Rational Choice Theory and Large-scale Data Analysis*, Boulder: Westview Press, 31–53.

———. 2000. *On Sociology*, Oxford: Oxford University Press.

———. 2001. "Causation, statistics, and sociology" in *European Sociological Review*, 17: 1–20.

Government of Latvia. 1999. "National report submitted by the government of Latvia" in *Population in Europe and North America on the Eve of the Millennium*, Geneva: UN-ECE, 123–129.

Granger, C. W. J. 1969. "Investigating causal relations by econometric models and cross-special methods" in *Econometrica*, 37: 424–438.

Hedström, P. 1995. "Rational choice and social structure: On rational-choice theorizing in sociology" in B. Wittrock (ed.), *Social Theory and Human Agency*, London: Sage.

———. 2005. *Dissecting the Social: On the Principles of Analytical Sociology*, Cambridge, UK: Cambridge University Press.

Holland, P. W. 1986. "Statistics and causal inference" in *Journal of the American Statistical Association*, 81: 945–960.

———. 1988. "Causal inference, path analysis, and recursive structural equation models" in *Sociological Methodology*, 18: 449–484.

Johnston, J. 1972. *Econometric Methods*, Second edition, New York: McGraw-Hill.

Kalbfleisch, J. D. and R. L. Prentice. 1980. *The Statistical Analysis of Failure Data*, New York, NY: John Wiley.

Katus, K. 1992. "Fertility transition in Estonia, Latvia and Lithuania" in W. Lutz, S. Scherbov and A. Volkov (eds.), *Demographic Trends and Patterns in the Soviet Union Before 1991*, London: Routledge, 89–111.

Kelly, J. R. and J. E. McGrath. 1988. *On Time and Method*, Newbury Park: Sage.

Kerlinger, F. N. and E. Pedhazer. 1973. *Multiple Regression in Behavioral Sciences*, New York: Holt, Rinehart and Winston.

Lieberson, S. 1985. *Making It Count: The Improvement of Social Research and Theory*, Berkeley: University of California Press.

Lillard, L. A. and L. J. Waite. 1993. "A joint model of marital childbearing and marital disruption" in *Demography*, 30: 653–681.

Macy, M. W. 1991. "Chains of co-operation: Threshold effects in collective action" in *American Sociological Review*, 56: 730–747.

Macy, M. W. and R. Willer. 2002. "From factors to actors: Computational sociology and agent-based modeling" in *Annual Review of Sociology*, 28: 143–166.

Manting, D. 1994. *Dynamics in Marriage and Cohabitation*, Amsterdam: Thesis Publishers.

Marini, M. M. and B. Singer. 1988. "Causality in the social sciences" in C. C. Clogg (ed.), *Sociological Methodology*, 347–409.

Mayer, K. U. and J. Huinink. 1990. "Age, period, and cohort in the study of the life course: A comparison of classical A-P-C-analysis with event history analysis or farewell to Lexis?" in D. Magnusson and L. R. Bergmann (eds.), *Data Quality in Longitudinal Research*, Cambridge: Cambridge University Press, 211–232.

Mills, M. 2000. *The Transformation of Partnerships: Canada, the Netherlands and the Russian Federation in the Age of Modernity*, Amsterdam: Thela Thesis Population Studies Series.

Mills, M. and F. Trovato. 2001. "The effect of pregnancy in cohabiting unions on marriage in Canada, the Netherlands, and Latvia" in *Statistical Journal of the United Nations ECE*, 18: 103–118.

Pötter, U. and H.-P. Blossfeld. 2001. "Causal inference from series of events" in *European Sociological Review*, 17(1): 21–32.

Rohwer, G. 2007. Statistical social research: Basic concepts and models, Fakultät für Sozialwissenschaft, Bochum: Ruhr-Universität Bochum (unpublished manuscript).

Rubin, D. B. 1974. "Estimating causal effects of treatments in randomized and non-randomized studies" in *Journal of Educational Psychology*, 66: 688–701.

———. 1978. "Bayesian infernece for causal effects: The role of randomization" in *Annals of Statistics*, 6: 34–58.

———. 1980. "Discussion of 'randomization analysis of experimental data in the Fisher randomization test' by Basu" in *Journal of the American Statistical Association*, 81: 961–962.

Schneider, B., M. Carnoy, J. Kilpatrick, W. H. Schmidt and R. J. Shavelson. 2007. *Estimating Causal Effects: Using Experimental and Observational Designs*, Washington DC: American Educational Research Association.

Shadish, W. R., T. D. Cook and D. T. Campbell. 2002. *Experimental and Quasi-experimental Designs for Generalized Causal Inference*, Boston: Houghton Mifflin.

Steele, F. 2003. "A multilevel mixture model for event history data with long-term survivors: An application to an Analysis of Contraceptive Sterilisation in Bangladesh" in *Lifetime Data Analysis*, 9: 155–174.

Stinchcombe, A. L. 1968. *Constructing Social Theories*, New York: Harcourt, Brace, and World.

Tuma, N. B. and M. T. Hannan 1984. *Social Dynamics: Models and Methods*, Orlando, FL: Academic Press.

Willekens, F. J. 1991. "Understanding the interdependence between parallel careers" in J. J. Siegers et al. (eds.), *Female Labour Market Behaviour and Fertility*, Berlin: Springer-Verlag, 11–31.

Yamaguchi, K. 1986. "Alternative approaches to unobserved heterogeneity in the analysis of repeatable events" in N. B. Tuma (ed.), *Sociological Methodology*, 213–249.

———. 1991. *Event History Analysis*, Newbury Park: Sage.

Zhang, W. and F. Steele. 2004. "A semiparametric multilevel survival model" in *Journal of the Royal Statistical Society*, Series C, 53: 387–404.

NOTES ON CONTRIBUTORS

Hans-Peter Blossfeld holds the Chair of Sociology I and is the Director of the State Institute for Family Research, both at Bamberg University. He has published 20 books and over 150 articles on social inequality, youth, family, and educational sociology, labor market research, demography, social stratification and mobility, the modern methods of quantitative social research and statistical methods for longitudinal data analysis. Currently, he is interested in the flexibilization of work in modern societies, the division of domestic work in the family, and the development of individual competences and the formation of educational decisions in early school careers.

Raymond Boudon, Professor Emeritus at the Sorbonne, has worked on education, social mobility, beliefs, values, sociological theory. He belongs to the Institut de France, the Academia Europæa, the British Academy, the American Academy of Arts and Sciences, the Royal Society of Canada, the Académie internationale de philosophie des sciences. He has been a fellow at the Stanford Center for Advanced Study in the Behavioral Sciences, and invited professor notably at Harvard, Oxford and the universities of Geneva, Chicago and Stockholm. His publications include: *Education, Opportunity and Social Inequality; A Critical Dictionary of Sociology; The Origin of Values; The Poverty of Relativism; Tocqueville for Today* and *Towards a General Theory of Rationality*.

Richard Breen is Professor of Sociology at Yale University and Co-Director of the Center for Research on Inequalities and the Life Course (CIQLE). His research interests are social stratification and inequality, and the application of formal and quantitative models in the social sciences. He is a Fellow of the British Academy and a Member of the Royal Irish Academy. Current research projects include the study of trends in social mobility and educational inequality in the 20th century and analyses of the role of demographic factors in accounting for change in income and earnings inequality.

Christofer Edling is Professor of Sociology at Jacobs University. He was Torgny Segerstedt Pro Futura Fellow at Swedish Collegium for

Advanced Study in 2002–2006. His research interests are focused on sociological theory and social network analysis.

S. N. Eisenstadt is Rose Isaacs Professor Emeritus of Sociology at the Hebrew University of Jerusalem and currently works at the Van Leer Jerusalem Institute. He has held teaching and research positions at universities and institutes all over the world and is the recipient of several awards and honorary doctoral degrees. In 2006 he was awarded the Holberg Prize. He has written extensively in historical, comparative and cultural social science. Recent publications include: *The Great Revolutions and the Civilizations of Modernity*, 2006; *Axial Civilizations and World History* (with Johann Arnason and Björn Wittrock, 2005) and *Explorations in Jewish Historical Experience: The Civilizational Dimension*, 2004.

Peter Gärdenfors is Professor of Cognitive Science at Lund University, and is the chair of their Ph.D. program in cognitive science. He has published numerous books and articles on decision theory, epistemology, belief revision, concept formation and the evolution of cognition. The most important books are *Knowledge in Flux: Modeling the Dynamics of Epistemic States*, 1988; *Conceptual Spaces: The Geometry of Thought*, 2000; *How Homo Became Sapiens: On the Evolution of Thinking*, 2003 and *The Dynamics of Thought*, 2005.

Jack A. Goldstone is the Virginia E. and John T. Hazel Professor of Public Policy at George Mason University. He is best known for his work on revolutions, social movements, and political conflict. He has won the Distinguished Contribution to Scholarship award of the American Sociological Association, and the Arnoldo Momigliano award of the Historical Society. He has won fellowships from the MacArthur Foundation, the Center for Advanced Study in the Behavioral Sciences, and the American Council of Learned Societies.

Philip Gorski is Professor of Sociology and Religious Studies and Co-Director of the Center for Comparative Research at Yale University. He is a comparative-historical sociologist with strong interests in religion, social theory, historical methods and the philosophy of social science. The primary focus of his work is religion and politics in Western Europe and North America in the early modern and modern periods. Recent publications include *The Disciplinary Revolution: Calvinism and the Growth of State Power in Early Modern Europe*, 2003; *Max Weber's Economy and*

Society: A Critical Companion, 2004 and "The Poverty of Deductivism: A Constructive Realist Model of Sociological Explanation" in *Sociological Methodology*, 2004.

Ulf Hannerz is Professor Emeritus of Social Anthropology, Stockholm University, and has taught at several American, European, Asian and Australian universities. He is a member of the Royal Swedish Academy of Sciences and the American Academy of Arts and Sciences, and a former Chair of the European Association of Social Anthropologists. His research has focused on urban anthropology, media anthropology and transnational cultural processes. Among his books are *Soulside*, 1969; *Exploring the City*, 1980; *Cultural Complexity*, 1992; *Transnational Connections*, 1996 and *Foreign News*, 2004. He was Anthropology editor for the *International Encyclopedia of the Social and Behavioral Sciences* (2001).

Peter Hedström is Professor of Sociology and Official Fellow of Nuffield College, Oxford and Dean of the School of Social Sciences at Singapore Management University. His main area of interest is analytical sociology, with a special interest in complex networks, diffusion processes, and the principles of mechanism-based theorizing. He is one of the key contributors to the literature on social mechanisms and has numerous publications in leading sociology journals. He is Past President of the Swedish Sociological Association, the current President of the European Academy of Sociology, Fellow of the Norwegian Academy of Science, and the current Secretary-General of the International Institute of Sociology.

Hans Joas is Director of the Max Weber Center for Advanced Cultural and Social Studies at the University of Erfurt and Professor of Sociology and member of the Committee on Social Thought at the University of Chicago. He is a regular member of the Academy of Sciences in Berlin and a long-term Fellow of the Swedish Collegium for Advanced Study. Selected publications: *The Genesis of Values*, 2000; *War and Modernity*, 2003 and *Social Theory* (published in German by Suhrkamp 2004; forthcoming in English: Cambridge University Press).

Dietrich Rueschemeyer is Charles C. Tillinghast Jr. Professor of International Studies, Emeritus, at Brown University. His books include *Bringing the State Back In* (co-editor with Peter B. Evans and Theda Skocpol, 1985); *Power and the Division of Labour*, 1986; *Capitalist Development and Democracy* (coauthor with John D. Stephens and Evelyne Huber Stephens, 1992); *Comparative Historical Analysis in the Social Sciences* (co-editor with James Mahoney, 2003), and *States and Development: Historical Antecedents of Stagnation and Advance* (co-editor with Matthew Lange, 2005). He currently works on *Useable Theory: Analytic Tools for Social and Political Research.*

Jens Rydgren is Associate Professor of Sociology at Stockholm University. He has been a visiting scholar at Columbia University, Harvard University, Cornell University, and at the École des Hautes Études en Sciences Sociales in Paris. He is the author of *The Populist Challenge: Political Protest and Ethno-Nationalist Mobilization in France*, 2003 and *From Tax Populism to Ethnic Nationalism*, 2006. He has also published extensively on political sociology, ethnic relations, and sociological theory in journals such as *Annual Review of Sociology, Rationality and Society, Sociological Theory, European Journal of Social Theory*, and *European Journal of Political Research.*

Neil J. Smelser is University Professor of Sociology Emeritus at the University of California, Berkeley, and Director Emeritus of the Center for Advanced Study in the Behavioral Sciences at Stanford. His research interests include social theory, social change, social movements, economic sociology, sociology of education, psychoanalysis, and terrorism. He is a member of the National Academy of Sciences, the American Philosophical Society, and the American Academy of Arts and Sciences.

Aage B. Sørensen was Professor of Sociology and chair of the joint doctoral program in organizational behavior at Harvard University until his death in 2001. His research interests were in the areas of social stratification, the sociology of education, mathematical sociology, and in the sociology of the life course. The article included in this volume reflects his long-standing interest in social mechanisms and his concern for the widespread use of statistical models in sociology that do not reflect the mechanisms or processes that are being studied.

Richard Swedberg is Professor of Sociology at Cornell University. His two main areas of specialization are economic sociology and social theory. His books include *The Handbook of Economic Sociology* (edited with Neil Smelser, 1994 and 2005); *Max Weber and the Idea of Economic Sociology*, 1998 and *Principles of Economic Sociology*, 2003. He is currently working on a study of 19th century economics.

Piotr Sztompka is Professor of Theoretical Sociology at the Jagiellonian University in Krakow, and of the J. Tischner's European University. He has taught at Universities in the US, Europe, Latin America and Australia, and has held several fellowships. In 2006 he received the highest Polish academic prize granted by the Foundation of Polish Science, known as the "Polish Nobel". His publications include: *System and Function*, 1974; *Sociological Dilemmas*, 1979; *Robert K. Merton: An Intellectual Profile*, 1986; *Society in Action*, 1991; *The Sociology of Social Change*, 1993; *Trust: A Sociological Theory*, 1999; *Cultural Trauma and Collective Identity* (with J. Alexander, N. Smelser et al., 2004).

Peter Wagner is Professor of Sociology at the University of Trento. His research focuses on social theory, historical and political sociology and the sociology of knowledge. In particular, he has aimed at analyzing the history of European societies in terms of transformations of modernity. His publications include *Modernity as Experience and Interpretation: A New Sociology of Modernity*, 2008; *Varieties of World-making: Beyond Globalization* (edited with Nathalie Karagiannis, 2007); *Theorizing Modernity* and *A History and Theory of the Social Sciences*, 2001 and *A Sociology of Modernity: Liberty and Discipline*, 1994.

Björn Wittrock is University Professor at Uppsala University and Principal of the Swedish Collegium for Advanced Study, Uppsala. In 2005 he was elected President of the International Institute of Sociology. He has published extensively in the fields of intellectual history, historical social science, and social theory. His publications include: *Eurasian Transformations, Tenth to Thirteenth Centuries: Crystallizations, Divergences, Renaissances* (with Johann Arnason, 2004); *Axial Civilizations and World History* (with S. N. Eisenstadt and Johann Arnason, 2005); *The Rise of the Social Sciences and the Formation of Modernity: Conceptual Change in Context* (with Johan Heilbron and Lars Magnusson, 1998).

AUTHOR INDEX

Annals of the International Institute of Sociology (IIS)

7. Scheuch, Erwin K. and David Sciulli (eds.). *Societies, Corporations and the Nation State.* 2000. ISBN-10 90 04 11664 8; ISBN-13 978 90 04 11664 1.

8. Ben-Rafael, Eliezer with Yitzhak Sternberg (eds.). *Identity, Culture and Globalization.* 2002. ISBN-10 90 04 12873 5; ISBN-13 978 90 04 12873 6.

9. Skąpska, Grażyna, Annamaria Orla-Bukowksa and Krystof Kowalski (eds.). *The Moral Fabric in Contemporary Societies.* 2003.
    ISBN-10 90 04 13114 0; ISBN-13 978 90 04 13114 9.

10. Tiankui, Jing, Masamichi Sasaki and Li Peilin (eds.). *Social Change in the Age of Globalization.* 2006. ISBN-10 90 04 15143 5;
    ISBN-13 978 90 04 15143 7.

11. Hedström, Peter and Björn Wittrock (eds.). *Frontiers of Sociology.* 2009.
    ISBN 978 90 04 16569 4.

Axial Civilizations and World History

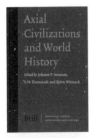

Edited by Johann P. Arnason,
S. N. Eisenstadt, and Björn Wittrock

• November 2004
• ISBN 978 90 04 13955 8
• *Hardback* (x, 574 pp.)
• List price EUR 151.- / US$ 225.-
• Jerusalem Studies in Religion and Culture, 4

The overarching theme of the book is the historical meaning of the Axial Age, commonly defined as a period of several centuries around the middle of the last millennium BCE, and its cultural innovations. The civilizational patterns that grew out of this exceptionally creative phase are a particularly rewarding theme for comparative analysis. The book contains essays on cultural transformations in Ancient Greece, Ancient Israel, Iran, India and China, as well as background developments in the core civilizations of the Ancient Near East. An introductory section deals with the history of the debate on the Axial Age, the theoretical questions that have emerged from it, and the present state of the discussion. The book will be useful for comparative historians of cultures and religions, as well as for historical sociologists interested in the comparative analysis of civilizations. It should also help linking the fields of classical, biblical and Asian studies to broader interdisciplinary debates within the humanities sciences.

Johann P. Arnason, dr.habil. in Sociology, University of Bielefeld 1975 is now Emeritus Professor in Sociology at La Trobe University, Melbourne.
S.N. Eisenstadt, Ph.D. (1947), Jerusalem, is Professor Emeritus at the Hebrew University of Jerusalem. He is member of many academies, recipient of honorary doctoral degrees of the Universities of Tel Aviv, Helsinki, Harvard, Duke, Budapest and Hebrew Union College.
Björn Wittrock, Ph.D. (1974), formerly Lars Hierta Professor of Government at Stockholm University, is now University Professor at Uppsala University and Principal of the Swedish Collegium for Advanced Study in the Social Sciences, Uppsala.

BRILL

* Discount is valid until December 31, 2009